YOU CAN'T LOSE
TRADING COMMODITIES

by
ROBERT F. WIEST

Robert F. Wiest
PO Box 3882, Westlake Village
California 91359-0882

ISBN 0-9641253-0-7

Dedication

I have been involved in commodity futures trading for about thirty-five years, and I must admit quite frankly that I have never seen anyone make money *consistently* trading commodity futures. I have seen a few traders who pyramided numerous consecutive winners and temporarily accumulated a sizable profit, others whose faddish systems worked for a while, and the few who got just plain dumb lucky and hit a big one. But — just like the Las Vegas slot machine player who hits a jackpot on the first coin — they usually stay around long enough to lose all the winnings, plus more.

It is the commodity broker's favorite pitch to tell the prospective commodity trader that the client will show a net profit for all of his trading if he catches as few as three winners out of each ten trades, and that all he needs to do is "to cut the losses short and to let the profits run." That's a lot of baloney. The only thing *that* system does is to generate commissions for the broker and his brokerage house. It guarantees failure for the client.

As far as I am concerned, there is but a single axiom that applies to commodity trading. It is: If you trade commodity futures contracts, it is a virtual certainty that you will lose. More simply stated: If you trade, you lose.

The reason nearly everyone trading commodities loses is because he takes $5,000 or $10,000 and tries to run it into $100,000 in six months. Every once in awhile someone succeeds. Unfortunately it happens just often enough for the stories to get around and make the others believe it can happen to them. Commodity brokers exist only because this $100,000-for-$10,000 phenomenon occurs just often enough for them to retell the tale to the new sheep who have lined up for the shearing.

For each trader who wins $100,000 there are hundreds who lose a few thousand each. Even the $100,000 winners will eventually surrender their winnings. All of this is as certain as tomorrow's sunrise.

It is for these thousands — indeed, *tens of thousands* — of losers that this book is respectfully dedicated. They should have learned by now that "You Can't Win Trading Commodities."

But if you will take the time to read this book I will demonstrate to you how "You Can't Lose Trading Commodities."

*   *   *

Also lovingly dedicated to:

Helen E. Wiest
Dorothy Gatlin Wiest
Frances L. Antonio
Helen F. Castro

Table of Contents

Foreword

I studied aeronautical engineering in college with a major in mathematics. As a mathematician, naturally, I was fascinated by gambling systems. I even worked in Las Vegas awhile and had an opportunity to observe hundreds of systems. Most of them I could eliminate quite readily, but a few offered some merit and warranted closer scrutiny. I narrowed it down to two or three that I occasionally play when I visit Las Vegas.

I only try to make expense money with a system in Las Vegas, and I usually grind that out during a weekend. However, the inevitable occurs sooner or later, and I lose a bundle. Over the long haul I lose more than I win, as is true of all gamblers whether they use a system or not. The amount that I lose is what I consider the entertainment tax, for I enjoy Las Vegas.

Winning or losing a few hundred dollars in Las Vegas is one thing, but losing tens of thousands in the commodities market is something quite different. There is no "thrill of the chase" in losing that kind of money. That is not an entertainment tax. That is serious money. It is heartbreaking (and even home-wrecking) to suffer losses of that magnitude.

When I worked as a commodity broker, it troubled me deeply that all of my clients lost money trading commodities. It made no difference whether they followed my firm's recommendations, my personal advice, their own hunches, used some exotic computer system, followed the recommendations of a professional advisor, or listened to a guru on a mountaintop in Tibet. They all lost.

Then one day while reflecting upon one of my Las Vegas systems, it suddenly occurred to me that it would adapt itself perfectly to the commodities market. I knew the flaw which kept the system from being infallible in Las Vegas was that the laws of chance dictated that upon occasion runs of losers would occur against me that even the U.S. Treasury could not bankroll. I reasoned that all I needed for my gambling system to be successful every time I played it would be for Nevada to pass a law that made it mandatory that after a certain number of losers had occurred against me, the table must now reverse and award me a certain number of winners. Obviously, no such law exists in Nevada. But it *does* in the commodities market.

That *Law* is called "The Law of Supply and Demand."

My system is based upon that Law, a Law as immutable as the sunrise. The logic behind the system simply relies upon the fact that low prices must ultimately result in a reduction in supply as costs make it unprofitable to produce that commodity. The low prices will in turn increase demand. This combination of reduced supply concomitant with increased consumption must ultimately result in higher prices.

If you balk at the thought of trading commodity futures you are correct in your thinking. Ordinarily, most commodity traders sooner or later are destroyed financially. But I do not consider the people who use my system to be commodity traders. As previously indicated, I would use this system in Las Vegas if the Law of Supply and Demand applied there, but it doesn't. It only applies to the commodities market. Therefore, I merely use the commodities market as my vehicle to profits.

The basic system is described in Chapters II through VIII. All you need to do is to read and learn the concept as presented in those chapters, and you will make money trading commodities. The subsequent chapters present the subtleties of sophistication which you may or may not choose to employ after you have become comfortable with the basic system. You will increase the return on capital using the advanced techniques, but the basic system will prove adequate for a beginner. It will make money for you even if you know virtually nothing about commodities trading and have never traded before.

I

An Introduction to Commodities Trading

Most of the readers of this book will be experienced commodity traders, but the system which will be described is so simple that any person — whether he has traded commodities or not — will be able to trade profitably; however, for the benefit of the person who has never traded commodities but would like to start, I will devote the first few pages to a brief introduction to commodities trading.

The primary function of the commodity exchanges is to provide a marketplace wherein producers, processors, manufacturers, distributors, importers, exporters and other handlers of commodities may hedge the risk of inventory loss due to price changes during their period of ownership of the physical commodity. To best illustrate a series of hedges, I offer the following examples:

During the month of January a wheat farmer may calculate his cost to produce each bushel of wheat at $3.00, including expenses for seed, fertilizer, fuel, labor, machinery depreciation, interest on loans, and shipping expense to deliver the wheat to Chicago, etc. He notes that wheat futures contracts for July delivery on the Chicago Board of Trade are trading at $3.20 per bushel, so he sells all or a major portion of what he estimates his crop will be by instructing his commodity broker to execute futures contracts totaling sales of that amount. He has guaranteed himself a profit of $0.20 per bushel, and he has very little further concern for the fluctuations in the price of wheat. He is hedged and has assured his profit.

By the time this farmer's wheat is harvested in May, he may decide that he does not want to bother with the shipping of the wheat to Chicago, so he may simply sell the wheat to the local grain elevator operator. Since the farmer no longer owns the wheat he no longer needs the hedge, so he will lift the hedge by simultaneously instructing his commodity broker to cover the position by making an offsetting futures contract to take delivery of the same amount of wheat as originally contracted for in the initial contract. The initial contract was to make delivery of (sell), say, 40,000 bushels of wheat in July in Chicago; the offsetting contract was to take delivery of (buy) 40,000 bushels of wheat in July in Chicago. One cancels the other and the farmer has no further obligation to either deliver or to take delivery of wheat in July in Chicago.

During the period that the farmer was hedged, he had eliminated the risk of price fluctuations, for while a rise in the price of wheat would cause him to lose money on his futures contracts, the loss would be offset by the corresponding rise in the value of his physical wheat. The opposite is also true: a decline in the price of wheat would result in a profit on his futures contracts and a corresponding loss on the physical wheat. The farmer was only interested in a profit of $0.20 per bushel, and he guaranteed that in January while the crop was still growing.

When the farmer sells his wheat to the local grain elevator operator, the elevator operator has assumed the risk of ownership. Because the elevator operator is in the business of storing grains for storage charges only and has no interest in speculating on price fluctuations, he will now hedge his position. In the aggregate the elevator operator may have purchased as much as one million bushels of wheat. If he does not hedge that position and the price of wheat declines $0.10 per bushel (which would be a very modest price change for wheat), the elevator operator will lose $100,000 on his million bushels of wheat — a catastrophic loss. Therefore, the elevator operator — like the farmer — will hedge his inventory risk by selling futures contracts for an amount equal to his inventory. Once he has hedged, he has little concern for the fluctuations in the price of wheat, for gains or losses in the cash price for physical wheat will be offset by corresponding losses or gains in his futures contracts. As time passes and the elevator operator sells physical wheat from his elevator inventory he will lift portions of his hedges so that he stays fully hedged between physical inventory and futures contracts.

Among the customers who may be buying wheat from the grain elevator operator might be a miller who will grind the wheat into baking flour. The miller may be making contractual commitments with his customers to deliver flour many months from now at specific prices. If the miller does not hedge against these contracts he may suffer substantial losses if the price of wheat advances sharply before he is able to buy his necessary wheat for grinding to meet his contractual obligations. Like the farmer and the grain elevator operator, the miller will also hedge to avoid inventory risk, but his hedge will be opposite to theirs. The first two hedges were selling hedges because the farmer and the elevator operator sold futures contracts, but the miller's hedge will be a buying hedge because he will be buying to guarantee acquisition of the physical commodity at a future date at a specific price which will assure him of the ability to meet his contractual obligations profitably. Once the miller has hedged his position he has no further concern for the price fluctuations in wheat, for inventory losses or gains will be offset by corresponding gains or losses on his futures contracts.

Meantime, the baker who will buy the flour from the miller is making contracts for delivery of bread, cakes and other goods at some future date, so he must also hedge against these contracts by making buying hedges. His inventory losses or gains will also be offset by corresponding gains on his futures contracts.

If it were not for the benefit of price protection offered by hedging, users of wheat would be forced to trade with higher markups (profit margins) to offset inevitable losses which would come in bad years. Price swings would be sizable, and it would be difficult to conduct business.

To further reduce the broad swings and the day-to-day or minute-to-minute price fluctuations, another type of commodity trader has been invited to trade. He is known as the speculator. He rarely owns or ever deals in the physical commodity, but he speculates on what he believes will be the price changes. If he feels the price of wheat may advance, he makes a contract to *take* delivery of (to buy) wheat in Chicago at a specific price on a specific date. He has no intention of ever taking delivery of wheat, so sometime before the delivery date arrives he will make an offsetting contract to *make* delivery of (to sell) wheat in Chicago at a specific price on the originally specified date. One contract cancels the other, and the only matter to be settled is the profit or loss on his contracts. If his selling price is greater than his buying price, he has a profit; if the selling price is lower than the buying price, he has a loss.

The volume of trading accounted for by speculators is enormous in commodities trading and assists commodity users in exchanging the physical commodity or manufactured product at the lowest possible competitive prices.

When an individual decides that he would like to become a commodity speculator (trader), he goes to a commodity broker to open an account. This commodity broker may be the same broker who handles this individual's stock business, or it may be a firm which does commodity brokerage business exclusively. The individual signs the standard forms to open the account and makes the initial deposit — usually a $5,000 minimum. If the account is opened with a cashier's check, trading may commence immediately.

Since we have been talking about wheat, let's use a wheat contract for our illustration of the purchase and subsequent sale of a commodity futures contract. If we assume that the client has determined that the price of wheat may advance during the year, we will start with the assumption that he will give the broker an order to buy a contract of wheat. The logistics of the purchase are much the same as a stock purchase. The broker sends the order to the floor of the Chicago Board of Trade, and a trade is executed. The terms of the trade are then communicated back to the broker for confirmation to the client.

Basically, there are two differences between the purchase of shares of stock and the purchase of a commodities futures contract.

The first difference is that the stock purchase is permanent so that the new owner may hold the stock for as long as he chooses, whereas, the commodity futures contract purchaser has merely made a *contract to purchase* and will not become the owner until expiration of that contract. Then he becomes the owner and may hold it for as long as he chooses.

The second — and far more important — difference lies in the use of the word "contract." The commodity futures contract buyer does not purchase anything physical. A wheat buyer does not actually buy wheat. He merely makes a contract to buy wheat for delivery (or receipt) at a specified location on a specified date for a specified price. For example, if the speculator notes during August that wheat for delivery in Chicago in December is currently being traded (contracted for) at $3.00 a bushel, and if he thinks wheat will be going up in price before December, he may instruct his broker to "buy Chicago December wheat at $3.00." What he is saying is, "I want to make a contract to receive 5,000 bushels of wheat in Chicago in December at $3.00 per bushel."

Once the order is executed, the client has made that contract and has until December to decide whether he wants to fulfill the contract by actually receiving the wheat (unlikely if he is a speculator) or to cancel the contract by entering an offsetting sell contract, which is accomplished by giving his broker an order to "sell Chicago December wheat at $3.40." What this order says is, "I want to make a contract to deliver 5,000 bushels of wheat in Chicago in December at $3.40 per bushel." When both orders are executed — though the executions may occur months apart — they cancel each other as far as receipt and delivery are concerned, and the price difference represents the profit (or loss) for the speculator. In this case, the first contract was entered into at a buying price of $3.00, and the second (offsetting) contract was entered into at a selling price of $3.40, so the speculator has a profit of $0.40 per bushel on his 5,000 bushel commitment, a profit of $2,000, less commissions and fees.

Obviously, the speculator does not buy at $3.00 and sell at $3.40 on the same day. It takes time for the price to move through such a broad range, and there will be many factors that will enter into consideration which will cause the price to rise and fall on a daily basis before it eventually reaches the speculator's price objective — if ever. The trend of prices during the period of time that the speculator holds the contract might go something like this:

Shortly after entering into his contract to buy at $3.00 a U.S. Government report is issued which indicates that the recently-harvested wheat crop was larger than previously estimated, so the overabundance of supply causes the price to decline, and December wheat drops to $2.80. By September word is circulating that Australia and Argentina are having problems with their wheat crops. (Remember, both of these countries are big producers of wheat, but their crops are harvested six months later than ours because they are in the Southern Hemisphere.) This rumor of possible crop damage causes the December price to rise, for it indicates the possibility of a reduction in the overall world supply. Shortly thereafter, there is a rumor that Russia is about to make large-scale purchases of wheat in the world markets. This causes the price to rise. Then the rumors appear to be unfounded, and the price declines. Then word comes out of Washington, D. C., that some senators from wheat-growing states are going to push for higher support prices for wheat farmers for the coming year, and the price runs up again. Later word out of Washington indicates that some senators from cotton-growing states intend to oppose the higher wheat supports unless something is done to aid cotton growers, so the price drops. Then a government report on inflation indicates this problem is intensifying, so people rush to buy "things" — including commodities — with their depreciating dollars; consequently, the price of wheat rises. A seriously deteriorating situation is revealed as the U.S. balance of payments is announced, indicating worsening problems ahead for the U.S. dollar overseas. But a declining dollar makes purchases of U.S. products cheaper for foreign holders of U.S. dollars, so they buy U.S. wheat instead of Canadian, Australian or Argentine wheat. This boosts the Chicago price of wheat. Add them all together and you probably will find that the events which caused a price increase outnumbered those which caused a price decrease. Thus, before December rolls around, the price may have advanced to $3.40 for December wheat, and the speculator is able to close his position profitably.

It is important that you note that I mentioned that the price declined before it rose. In my illustration the price declined from $3.00 to $2.80 before rising through a series of oscillations to a price of $3.40. It is that initial decline which destroys most commodity speculators. The broker cautions the speculator that wheat might undergo a severe decline, and the speculator is admonished to enter a protective "stop-sell" order which instructs the broker to close out the client's position if the price drops a certain minor amount. (This is where that "keep your losses small and let your profits run" foolishness comes from.) The use of stop-sell orders is an exercise in vanity, for the user has convinced himself that he has the ability to make every purchase precisely at the bottom and that stop-sell orders placed slightly lower are unlikely to be reached. I maintain that it is virtually impossible to buy always at or near the lowest price, so the system of using stop-sell orders will guarantee repeated losses and extermination of the account.

You should also note that I mentioned a series of news events which would cause the price to fluctuate. These are normal occurrences, and commodity prices will fluctuate in response to them — the same as stocks fluctuate in response to news events. It is these minor price oscillations which led me to develop the system which will be described in this book.

One thing which is important for the neophyte commodity trader to appreciate as a difference between commodity and stock trading is the handling of margin. In stock trading, margin requirements are generally 50%. This means that $10,000 worth of stock may be purchased with a deposit of $5,000, and the stock broker arranges a loan of $5,000 for the client to complete payment for the stock purchase. The client is obliged to pay interest on the borrowed $5,000, which is called his debit balance.

There is no such thing as a debit balance incurred in the purchase of a commodity contract. You will see this immediately if you remember that there was no actual purchase made of any physical commodity. Only a *contract to purchase* was made. Since no actual change of ownership occurs, no one is required to pay for the purchase of anything. Therefore, without any cash changing hands, there cannot possibly be a debit balance. *No interest charges can possibly be incurred.*

The only reason the commodity trader is required to make a margin deposit is to guarantee payment of the loss in case the contract is closed out at a selling price which is lower than the buying price and therefore results in a loss. Margin deposits are actually earnest money. Both parties — the buyer and the seller — are required to make margin deposits with their respective brokers to guarantee payment of profits to the winners from the losers.

When I speak of two parties being involved in a trade, I do not want to create the impression that it is necessary for the parties on opposite sides of the trade to agree to offset their positions at precisely the same time. An example I like to use to convey the concept of commodity trading is to ask my listener to visualize a large gymnasium filled with commodity traders. These traders would include producers, shippers, processors, exporters, importers, all of the other people who might be involved in the handling of the commodity from raw material to finished product (these are the hedgers), and the inevitable speculators. There might be 1,000 or more traders in our hypothetical gymnasium. If we use wheat as an example, the traders would include all of the hedgers mentioned earlier in this chapter.

When trading commences, one of the 1,000 traders will be a buyer making a contract to take delivery at a specific location, date, and price; someone else in the gym will make the other side of the contract, agreeing to make delivery at that same location, date, and price. Other pairs of traders join in, always with a buyer on one side of the trade and a seller on the other. When buyers are the more aggressive traders, the price will rise; when sellers are the more aggressive, the price will fall.

As time passes and prices rise and fall, buyers and sellers choose to close out their respective positions — some with profits, and some with losses. When a trader chooses to close out his position, it is unnecessary for the party who was originally on the opposite side of the trade to close out his position simultaneously, for another trader will step in and take that opposite position at whatever the prevailing price is at that time.

Over a period of time all of the people in the gym conclude whatever trading they intend to do, and they leave the room. The last two people remaining in the gym are the person owning the wheat who intends to deliver it and the person who intends to accept delivery of the wheat. The farmer, the grain, elevator operator, the miller, the baker, all of the other hedgers — as well as the speculators — have used the futures market for better or worse, and the trading in that particular contract has expired. However, trading continues, for all of the hedgers and speculators have met in another gym and are now trading futures contracts against wheat for delivery at some date in some deferred delivery month. It goes on forever.

While trading in that gym, all of the hedgers and speculators were obliged to deposit margin money with their brokers, who in turn deposited the money with the clearing house for the exchange which trades that particular commodity. While traders held positions they were required to deposit additional margin (this is called a "margin call") to cover paper losses resulting from price movements which were adverse to their positions; conversely, they were permitted to withdraw excess funds which may have accumulated during those periods when paper profits were generated by favorable price movements. As each trader left the gym, he would stop by the cashier's window — which represents the clearing house — to pick up a check representing his margin deposits, plus or minus his profits or losses.

In my illustration of trading I have always shown the initial trade to be on the "buy" side, but that is not a requirement. In stock trading most people sell only stock they own and rarely — if ever sell before buying (called a "short sale"), but short sales are a common practice in commodities trading. If, in my example, the trader had expected the price of wheat to decline, he could have sold first with the hope of buying later at a lower price. This is also referred to as a short sale in commodities trading, but it has the advantage of not requiring an "up-tick"* such as required in stock market trading.

It would be nice to be able to say that all of the money which changes hands comes out even, that the total amount of profits equals the total amount of losses, but that is not the case. The gross profits and losses will be equal, but the net losses will far exceed the net profits, for there is a commission charged on every transaction to both buyer and seller. The effect is a reduction of profit for the winners and an increase in loss for the losers. The brokerage houses are the only true winners. This is another reason why it is so difficult for the average person to win at commodity trading. If his poor judgment does not get him, the commissions will.

---

* In the 1929 stock market it was permissible for speculators to make unrestricted short sales by borrowing and selling huge blocks of stock as the market fell. It was their intention to repurchase the stock at a lower price, to return the borrowed stock to the lender, and to pocket the profit. This practice was a major contributing factor to the stock market's collapse.

To prevent a recurrence of that debacle, short sales in the stock market presently may be made only on an up-tick, which means at a price higher than the last previously different price.

No such restriction is placed upon commodity markets.

It should be noted here that one of the major attractions of commodity futures trading is the clearing house system. It is comforting to the speculator to know that his margin money is deposited with a clearing house which acts as referee and custodian of all funds so that all winners are assured of receipt of their profits. Thus, the speculator need have little fear for the financial condition of the firm with which he trades, for the financial integrity of his account is made secure not only by the deposit of his own funds with his own brokerage firm, but also by (1) the guaranty funds which each brokerage firm is required to deposit with the clearing house, (2) the clearing house's own substantial cash reserves, and (3) the joint responsibility of the collective membership of the clearing house. It is because of all of this collective protection that the commodity industry may claim with pride that no customer has ever lost a single cent as the result of the failure of any commodity clearing house.

I also want to call your attention to the magnitude of commodity futures trading, to encourage you to take a long and serious look at commodities trading if you have never traded before. Most persons are familiar with the workings of the New York Stock Exchange, and we accept it as being the world's largest securities market in which the stocks of the world's largest corporations are traded daily in dollar amounts which almost defy comprehension. But are you aware that there are several commodities which by themselves account for more dollar volume of trading in a single day than the aggregate dollar volume of all stocks on the NYSE on a single day?

On an average day the NYSE may have a turnover of 150,000,000 shares at an average price of $20 per share. That is a total dollar value of $3,000,000,000. That is $3 billion.

Consider corn. A typical trading day for corn on the Chicago Board of Trade will show a turnover of about 80,000 contracts, and volume far in excess of 100,000 contracts is not uncommon. Each contract is for 5,000 bushels of corn at an average price of around $3.00 per bushel. Thus, an average day's trading of 80,000 contracts of corn would equal about $1.2 billion, while a single day's volume of 130,000 contracts would equal $1.95 billion. This means that corn *alone* trades a dollar value equal to 65% of *all* stocks on the NYSE *combined*!

But corn is chicken feed. Chicago Board of Trade volume in soybeans will easily exceed 100,000 contracts of 5,000 bushels each.

With soybeans trading around $7 per bushel, that is $3.5 billion, or nearly 20% more than the total dollar value of the NYSE turnover.

The hysteria for gold and silver speculation has subsided, but it will come again. Even now, with gold speculation virtually nonexistent, typical daily volume on the New York Commodity Exchange (Comex, for short) runs 50,000 contracts daily, with 100,000 contract trading days not uncommon. At $400 per ounce for the 100 ounce contract, the contract has a value of $40,000, and the dollar value of 100,000 contracts is $4 billion. *That is a single day's trading!* 1.33 times the NYSE trading *in an inactive commodity.*

Silver was the darling of the speculators when everyone wanted to ride the coattails of the Texans when they tried to corner the silver market in 1979. Daily trading volume of the 5,000 ounce Comex contract at that time averaged about 40,000 contracts. Silver's price was about $12, giving the daily trading volume a value of $2.4 billion. Today silver trades around $5, so its daily dollar value is about $1 billion, but that is still one-third of the value of *all* trades on the NYSE, and that is in a *dead* commodity. Speculation will return to gold and silver, and if silver trades again at $15 (it hit $50 in the 1979-80 run) the volume probably will leap to more than 100,000 contracts daily, and the dollar volume will exceed $7.5 billion.

Raw materials are not the only commodities traded on commodity exchanges. Crude oil is a contract which trades very actively on the New York Mercantile Exchange, averaging about 100,000 contracts for 1,000 barrels daily. At $20 per barrel, that is $2 billion daily, or two-thirds of the dollar value of *all* stocks trading on the NYSE.

Financial instruments began trading just a few years ago, and their volume has proved astounding. The German mark trades about 60,000 contracts for 125,000 marks each on the IMM daily. At $0.62 per mark, the dollar value is $4.65 billion. The Japanese yen trades 40,000 contracts of 12.5 million yen on an average day. At 100 yen per dollar, that is $5 billion worth of trading.

Stock indices are relatively new traders, but the Standard & Poor's index of 500 stocks trades 50,000 contracts daily. At 460 on the index, the market value of these trades is $11.5 billion *daily* . A single stock market index trades nearly four times the volume of all of the NYSE stocks put together! And that's only *one* index; there are also the NYSE Composite, the Standard & Poor's Midcap 400, the Value-Line, the MMI Maxi, the Standard & Poor's 100, etc.

The three-month U.S. Treasury bills frequently trade 10,000 contracts in a day. At $1 million per contract, that is $10 billion, or 3.3 times the trading on the NYSE. The combined trading for two-year, five-year, and ten-year U.S. Treasury notes averages well over a combined 100,000 contracts per day. At $100,000 per contract ($200,000 on the two-year), that is also a dollar volume of well over $10 billion daily. The U.S. Treasury thirty-year bond contract averages 350,000 contracts per day. At $100,000 per contract, that is a dollar value of $35 billion, or *twelve times the value of all stocks traded on the NYSE*!

Are you ready for this one? The Eurodollar, which trades on the International Monetary Exchange in Chicago, averages 300,000 contracts traded daily. At *$1 million* per contract, that is a volume of $300 billion daily. By comparison, the $3 billion of value for *all* stocks traded on the New York Stock Exchange in a day pales into insignificance.

If you are not trading commodities, you are missing something. It is the biggest market in the world. There are countless opportunities for profit here. Many people abuse its qualities of leverage and time compression to turn their trading into outright gambling, but I use it almost as a long-term investment vehicle. You, too, should take advantage of the commodities markets to earn an above-average investment return with below-average risk.

Before closing this chapter on an introduction to commodities trading, I would like to comment further on the features of commodities trading which make it so attractive to a large and rapidly expanding segment of the population. I previously described the fluctuations caused by news events, rumors, crop reports, etc. You may have inferred from my description that commodities, per se, are extremely volatile. Such is not the case. Once in awhile a particular commodity will make a very substantial price run, but generally commodity prices move in amounts which are no greater than the price swings we see (and accept as normal) in stocks. A price swing for wheat within a range of $3.00 on the low for the year to a high of $4.00 is the same as a price swing for a stock through a range from $30 to $40. It is the 5% to 10% (sometimes as low as 2%) margin requirements which make commodities trading attractive, for this low margin amplifies moves by a factor of ten to twenty times, allowing for huge percentage gains (and losses). This enormous leverage is also reflected in the compression of the amount of time required to realize certain percentage moves. Whereas it might require a year or more for a stock purchased for cash (100% "margin") to appreciate 100%, a commodity futures contract purchased on 5% margin may show the same results in one-twentieth the time. It is the combination of super leverage and time compression which makes commodities trading attractive.

Certainly another attractive feature of commodities trading is the abundance of information available to *everyone*. There is virtually no such thing as "insider information" in commodities trading, for the information which affects commodities prices — information such as a government report on the predicted size of the corn or soybean crop — is so massive in scope that it would be impossible for anyone other than the U.S. Government to accumulate such data, and when that information is collected it is released after the close of trading and with equal distribution to all persons. Prior to the release of such reports the precautions taken to insure protection against leakage of the information are akin to something that might come from a James Bond novel. Data are collected in windowless rooms which have no telephones or other means of contact with the outside world; meals, ordered in advance, are passed through chambers which are otherwise sealed so that no contact can be made between those compiling the information within the sealed room and outsiders. The entire process of protecting the secrecy of these reports is a fascinating story that could fill a book by itself.

(Note: The foregoing paragraph was repeated verbatim from the previous editions of this book. Although generally still true, I will mention later in this book about my suspicions that there is now leakage.)

These reports, and all other news events having a bearing upon commodities, are reported continuously in media offices and brokerage houses through such services as Dow Jones, Reuters, Associated Press, and United Press International. Commodity prices and news are reported daily in the financial sections of all major newspapers. Because developments within industrial corporations usually require lengthy periods of time, the day-to-day happenings do not require daily reporting. Also, due to the limitations of time or space for financial reporting in the media, it is impractical — indeed, impossible — to publish daily reports on the tens of thousands of corporations which have public stock outstanding. News affecting the stocks of major corporations may appear no more frequently than once each few weeks, while news of minor corporations may appear but once each few months. Major corporate news developments — such as an earnings report — are known to countless insiders such as the internal accounting department, the external auditors, corporate officers and directors, and the printers — and to all of the friends of those insiders — long before release of the news to the general public. Such is not the case for commodities, for with only fifty commodities to be reported upon, and with news from throughout the world affecting commodity prices, it is common for *daily* reports to appear in the media on each commodity. Without such broad coverage of commodity news, commerce would be impossible.

If you still harbor any doubts about commodities futures trading as an investment vehicle for the employment of your funds, I should remind you of perhaps the most compelling reason of all: inflation. The system which I will describe in this book uses only the long side (the buying side) of the commodities markets. Therefore, steadily increasing prices are a plus factor which will work in the favor of all traders and should make it possible for even the most unskilled trader to make profits.

II

The Las Vegas System

This book describes a highly successful and profitable system for trading commodity futures contracts. However, it is a system which has its mathematical roots in a Las Vegas gambling system, so to help the reader understand the technique of the commodities system it is appropriate to begin with a short discussion of the Las Vegas system.

I did not invent the Las Vegas system, so I may only speculate on how it was developed. I imagine someone observed that a person playing at a gaming table and betting only even-money bets usually broke about even after playing for any relatively brief period of time. That would indicate that the number of winners and losers would be approximately equal. That would be statistically correct, for the house percentage is very low, and a player should lose only a relatively small amount during a brief play.

The curious observer who wanted to capitalize upon the probability of winners approximately equalling losers must have carried his empirical analysis a step further to note that the player making repeated bets of equal size would at times be slightly ahead, while at other times he would be slightly behind. On some occasions the player would be ahead or behind a large amount, and on a very few occasions he would be ahead or behind a substantial amount. However, sooner or later his bankroll would restore itself to approximately its starting amount because of the statistical probability that the winners and losers would equalize over an extended period of time.

The developer of the system probably reasoned that he could capitalize upon this statistical probability of winners and losers being equal by inventing a progressive betting method which would insure that his winning bets were for amounts that would be slightly greater than the amounts of the losing bets. If nothing else, his progression is beautiful in it simplicity.

Other than the straight Double Up system, this progression which is called Chops, Stair Step, or Pinch and Press, is probably as simple a progression as a person could find. The Double Up system calls for the player to wager a single unit for the first bet and then double up each time he loses a bet, with the theory being that eventually he will win one bet which will recover all of his losses and reward him with a single unit of profit. Those who play that system like it because it requires only a single winner to recoup all losses, but it is probably one of the worst progressions ever developed, for it takes a run of only a few consecutive losers for the player either to reach the table limit (so that he may no longer continue his progression) or to expend his total bankroll. Anyone who tries the Double Up system usually goes broke within the first few hours of play.

One facet of the Double Up system which should be noted at this time because of its bearing upon the Chops system is the mathematical probability that the player will — during the time he survives and before he goes broke — win one unit for each two bets that he makes. If he plays long enough to make 100 bets, it is probable that he will win about 50 units; about half of his bets will be losers, requiring that he double up, while the other half will be winners, giving him his single-unit profit and allowing him to reduce his bet to the starting level again. There will be times when he loses six bets in a row, requiring that he double up six times, but there will be other times when he wins six consecutive times. He still wins one unit for each pair of bets.

Chops is a much better system than Double Up because it produces the same profit with a far smaller bankroll. Here is how it works: The player starts with a basic bet and simply increases his bet a single unit each time he loses and reduces his bet a single unit each time he wins. For example, he might start with one dollar and lose his first bet. His next bet would be two dollars. If he wins, he drops back to a single dollar bet. If, instead, he loses the two-dollar bet, he goes up to three. If he wins the three-dollar bet he goes down to two, but if, instead, he loses the three-dollar bet, he goes up to four. If he wins the four-dollar bet, he drops down to three. The theory behind this progression is that the winners and losers will eventually even out so that the player will have, say, 100 bets with fifty winners and fifty losers and win $50, for each winner is $1 more than some corresponding loser.

As with the player who used no progression in his betting but maintained the bet at a fixed level, the Chops player will at times be behind by six, eight, ten, or even twenty bets, but usually the number of winners and losers will equalize so that he returns to his starting level and — like the Double Up system player — has one dollar of profit for each *pair* of decisions. Thus, if he is there for 100 decisions he will win 50 units; 200 decisions will produce 100 units of profit; etc.

To be more precise, the house percentage is about 1.4% on the craps table, but let us call it 2%. That means the house will win two more bets than it loses out of each 100. In 100 decisions on the craps table the house should win about 51 times and lose 49. That means the Chops player making wagers in dollar units should win about $46 in 100 decisions, which is $49 for the combination of 49 winners and 49 losers, less the $3 for the two percentage losses which caused him to lose an extra $1 bet, an extra $2 bet, and pushed him up to a new basic $3 bet. If he stays for another 100 decisions he will win only $42 on this series, for he should again have 49 winners and 49 losers for a $49 profit, less the $3 and $4 bets the percentage forces him to lose, and now his basic bet has been upped to $5. Eventually, if the player is greedy and plays so long that his basic bet is pushed above $25, even the system can no longer provide the player with a profit, for the two percentage losses would now exceed the basic $49 profit per 100 decisions.

Obviously, Chops is intended as a system to grind out a nominal profit, nothing more. Hit and run. It works for me frequently, but on some occasions the bet just keeps getting larger and larger, and prudence forces me to quit with a sizable loss, for there is no law that says I must now start to win simply because I have been losing awhile. (This brief description of the Chops system lacks the additional sophistication that I employ when I play the system, but that has been purposely omitted to keep the treatise to minimum length.)

The Chops system will produce frequent small winnings, but it must inevitably produce some large losses. I play it for entertainment, not for profit. When it comes to profit, I play the commodities market, for in commodities I know there is a Law on my side that says I can depend upon winners to come my way after I have some losers. That Law is the Law of Supply and Demand, and when it is coupled with the Chops betting progression, it assures profit.

III

Supply/Demand

Mathematicians are continually experimenting with systems to beat the stock and commodity markets. Their technical skills include highly sophisticated computer techniques. However, few, if any, of these techniques have proved consistent because the analysis is directed toward the *effect* rather than the *cause* of price fluctuations. In other words, the study of price movements, which is called technical analysis, is a study of effect, being a study of prior price action, volume, chart patterns, etc., and the effect which these factors will have upon future prices; therefore, technical methods of price predictions — including computer systems — have proven woefully inadequate because it is impossible for such methods to anticipate unexpected changes in supply and demand, which are the true cause of price fluctuations.

Think about it. Let's say corn has been trading around $2.60 during June, but we run into three weeks of blistering heat throughout the Corn Belt in the first part of July. The price advances to $2.90. Then a week of gentle rains throughout the Corn Belt breaks the drought and sends corn's price back to $2.60. Chartists would now call $2.90 a "resistance level," and they would tell you that you should sell corn if it returns to the $2.90 level "because that is where it met resistance on the chart." That is preposterous! We might get *four* weeks of blistering heat at record levels *in August* without a drop of rain anywhere in the entire Corn Belt. We can't know during the first few days of the new drought that it is going to last a month, but the price will begin to inch slightly higher. As the drought extends itself to about two weeks, the price increases to $2.90. If you are foolish enough to believe that $2.90 will again be the point at which corn's price will reverse simply because it is a *resistance level* and you sell corn short, you will have another whopping loss two weeks later when the new drought is four weeks old and corn is selling at $4.00!

The chart had nothing to do with the first $2.90 top. It was the *rain!* The chart had nothing to do with the second $2.90 — which was not a top. This time it was the *lack of rain.* The only way corn was going to reverse and turn down a second time from $2.90 was if it had rained again. Rain — or the lack thereof — is what *caused* the price movements. The movements themselves were only the *effects*.

Consider another scenario: Gold is declining because of over-production and a glut of supply. It has drifted from $450 per ounce down to $420. Then someone assassinates a world leader and the price of gold leaps to $440. In a week or two world tensions have subsided, and gold has resumed its downward movement because of the glut of supply. A chartist would have you believe that the price will bottom again at $420 because that "proved to be a support level last time." During the few weeks that tensions are high, a report on worldwide gold production may have been released, and it indicated that gold production is declining because of low prices while consumption is increasing for the same reason. By sheer coincidence the report was released just as the price of gold had fallen to $420, and it rallies on the news. That convinces the chartist that $420 was a true "support level." Indeed, if gold stays between $425 and $475 for the next four years and then declines again to $420, the chartist will tell us that gold should find support again at $420 simply because that is what it did four years earlier. That, too, is preposterous, for we might now be in an economic recession and gold consumption is low, creating another surplus of supply. Gold will ignore the $420 support level and go straight to $350 — unless the chartist is saved by a different kook who shoots a different world leader.

You must realize that it is only the available (or prospective) supply of a commodity and the demand for that commodity which can possibly affect its price. Supply and demand *cause* price movements; the price movements are only the *effect* of supply and demand.

Thus, to be successful in predicting future prices in stock and commodity markets it is essential to preface technical analysis with fundamental analysis, which is the study of supply and demand factors. Unfortunately, fundamental analysis fails miserably in the stock market because of the specialist system the market employs and the influence of insider trading. Those two factors make it extremely difficult for members of the public who have no access to the specialist's book or to insider information to make profits in the stock market. In recent years the public has become increasingly aware of the stranglehold which specialists and insiders have upon stocks, and this probably accounts, in part, for the public investing so heavily in mutual funds — where *all* knowledge is insider information.

But the specialist system and insider trading are not the only factors making fundamental analysis of the stock market so difficult. The overwhelming powers which dictate stock prices are the two emotions called FEAR and GREED. No matter how cautious and studied the analytical methods one employs in the stock market, the results will have a very low predictability rate and will bear more relationship to mere chance than to anything else because of the unpredictability of the fear and greed emotions of investors. Fear and greed will continue to dominate the stock market as investors — including professional managers — chase stocks in rising markets and unload in falling markets, thereby amplifying the very price extremes they had sought to avoid.

"Buy on dips" is the standard recommendation of securities analysts, but people tell me they get sick and tired of spending long hours analyzing a list of stocks before isolating one and deciding to make an investment in that stock, only to find that when they thought they were buying on a dip they were actually buying into the beginning of a decline brought about by massive insider selling. The insiders and their friends knew well in advance of a pending public announcement that the company was facing a problem which would adversely affect the price of its stock, and they sold to the unsuspecting public.

Conversely, investors sometimes hold stocks for extended periods of time while that stock rests in a static range, not going low enough to buy more nor high enough to sell profitably. The holder of the stock becomes restive. Then one day the stock moves up two points and the holder sells, feeling greatly relieved that he is finally able to unload the stock with a reasonable return for the time the money was invested. During the next few days the stock jumps three more points, and then there is a news announcement of a technological breakthrough which will enhance the company's competitive position in its industry and ultimately increase it earnings; or there is a buyout offer; or any one of dozens of other events which could inflate the stock's worth. Only the insiders knew, and they took advantage of their information at the expense of the general public.

I have a personal distaste for the stock market because of its volatility. Has it ever occurred to you that stocks are far more volatile than commodities? Most people would scoff at that statement, but it is absolutely true. I once did an 8,000-word study for the Department of Corporations, State of California, to demonstrate that particular fact. The facts presented in that treatise are not important to this book, but it suffices to say that it is obvious that it is only the *leverage* which may be employed in commodities trading that gives commodities markets the APPEARANCE of greater volatility. A commodity such as corn might go through an entire season with a low of $2.00 and a high of $3.00 per bushel (which would be a *monstrous* move for corn), while a company which uses corn as an ingredient in its product line might see its stock range from a low of $20 to a high of $40 during the same year. That means the stock is twice as volatile as the commodity, but people never seem to notice that since they are accustomed to buying stock and paying 100% cash while they think in terms of trading commodities on 5% to 10% margin. Stocks actually were carried on 10% margin in the 1920's, which was one of the primary causes of the 1929 stock market collapse.

Commodities may be carried on 5% to 10% margin, but that does not make them all that great a risk if the leverage is used properly. That great leverage makes it possible for the trader to control large quantities of commodities with small amounts of cash and thereby realize substantial profits (or losses) from the relatively small ranges of prices through which most commodities swing. This subject is covered in Chapters I and XXV, but I wanted to mention it now in the context of comparing stock and commodity markets.

Commodities markets adapt themselves ideally to fundamental analysis because price variations occur in almost perfect relationship to SUPPLY/DEMAND factors. Conversely, supply and demand will ebb and flow in direct relationship to prices. In commodities, low prices result in low profitability for producers and force production restraints, thereby reducing supply. Concomitantly, low prices encourage consumption, thereby increasing demand. The necessary result of this "low price/supply reduction/demand increase" situation is an inevitable price increase. Ultimately, the price will rise to such a level that it will prompt production increases due to higher profit margins, and a corresponding decrease in consumption as potential consumers are priced out of the market. Then the cycle reverses.

If you are seeking a vehicle for employment of techniques of fundamental and technical analysis (99% fundamental and 1% technical) for the highest degree of predictability, you should concentrate on the commodities markets where SUPPLY/DEMAND factors — rather than FEAR/GREED factors — dictate prices. You should further concentrate your activities by confining your attention primarily to *cause* factors (supply/demand) with only a minor consideration to *effect* factors (price).

It can be stated without equivocation that supply and demand bear such a high degree of influence upon commodity prices that reasonable ranges may be predicted with a high degree of accuracy for the foreseeable future. This definitely is not true of the stock market, but it has been true of commodity prices since the dawn of history and will be true until the end of time. This is the foundation upon which my commodity trading system has been built.

IV

The Scale Trading System

Keeping in mind that commodities trading at prices which are unrealistically low by historical standards must trade at higher prices eventually, purchase of such commodities should offer great potential for profit to the patient investor. In fact, accumulation of additional holdings on further price deterioration should substantially increase the probability of profit as the ultimate turnaround in price approaches certainty, offering the investor an even surer opportunity to take profits on the inevitable rally. This is known as "scale trading" — buying on a scale down and selling on a scale up. A scale trader with sufficient capital to withstand severe declines will ultimately show a profit as falling prices *must* alter SUPPLY/DEMAND and ultimately result in a rallying price. It has been said, "The best cure for a low price *is* a low price," and with that truism in mind we recognize why a conservative program of scale trading of commodity futures contracts must show profits.

For example, consider corn prices. Corn formerly traded in the range of $1.00 to $2.00 per bushel, but that was when Iowa farmland, which presently sells for $1,200 per acre, sold for $700 per acre; when the worldwide price for oil to fuel tractors and to manufacture fertilizer was $2.00 per barrel instead of the present $20; and when the minimum wage was $1.00 per hour instead of $4.25. For at least the last decade corn has traded through a range of about $1.40 on the low and $3.80 on the high, so it is realistic to assume that this approximate range will be maintained until another burst of inflation raises it. Whenever corn trades in the lowest third of that range — assuming the available supply of corn is around the normal level — the lowest probable price can be accurately projected at $1.40, and the probable risk in buying can be predetermined. With the range being from $1.40 to $3.80, a total of $2.40, one-third of the range would be $0.80, and the bottom third would be anything below $2.20 ($1.40 + $0.80 = $2.20). Thus, the conservative speculator would begin to accumulate corn at $2.20 per bushel, and subsequent purchases would be made upon each further decline of $0.10. As with the Las Vegas Chops system, each position so acquired would be liquidated at a price $0.10 above the corresponding purchase price. The commodity futures corn contract is for 5,000 bushels, so the $0.10 gain per bushel means $500 of profit for the scale trader.

(Note: The reader should be aware that trading results as presented throughout this book will ignore commissions and consider the gross profit to be the same as the net. The reason for this is the frequent gap openings which give the trader bonus executions. These bonuses, when cumulated over an extended period, will generally come very close to covering the trader's commission costs. For example, corn may close at the high of the day, $2.49, when the scale trader has a resting order to sell a contract at $2.50. The next morning corn may gap open at $2.52, giving the scale trader an execution at that level instead of the expected $2.50, for a 2 cent bonus, which is equal to $100 on the 5,000 bushel contract. That would be enough to cover about two round turn corn commissions. This may happen on either the buy side or the sell side, and although it does not happen every time, it happens frequently enough to cover the major portion of the commissions.)

The scale trader must not adhere so strictly to the rule of trading only in the bottom third of the last decade that he becomes inflexible in selecting starting points. The bottom third applies when there is a *normal* supply of corn available, but in the year following the 1983 drought corn raced above $3.50 and did not fall below $2.00 until the bumper crop of 1986. The drought of 1988 sent corn racing to $3.60 again, and it took four years of bumper crops to bring the price down to $2.00. The flood of 1993 took corn up to $3.10, but it didn't go higher because of the record crop harvested in 1992, which provided a cushion against the flood losses. Under conditions which prevail as this is written in early 1994, it is unlikely that corn will trade under $2.00 for at least another year or two, and scales could commence around $2.65 instead of $2.20.

What makes this trading method succeed is the SUPPLY/DEMAND influence described earlier. Any time the price of corn falls to near $2.00 per bushel, farmers will reduce their corn plantings and either fallow the fields or switch to other more profitable field crops, thereby decreasing the corn supply for the next season. Meantime, livestock feeders will breed their animals instead of slaughtering them to take advantage of the low corn prices and high profit margins. The increasing number of animals will increase the demand for corn. Obviously, these factors of decreased supplies during a period of increasing consumption *must* cause corn's price to rise. Once the price has risen enough, the cycle will reverse itself, and then prices must fall.

During that period when the corn price has risen because of relatively low supply and higher demand it is imprudent for the scale trader to trade corn. Does this mean he must sit on the sidelines and wait for the cycle to reverse itself and for the price of corn to return to a level which complies with the rule of buying only in the lowest third of the range? Of course not. First of all, it is possible that livestock prices may have moved through a similar but exactly opposite cycle. When corn prices are high, livestock feeders will be slaughtering their animals because of low profit margins. This surplus of slaughter animals drives livestock prices down and makes any one of the several meat commodity futures contracts attractive for scale trading. As corn farmers increase plantings to take advantage of the high corn prices, they start the downward phase of the cycle in livestock prices. As soon as it becomes apparent that corn supplies will be increasing and corn prices declining, livestock feeders will begin to withhold animals from slaughter, saving them for breeding. This creates a temporary shortage of slaughter animals, starting the upward phase in the cycle of meat prices. As long as corn prices decline and meat prices rise, livestock feeders will be increasing breeding. Eventually the number of animals consuming feed will be great enough to cause the two cycles to reverse again as corn prices rise because of the increased demand, and as meat prices fall because of the excess supply of livestock. While this example may have been presented too simplistically, the principle is invariable and requires only time for realization.

Furthermore, there are more than forty commodities in which futures contracts are traded. If corn and livestock prices are midway in their respective cycles, making neither of them attractive for scale trading at the moment, there will probably be several totally unrelated commodities which are perfectly suited for scale trading. I cannot recall ever having seen the time when there were not several commodities that were attractively situated for the commencement of a scale trading venture.

V

Why You Can't Lose

There will surely be those who will scoff at the title of this book and maintain that there is absolutely no system that will insure against losses, so I will take just a few paragraphs to illustrate the truth of the statement that, "You can't lose trading commodities using the scale trading system."

It is obvious that the person with unlimited wealth could scale trade forever and never be the least bit concerned about the possibility of losing money. He would only need to pay *cash* for his purchases and hold them for whatever time necessary until they rose above his purchase prices, allowing him to cash his profits. It would be impossible for that trader to lose.

However, few people have sufficient capital to finance an all-cash scale trading operation; furthermore, the return on invested capital would be very low percentage-wise. The reader will more likely be a person with $10,000 to $100,000 available for scale trading, so I will show you the method to use to insure that your capital will never be exhausted and that your profits will be assured.

The prospective scale trader with as little as $5,000 of capital should confine his trading to the smaller contracts which trade on the

MidAmerica Commodity Exchange, the 1,000 ounce Chicago Board of Trade silver contract, or commodities with low volatility such as corn or oats. The MidAmerica Commodity Exchange is covered more completely in Chapter IX, but I will use the MidAm 1,000 bushel corn contract for my examples in this chapter.

The key to every successful scale trade is advance selection of a proper scale. If the numbers are worked out in advance and planned so that all possible contingencies may be met without hazard to the capital in the account, it is impossible to lose. For example, if the person with $10,000 to invest buys his first MidAmerica contract of corn at $2.50 and plans to buy another contract each $1.00 down, he will have acquired contracts at $2.50, $1.50, and $0.50 if corn goes to $0.01. His paper losses would be $2,490 on the first contract, $1,490 on the second, and $490 on the third. That's an aggregate loss of $4,470. This person would still have $5,530 of his capital intact. All he has to do is to hold these contracts until they recover in price so that he may sell them profitably. There may be times when the scale trader is forced to hold a position of several contracts for a very long time — perhaps until the contracts expire — but he needs only to roll them over by selling the expiring contracts and purchasing the same number of contracts of a deferred delivery month. Eventually the Law of Supply and Demand will push the price high enough for him to sell at levels which will permit him to recapture the previously taken losses and to cash his profits.

Obviously, it is ludicrous to even consider the possibility of corn going to $0.01 per bushel, but I wanted to end any possible debate over the "can't lose" claim immediately by demonstrating that it is impossible to lose if the capital is adequate.

A more realistic attempt at establishing a workable scale would be to start scaling corn with purchases at $2.50 and allowing for a price drop to $1.50. This is about $0.50 below any reasonable expectation, but it allows for the unexpected. If purchases are made each $0.25 down from $2.50 to $1.50, the buy points are $2.50, $2.25, $2.00, $1.75, and $1.50. The paper losses are $1,000 ($10.00 for each penny decline) on the first contract, $750 on the second, $500 on the third, $250 on the fourth, and zero on the last. The aggregate loss is $2,500. There is still $7,500 available after corn has declined to $1.50, which is some $0.50 below any reasonably expectable price level. This means the scale is too broad. It should be tightened, buying more contracts at smaller decrements.

After you have worked a few trial scales for yourself, you will get a feel for them, and you will not go through all of the tedium that I am demonstrating, but I must do it here for the sake of illustration. An example of a really tight scale would be to buy MidAmerica corn contracts each $0.05 down, from $2.50 to $1.50. This would accumulate 21 contracts, and the aggregate paper loss would be $10,500, not even considering the required $80 margin per contract. It is quite unlikely that corn will decline to $1.50 anytime in the next few years, but we must admit to the possibility that it could reach that level; thus, the prudent scale trader would abandon the attempt to buy corn on a 5 cent scale with only $10,000 of capital in his account.

Try each $0.10 down. At $1.50, eleven contracts have been accumulated, and the paper loss is only $5,500. The $80 margin required for each of the eleven contracts totals another $880, which means a total of $6,380 is required to maintain the position out of $10,000. There is still $3,620 in reserve. Conditions are always subject to change, but under conditions which prevail as this book is written in early 1994, it is safe to say that corn will not fall to $1.50 soon. It would be impossible for the scale trader using this $0.10 scale to go broke. The worst that could happen to him would be that he is forced into the position of making repeated rollovers of expiring contracts if huge grain surpluses develop, causing corn prices virtually to stagnate. This would cost him extra commissions, but the minor oscillations seen throughout that holding period would generate enough profits to more than cover those commissions and even the carrying charges. (Carrying charges and commissions will be covered in Chapter XVI, "The Rollover.") Eventually and inevitably the surpluses would be eradicated, and the price would rise to $2.60 or higher. That's all it takes to recapture all of the losses and to nail down the desired realized gains.

I repeat: You can't lose trading commodities if you use the scale trading system and properly budget your capital not only to accommodate the worst foreseeable decline, but also to have an emergency reserve to withstand the unforeseen.

VI

The Bankroll

If four people experimented with a gambling system at home with
the intention of forming a team to play that system in Las Vegas, they
might find that the maximum dollar amount ever required under the
worst conditions was, say, $1,000. That occurred either when they
got really strung out with losers before they started catching winners, when they reached the table limit and were restrained from betting more even if they had a larger bankroll available, or when they
had reached a practical limit beyond which they cared to risk no
further capital.

They might then travel to Las Vegas with the mutual understanding that they would each contribute a share of the $1,000 bankroll,
split profits proportionately, and under no circumstances go beyond
the original $1,000 risk. At the end of the weekend they might find
they had a satisfactory profit and had been extended near to the limit
of the $1,000 bankroll on only two or three occasions, rarely being
extended beyond a few hundred dollars, usually less than $100. They
decide to try again next weekend.

During the week one of the team members suggests that they
had wasted a considerable portion of their allotted gambling time by

having a single team member play while the others stood by and watched. He reasons that with an additional contribution from each member they could play simultaneously on a second, third, and fourth table, possibly increasing their profits fourfold. The team members agree. Noting that they were rarely extended to a point near to the limit of their $1,000 bankroll, they conclude that it would not require a full $1,000 to play four games simultaneously. After all, they needed the full $1,000 the first weekend on only a few occasions. They decide they can cover themselves if they carry a bankroll which would be sufficient for a full $1,000 extension on one table, $600 on another, and $400 on each of the other two, reasoning that it is unlikely that they would ever be extended on more than one or two tables simultaneously. Their reasoning is logical.

The same applies to the commodities markets. It takes a substantial bankroll to scale trade a single commodity, but a second *unrelated* commodity may be traded simultaneously with less money than was allotted for the original. Even less is required for a third, a fourth, and so on. The reasoning is the same as it was for the Las Vegas play; it is unlikely that scale trading of *unrelated* commodities would cause the trader's bankroll to become fully extended on all of his positions simultaneously. Perfect growing conditions in the Midwest may produce a record corn crop, depressing the price and fully extending the trader who is scaling corn, but those perfect conditions for growing corn are hardly likely to affect the price of copper. Conditions which may depress cattle prices are unlikely to affect world sugar. An abundant orange crop in Florida may depress frozen concentrated orange juice prices, but that hardly affects interest rate futures or the price of gold. A slowdown in housing starts may depress lumber prices, but that shouldn't affect soybean oil prices. Etc., etc., etc.

I have found that $30,000 is adequate to scale trade a single commodity safely. A second unrelated commodity may be traded simultaneously for an additional $20,000. A third for another $10,000, and each succeeding commodity for $10,000. Thus, a person with $50,000 could trade two commodities simultaneously, while $100,000 would accommodate seven, $150,000 would cover twelve, etc.

The estimated $30,000 bankroll for a single commodity has been determined through many years of empirical analysis, theoretical experimentation, and practical application. However, that number is not inflexible. It is simply the amount which I have found to be nearest to ideal.

A person with only $20,000 may also scale trade, but he would have to make adjustments, such as initiating positions from a lower starting level, using a wider scale, or plainly assuming greater risks. For example, the trader with $30,000 might begin scaling soybean oil at 21 cents, purchasing each 1.5 cents down to about 13 cents without jeopardizing the bankroll. The trader with only $20,000 would be more prudent to initiate his scale at 20 cents, or he might scale each 2.2 cents down, or he might just pray that soybean oil never drops low enough to exhaust his bankroll. Obviously, a trader who tries to scale soybean oil with only $10,000 would have to make even greater adjustments.

If two traders are scaling the same commodity, one with a $30,000 bankroll and the other with $15,000, the person with the $15,000 bankroll should use a scale twice as wide as the person with $30,000. It might seem that the only difference will be that the man with the $30,000 bankroll will make twice as many trades and therefore collect twice as many profits but realize the same percentage return because he had twice as much money invested. Unfortunately, that is not necessarily so. This is because oscillations in price might be so narrow that they frequently touch the double-bankroll trader's prices without ever approaching the single-bankroll trader's wider scale. It is even possible for the trader using the larger bankroll and narrower scale to have a great many trades while the trader with the smaller bankroll has virtually none.

Take soybean oil as an example. A trader with adequate capital might determine that his ideal scale would be to buy each 1 cent down and to sell each 1 cent up. A trader with only half the bankroll but using the same methods of fundamental analysis would necessarily come to the conclusion that his best scale is to buy each 2 cents down and to sell each 1 cent up. Both begin at 20 cents. At 19 cents the first trader acquires a second contract. It is possible that during the life of the contract the price might never dip below 18.01 cents, so the second trader never gets to buy his second contract (nor the first trader his third contract). The price may rally to 20 cents again, cashing a profit for the first trader. Then the cycle is repeated again and again as the price oscillates from slightly below 19 cents to slightly above 20 cents. The first trader cashes numerous profits while the other trader sits on his original position.

It is also possible that the price might swing back and forth from 20 cents down to 18 cents and back to 20 cents without interim oscillations, giving the trader with the half-bankroll exactly half as many winners as the trader with the larger bankroll if they are both selling on 1 cent advances. This gives them identical percentage gains. It is also possible that the trader with the smaller bankroll will opt for 2 cent profits and cash half as many winners but will realize exactly the same gross dollar profit as the trader with the larger bankroll under the ideal conditions of the 20-cent to 18-cent to 20-cent swing. This gives the larger trader two 1 cent winners and the smaller trader one 2 cent winner, which means the smaller trader has twice the percentage return because of making the same dollar profit on half the bankroll. But it rarely works that way. Believe me, although a trader with limited capital may earn a high return, he may also earn a low return, for he has no way to foretell the results, but a trader with a very large account may almost predict his percentage return.

It is likely that you, as a prospective scale trader, will make your decisions for setting scales through a series of compromises. You might want to initiate the scale at existing prices for a particular commodity, but recognizing the possibility that the price may be just a little risky for carrying through to a possible bottom, you might elect to wait for a lower price to begin. You might use a broader scale. You might use a complex scale (as described in Chapter XIII). You might abandon the particular commodity altogether and trade a different one with less risk. Only you can make these determinations, and you should make your decisions only after considering all factors such as different scales (considering profit potential as well as risk), fundamental conditions (what should the price range probably be, based upon supply and demand?), perhaps a little technical analysis (is the respective commodity currently oversold so that it has a better chance of a price advance?), your "comfort factor" requirements, an alternative commodity which appears more attractive, etc. (The comfort factor is the amount of cash reserve you deem necessary for you to feel comfortable and not to worry about your paper losses.)

There are other alternatives. The most obvious is for the scale trader to use a larger bankroll, but if he has already reached the limit

of his personal commitment, this is impractical unless he seeks partners. The combination of several relatively small traders into a comparatively large pool will benefit all participants. Partnerships and
their advantages are discussed in detail in Chapter XXIII.

The requiring of $30,000 for scaling a single commodity is based
upon the assumption that full-sized Chicago Board of Trade, Chicago Mercantile, New York Commodities Exchange, etc., contracts
are to be traded. Another alternative to the $30,000 requirement is to
trade the smaller MidAmerica contracts where as little as $5,000
should prove adequate. This is the subject of Chapter IX, "The
MidAmerica Contract."

In the past few years I have found that I can be more flexible on
the $30,000 initial commitment rule by being slightly more cau-
tious about starting points for initiating scales. By adhering rigorously to the "unrelated" rule and initiating scales about one decrement below my preferred level I have been able to use a "$10,000
per commodity" rule of thumb for scale trading accounts of any
size. A $50,000 account trades five commodities, while a $100,000
account trades ten. There have been a few occasions when I was
trading five commodities with a $50,000 account and began to ac-
cumulate paper losses in one position while a different position, in
an unrelated commodity, was rising sufficiently to scale out of all
contracts of that commodity. I then cancelled all buy orders in the
sold-out commodity and reduced the number of commodities being traded by that account to four until the imperiled position recovered. If that position worsened, I would reduce to three the number of commodities that I was trading as soon as another of the four
reached a level high enough to scale out of the last of its contracts.
Experience will give you the necessary skill to determine optimum
employment of your capital.

It is possible to trade five commodities quite easily in a
$50,000 account by using two or three MidAmerica commodities
with three or two full-sized contracts from one of the other exchanges. For example, you might trade mini-contracts of wheat
and hogs on the MidAm, the 1,000 ounce contract of silver on the
CBOT, and full-sized contracts of oats and cocoa on their respective exchanges. Diversification is one of the key elements to the
success of a scale trading account, so it is desirable to maximize

the number of commodities being traded within the limitations of risk. Again, you will learn from experience.

*   *   *

The foregoing text in this chapter has been reproduced *exactly* as it appeared in the original printing of this book with the 1980 copyright. The next eight paragraphs have been reproduced *exactly* as they appeared in the hard cover edition — 1984 through 1993 copyrights. (A few minor changes were made in the wording for clarity.) My comments for the 1994 edition will appear at the end of this chapter.

*   *   *

In using the scale trading system, I adhered rigidly to the $30,000, $20,000, $10,000 rule for the first few years, but then it became apparent that by diversifying properly with *unrelated* commodities, there was enough flexibility for me to waive the necessity for reserving $30,000 and $20,000, and instead to go directly into $10,000 for each commodity. The final two paragraphs above were added almost as an afterthought as the original text was about to go to the printer.

It was absolutely true that separate commodities could be traded for $10,000 each under *normal* market conditions; unfortunately, we have not had normal market conditions since that was written. Some day we may return to normal market conditions, which would make the preceding $10,000-per-commodity suggestion appropriate again, but until that time you should consider the following:

We have had totally abnormal markets for several years because of the Federal Reserve's meddling policy of trying to fine-tune the economy by adjusting interest rates. Some idiot Federal Reserve chairman (that's a redundancy) got the idea that he could slow inflation with high interest rates, the theory being that that would reduce borrowings. About all that accomplished was to draw the entire world to the brink of economic collapse.

One devastating effect of this ludicrous experiment was to cause interest rates to *dominate* commodities markets. There were no such things as *unrelated* commodities; when interest rates rose, *all* commodity prices *had to rise* for a while; then they collapsed. When interest rates fell, *all* commodity prices *had to fall* for a while. They may soon turn upward. Supply and demand began to have less of an effect on commodity prices than the unnatural manipulations of the economy by the Federal Reserve.

Even the $30,000, $20,000, $10,000 distribution plan did not work, because a trader trying to scale seven commodities with $100,000 suddenly found that he needed $30,000 for *each* commodity because they were all in a tailspin together. $10,000 per commodity was out of the question.

Today's interest rates at about 10% are somewhat more manageable, and for the first time in several years we are beginning to see supply/demand factors carrying a greater influence over commodity prices than interest rates, but we are not totally out of the woods. Not until we see 6% rates again would it be advisable to trade a large portfolio of commodities with $10,000 each.

If you are diversifying and have allotted $10,000 for each commodity, or even if you have used the $30,000, $20,000, $10,000 plan of distribution, a sudden return to high interest rates could cause you to suddenly need $30,000 for *each* commodity — unrelated or not. This can force you into premature liquidation of some positions. Indeed, it might be best to use your entire capital to scale trade a single commodity. That way there is no possible chance of your running out of capital because of outside surprises. For example, the trader with $50,000 who is ready to trade two commodities, following the $30,000-$20,000 plan could find himself in a bind if a return to high interest rates causes a decline in the price of both of his *unrelated* commodities, but there cannot possibly be a surprise if he has calculated a single scale in advance and set it to go all the way down. If he calculates a scale for pork bellies all the way down to 15 cents and applies his entire capital to this one scale, he should never worry.

Incidentally, I cannot resist proffering my comment about the Federal Reserve and interest rates: I contend that it is absolutely impossible to accomplish anything by raising interest rates except to make bankers rich. When the United States raises its rates, so do all of the other countries. The Fed has put out the propaganda that we must keep our rates high to stay competitive with other nations and their high rates. Hogwash. All that happens when we raise interest rates is that other nations raise their rates to stay competitive with *us*. It is like a gasoline war at the corner filling stations. The United States is the banker to the world — the primary lending source. If we dropped our rates to 6%, the rest of the world would come down to 7% overnight. I may be an iconoclast, but no one will ever convince me that it serves any purpose to hold interest rates high!

* * *

When the foregoing paragraphs were written, short-term interest rates were 10%, silver was $12, soybeans $9, etc. I admonished readers to use broad scales, to trade only with large amounts of capital, and to keep plenty of cash in reserve. Today short-term interest rates are around 3%, and commodity prices have fallen sharply. Silver is under $5, soybeans are in the $6 range, etc. Before the 1993 flood, grain prices were 25% below current prices, but it will not be long until we see them there again. Under those conditions it is easy to scale trade with as little as $5,000. Over the past few years our newsletter, *The Scale Trader*, has suggested numerous scales for accounts of $5,000, and all of the scales were profitable.

Later in this book I will delve deeply into the effect interest rates have on commodity prices, but for this chapter I will simply say that interest rates have been stable for a while, and commodity prices have returned to their normal status of being influenced by supply/demand factors. Thus, it is again safe to trade $10,000 scales, and selected commodities (full-sized corn and oats, half-sized hogs, and mini-sized wheat, soybeans, and silver, and half-sized cattle, if the price falls) may be traded with $5,000.

Before leaving the subject of "the bankroll," I want to offer my thoughts about commodity trading in general:

You *must* treat commodity trading the same as you would any other business. You would never consider going into any business undercapitalized, but I see it happen every day in commodities trading. I have been one of the guest speakers at commodity seminars, and after I give my speech explaining scale trading, they take a break. Attendees will come to me and say, "I like your trading method, but I have only $3,000 with which to work." That shocks me! This person paid $800 to attend the seminar, possibly spent $800 on an airplane ticket, $500 on the room and meals for three days, and all he has for the business of trading commodities is $3,000!

He hasn't a chance to succeed with just a $3,000 bankroll. He would be better served to donate it to the American Cancer Society. At least he would get a tax write-off.

The reason this person thinks he can trade commodities successfully with just $3,000 is that he has been bombarded with mailers from unscrupulous commodity people who claim that they have clients who turned $3,000 into $300,000 in eighteen months, quit their jobs, and now do all of their commodity trading from their yachts in the Caribbean. The people who mail that garbage should be put in jail. You have as much chance of turning $3,000 into $300,000 as you have of winning the lottery.

I once received a letter from a man who said he was quitting his job so that he could devote full time to commodities trading. He said he had $7,000 of capital. It is difficult for me to answer all of my mail, but I dropped everything and *telephoned* that man to plead with him not to quit his job.

As I will explain later in this book, you must be content with a very modest 20% to 30% return annually. *That is all!* Unless you have at least $200,000 with which to work, you must not rely upon profits from scale trading for your sole livelihood. Scale trading is intended only to supplement your ordinary income, not to replace it.

Before closing this chapter on capital requirements, I must also comment upon your personal psychological approach to commodities trading. I'll start by giving an illustration of what happens to the person who sits on the floor in his living room and rolls the dice 10,000 times to see how the Double Up system would work if he were in Las Vegas. A few times he had to bet $256, twice he had to bet $512, and once he had to bet $1,024. He was never pushed higher than that. The system is a piece of cake. It's no big deal to go to bets of $256 and more because he always won within the next bet or two and could drop back down to a $1 bet. So he cashes a check for $2,000 and heads to Las Vegas to play the Double Up system.

When I dealt craps I saw these people all of the time. They had no trouble with the $16 or $32 bets, but when they lost a $32 bet and were forced to wager $64, I could see the beads of sweat on their foreheads. When they lost the $64, they became so nervous they could not count out $128 in checks (chips). The dice would be in the air, so I would shout to them, "$128 goes?" They would answer in the affirmative, and I would say, "You have a bet." When they lost the $128 bet, we had to call the paramedics. 911! Even though they had the cash in their pockets, there was no way they could make the $256 bet or the $512 bet. The $1,024 bet was out of the question. It was easy on the living room carpet, but not with the real money.

I see the same thing all of the time with scale traders. They see a scale in *The Scale Trader* to purchase up to eight contracts which could be accommodated with $10,000. The maximum paper loss would be $3,500. But as soon as they hold four contracts with a $1,200 cumulative loss, they are on the phone to me asking what to do.

Unless you are emotionally equipped to ride out the losses which you projected on paper, do not scale trade. You will inevitably trade something which will surprise you and show a large paper loss. *You must be emotionally prepared to ride it out.*

I will give you a perfect example: During 1993 before the crude oil collapse, I received a call from a man who had opened his commodity trading account with $800,000. It was his intention to scale trade. He took a subscription to *The Scale Trader* and traded everything we traded, except that his scales were ten times tighter than ours because of the enormous amount of money with which he was working. He had several hundred consecutive winners in our various scales, including crude oil, heating oil, and unleaded gasoline. Because of the large upside moves in most prices as a result of the flood, we (and he) were sold out of all but our petroleum group scales.

This gentleman informed me that he had made so much profit in his early scales that he had doubled up on crude oil, heating oil, and unleaded gasoline. While the newsletter was recommending buying one contract of crude oil each 50 points down, he had started buying one contract each 5 points down, but now he was buying two contracts each 5 points down. That was twenty times more aggressive than the newsletter recommended, but he said he had worked the scales on spread sheets on his computer, and he had determined that he could ride out all three scales if the crude oil price dropped all of the way to $8. As soon as crude oil's price dropped $2, he lost his nerve and liquidated the entire account, taking a huge loss. As was the case with the chap rolling the dice on the living room carpet, there was no limit to the risk he was willing to take on the computer, but he choked when he tried it with real money.

The moral: You must predetermine your ability to take a realistic risk and pledge to yourself that you will ride it out. Don't get greedy. Scale trading will never make you rich unless you do it for years and keep all of the profits in the account. You should think of scale trading profits as a mere supplement to your income, giving you enough profit to pay for a nice car, a family vacation, new furniture for the house, or some other luxury item which you would not otherwise buy.

VII

Selecting The Scale

My basic rules for selecting a scale are set in three stages. First, I try to determine the price that would be a *probable bottom*, and I set a scale which will consume 50% of my capital at that price level when paper losses and full margins are totaled. Second, I estimate the limit to which I think the price could *possibly decline* if everything went awry. At this *possible bottom* I still want to have committed only 70% of my capital. Third, the remaining 30% of the capital will give me the margin for error that would be necessary if my estimates prove to be incredibly inaccurate.

I start by determining the recent historic range for the commodity under consideration. The easiest way to ascertain this range is to look at a ten-year chart of the commodity. Another way is to check the statistics as presented in numerous commodity yearbooks or government reports. I prefer to look at a chart because it gives me an all-inclusive view, including annual ranges. It is particularly helpful to look at the chart because of the price aberrations which are obvious in a picture but may not be quite so easily noticed when presented in statistical form.

Soybean oil, as an example, has traded from the mid-teens to above 50 cents per pound in recent years. However, a check of a chart will show that the run above 50 cents occurred in 1974, and the prospective scale trader might remember that 1974 followed the 1973 year in which President Nixon emptied our grain elevators by selling nearly all of our reserves to the USSR early in the year, only to see a terrible drought hit the Midwest that summer. The upward surge in grain prices triggered a broad upward movement in virtually all commodities as many prices ran to extreme levels, and it became popular that year to declare that the United States and the rest of the world were headed for economic ruin through a combination of worldwide depression and simultaneous inflation. Soybean oil's *practical top* should be considered to be the 42 cents level reached in 1984, following the drought in 1983. The 50 cent price for soybean oil should be eliminated from consideration as the top of the range — at least for the time frame in which this book is being written.

I like to consider the range of the last ten years, so a quick perusal of the 15-year soybean oil chart (Chart XIII, page 64) will reveal that soybean oil traded as low as 16 cents in 1983, then shot up to 42 cents in 1984 because of the 1983 drought, dropped back to 12 cents in 1986 as oilseed growers throughout the world took advantage of the high 1984 prices and produced a record crop (the Law of Supply and Demand in action), and then hovered between about 18 cents and 25 cents for the last six years. The exception was the run to 34 cents in 1988, another severe drought year.

Thus, the practical range for soybean oil for the last ten years of the chart is from a low of 16 cents to a high of 25 cents, or a 9 cent range. The lowest third of that range would be from 16 cents to 19 cents. In this case the *probable bottom* would be 15 cents, but I would allow for a *possible bottom* at 13 cents. With these parameters in mind, I would try to set a scale which would begin at 19 cents and could consume approximately 50% of the capital if the price declined to a level nearing 15 cents. The possible further decline to 13 cents would consume no more than another 20% of my capital so that there would be a 30% cushion remaining.

Assuming a $30,000 bankroll has been set aside to scale soybean oil, I would make a first rough-draft approximation of the results of a scale and then put in the necessary adjustments. The simplest scale would initiate the buying at 19 cents and buy each 1 cent down. The scale would appear as in Chart I.

43

CHART I

EXAMPLE OF A 1-CENT SOYBEAN OIL SCALE

1	2	3	4	5	6	7	8
19.00	1	0	0	0	0	700	700
18.00	2	1	600	600	600	1,400	2,000
17.00	3	2	600	1,200	1,800	2,100	3,900
16.00	4	3	600	1,800	3,600	2,800	6,400
15.00	5	4	600	2,400	6,000	3,500	9,500
14.00	6	5	600	3,000	9,000	4,200	13,200
13.00	7	6	600	3,600	12,600	4,900	17,500

COLUMN 1 represents the price at which I intend to buy my soybean oil contracts, expressed in cents per pound.

COLUMN 2 represents the number of contracts accumulated to date when the price reaches the level in COLUMN 1, assuming a single contract is purchased at each of the scale levels.

COLUMN 3 represents the number of contracts held which have losses in them *since the last previous purchase.* This number is always one less than COLUMN 2 because the newest contract does not have a loss in it yet.

COLUMN 4 represents the dollar amount of loss for a single contract falling from the previous purchase level to this level. In this example, the soybean oil contract is for 60,000 pounds, so the decline of 1 cent per pound equals $600.

COLUMN 5 represents the dollar amounts of loss in the aggregate contracts from the previous purchase level. Multiply COLUMN 3 and COLUMN 4.

COLUMN 6 represents the aggregate dollar loss of all contracts purchased to date. Cumulate COLUMN 5.

COLUMN 7 represents the margin requirements to *initiate the* aggregate positions. Soybean oil margin, as with all margins, is subject to change, but in early 1994 it is $700 per contract, initial margin. Multiply COLUMN 2 by $700.

COLUMN 8 represents the total cumulative margin requirement to cover the accumulated paper losses and initial margin at the indicated price level. COLUMN 6 plus COLUMN 7.

CHART I is carried all of the way down to 13 cents so that I may determine whether my scale is proper for my capital. I had assumed a $30,000 bankroll, and I had wanted to have about $15,000 of that remaining if soybean oil declined to 15 cents. I had also wanted to have about $9,000 remaining if the price dropped all the way to 13 cents. Inspection of the scale shows only $9,500 (about 32%) committed at 15 cents, and $17,500 (58%) committed at 13 cents. This scale is too loose. I can afford to tighten it.

The Great Flood of 1993 curtailed soybean production and created a relative shortage of soybeans (from which soybean oil is derived). It is unlikely that we will see a 13 cent price soon, and probably not even a 15 cent price for at least several years. Therefore, an aggressive trader could make alterations in the scale by using a higher starting price of, say, 21 cents and a possible bottom of 15 cents. That means he would be using the identical numbers shown in CHART I, except for the buy prices shown in COLUMN 1. Even then, it would still be a very loose scale because a 15 cent bottom would still commit only 58% of his capital. However, there is the *possibility* that soybean oil might decline to 13 cents, so I would stay with my 13 cents to 19 cents parameters and calculate a tighter scale, as depicted in CHART II, below.

In this example, when soybean oil has reached 15.25 cents I have committed $10,950. If the price declines another 0.25 cents, my paper loss (COLUMN 6) has increased by $900 (0.25 cents per pound x 60,000 pounds x 6 contracts = $900), with my commitment now totalling $11,850 (40%), which is well within my 50% target. At 13 cents my commitment is $22,500 (75%), or just barely beyond my desired 70%. I would proceed to trade this scale.

CHART II

EXAMPLE OF A 3/4-CENT SOYBEAN OIL SCALE

1	2	3	4	5	6	7	8
19.00	1	0	0	0	0	700	700
18.25	2	1	450	450	450	1,400	1,850
17.50	3	2	450	900	1,350	2,100	3,450
16.75	4	3	450	1,350	2,700	2,800	5,500
16.00	5	4	450	1,800	4,500	3,500	8,000
15.25	6	5	450	2,250	6,750	4,200	10,950
14.50	7	6	450	2,700	9,450	4,900	14,350
13.75	8	7	450	3,150	12,600	5,600	18,200
13.00	9	8	450	3,600	16,200	6,300	22,500

In the previous editions of this book I gave examples of numerous soybean oil scales as I offered exercises for neophyte scale traders to attempt as they searched for appropriate soybean oil scales which started at 21 cents, went down to 13 cents, and could be accommodated with $30,000 of capital. The final example I used said, "Try starting at 21 cents and purchasing each 1.5 cents down, as illustrated in CHART II (of those editions). At 15 cents the commitment is $14,000, which is less than the 50% allocated, and at 13.5 cents the commitment is $19,500, or just 65% of the allocated capital. (Note: Soybean oil margin was $1,000 at that time and in those examples.) Taking it to the next purchase level, 12 cents, which is a full cent below our *possible* level, the commitment is only $25,900, which should be within almost anyone's comfort range. This is the scale I would use for the most conservative investor who asked me to select a scale for him which would generate reasonable profits without unreasonable risks. *Using this scale, and assuming today's commodity market conditions, that conservative investor would never lose.*" (Italics added for emphasis.) As you see from the 15-year soybean oil chart on page 64, soybean oil has not traded under 13 cents since that was written in 1979. Thus, a scale trader using that scale would have gone from 1979 to the present *WITHOUT A LOSING TRADE!*

There are three additional "fudge factors" that provide the scale trader a further degree of safety. I do not invoke these while doing the preliminary calculations, but I am cognizant of their existence and I keep them in the back of my mind. The first is the maintenance margin requirements as opposed to the initial margin requirements. In all of my scale calculations I assume that I am depositing full initial margin and will maintain full margin. However, once the initial margin requirements are met, the brokerage house *customarily* will require the commodities trader to maintain only about 70% margin, which is called the maintenance margin level. If they didn't do this, they would be forced to issue margin calls every time the commodity price dipped even the smallest fraction. Thus, the first fudge factor would be that I could probably depend upon my account having additional reserves by estimating my margin requirements at 70% of those actually shown in COLUMN 7.

CAUTION: Different brokerage houses treat maintenance margin requirements differently, so it would be imprudent for you to assume that you could carry your positions at 70% margin levels. Some brokerage houses will insist that you restore your account to full *initial* margin levels if your account has penetrated below maintenance margin levels. Discount brokers are notorious for raising initial margins to trigger maintenance margin deficits so that they can force you to send substantial additional margin. I merely mentioned the subject to inform you that there is probably a built-in comfort factor for you.

The second fudge factor, which also should never be relied upon but which possibly could come into play, is the probability that the commodity exchanges would reduce margin requirements after prices have fallen severely. For example, if soybean oil had fallen all the way to 15 cents or lower, the decline would most likely have been caused by an enormous oversupply of soybean oil. It is also likely that soybean oil prices would be fluctuating through only a very narrow range. Since margin requirements are usually set according to the volatility of each respective commodity, it might be safe to assume that the soybean oil margin would be reduced, giving the account additional reserve. But don't count on it.

The third fudge factor is the probability that the account will realize some profits from the price oscillations which usually occur, even in declining markets. Each scale example presented in this book assumes a vertical drop in price without any profitable oscillations along the way. That would be a highly unusual circumstance. The account should garner some oscillation profits during the decline. This increases the reserve capital. But don't count on it.

Some commodity traders question why we are so conservative and keep so much capital in reserve. They feel it is wiser to trade more aggressively and to allow the winners to increase the reserve. It is our conservative approach which holds our annual profits to 20% to 30% instead of the 100% they seek, but it is also our conservative approach that keeps us in the game.

For example, I have had people tell me they used $10,000 of capital to realize a $10,000 gain for the year, which they say is a 100% return. They say they did four times better than I because I used $40,000 to make the same $10,000 profit, or only 25%. Then I ask them if there was ever a time during the year when they had to add capital to the account. They answer that there was a brief period when everything went against them, they received a margin call, and they were forced to add another $10,000, to make their total commitment $20,000. Fortunately, though, prices moved their way, and they were off call as soon as the broker received their margin check. The check cleared in a couple of days, and they were allowed to withdraw the second $10,000, so they never really considered that part of the account capital. Then I ask if they would have been willing to commit additional capital if things had gotten really bad. They usually say they were prepared with another $10,000 from a savings account and could have liquidated $10,000 from a mutual fund investment. In truth, they were working with $40,000, counting the $20,000 which they actually committed and the $20,000 they had in reserve. Therefore, their $10,000 profit is a return on capital of 25%, the same as mine.

If you really want to accelerate performance, keep plenty of reserve in the account, and once trading profits are realized, the scales may be tightened, as discussed in Chapter XXXII, under the question about pyramiding profits.

VIII

Worth 10,000 Words

I have used the scale trading system sporadically since 1962, but in 1975, when I had been using the system full-time for about a year, I wrote a four-page brochure on the basics of the system and distributed several thousand copies of it. To save 10,000 words, the write-up included a picture of a chart of a typical commodity to illustrate the system in graphic form. I am reprinting the original chart and the precise wording from the original write-up. (See Chart III.)

It reads, in part: "Consider the accompanying chart of soybean oil. A futures contract of soybean oil is for 60,000 pounds, so each penny change in price is equal to $600. In 1974 soybean oil sold for as much as 51 cents per pound, but by February, 1975, the price had fallen to half that level. In that area the price seemed low, and a scale trader might have chosen to start accumulating at 24 cents, purchasing each 1 cent down and selling those contracts each time at a price 1 cent above a corresponding previous purchase. Following this system, purchases would have been made at each point shown by an "x" on the chart, and sales would have occurred at the points marked "o." Please notice that in April through June the price decline was nearly uninterrupted, so a large paper loss was accumulated quickly.

These losses were recovered entirely when the price rose above 25 cents in August. Assuming the scale trader resumed his purchases when the price fell again to 24 cents, he would now hold six positions acquired at 24 cents, 23 cents, 22 cents, 21 cents, 20 cents and 19 cents. With the current price hovering near 19 cents, the accumulated paper loss losses would total 15 cents (5 cents, 4 cents, 3 cents, 2 cents, 1 cent and 0 cents). At $600 per penny, the unrealized loss would total $9,000. However, the 27 1-cent profits (count the 0's on the chart) would have produced a realized profit of $16,200, or an overall gross profit of $7,200 in a market which has fallen from 24 cents to 19 cents, or 21%. Sooner or later the price should hit 25 cents again, recapturing all of the paper losses, netting a 1 cent profit on each of the six current open positions, plus 1 cent gains from any additional oscillations. That would result in a total gain of at least an additional $12,600, or a grand total of $28,800.

CHART III

DECEMBER 1975 SOYBEAN OIL

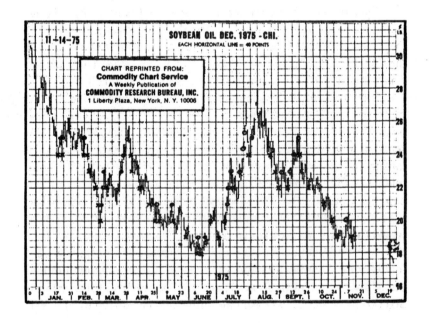

"When soybean oil rose to 51 cents per pound, margarine (of which soybean oil is the primary ingredient) sold at the same price as butter, and many homemakers switched to butter, thereby decreasing soybean oil consumption. Farmers who wanted to benefit from high soybean prices planted and harvested a record crop. The combination of decreased consumption and increased production precipitated a price decline. Today margarine sells at half of the price of butter, which will prompt homemakers to switch again, increasing soybean oil consumption. The recent 65% drop in soybean oil prices may also prompt farmers to reduce plantings in 1976. The combination of these factors should cause the price to rally."

I had purposely selected the December 1975 soybean oil contract because I wanted to demonstrate that — as with the Chops gambling system — it was possible to make a net profit while taking more losers than winners. Notice, however, that I left the question of recapture of paper losses open when I stated, "Sooner or later the price should hit 25 cents again, etc." Did the price ever hit 25 cents again? I'll say it did! In 1976, 1977, 1978 and 1979. And, as this book is written in 1980, all futures contracts have topped that level, with some of the nearby contracts approaching 29 cents.

Thus, the six open contracts of soybean oil held in the original example would have been rolled over to 1976 contracts, and all of the $9,000 of paper losses would have been recaptured along with the $3,600 of realized profit for the six open positions. That puts the final tally for 1975 trading at well over $30,000 of profit.

The December 1975 contract of soybean oil expired at about 16 cents, so the dollar amount necessary to carry the scale through to the bottom would have been $30,600 (see Chart IV). The $30,600 represents the projections set in advance by the scale trader who — when he initiates his scale at 24 cents — assumes that soybean oil may fall to the mid-teens without any oscillation profits along the way. His maximum exposure would be $30,600 at 16 cents. As we have seen, though, he had already captured $16,200 in realized profits, so his cash commitment would have been no greater than $14,400 at that 16 cent bottom.

If you will notice on the pictured Chart III, there is an 18 cent low in June. That would have necessitated a $19,600 commitment, but by that time eleven $600 winners had been taken, for a profit of $6,600. Thus, the actual cash commitment was reduced to $13,000.

CHART IV

EXAMPLE OF A SOYBEAN OIL SCALE*

1	2	3	4	5	6	7	8
21.00	1	0	0	0	0	1,000	1,000
20.00	2	1	600	600	600	2,000	2,600
19.00	3	2	600	1,200	1,800	3,000	4,800
18.00	4	3	600	1,800	3,600	4,000	7,600
17.00	5	4	600	2,400	6,000	5,000	11,000
16.00	6	5	600	3,000	9,000	6,000	15,000
15.00	7	6	600	3,600	12,600	7,000	19,600
14.00	8	7	600	4,200	16,800	8,000	24,800
13.00	9	8	600	4,800	21,600	9,000	30,600

Charts V, VI, VII and VIII show the action of December 1976, 1977, 1978 and 1979 soybean oil contracts. These charts give us an idea of what would have happened for anyone who had traded soybean oil continuously since 1975. Assuming he had rolled over any open positions at the end of each year, he has continued to buy each 1 cent down from 24 cents and sell each 1 cent up. As you see, in addition to the 27 winners captured in 1975, there would have been 25 winners in 1976, 15 in 1977, 18 in 1978, and one in 1979. That is a total of 86 winners of $600 each, or a total of $51,600 in five years. That is an average annual gain of 34.4%. If the person doing scale trading as described had also deposited U.S. Treasury bills as margin, in lieu of cash, he would have averaged about another 10% annual return during the five-year span. That is a net return of about 45% annually, which certainly should be considered generous for such a low-risk investment.

---

* This scale was used with Charts III, V, VI, VII, VIII, IX, X, XI and XII.

CHART V

DECEMBER 1976 SOYBEAN OIL

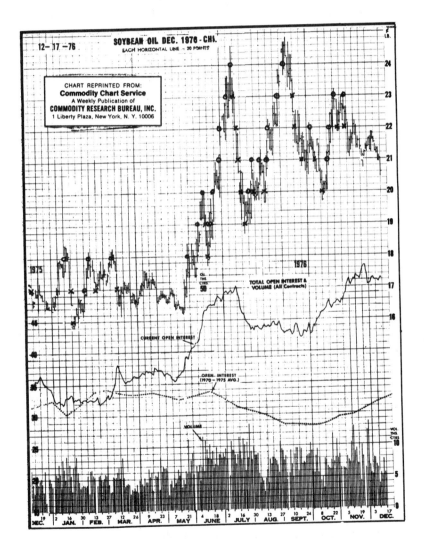

Perhaps you are thinking that I have chosen soybean oil to illustrate the system's performance because soybean oil has been an ideal trader. It is standard operating procedure for chicanerous commodity advisors to devise a basic method for trading a particular commodity and then apply it to several recent years of trading to prove that it would have been successful if used during that period. They even modify the basic strategy whenever necessary to accommodate the periods when prices would have failed to produce profits. All of this is done *after the fact*, but then the system works about 50% of the time when it is finally used with actual cash commitments — results no better that those which would be derived from coin-flipping. Such is not the case with my example, for I have shown the results of a system which has remained unaltered since I originally offered it as an advertisement on a television show I did during 1975 and was distributed to thousands of viewers. The original write-up used soybean oil as its example simply because it was easier to illustrate by using simple numbers such as 24 cents, 23 cents, 22 cents, etc., keeping the scale limited to one penny down and one penny up. Similar results would have been obtained by using any one of a dozen or more commodities. Silver was ideal until it moved above $5.00. Copper was perfect, as were all of the grains and the soybean complex. Indeed, it is easier to name the ones that have *not* been good. This is not because they produced losers, but only because they moved too high to scale trade. There were but five: cocoa, coffee, lumber, orange juice and plywood.

Note: An astute reader may have noticed that the five graphs illustrated in this chapter indicate eighty x's denoting buy points and eighty-six o's denoting sell points. The reason for this discrepancy is the price differences which prevailed at the time of the rollovers. In three out of the four rollover situations the price of the new contract was lower than the expiring contract; therefore, it would have been necessary for the scale trader to roll over all existing positions and also to add two extra contracts each of the three times that the new price was 2 cents lower. This would have permitted him to adhere rigorously to his 25 cent selling objective each year.

In actual practice, rollovers would not be made from December contracts to the succeeding December contracts, for the deferred contracts usually lack the desired liquidity which nearer contracts provide. The rollovers would likely be made from December to the succeeding July. The July contracts, in turn, would be rolled to the succeeding December as July approaches expiration.

CHART VI

DECEMBER 1977 SOYBEAN OIL

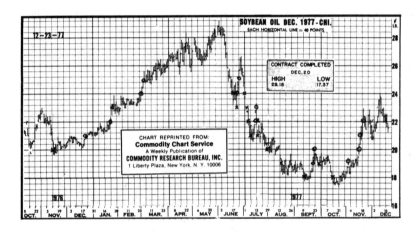

CHART VII

DECEMBER 1978 SOYBEAN OIL

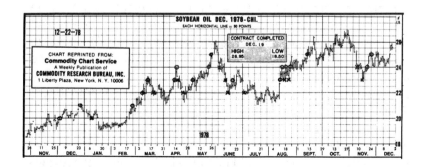

CHART VIII

DECEMBER 1979 SOYBEAN OIL

Please note that all these graphs are presented for illustrative purposes only.

* * *

The foregoing part of this chapter is repeated verbatim from the original (1979) edition of this book. This middle portion of this chapter is repeated verbatim from the 1984 edition of this book. The final portion of this chapter is entirely new, and it is intended to show you the trading results you would have had by scale trading soybean oil from 1983 through 1993 *with a system which remains unaltered since 1975.*

* * *

I could have consolidated the 1975 through 1980 years with the 1981 through 1983 years for a summary, but it serves a purpose to

56

separate them, for conditions changed in the latter half of the period, and it should prove useful to observe the two different situations.

Prior to 1981 the nearby contracts sold at premiums over the deferred contracts, making rollover situations simple to accomplish. In this circumstance, it is unnecessary to drop contracts to compensate for carrying charges; indeed, it is sometimes advisable to *add a* contract or two because of the very low risk.

However, during 1981 and thereafter, soybean oil prices returned to normalcy with all deferred contracts selling at premiums to nearbys. This was true not only for the expiring 1981 contracts, but again in 1982, 1983, and with the new 1984 contracts. In this circumstance it becomes mandatory to take an occasional carrying charge loss as described in Chapter XVII, "Compensating for Carrying Charges," to avoid accumulating a large number of contracts in a desultory market.

CHART IX

DECEMBER 1980 SOYBEAN OIL

The year 1980 was an uneventful year for soybean oil. The December, 1980, contract opened trading above 26 cents and held above 24 cents until late March. A brief declining period carried the price down to 22 cents, allowing for four purchases and sales, for a very modest $2,400 profit for the entire year, or only an 8% return on the assumed $30,000 of capital. However, interest rates were exceptionally high that year, with U.S. Treasury bills earning around 15% for most of the year; thus, the overall return was a respectable 23%.

The December, 1980, soybean oil went off the board with a plunge in price, but by that time the scale trader would have been forced (by expiration) to move forward and would have been trading 1981 contracts, which were about 2 cents higher in price. This would have kept scale traders from purchasing any 24 cent contracts until June of 1981. Seven contracts would have been purchased at prices ranging from 24 cents down to 21 cents, with three winners having been cashed and the remaining four rolled over to December, 1982, contracts. The three winners would have returned only an $1,800 profit, or merely 6%, which would have totaled 18% when combined with the 12% T-bill yields of 1981.

CHART X

DECEMBER 1981 SOYBEAN OIL

A purchase of a fifth contract of December, 1981, soybean oil at 20 cents would have been necessary except that it would have occurred in late November, by which time the scaler would have begun his rollover. Again, December, 1982, soybean oil contracts were trading 2 cents above the December, 1981, contracts, so the experienced scale trader would have jettisoned a contract or two. The loss would have been minor — 3 cents if dropping one contract (the highest priced) plus an additional 2 cents if dropping a second contract (the second highest priced) — but even dropping one contract to accept a 3 cent loss would have wiped out the profit for the entire year (excluding T-bill interest), so the trader might have stubbornly hung onto his position and rolled all of the four contracts into the new year. This rollover would have occurred at approximately 22 cents, from which level the price dropped to 21 cents before rallying to 22 cents again to allow for the cashing of a single winner. A few more oscillations would have allowed for the capture of two more winners by May, and then the price went into an extended slide which continued until the expiration of the contract. (Trading for the month of December, 1981, in the December, 1982, contract is shown by the single bold line on the far left side of the chart where each bold line represents a month of trading instead of a single day.)

The combination of the four contracts rolled over from 1981 plus the six new contracts accumulated during 1982 gave the scale trader an inventory of ten contracts near the end of the 1982 trading year, and this would have made it mandatory that he jettison a contract or two. If he drops two contracts, he loses 9 cents on one and 8 cents on the other, which leaves him with a 14 cent realized loss for the year after allowing for the three one-cent winners he captured early in the season. This $8,400 realized loss is the only loss that he has incurred since he began using the scale trading system in 1975; however, he also holds a $16,800 unrealized loss on the eight contracts still in inventory, and he has had to dig into his reserves to supplement his $30,000 capital account.

If you will add one more purchase line to Chart IV, you will see what his position is after purchasing a full ten contracts. Although the price is only down to 17 cents, it is the equivalent of 15 cents on the scale because of the 2 cent premium at the time of the rollover. T-bills again averaged about 12% throughout 1982, for a return of $3,600 interest on the $30,000 bankroll, plus the three winners would have added $1,800 for a *realized* increase of $5,400 for the year, which means that the scale trader would actually have had to supplement his $30,000 bankroll with only $1,600 to hold all ten contracts if again he were stubborn enough to refuse to drop a contract or two to compensate for carrying charges.

CHART XI

DECEMBER 1982 SOYBEAN OIL

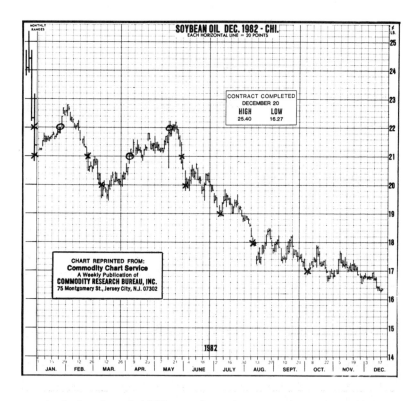

As it developed, 1982 was the only contentious year which the scale trader would have experienced from 1975 through 1983. We have assumed that he started scaling soybean oil each time it was available at 24 cents and that he maintained his penny-down/penny-up scale throughout the entire period. Soybean oil traded at 25 cents or higher in every year of the period except 1982, so there was never a problem year except 1982.

If the scale trader continued his scale into 1983, he was fully rewarded for everything, no matter how he handled the rollovers. As you see from the latest available chart, the price of December, 1983, soybean oil topped 36 cents, permitting him to sell all of the contracts which were rolled over at a level of about 18 cents. He would have had no difficulty in selling either eight *or ten* contracts — or eighteen, for that matter.

CHART XII

DECEMBER 1983 SOYBEAN OIL

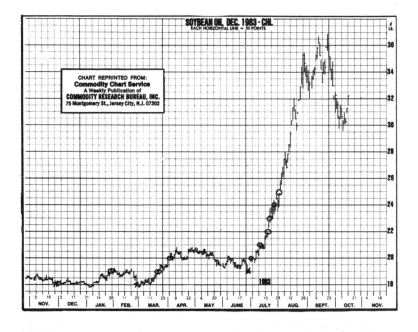

I prefer the cautious approach, so I personally would have been discarding a contract each year instead of rolling all of them over, but in our illustration we assumed the scaler was stubbornly holding them all. With that being the case, he would have recaptured the

$27,000 of paper loss carried over from 1982, plus two $600 profits from oscillations during 1983, for a profit of $28,200 during 1983. Add to that another $3,000 of interest from the T-bills, and the net return for the year is $30,600, or 102%.

The explosion in price during the summer of 1983 is attributable to the combination of the government setaside program (PIK) and a severe drought occurring concomitantly. Detractors might call that luck, but the PIK program was designed to raise prices in the first place, and droughts do occur regularly. Scale traders do not concern themselves with what causes the rallies; they just wait patiently for them to occur.

* * *

All of the foregoing text in this chapter was repeated verbatim from the four-page pamphlet I wrote and distributed in 1975, the soft cover edition of the book from 1980, or from the hard cover edition written in 1984. The wording describing this trading method will remain unchanged for 1,000 years unless The Law of Supply and Demand is repealed before that time. My sole purpose in repeating everything is to show you the difference between my trading method — which has remained unaltered from its first publication in 1975 through today — and the theoretical results presented by other publishers who use *known* results and develop a trading system built around historical data and then alter their trading methods annually to compensate for another year of poor trading results. I will comment further on this in Chapter XXIV "Trend-Following Systems."

For this 1994 edition of the book I will simply print a chart showing the trading results for soybean oil as far back as the chart goes, 1979. Please remember that we started our scale each year at 24 cents; therefore, we needed a top of only 25 cents to complete our scales and to liquidate all contracts profitably. As shown earlier in this chapter, soybean oil exceeded 25 cents in price in 1975, 1976, 1977, and 1978, 1979, 1980, and 1981, missed in 1982, but then roared to 37 cents in 1983 and 41 cents in 1984. Whenever the price reached 25 cents we were completely sold out, and we would either go to the sidelines or look for another commodity to scale trade. When the price of soybean oil later dropped back to 24 cents, we would resume scaling.

Remember the quote, "Sooner or later the price should hit 25 cents again..."? Did it hit 25 cents after 1984? Yes, in 1985, 1988, 1990, 1993, and already in 1994 contracts.

Detractors who dislike scale trading — usually commodity brokers who try to dissuade clients from using the system because the broker can't earn enough commissions from it — say carrying charges at rollover could eventually bury you. Rollovers were not a problem in 1986 and 1987 because we had *inverted markets*. An inverted market occurs when the nearby contracts trade at a premium over the faraway contracts because current supplies are tight, but the new crop which will be harvested in a few months will relieve the supply tightness. When you do a rollover in an inverted market you do not pay a carrying charge premium; indeed — as discussed earlier in this chapter — you roll to a cheaper contract and might elect to take advantage of the situation by *adding* extra contracts.

As for the dip in 1991-92, the situation was the same as 1981-82 (described earlier in this chapter) so that you would have been commencing scales at 21 cents instead of 24 cents; besides, soybean oil never traded below 18 cents in those years, so you would have had no trouble in completing the scales, regardless of whether you had started fresh at 21 cents or were carrying old contracts from 1990 purchased at 24 cents.

It is impossible to estimate the number of winning oscillation trades you could have had in those years, but it is *certain* how many losing trades you would have had: ZERO. Some years you would have had fewer than ten winners, but in some years — e.g., when rumors formerly circulated about the then-USSR buying or not buying commodities from the U.S. — you might have had forty or fifty winners. A fair estimate would be an average of about twenty oscillation winners per year, or $12,000. That would be nineteen years of trading *without a losing trade*, 380 consecutive *winning* trades, and $228,000 of profit on starting capital of $30,000.

Note: Please do not be deceived by lines on the chart which make it appear that the price collapsed in a single month. That usually means that the *final* delivery contract for the old crop expired while trading at a very high price because of a tight supply while the *first* delivery month of the new crop contracts opened trading at a relatively low price because of a bountiful crop assuring an ample supply.

CHART XIII

SOYBEAN OIL 1981 - 1993

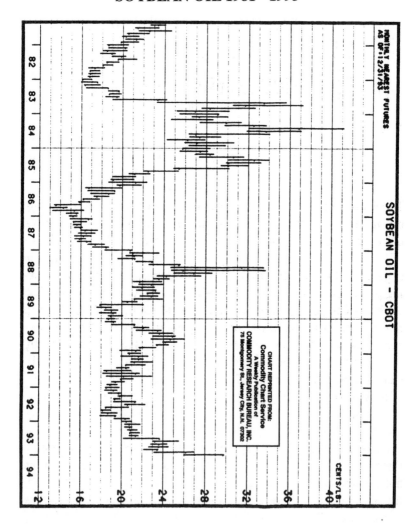

IX

The MidAmerica Contract

The MidAmerica Commodity Exchange is more than 100 years old, but it had not come into prominence until after 1973 when grain prices advanced to such levels that a Chicago Board of Trade (CBOT) futures contracts for 5,000 bushels of grain became so expensive that futures speculators with limited resources were being priced out of the market. The MidAmerica contract is for 1,000 bushels of corn, wheat, or soybeans; 20,000 pounds of live hogs or live cattle, half of the size of the Chicago Mercantile Exchange contracts; 1,000 ounces of silver, one-fifth of the New York Commodity Exchange contract; 33.2 ounces of gold, one-third of the standard 100 ounce contracts; $500,000 of 90-day U.S. Treasury bills, half of the size of the International Monetary Market contract; and $50,000 of U.S. Treasury bonds, half of the size of the CBOT contract.

(Note: Under present conditions with gold and silver trading so light on the New York Commodity Exchange and trading virtually nonexistent on the MidAm, if you want to trade small contracts, trade the 35.27 ounce — one kilogram — CBOT gold contract and the 1,000 ounce CBOT silver contract.)

Trading activity on the MidAmerica had expanded to the point where several major commodity brokerage houses bought memberships on this exchange and executed a fair volume of trade there. Unfortunately, many of the small commodity traders who entered the market in 1979 because of the publicity attendant to the Texans' attempt to corner the silver market either lost their money in the twelve-year decline in commodity prices from 1981 to 1992, or they went into professionally managed commodity pools (funds). This has caused the volume on the MidAm to fall, decreasing liquidity; however, some event will occur which will restore inflation and attract small — as well as large — speculators back to the commodities markets. There is no way to know when that will happen, but to insure that you are prepared for it, I will complete this description of trading on the MidAmerica Commodity Exchange.

Minimum margin requirements for commodity futures trading are set by the respective exchanges and adhered to by the exchanges' member firms. The individual firms have the right to require additional margin above the minimum, but they may not require less than the minimum. The MidAmerica generally requires a margin deposit which is prorated upon the requirements of the exchanges which trade the standard contracts. For example, if the Chicago Board of Trade requires $1,000 for the 5,000 bushel wheat contract, the MidAmerica will probably require $200 for its 1,000 bushel contract.

With the margin requirements being — in the case of wheat — one-fifth of the requirements for the full-sized contract, and with the cumulating paper losses being precisely one-fifth, the scale trader with only $6,000 trading on the MidAmerica can use the identical scale employed by the scale trader with the $30,000 bankroll who trades on the CBOT. Assuming there are executions for both scale traders at all respective levels, they will show identical percentage results, exclusive of commissions.

It costs the brokerage houses the same amount of overhead to process a customer's execution on the MidAmerica as it does on any other exchange, so they are obliged to charge nearly the same commission for the execution of the 1,000 bushel MidAmerica wheat contract as for the 5,000 bushel CBOT wheat contract. They may charge $20 to $40 for a MidAmerica execution and $50 to $80 for the CBOT (round turn). This is a disadvantage for the MidAmerica scale trader, cutting into his percentage profits, but there can be an enormous advantage if the CBOT scale trader converts to MidAmerica trading. Here's how:

Let us assume that a CBOT scale trader has set his scale to buy each 10 cents down and to sell each 10 cents up on corn. Swings of 10, 20, or even 30 cents are not uncommon in corn in early 1994 following the "500-year flood" and with corn trading above $3.00, but in a year or two we will see large crops again, and the price will return to a more normal $2.50, so let us use $2.50 corn for our illustration: He acquires his first contract at $2.50, but the price only falls to $2.41 before rallying to $2.59, and then it falls away again. He has watched corn swing through a 9 cent decline, an 18 cent rally, and a subsequent decline. This would be a very broad swing for corn in the $2.50 range, but the CBOT scale trader has not cashed a single winner because he has made no trades subsequent to the initial purchase. He would have been amply rewarded, however, if he had split his 5,000 bushel CBOT order into five 1,000 bushel MidAmerica decrements. Instead of scaling one 5,000 bushel order at each 10 cent decrement, he could have scaled 1,000 bushel MidAmerica contracts at each 2 cent decrement.

This way, he would have made the initial purchase at $2.50, and subsequent purchases at $2.48, $2.46, $2.44, and $2.42. He, too, failed to get an execution at $2.40 because the price never got that low. On the rally, he is able to sell at $2.52, $2.54, $2.56, and $2.58. He, too, is unable to sell at $2.60 because the top of the rally is $2.59. A CBOT scaler gets no executions, but a MidAm scaler cashes four winners of $100 each. After paying a commission on each trade, the MidAm scaler nets $300 or more, while the CBOT scaler has yet to complete a trade.

Under the conditions described above, the CBOT scaler needs a 20 cent move to be assured of at least one trade, while the MidAm scaler needs only 12 cents. There will be far more 12 cent swings than 20 cent swings, obviously.

The corollary to the above situation would be if corn's price drops from $2.50 to $2.39 and then rallies to $2.51. Each of the two traders cashes one winner, the CBOT trader garnering a $500 winner and the MidAm trader garnering a single $100 winner.

The MidAmerica trader — whether scale trading or using *any* other system — may have another problem to face: The higher commission expense has already been mentioned, but of greater concern — at least in my experience — is the problem of questionable executions on the MidAm. People in the commodity brokerage industry with whom I have discussed this matter seem to be in general agreement that the CBOT price must actually penetrate your limit before you may feel reasonably assured of getting an execution on the MidAm. If you have a resting order to buy a contract of corn on the MidAmerica at $2.50, you may see it trade repeatedly at that price on the CBOT tape, but sometimes you may not receive confirmation of an execution until the price runs down to $2.4975 or $2.4950. One reason why this problem exists is that the trading volume on the MidAm is so low, there is not enough volume on the MidAm to guarantee prompt executions at your limit. The second reason is that the MidAm floor broker is probably holding five unexecuted orders and will wait until the price dips one-half cent below their limit before filling them by buying five 1,000 bushel orders on the MidAm at $2.4950 and simultaneously selling one 5,000 bushel order on the CBOT at $2.50 (or vice versa), scalping $25. Without bothering to thank you, he goes on a break and has a $25 lunch.

In defense of the MidAm, I should comment that on some occasions I have bought a MidAm contract below the low of the day on the CBOT or sold above the CBOT high. It happens infrequently, but it does happen.

Processing costs for the brokerage firms continue to rise, and the amount of commission which they are forced to charge is difficult to overcome when trading the one-fifth size MidAm contracts. For example, a person scaling the CBOT soybean contract will net $430 profit on a 10 cent move from his buy price to his sell price after paying a $70 commission, which is 86% of the gross; however, the MidAm trader might need a $\frac{1}{2}$ cent penetration for the CBOT price on *both* the buying and selling sides of his MidAm trade, plus he could be paying a $40 commission, which is equal to another 4 cents, so that he is giving away 5 cents of the 10 cents CBOT move (actually 11 cents) to net $60, or 60%. That 28% differential is an enormous sacrifice just to trade the smaller contracts. If you plan to trade with limited resources, you would be better advised to join with several other persons to form a partnership and trade the full sized contracts instead of paying the high commissions on the MidAmerica.

There was a time when I did most of my trading — even for my largest managed accounts — on the MidAm, but the increase in commissions has caused me to drift away from it. You may still want to trade there while you are learning the system, but eventually you will probably want to trade the regular contracts.

You might also consider the CBOT oats contract as an alternative to other MidAmerica grain contracts. The grains and soybeans usually move in quite similar patterns, all rising or falling together. If you take into account the rule of thumb price ratios between soybeans and corn as well as between corn and oats, the soybeans:oats ratio is easily determined. The normal ratio between soybean and corn prices is 5:2, meaning that when soybeans sell at $5.00 per bushel, corn should sell at $2.00 per bushel. The ratio of corn to oats is 2:1, so that $2.00 corn equals $1.00 oats. Thus, if the soybean price is $6.00, the corn price should be $2.40, and oats should be $1.20.

At the time of this writing the 1994 soybean contracts (1993 crop) are trading around $7.00, but the 1995 contracts (1994 crop) are trading closer to $6.00. I suspect that we will see soybeans hover around $6.00 for at least a couple of years. With soybeans at $6.00, the value of the MidAmerica 1,000 bushel soybean contract is $6,000, but the parity price for oats would be $1.20, or $6,000 for the 5,000 bushel CBOT contract. A 5 cent move in the soybeans would probably be matched by a penny move in oats, and in both cases that is a $50 change in the value of the respective contracts. In other words, the price movements for daily fluctuations would be about equal in dollar results.

As for the margins, when the margin requirement is $1,500 for the CBOT soybean contract, it is probably $600 for corn and $300 for oats, which is consistent with the 5:2:1 ratios. The MidAmerica soybean margin would be one-fifth of the CBOT requirement, or $300, which is identical to that of oats.

There will be times — such as in 1983 — when soybean prices will explode and run away from oats, but that is not important, for the initial part of that upside move will sell you out of all of your scales in either soybeans or oats. During normal times, the 5:1 ratio will prevail, and you will do as well trading CBOT oats as MidAm soybeans; indeed, with the commission difference, you will do better.

Here is a way that I combine MidAm contracts with CBOT contracts: Let's say that soybeans are currently trading at $6.50, and I want to commence a scale. I am a little uncomfortable about starting so high because the South American harvest will soon commence, and the rumor is that it will be a record crop. Perhaps I doubt the veracity of the South American rumor, so I am willing to scale trade the soybeans, but I really would prefer to start at $6.25 instead of $6.50. I will start with a MidAmerica scale buying 1,000 bushel contracts at $6.50, $6.40, $6.30, $6.20, and $6.10. My average cost per contract is $6.30, which is not that much worse than the $6.25 I was willing to pay for the CBOT contract. If the price bounces around between $6.30 and $6.60, I will pick up a few oscillation profits, which will soon bring my average cost down to $6.25. Perhaps the South American rumor proves false, and soybeans never come down to $6.25. I will have picked up a few $100 winners in the MidAmerica scale. But, if the price continues to decline to $6.00, I switch to CBOT contracts and buy on the same scale I would have been using for CBOT contracts.

Don't worry if you have only $5,000 with which to scale trade. That was insufficient capital when the earlier editions of this book were written because we were still coming down from the sky high prices brought about by the silver cornering operation. But in the past year or two, prices have fallen back to twenty-year lows. In fact, when adjusted for inflation, these prices are on a par with those which prevailed at the time of the Roman Empire. With $5,000 you could trade CBOT corn or oats, MidAm wheat, soybeans or hogs, or the 1,000 ounce silver contracts on the CBOT. I frequently recommend $5,000 scales in the newsletter, *The Scale Trader*, and we do very well with them.

Before leaving the subject of MidAmerica scale trading, I must tell you about the Texas optometrist who sold his practice while in his early forties and retired. (True story.) His wife got tired of his lying around the house, so she called him a bum and told him to go out and get a job like everyone else. He had read this book and had been successfully scale trading from home, so instead of working for someone else he rented a small office in a high-rise office building, installed a commodity quote machine, and scale traded commodities for a living. He specialized in MidAmerica contracts, taking small profits — e.g., $80 in soybeans to net $55 after the commission or netting $100 on a T-bill trade — but capturing two or three every day. He told me he was making more money than he had ever earned by working for a living.

As time passed the word got out that he had a quote machine in his office, so many of the people in his building would stop by at noon to get quotes on their holdings. He told me they teased him because he was "fooling around" picking up so many $50 to $100 winners each day. I suggested to him that the next time someone said that, he should take that person out to the sidewalk in front of the building and ask that person to look around to see how many $100 bills he saw falling on the ground. Then they could go back into the office and await the broker's call informing him that another $100 had fallen into his lap as he cashed another winner. He told me they stopped teasing him when he did that.

X

Taking a Profit

A great deal of consideration must go into setting the scale for taking profits. One may not set a rule which applies for all commodities at all price levels. The factor of volatility is probably the most important consideration. Wheat will be more volatile above $5.00 per bushel than below $3.00. Pork bellies at any price is likely to be more volatile than gold. Soybeans at $7.00 may provide more trading opportunities in one month than corn at $2.00 will provide in an entire season. The commission on one commodity may be disproportionately high in relation to its volatility, while another may be low. All of these things must be considered.

The scale trader possibly may want to tailor his profit taking to his capital. He may attempt to capture a fixed dollar profit from each trade, or he may seek a certain percentage of the bankroll as his profit target, reasoning that a certain number of trades in a year will give him the percentage return he desires.

Whatever method you use, your primary consideration should be the volatility of the commodity being traded.

The simplest method of determining the proper selling scale to use is to observe the margin requirements set by the exchanges for the different commodities. As a particular commodity becomes more volatile, the exchange will require more margin. As the commodity loses some of its volatility the margin will be reduced. For example, if wheat margin is $1,000 on the CBOT 5,000 bushel contract, that is equal to a 20 cent move. You might set your selling scale at half the margin requirement, which would be $500, or 10 cents. If wheat margin is raised to $1,200 because it has become more volatile, you would raise your selling scale to 12 cents. If the wheat margin is raised to $1,500, you would raise your selling scale to 15 cents, etc. When the volatility of wheat lessens, the exchange will reduce the margin requirement, and you automatically reduce your selling scale. I have found a good rule of thumb in using this method is to seek a profit equal to 40-50% of the *exchange's* required margin.

Note: You must remember that each brokerage house may set its own margin requirements at any level it chooses so long as it is at least equal to or greater than the exchange minimum. Some firms which treat commodities as a mere sideline to their major business of securities trading will set abnormally high margin requirements. Some firms actually require margin deposits which are double exchange minimums. You should request that your broker inform you of the exchange minimums so that you may tailor your 40-50% profit goals to the exchange minimums rather than to the arbitrary margin requirements of the individual house. Otherwise, you would be seeking profits which might be virtually impossible to obtain.

Another method of setting selling scales that is both effective and simple is to make the increments a percentage of the price. The logic behind this method is that all commodities futures contracts are tied to a cash market wherein price fluctuations are usually quickly reversed as wholesale dealers buy and sell on the slightest price variations, generally confining the price oscillations to a relatively narrow range for brief periods of time. The range seems to be equal to the profit margins upon which wholesale dealers operate, which is a very low percentage. A good percentage figure to use, I have found, is around 2% to 3%. Thus, when silver trades around $5.00, the desired increment would be 10 cents ($500). Copper at 70 cents would indicate about a 1.5 cent ($375) profit goal. Soybeans between $5.00 and $6.00 would sell on a scale of about 12.5 cents or 15 cents ($625 or $750). Corn at $2.50 should be good for 7 cents ($350). Oats at $1.40 should be good for 4 cents ($200). Etc., etc., etc.

Chapter XIII deals with complex buying scales, but it is appropriate at this time to mention complex selling scales. As a commodity changes in price, its volatility will change. As stated earlier, when wheat is trading between $2.00 and $3.00 per bushel, its volatility will not be as great as when it trades between $3.00 and $4.00. It is even more volatile between $4.00 and $5.00. Therefore, positions bought below $3.00 might be sold on a scale of 8 cents per trade, while those to be sold between $3.00 and $4.00 would be sold with 10 cent profits. In the range from $4.00 to $5.00 you might seek a 12 cent gain. Above $5.00 the target might be 15 cents profit.

(The preceding paragraph may seem to be in contradiction to what I have previously said about scaling only in the lowest third of the recent historic range, for it would be impossible to be scaling wheat near $5.00 if you are following that rule, but in Chapter XV, I will demonstrate how it is possible to scale every commodity at virtually any price.)

Another easy method you might use to establish a good selling scale is to study charts showing the *daily* range of trading for the last several years. These charts are available in most commodity brokerage offices. If you are trading silver, ask your broker to make several photocopies of the silver charts for you. Then take them home and actually count the number of trades that would have been completed during the past several years if you had been buying on a certain scale down and selling on a certain scale up.

Experiment with scales. One scale trader once told me that he purchased computer tapes which gave him *every tick* for gold in the last ten years. He wrote his own program to scale trade gold using many different buying and selling scales. He discovered that he would have made more money — net after commissions — by buying each $2 down and selling each $2 up than he would have made buying each $3 down and selling each $3 up.

Your buying scale was determined by your capital, and the trading is assumed to be done only in the same range as seen in recent years, so it is simple enough to use the charts given to you by the broker and to mark on one chart the point where the initial purchase and all subsequent purchases, plus all of the sales, would have been made if you had been trading silver that year. I like to use red and green felt pens for my marking — red dots for the purchases and green dots for the sales.

For the moment, let us assume that you are considering buying silver each 10 cents down, starting at $4.50, and selling each acquired contract 10 cents above the *scale* purchasing point. (If you buy below the scale price, you should still enter your sell order 10 cents above the *scale* price. Use the bonus to take your spouse or your sweetheart out to dinner. If the bonus is large enough, take them both out to dinner. But not at the same time!) Start with a red dot at the point where silver first dipped to $4.50. Then move across the chart and put in either a green dot if silver hits $4.60 or a red dot if it drops to $4.40. Let's assume it drops to $4.40 instead of rising to $4.60. You have marked the red dot at $4.40, and now you look to see whether $4.50 or $4.30 occurs next, marking the appropriate color dot. This time the assumption is that the price has risen to $4.50, so a green dot is marked, and now you look to see whether the next price level touched is $4.60 or $4.40. This technique is carried across the entire chart. As long as the price stays below $4.60 there should be frequent trades, but once the $4.60 level is surpassed all of your positions will have been liquidated and no trades will occur until the price returns to $4.50 and you resume buying.

Add the number of red and green dots on the chart. If the price is $4.60 or above, the red dots and the green dots should be equal. Each green dot is at least 10 cents above a corresponding red dot, so there is a gross profit of $500 for each trade if you were trading the 5,000 ounce contracts or $100 if you were trading the 1,000 ounce contracts. You need only to deduct the commissions to determine the theoretical profit, although it is possible that the commissions were covered by the bonus executions caused by gap openings or fast moving intraday markets.

Next, do what the gold trader did. Use another copy of the same silver scale but assume an 8 cent selling scale. The buying scale was tailored to your bankroll, so it remains exactly the same, but the target for each sale is set only 8 cents above its corresponding buy price. For example, if purchases are made at $4.50, $4.40 and $4.30, sell orders should be entered at $4.58, $4.48 and $4.38. After inserting all of the appropriate red and green dots, total them again to determine gross profits, and then deduct the commissions. There should be more winning trades with the 8 cent selling scale than with the 10 cent selling scale, but did the extra winners produce enough extra profits to overcome the 2 cent-less profit per trade and the extra commissions?

Now try it with your same buying scale but with a 12 cent selling scale. There will be fewer completed trades at 12 cents than at 10 cents, but the profits will be larger and the total commissions will be less. Does the lesser number of profitable trades — even though they are larger profits — produce the same total dollar profit? Only you can determine this to your personal satisfaction. Only practice and actual trading can give you the skill to set your selling scales properly.

Just remember that selling scales set too narrow will net too little after commissions, while selling scales set too wide will produce too few profitable trades. I have seen people who thought they were "playing it safe" by buying and selling on very broad scales, only to find that after acquiring a contract or two they never bought any additional contracts and never sold any of their inventory; carrying charges ate them up. For example, because they were working with limited capital, they wanted to play it safe by using a very broad buying and selling scale in silver. They were buying each 25 cents down and selling each 25 cents up. Silver is not as volatile today as it was in the 1980's, so it could take weeks — or even months — to swing through such a broad range. They were forced to hold their positions for a very long time and watched their losses mount because of the rollover premiums they were forced to pay. There would have been less risk for them to have traded a "tight" scale in oats or corn.

It is important that you consider the commissions in setting selling scales. You certainly can trade the MidAmerica 1,000 bushel contracts and net a reasonable reward after commissions by trading soybeans for 12.5 cents or wheat for 10 cents, but your profit begins to narrow if you take 8 cents ($80) in corn, less a $20 to $40 commission. You would be forced either to maintain a 10 cent selling scale in MidAmerica contracts or to switch to CBOT contracts with an 8 cent selling scale, which is $400 profit less only a $60 commission.

XI

How Can I Lose?

I remember the time a doctor telephoned my office to introduce himself and to solicit some help in getting out of a managed commodity account he was carrying with an advisor who was using a trend-following system that was generating substantial losses in his account. During the conversation I couldn't help commenting upon my own scale trading system with the boast that it was impossible to lose while trading with this method. I offered to mail this gentleman the four-page pamphlet version of the system, and he accepted.

The very day the doctor received the write-up he rushed to my office wanting to talk about my trading method, and early in the conversation I once again made the claim that it was impossible to lose while trading commodities if one stuck to the scale trading method, following the rules rigorously and without deviation. The doctor looked me in the eye and admonished me to please refrain from repeating that "can't lose" boast because I "sacrificed professionalism with such ridiculous claims."

We spent the next two hours discussing the system as I attempted to answer all of his questions and objections and, in general, to clarify his misconceptions about the system. At the end of the two hours he merely sat there looking at me and confessed, "This is incredible. It's really incredible. With this system you really can't lose."

I relate that tale only for the benefit of the skeptics. It is true that a properly managed scale trading account cannot lose. However, an improperly managed account will lose at scale trading or at any other method of trading. The key to the whole matter is in the management of the available capital. The only way that a person using the scale trading method can lose is either by setting his scales too tight — buying more contracts than the capital can accommodate — by scale trading too many commodities at once with limited capital, or by losing his nerve and quitting when the commodity being accumulated falls to such a level that substantial paper losses have been accumulated.

There is no other way to lose. If the scale trader has properly set his scale within the limit of his available capital and provided a reserve as described in Chapter VII, it is impossible to lose, for eventually and inevitably the price must rise to a level sufficient to allow him to liquidate all of his positions profitably.

In 1975 I was accumulating wheat, using MidAmerica contracts. I was purchasing each 2 cents down, intending to sell each 10 cents up. I purchased fourteen contracts before the first rally came. But that rally was only 10 cents, so I was able to sell only a single contract before the decline resumed. I was forced to purchase eight more contracts before wheat prices finally flattened out and terminated the decline. Then a series of events occurred that put me in the money.

First it was the *Mayaguez* incident. (Do you recall the U.S. freighter that was attacked by the Cambodian gunboats? That was the *Mayaguez*. The names of the Cambodian gunboats were never revealed, but I presume they were *The Nina, The Pinta, and the Santa Maria.*) With that sudden and shocking news, most commodities prices rallied sharply to close with substantial gains for the day. This is a typical response to a threat of war. The upward thrust in wheat prices got me out of four contracts.

By sheer coincidence, *the very next day* a rumor circulated that representatives of the USSR were in Washington to discuss the purchase of wheat. With the memory of the 1973-74 explosion in grain prices still fresh in the minds of traders, there was another surge of prices in a short-covering rally. Wheat was up the limit. This allowed me to cash ten more winners.

By the end of the day word was circulating that the Russian story was nothing but rumor, and prices settled back to about where they had closed the previous night. Because I had reinstated all of the buy orders upon execution of each sell order, I was able to repurchase four contracts of wheat on the retracement.

The price of wheat fluctuated for a few weeks as rumors and counter-rumors circulated, but then came word that the Russian news was not a rumor after all but was in fact true. Prices climbed steadily for several weeks, and I was able to sell all of the positions. There had been well over fifty winning trades.

All that it took was patience. Fortunately for me, my reward came in a matter of a few months, but it may occasionally be necessary for you to wait much longer and even to do some rollovers as described in Chapter XVI. It is most important that you realize that sooner or later some event will occur — whether it be a drought, the threat of war, insect infestation, political palliatives to assuage special interest groups in an election year, simple inflation, or whatever — which will force commodity futures prices higher and allow you to dispose of all of your previously acquired positions profitably.

The story I just related concerned an account over which I had absolute control and had no fear of accumulated paper losses. Now I will relate a story to you about an account which I managed but over which I had very little control. I had scale traded the account, but the account took a merciless beating. Here is how it happened:

I had formed a limited partnership for the purpose of trading commodity futures contracts. It was publicly offered to Californians only. When we commenced trading we had about $200,000 in the fund. I divided the money three ways: $70,000 each to two unaffiliated advisors to the fund and $60,000 which I was to manage personally. One advisor was to use technical analysis, the other was to use fundamental analysis, and I was to scale trade.

It took only six weeks to confirm what I had always suspected about commodity advisors — that they do as poorly as anyone else in commodities trading. The advisor using the technical approach lost more than $46,000 of his $70,000 in that short span of time. Our partnership units (similar to shares), which had been priced originally at $500 apiece were down to $350. I fired both of the outside advisors and assumed total control of the fund's management. I committed the fund's entire assets — which after a few small redemptions had dropped to $135,000 — to a scale trading program.

During the next six months there was no particular trend in commodity prices, neither up nor down, which was ideal for scale trading. I had the unit value above $425 again. That may not sound like much, but that is an annualized rate of appreciation of better than 42%.

This creditable performance record began to attract new money to the fund, putting our total assets near $300,000. I continued using the scale trading method as commodities prices went into a declining phase. I was accumulating substantial positions in a number of commodities, and I was accumulating some substantial paper losses. This was akin to the wheat accumulation described earlier in this chapter, so it did not alarm me. However, many of the fund's eighty partners became panicky, remembering the $150 decline they had witnessed in the first six weeks of our operation, and — fearing another such loss — they requested redemption because they did not comprehend the principle of scale trading. The redemption requests were overwhelming. This was catastrophic to the fund. The redemption requests were so large that it became obvious that the fund would be unable to continue to function with the limited remaining resources. We closed out all positions and liquidated the fund.

Post-mortem: Among the positions which the fund had begun to accumulate and which had accumulated substantial paper losses were gold, cattle and orange juice. I had started buying gold at $130 with the intention of buying each $2 down and selling all positions with $5 gains, for a $500 profit on each contract traded. I expected to see gold oscillate below $130 while we cashed repeated profits. I was confident that gold's price would eventually reach $135, by which time I would have liquidated all of the positions profitably. The decline in the gold price caused us to acquire ten contracts at prices all of the way down to $112, and when the price reached $111 the total paper loss was exactly $10,000. That wasn't much of a loss, but similar losses were beginning to build in other commodities too, and that was when the avalanche of redemption requests buried us. I had no choice but to begin liquidating all positions — including gold at $111 — to liquidate the fund. I don't have to tell you that the bottom for that particular contract was $108 and that the price eventually went above $900 per ounce. All I needed was $135.

Cattle: I had begun buying cattle at 46 cents and had added positions, as I recall, each half-cent down, with the intention of selling each contract on a penny advance to gross $400 profits. Because of the redemptions, I was forced to begin liquidating those positions at 38 cents. All I would have needed to close all positions profitably was a 47 cent price to liquidate the final contract. The price hit 75 cents. Too late, we were already out of business.

Orange juice: This story would make strong men cry. I had begun accumulating OJ at 63 cents with the intention of scaling purchases each 1 cent down and selling on a scale each 3 cents up. The forced liquidation began near 50 cents. The bottom was 48 cents. All I needed was 66 cents to be out of the entire position profitably. OJ went to $2.00!

I had similar but smaller positions in numerous other commodities. I was forced to liquidate every position and to dissolve the fund. There is no telling what kind of asset value per unit we would have today if we had stayed alive. The value of the original $500 units would have to be near $8,000 apiece.

The moral of the story is simple. In fact, there are two: (1) If you plan to scale trade you must be prepared to endure and to ignore the accumulation of a large paper loss. This will never be a problem if you have carefully budgeted your bankroll and provided an adequate comfort factor; (2) Trade without partners, or if you elect to take on partners because of the obvious benefits of a larger bankroll, be sure they are not going to panic on the first decline. The partnership agreement must provide for nothing more frequent than annual withdrawals, and then only with ninety days written notice.

The subject of partnerships will be covered more extensively in Chapter XXIII.

* * *

All of the text in this chapter has been repeated verbatim — except for minor changes for clarity — from the previous editions of this book. *AMAZINGLY,* the problem persists. Even though the people have read the book and should have read this chapter, they still lose their nerve and sell out just when The Law of Supply and Demand is about to take over and send prices higher. I suspect that the reason for this is that they have been schooled by commodity brokers *al-*

ways to use stops to "protect" themselves. This has been drummed into their minds so incessantly that they cannot think any other way. They would never *think* of using a stop on any of their stock holdings because they feel that the stocks will always come back, but for some unfathomable reason they are convinced that commodity prices *never* come back. They should remember that stocks *can* go to zero but commodities *cannot*.

I am compelled to warn you that you *must* be prepared to ride out all storms when scale trading. You will almost surely have a paper loss in your account when you start scale trading because you must accumulate inventory. If you have no inventory, you cannot cash winners. If you have inventory, there will be the inevitable paper losses. If there are only paper profits, they will be sold on your selling scales.

I have seen some accounts which are lucky enough to have to buy only a contract or two each time, and the rallies come almost immediately. These accounts move onto the profit side of the ledger rapidly, but the norm is for your account to take three months or so to capture enough oscillation winners to overcome the omnipresent paper losses.

You must also expect that there will be regular times when commodity prices have moved to overbought conditions and you have cashed most of your contracts with profits, only to be followed by periods of declining prices during which you are forced to reload your scale positions. During those declines you will accumulate paper losses again, but that is part of the system. Think of it as "one step back, followed by two steps forward." Your chances of success as a scale trader are going to be greatest if you ignore the accumulation of paper losses and just remember that when the declines begin you will be owning one or two contracts, but when the rallies begin you will be owning six or eight contracts.

The four preceding paragraphs refer to people losing their nerve and taking losses with scale trading. I could cite many examples of over-trading the available capital, but this one should make my point: A man called me one time and asked me what I thought of his scale for pork bellies, which was to buy each 2 cents down and to sell each penny up. He said he was using $35,000, and with pork bellies in the mid-30's, I told him he was borderline but could probably make it. Then he asked me to critique his cocoa scale. I asked how much capital he had set aside for cocoa, and I was amazed when he said that was

was part of the $35,000. By the time we finished talking, he had informed me that he was trading *seven* commodities in his $35,000 account. He was delighted with the super bounty of oscillation winners he was taking, but I warned him that he was destined for inescapable disaster. Naturally, he ignored me. Two months later he called to say he wished he had listened to me because he had been wiped out. It's corny, but the old saw about the bulls making a little and the bears making a little while the hogs get slaughtered is absolutely true when it comes to scale trading. If you are conservative in the employment of your capital you will do well for a very long time. If you trade aggressively you will do *very well* — for a while.

One sad anecdote about a partnership: I was managing a partnership which had started with $60,000, had appreciated about 60% in a year, had attracted new capital, and now had assets of $480,000. An airline pilot invested $220,000 in the partnership, increasing our assets nearly 50%, to $700,000. I could not sit on all of that cash, so I began to use some very conservative scales, but we were in an overbought market, and most commodity prices began to decline. By the end of the one-year decline the units had fallen from $160 to $112, and we had a large inventory of new positions and a substantial paper loss in most of those positions. He liquidated over half of his units! That was devastating to the partnership. Whereas we had had probably fifty contracts in inventory in the $480,000 account, we were now faced with the prospect of holding about 100 contracts in a $415,000 account. The risk was too great for the existing partners, so again I was forced to liquidate substantial positions.

I told him that he was doing it backwards, buying at the top and selling at the bottom. I was stunned by his response: "Isn't that human nature?" I had done a little flying in the Navy during the war, and because Navy pilots have to land a plane on a postage stamp which is bobbing in high seas, we didn't have much respect for airline pilots who land on a three-mile runway. We used to say that when an airline hired a new pilot they gave him an IQ test and measured him for a uniform at the same time. If his IQ was greater than his sleeve length, he was automatically disqualified. I don't know which airlines this chap flies for, but I hope I never ride on his airplane!

XII

Taking A Loss

If you follow the scale trading rules which are propounded in this book you will have a virtually unblemished record of trading with only an occasional losing trade. Rollovers may be treated as losses for tax purposes, but they will ultimately result in winners for the patient scale trader, so there is no need to consider them to be true losers. However, it is necessary to take an occasional loser which stands forever on the record as a loser and is irretrievable.

The most frequently appearing losses come either from price discrepancies that occur with rollovers or from carrying charges.

The best way to explain the problem of price discrepancies is to give an example. In 1991 I was managing a large partnership which scale trades pork bellies only. (We call it "Bellies Up.") Pork bellies had gone into an extended slide so that we owned nineteen contracts. The bellies were trading in the low 40's, but we were approaching the expiration date for our old-crop contracts and were faced with the prospect of rolling to the new-crop contracts in the low 50's. The price difference was 11 cents. Two years earlier we had seen pork bellies trade at a record low of 24.6 cents, and with the current expansion of hog herds I feared a return to the 25 cents area, in which case we would be forced to buy a huge number of additional contracts. Discretion being the better part of valor, I elected to jettison a few contracts, actually taking losses. As it developed, it was a good thing that I did, for the price dropped to 28 cents before staging a big rally.

That is an example of dropping a few contracts as a defensive measure. A similar tactic would be if we had held, say, only a pair of contracts. To avoid forcing ourselves to continue the scale 11 cents above current prices and thereby possibly exposing ourselves to greater risk, we might have elected to jettison both contracts, taking losses on each, and simply looking for a "safer" commodity to scale trade. This option is infinitely more palatable if you have already cashed several oscillation profits.

This type of deliberate loss is less frequent that the "carrying charge" loss, which occurs with a fair degree of regularity.

Once again, it is best to give an example to describe a carrying charge loss. You will find that most commodities trade in a normal "carrying charge market," which simply means that each successive delivery month trades at a slight premium to the preceding month with that premium being equal to the cost of carrying that commodity in storage. The scale trader who makes no allowance for carrying charges may eventually accumulate an enormous number of contracts which would be virtually impossible to liquidate on an upside scale without the benefit of a substantial price increase.

The major portion of the carrying charge is attributable to interest rates, with insurance, storage, and miscellaneous fees accounting for the minor balance. Thus, if the prime interest rate is hovering near 6%, the annual carrying charge on a commodity such as silver would approximate 6%. If spot (cash) silver is $5.00 per ounce and the prime interest rate is currently 6%, the annual carrying charge should be about 30 cents. For example, in the month of January, the January silver contract for the present year is virtually the equivalent of the spot market and would be trading at $5.00 if the cash silver price is $5.00. If the prime interest rate is 6%, the January silver contract for the *succeeding* year would be trading around $5.30, which would be a carrying charge of 30 cents, or 6%, spread over twelve months. Each contract from nearby February through next January will trade at a 2.5 cent premium to the preceding delivery month.

The current January is $5.00, February $5.025, March $5.05, April $5.075, etc., to the next January at $5.30.

Under these conditions you might elect to initiate a scale in silver. You choose to begin with the deferred January contract at $5.30, with the intention of purchasing each 10 cents down. You intend to take a profit each 10 cents up.

You buy your first contract at $5.30, and then an incredible circumstance occurs. The circumstance is that spot silver ceases to oscillate through its normal volatile range and virtually locks for a year or longer within the range of a few cents of $5.00. At the end of four months, spot silver is hovering near $5.00, and the May contract has become the spot delivery month, so it has drifted down to $5.00, and all other months have declined a corresponding 10 cents. Your January contract is now down to $5.20, and you have made a second scale purchase at that level. Four months later, the spot September contract is down to $5.00, and each of the other contracts is also down another 10 cents. Your January contract is down to $5.10, and you have acquired your third contract, at $5.10. If spot silver hovers near $5.00 for the entire year, your January contract will ultimately fall to $5.00 when it becomes the spot month, and you will have four contracts in your account. Silver went through an entire year without declining, but you have four contracts in your account with accumulated losses of $0.30, $0.20, $0.10, and $0.00. That is a cumulative total of $0.60, which is $3,000 in the 5,000 ounce contracts, or $600 in the 1,000 ounce CBOT contracts. Silver is unchanged in the spot market, but you have a large loss.

If you did a normal rollover with these four contracts, and if silver hovered near $5.00 for another year, you would acquire three more contracts with a pyramiding loss of $10,500 (or $2,100 in the small contracts). Silver would have to advance from its present $5.00 level to $5.80 an ounce (spot) to bail you out of your seven accumulated contracts profitably. That is quite an expectation when you consider that you had originally sought only an advance to $5.10 as you initiated this scaling venture.

If you are forced to roll over another year, the loss reaches $22,500 ($4,500), assuming again that spot silver hovers near $5.00.

Actually, silver would no longer need to hover near $5.00 to create the above situation. All it needs to do is to keep from rising to a level which would permit you to sell your highest-priced contract. After you have acquired seven contracts, silver could rally to $5.69, and you would still hold a single contract. If you have accumulated a dozen contracts, the price need only stay below $6.20 to keep you locked in and to set up your ultimate demise. For this reason it is absolutely essential that you dispose of a contract from time to time and absorb a small loss on it before it becomes a big one. There are several ways to accomplish this:

The ideal way requires some cooperation from silver. If, under normal conditions with silver prices oscillating, the price advances sufficiently for you to liquidate all positions on your normal scale, do *not* reinstate your buying scale in the same delivery month at the same price. Allow for the carrying charge difference. In other words, if carrying charges are running at a normal $0.30 annual rate and it has been four months since you began your scale, either lower your scale 10 cents (one-third of the annual rate) and trade the same delivery month, or use the original scale but trade the delivery month which is four months later than the one you originally used.

If silver is not cooperating, you might absorb a loss. If you are scaling with 10 cent increments and the carrying charge is approximately 30 cents per year, or slightly over 0.5 cents per week, you must absorb a loss on one contract by selling one out of your inventory each twenty weeks without regard to your scale. That means that you will have a nominal loss once each twenty weeks, but the way silver oscillates under normal conditions you may average a winner each week or two, so you can easily afford that single loss. In a year's time you could capture thirty winners in silver, so the two or three losses you absorb for carrying charges become inconsequential.

After you have acquired enough skill in scale trading, you will probably want to absorb the carrying charges by altering your scale through the year. This has the advantage of possibly eliminating the losses altogether. With this technique, if the price of silver has declined and you see that you are holding some positions, do not reenter a buy order upon the sale of one of those positions. For example, if you have been buying at $5.00, $4.90, $4.80, and $4.70, and the price rises to $4.80, allowing you to sell the contract you bought at $4.70, do not reenter a buy order at $4.70. Your next purchase will not be made until silver falls to $4.60. If you abstain from reentering one buy order each four months or so, you will not accumulate the large inventory of silver contracts mentioned earlier. If your scale buying was initiated at a reasonable level, the price will eventually rise above your initial purchase price so that you will have liquidated all of your positions profitably, and then you would reassess the silver situation and trade a deferred delivery month with the appropriate scale.

The drawback to the technique of abstaining from reentering certain buyback orders is that you widen the gap between buy and sell orders, making it easier for silver (or any other commodity) to make broad swings without permitting you to either buy or sell. For example, if you are scaling silver by buying each 10 cents down and selling each 10 cents up, the maximum gap through which silver may swing without you either buying or selling is 19 cents; however, if you choose not to reinstate a buy order, your gap becomes 29 cents. With a gap so broad, you might go for long periods between trades; meanwhile, the carrying charges are steadily eroding your equity. If you remember my earlier comment about the man who said he made more money trading gold on $2 swings than on $3 swings, you might decide simply to take all the silver oscillation profits you can get and then simply jettison an occasional contract when you are doing a rollover.

If this system of omitting buy orders to keep your inventory at manageable levels fails to accomplish its goal because you started buying at too high a level, at least the number of contracts that you will be forced to roll over will be relatively modest. In the illustration above, you would be rolling over no more than a contract or two per year rather than six or seven. Assuming you actually started scaling at a reasonable level, it is proper to expect that a modest rally will occur sooner or later, affording you the opportunity to dispose of all of the rolled-over contracts. Then you again assess the silver situation, selecting a proper scale and delivery month, and you resume your trading activity.

CAUTION: It is important that you note that I used January to January in my example for carrying charges only because it is easier to demonstrate a full year of carrying charges and then divided by twelve for the months. In the days when silver and gold were the hot trading items and the prices were reported each night on the evening news, the trading activity was substantial, and the deferred contracts had sufficient liquidity for you to trade them. Unfortunately, silver and gold trading has diminished to a level where you should not trade delivery months which are more than six months away on the calendar. This is probably true of the Comex 5,000 ounce contracts, but it is *absolutely* true of the CBOT 1,000 ounce contracts.

XIII

The Complex Scale

In Chapter VII, I described the basic method of setting a simple buying scale to accumulate a commodity as its price declines. This simple scale method will prove adequate for beginning scale traders, but as you become more familiar with the system you will find that it becomes more profitable — without increasing the risk — to tighten the buying scale in certain circumstances.

A commodity price is much like a spring in that the more it is depressed the more it will snap back when the pressure is released. For that reason a scale trader might be wasting an opportunity if he maintains a wide scale after the commodity he is accumulating has undergone a steep decline. For example, if you are scaling wheat and the price has fallen to a level near the government loan, you should be accumulating substantially more contracts at that low level because of the very low risk.

Another instance when it would be advantageous to employ a complex scale would be when the price is at a level which fails to instill ultimate confidence in your initiating purchases. You might want to try the toe-in-the-water approach by buying the first few contracts on a very broad scale and then tightening the scale after the price has fallen to a level where you can afford to get serious. It happens very frequently that the price will hover just above the level where you would like to begin scaling, and as it oscillates you feel that you are missing numerous opportunities for profit.

In case you should ever be tempted to start a scale slightly above the price which you truly consider best, just be sure that you have taken the precaution of computing your maximum exposure before buying. That high-priced extra contract may result in the subsequent accumulation of a paper loss larger than anticipated, but if you are adequately capitalized, it will be no problem. You may find that the single extra contract (or two or three, if you really extend yourself) provides numerous extra profits if the price continues to hover and oscillate at that level.

Chart XIII is an example of a complex scale for MidAmerica 1,000 bushel contracts of wheat where each 1 cent is equal to $10, and the margin requirement for a contract of wheat is $200. It is good, but not ideal, to begin a wheat scale at $3.00, so I start with purchases at 10 cent decrements. As the price declines the inevitable price rebound comes closer, so I may tighten the scale and make the new purchases each 5 cents down. Eventually, if the price penetrates the government loan level (which can happen), the risk is reduced to near-minimum, and I will reduce the decremental purchases to 3 cents or even 2 cents.

The key to the complex scale is COLUMN 4. (See Chart XIV.) In the simple scale the decremental loss was always equal; in the complex scale it changes. For example, if you are scaling MidAmerica 1,000 bushel wheat contracts, each 1 cent is equal to $10, so if the buying decrement is 10 cents, the decremental loss is $100. If you tighten the scale and start buying each 7.5 cents down, the decremental loss becomes $75. If you further tighten it to 5 cents, the decremental loss becomes $50. Etc., etc., etc.

The particular reason for illustrating the compressed wheat scale is that this example has shown the price declining to approximately the probable bottom. For 1993 the national average government loan level for wheat was $2.86 per bushel, F.O.B. the farm. Allow about $0.26 to ship into Chicago, and you are talking about $3.12 for wheat that did not see storage, or the first of the "new crop" months, which was July 1993. At the time this book is being written, it appears the

CHART XIV

EXAMPLE OF

A COMPLEX MIDAMERICA WHEAT SCALE

1	2	3	4	5	6	7	8
3.50	1	0	0	0	0	100	100
3.40	2	1	100	100	100	200	300
3.30	3	2	100	200	300	300	600
3.20	4	3	100	300	600	400	1,000
3.15	5	4	50	200	800	500	1,300
3.10	6	5	50	250	1,050	600	1,650
3.05	7	6	50	300	1,350	700	2,050
3.02	8	7	30	210	1,560	800	2,360
2.99	9	8	30	240	1,800	900	2,700
2.96	10	9	30	270	2,070	1,000	3,070
2.93	11	10	30	300	2,370	1,100	3,470
2.91	12	11	20	220	2,590	1,200	3,790
2.89	13	12	20	240	2,830	1,300	4,130
2.87	14	13	20	260	3,090	1,400	4,490
2.85	15	14	20	280	3,370	1,500	4,870
2.83	16	15	20	300	3,670	1,600	5,270

same loan level will prevail for 1994, so $3.12 is also the projected loan equivalent for the July 1994 contract. That is not an absolute bottom since many farmers did not qualify for the loan, and their wheat may be sold at levels below the Chicago $3.12 July price. I could see the July 1994 wheat contract going to a possible bottom of $2.83, but not much below that, so I have set up a scale to expend $5,370 at $2.83. My assumption is that a person with a $7,500 bankroll has committed about 50%, or about $3,910 at the $2.90 level, which I consider the probable low for July 1994 wheat. He could safely commit another 20% to the possible low of $2.83, so that he would have committed only 71.6% of the bankroll and still will have 28.4% in reserve in case my estimates are totally erroneous and the price falls below $2.83.

A $7,500 commitment to July 1994 wheat using the described scale would probably yield a $100 winner every two weeks or so. Doesn't sound like much, but that could be about $2,200 for the year, which would be about a 30% return. That is truly a remarkable return for such a low risk investment.

I should remind you at this time of the points I made in Chapter X about selling at different upside increments. In using the complex buying scale you might also choose to use a complex selling scale. When wheat trades below $3.00 you might elect to take only 8 cents profit, but between $3.00 and $4.00 (if you choose to trade in that range), you might want 10 cents. I mention this at this point because the traders with a bankroll larger than $7,500 would have very little difficulty in trading the July 1994 contract starting as high as $3.40 to $3.50.

If you choose to trade a deferred contract other than July, you may use any of the other delivery months by adding the carrying charges to the scale presented in Chart XIV. The carrying charge for wheat at this price level and with interest rates which prevail at the time of this writing approximate 1 cent per month, so the September scale may commence at $3.52, the December at $3.55, and the March, 1995, at $3.58.

CAUTION: The usual range for wheat trading is from about $2.50 on the bottom to $4.00 on the top; thus, the bottom third of the range would be from $3.00 down to $2.50. I can cheat a little on the 1994 contracts of 1993 wheat because of the damage the 500-year flood did to grain crops throughout the Midwest. The loss of corn, soybean, and sorghum production dropped available supplies to twenty-year lows and caused the prices of those respective commodities to rise sharply, causing livestock feeders to substitute wheat in their feed formulas under The Law of Substitution. 1994 is also expected to be a sub-par year for grain production because of the water still standing in some fields and the silt coverage in others, but the current high grain prices will encourage heavy use of fertilizer, and the total crops would be only slightly less than "normal" if the weather is "normal." This will bring grain prices back to normal ranges in

1995 futures contracts, which would indicate a bottom-third range again at $2.50 to $3.00 for wheat.

There may be a time when you — either by choice or by necessity — will hold some contracts of a commodity and will want to begin scaling that commodity. There could be a number of reasons for your owning the contracts before commencing the scale: primarily, you might have acquired a position as a long-term speculation, and it has gone sour; more likely, you may have been willing to start a scale in, say, copper when the price was 70 cents, but you were heavily involved with cotton and couldn't trade copper until you extricated yourself from the cotton. By the time you get out of cotton, copper has dropped to 60 cents, at which point you are willing to commence your scale with three contracts instead of one, realizing that you would now own six contracts if you had started at 70 cents and made purchases each 2 cents down.

It is a simple matter to construct this scale, for all you need to do is to enter the number of contracts you are starting with as the first number in Column 2 and enter a zero as the first number in Column 3. Construct your scale below by making the second entry in Column 2 one unit greater than the first entry, and make the second entry in Column 3 equal to the first entry in Column 2 (because it represents the number of contracts held which have losses in them).

To illustrate, if you have watched copper decline from 70 cents to 60 cents, and if you are willing to start a scale with three contracts in position, you buy those three contracts at 60 cents and construct your scale thusly: (See Chart XV.)

Each cent in copper is equal to $250, so the 2 cent decremental losses represent $500. The margin requirement for copper in this illustration is $750 per contract, so the scale starts out requiring $2,250 of margin to hold the three contracts. After that, everything is the same as the basic scale.

As for the price at which you should enter your first three sell orders, that is entirely up to you. This is a deviation from pure scale trading, and you did it on your own, so you must determine how you want to handle the sell orders. I suggest that if you *liked* copper at 70 cents you must *love* it at 60 cents; therefore, I would enter the three sell orders at 6200, 6400, and 6600. If realized, that would give you 12 cents of profit instead of 6 cents, or a $1,500 bonus.

CHART XV

STARTING WITH THREE CONTRACTS

1	2	3	4	5	6	7	8
60	3	0	0	0	0	2,250	2,250
58	4	3	500	1,500	1,500	3,000	4,500
56	5	4	500	2,000	3,500	3,750	7,250
54	6	5	500	2,500	6,000	4,500	10,500
52	7	6	500	3,000	9,000	5,250	14,250
50	8	7	500	3,500	12,500	6,000	18,500
48	9	8	500	4,000	16,500	6,750	23,250
46	10	9	500	4,500	21,000	7,500	28,500

Another variation on the manner of setting scales could be when you want to start trading something on the MidAmerica with the intention of shifting to the full-sized Chicago Board of Trade or Chicago Mercantile contracts if the price falls to a more desirable level. This could be useful if you are watching soybeans oscillating wildly above $7.00, and you want to get into the action, but you fear the possibility of a decline below $7.00. You would trade MidAmerica contracts over $7.00 and CBOT contracts under $7.00.

One adjustment you must make is caused by the fact that the MidAmerica soybean contract is for 1,000 bushels while the CBOT contract is for 5,000 bushels. My method of constructing scales requires that all contracts in the scale be of equal size, so an adjustment is necessary. This is simple. I merely express all contracts in MidAmerica sizes. Thus, Column 2 increases in single digits while I am accumulating MidAmerica contracts, but it increases in multiples of five when I start buying CBOT contracts. You must note that Column 4 is still expressed as the decremental loss for Mid-America contracts of 1,000 bushels, which keeps everything consistent because we multiplied Column 2 (and therefore 3) by five.

Chart XV is an example of a scale used to acquire single contracts of the 1,000 bushel MidAmerica soybeans, starting at $7.50 and each 5 cents down to $7.05 for the first ten contracts, and then it shifts to the 5,000 bushel Chicago Board of Trade contracts, starting at $7.00 and carrying down to $6.50. The margin requirement for a 1,000 bushel contract of MidAmerica soybeans is $300, and it is $1,500 for the CBOT 5,000 bushel contracts.

CHART XVI

EXAMPLE OF A SCALE COMBINING

MIDAMERICA AND CBOT SOYBEANS

<u>1</u>	<u>2</u>	<u>3</u>	<u>4</u>	<u>5</u>	<u>6</u>	<u>7</u>	<u>8</u>
750	1	0	0	0	0	300	300
745	2	1	50	50	50	600	650
740	3	2	50	100	150	900	1,050
735	4	3	50	150	300	1,200	1,500
730	5	4	50	200	500	1,500	2,000
725	6	5	50	250	750	1,800	2,550
720	7	6	50	300	1,050	2,100	3,150
715	8	7	50	350	1,400	2,400	3,800
710	9	8	50	400	1,800	2,700	4,500
705	10	9	50	450	2,250	3,000	5,250
700	15	10	50	500	2,750	4,500	7,250
690	20	15	100	1,500	4,250	6,000	10,250
680	25	20	100	2,000	6,250	7,500	13,750
670	30	25	100	2,500	8,750	9,000	17,750
660	35	30	100	3,000	11,750	10,500	22,250
650	40	35	100	3,500	15,250	12,000	27,250

Please note that Column 2 increases in single units from $7.50 down to $7.05, but it increases five units at $7.00 and for each subsequent purchase. This is because of the shift from 1,000 bushel contracts to the 5,000 bushel contracts. Each penny of decline per 1,000 bushels is equal to $10, so the incremental loss in Column 4 is $50 while the soybeans are declining 5 cents, and $100 while they are declining 10 cents.

Everything else remains the same: We will still multiply Column 3 times Column 4 to compute Column 5. Then we cumulate Column 5 to compute Column 6. Add the margin requirement from Column 7 to compute Column 8.

If single contracts of MidAmerica soybeans are too slow for you, you could buy two contracts each time, changing Column 2 from single units to double units, but it would serve the same purpose to buy each 2.5 cents down instead of each 5 cents. Obviously, there are limitless variations possible in scale trading.

You might ordinarily seek 10 cents profit on all of your soybean scales, but it is advisable to seek slightly more on the MidAmerica contracts because of the higher commissions. If you are seeking 10 cents on CBOT contracts, seek 12 cents on MidAmerica contracts. This slight increase in the profit goal would apply for any of the other commodities which you may trade on the MidAmerica.

It is not difficult to keep track of your scale for buy and sell orders if you are, say, buying soybeans each 10 cents down and selling them each 10 cents up; however, if you have shifted into a complex scale, or if you are trading several commodities simultaneously, it may be difficult to remember all of the scales without writing them down. I use a very simple logsheet to record the buy and sell prices, and I call them my "Buy/Sell Lines."

One quick glance at the logsheet tells me the number of buy orders I entered originally; the prices of the buy orders; how many buy orders have been filled and, therefore, how many contracts I hold; and the levels at which sell orders have been entered.

On a horizontal line I write all of the buy orders which I have entered. Thus, if I am buying July copper (Symbol: CPN) each 2 cents down, starting at 70 cents, my buy line would appear as follows:

Buy CPN	7000	6800	6600	6400	6200	6000	5800	5600	5400

Once the buy orders start to fill and I am entering sell orders, I simply write *above* the filled buy orders the corresponding sell orders I have entered. Thus, if I have bought the first three contracts, have cashed no winners so far (so that carrying charge adjustments are not yet required), and am seeking a 2 cent profit, my Buy/Sell Line looks like this:

Sell CPN	7200	7000	6800						
Buy CPN	7000	6800	6600	6400	6200	6000	5800	5600	5400

I can see at a glance that I hold three contracts bought at 7000, 6800, and 6600; that I have three sell orders entered at 7200, 7000, and 6800; and that I have six more open buy orders entered. (Note: Some of the executions may occur at bonus prices, but I always use the bonuses to cover commissions, and I continue to enter all orders precisely at scale levels.)

If the contract sells at 6800, I can see that I am to reenter a buy order at 6600. (This assumes that I am not adjusting for carrying charges.) The broker should also have an identical logsheet attached to my page in his account book so that he knows exactly where I want my orders entered in case he is unable to reach me. This is important, for if I have given him prior written limited power of attorney this grants him permission (indeed, *compels* him) to enter orders without the necessity for personal contact. (For example, if I am scale trading pork bellies and am on a transcontinental flight, I could be out of the reach of the broker for hours. Pork Bellies are so volatile that I could miss a winning trade or two if my broker doesn't keep Buy/Sell Lines on my scales.) If he keeps a log, I know that I am covered, even if I am out of contact for several days.

In the above example, if I want to adjust for carrying charges each time I sell a contract, I may use the method of reducing all of my open buy orders and the buy order about to be reentered by 100 points (one cent). In that circumstance, after the contract is sold at 6800, the repurchase order will be entered at 6500 instead of 6600, and all of the other buy orders will be lowered 100 points. The log now appears thusly:

Sell CPN	7200	7000							
Buy CPN	7000	6800	6500	6300	6100	5900	5700	5500	5300

If the 6500 buy order is filled, an order is entered to sell at 6700 and logged. If the 6700 sell order is later filled, and if I am still adjusting for carrying charges, I will reduce the repurchase order to 6400 instead of 6500, and I will reduce all other buy orders 100 points.

The sell orders are never reduced unless I have decided to jettison a contract or two to absorb carrying charge losses.

This may seem complicated, but it is really quite easy to follow after you have done it a few times. You probably will find the logsheet indispensable in helping you to remember your open positions. This will be especially true after you have done a number of trades in a scale series and the brokerage house's computer has taken the oldest contracts out first as you make sales, and the remaining contracts have no relation to the scale. I contend that the Account Executive must maintain an identical logsheet, but this may show you why it is so difficult to find a cooperative broker to handle scale trading accounts. If he is primarily a stockbroker and does only 10% of his business in commodities, or if he is a commodity specialist with dozens of large accounts who trade five or ten contracts at a time and never hold a position more than a few days, he just isn't going to fool around with all of the adjustments necessary for reentry of orders, cancelling of existing orders, adjusting for carrying charges, etc., especially because you are trading only one contract at a time.

I probably have placed too much emphasis on the subject of compensating for carrying charges — the subject of a full chapter later in this book — because you will more likely find that if you start your scales low enough you will be successfully sold out of your scales long before it is necessary to consider carrying charges, and you will simply cancel your scale in the delivery month you have been trading and move to a deferred contract, obviating the necessity for any adjustments.

XIV

Scaling From The Short Side

People frequently ask me the question, "Do you ever use the scale trading system to trade from the short side?" (To scale trade from the short side means to run a scale by selling into a rising market, hoping to make a profit by repurchasing on a decline.) I answer them, "Never. There is no limit to how high a commodity might rise, and eventually the accumulated loss may become too great for any person's capital if he is shorting that market."

I will give you an example: One man who learned about scale trading from watching my television show made a great deal of money with his very aggressive — in fact, reckless — variation of scale trading. He ignored the common sense dictates of careful planning and preservation of capital by using dangerously tight scales, by trading too many commodities simultaneously, and by using scales which involved short sales. For a while he had a picnic. I heard he made as much as 1,100% profit in one year trading pork bellies. I also heard that he made about $300,000 profit trading orange juice from both the long and short sides simultaneously. However, he was forced to pour on the coal in his short positions when orange juice set an all-time high in price as it topped $0.75 in 1977 following a disastrous freeze in Florida. He lost all of his previous orange juice profits and had a nervous breakdown when the price eventually reached $2.20 that year.

This same fellow eventually recovered his health and proved that he had learned nothing from the orange juice fiasco, for he began trading silver both long and short. Silver's price had never in history exceeded $6.00 per ounce, so he commenced a scale shorting silver above $7.00 in late 1979. He walked into a buzz saw, for that was the time the Texans were starting their attempt to corner the silver market, and silver's price shot to $50.00 per ounce in just four months. Fortunately for him, he had *another* nervous breakdown when silver approached $18.00 per ounce, and his broker was obliged to liquidate his account. There is no telling what his fate might have been if he had still been scale trading silver from the short side of the market when the price reached $50.00.

I would like to say that all I need to do to dissuade people from attempting to scale trade from the short side is to tell them the above story, but, unfortunately, that isn't so. Some people are stubborn and insist that they want to run a short-selling scale. I will continue to insist that you should not attempt it, but if you are one of the stubborn ones, I will offer a suggestion on how you might accomplish your goal:

Let us say that you have been watching spot copper trade around 65 cents, and you would like to commence a long scale at 60 cents, basis the spot contract. Spot copper keeps running up to 72 cents and falling back to 62 cents, but it just never seems to get down to 60 cents. You are properly cautious and do not start a scale above 60 cents, for you fear the possibility that the price could fall to 50 cents in a recession. For the sake of simplicity in this illustration, let us assume that this is the month of December so that the December (spot) futures contract is selling at 65 cents. Let us also assume that carrying charges for copper are running at 1 cent per month so that the May contract sells at 70 cents and the July at 72 cents. Let us assume that interest rates hold steady throughout the period during which we are running this scale (so that carrying charges do not change).

Note: Carrying charges on 65 cents copper would not run 1 cent per month unless interest rates approached 20% again, in which case you probably should not be scaling copper, but I am using 1 cent per month to avoid using fractions in the example.

We have assumed in the example that copper trades up to 72 cents on the high and then always falls to 62 cents. A reckless scale trader might be tempted to start shorting copper whenever it trades as high as 70 cents, reasoning that a scale designed to short every 2 cents up would cause him to be short no more than two contracts at any time. Unfortunately, a copper strike, a war threat, a sudden upside thrust in inflation, or any one of a thousand other circumstances could send the price of copper soaring. Even though this condition might be transitory, it could be severe enough to create substantial losses in your account, losses beyond the limits of your capital. This would bankrupt your account, leaving you without the capital means to recover.

As stated previously, there is a limit to how low a commodity may decline in price, but there is no limit to how high it may rise; therefore, if you insist upon scaling from the short side, you must find a way to limit your exposure during a price rally. This does not mean that you should commit yourself to a limitation of, say, shorting no more than four contracts of copper and then placing a buy-stop order above the top price so that you are assured of taking no more than a predetermined loss. If you attempt this method and are stopped out a few times, you will eventually exhaust your capital.

Instead of allowing yourself to become net short any contracts, you must find a way to carry short positions which are offset by at least a few long positions so that your inventory is usually net long and never worse than net even.

To illustrate, you might start by buying eight contracts of one delivery month and simultaneously shorting four contracts of a different delivery month. This has the effect of making you net long four contracts. If you are seeking a 2 cent gain on each winning sale, you would sell one of your long positions on a 2 cent rally and simultaneously short an additional contract in the delivery month in which you are doing the shorting. You are now long seven contracts and short five, or net long two. If the price continues to rise, you would cash another winner from your long contracts on an additional 2 cent rally, and you would simultaneously add one more short position. This reduces your long position to six contracts and expands your short position to six. You are now fully spread with a net position of zero contracts. If the price continues to rally, you take no further action, simply holding the spread positions until the price falls again into your trading range, allowing you to resume trading. As long as the price rises, you will suffer no losses, for the long and short positions will move in concert, giving you equal and offsetting profits and losses. If the price were to rise 20, 30, or 40 cents, you will have avoided financial disaster by merely holding the spread rather than continuing to short into the rally. You would not want to hold the spread position any longer, so you would close it out with commission losses only, and proceed to scale trade some other commodity.

If, instead of rallying, the initial move after we first establish our long eight versus short four positions is downward, we would purchase one additional long position and simultaneously cover one short position on each 2 cent dip. After the first 2 cent decline, we will have added our ninth long contract and reduced our four shorts to three, for a net long position of six contracts. A further decline of an additional 2 cents would cause us to add our tenth long, while reducing our shorts to two, so that we are now net long eight contracts. Another 2 cent decline gives us eleven longs and one short, for a net position of long ten. The final 2 cent decline makes us long twelve and short zero contracts, for a net long position of twelve contracts.

This is what I don't like about two-sided scale trading: the position of being net long twelve contracts after only an 8 cent decline. The exposure is terribly dangerous. A further decline would be costing you $3,000 for each penny of decline in copper's price. That would be if you ceased scaling and added no further positions. If you continued scaling, you could be increasing your paper losses and margin requirements substantially.

The construction of your scale would be slightly different than the simple scale. This is because you would be integrating a long scale and a short scale. Please see Chart XVII, "The Two-Sided Scale," and use the following columnar explanations:

COLUMN 1: The trading price of the commodity.

COLUMN 2: The number of contracts held long at this price.

COLUMN 3: The number of contracts held short at this price.

COLUMN 4: The unrealized profit or (loss) on open long positions at this price level.

COLUMN 5: The realized profit on closed long positions.

COLUMN 6: The unrealized profit or (loss) on open short positions at this price level.

COLUMN 7: The realized profit on closed short positions.

COLUMN 8: The net profit or (loss). (Add Columns 4, 5, 6, and 7.)

COLUMN 9: The margin requirement for the number of net long contracts and spread contracts held at this price level.

COLUMN 10: The total cash required at this price level. (Subtract Column 8 from Column 9.) Note: If this number is a negative, this means your profits are greater than the combined total of your losses and the margin requirement to hold your positions and/or your spreads. You would be permitted to withdraw this excess.

Let us now consider the two-sided scale (Chart XVII) to see how it would work in actual practice. Please remember that our assumption is that spot December copper has been hovering around 65 cents and that we are trading the deferred July contract, which has been trading around 72 cents. If you also remember the critically important fact that carrying charges are pushing the price down at a rate of 1 cent per month (in actuality it would be closer to $\frac{1}{2}$ cent per month, but even that is severe), you will recognize that the scale which I have presented is not even practical. It advocates a starting level of 64 cents, but that is 8 cents below the market. For July to fall to 64 cents, it would require spot December to fall to 58 cents, and our assumption is that December holds each time at 60 cents.

When our July copper contract trades at 64 cents we will purchase eight Julys long and simultaneously sell four contracts of a delivery month which is near to the July, either the May or the September. This gives us a net long position of four contracts and is shown on the third line on the chart. I am assuming that the margin requirement for a straight long or short position is $750, while the margin requirement for a spread position is $250; thus, with eight longs and four shorts, we have a net margin requirement of $4,000, being four times $750, plus four times $250.

CHART XVII

THE TWO-SIDED SCALE

1	2	3	4	5	6	7	8	9	10
68	6	6	6,000	1,500	(4,500)	0	3,000	1,500	(1,500)
66	7	5	3,500	500	(2,000)	0	2,000	2,750	750
64	8	4	0	0	0	0	0	4,000	4,000
62	9	3	(4,000)	0	1,500	500	(2,000)	5,250	7,250
60	10	2	(8,500)	0	2,000	1,500	(5,000)	6,500	11,500
58	11	1	(13,500)	0	1,500	3,000	(9,000)	7,750	16,750
56	12	0	(19,000)	0	0	5,000	(14,000)	9,000	23,000

If the price advances to 66 cents, as shown on the second line of the chart, we reduce our long position to seven contracts and increase our shorts to five. The 2 cent advance is worth $500 paper profit in each of the seven open contracts for a $3,500 gain (COLUMN 4) and a realized profit of $500 in the liquidated contract (COLUMN 5). This is partially offset by the paper loss in the four short contracts, which would be $2,000 (COLUMN 6). We have cashed no profits from short sales, so COLUMN 7 shows a zero. The combined total shows a $2,000 gain in COLUMN 8. The margin requirement for the five spreads is $1,250, and for the net two longs is another $1,500, for a total of $2,750, as shown in COLUMN 9. Subtracting COLUMN 8 from COLUMN 9, we see that our total cash requirement is only $750.

An additional advance of 2 cents in the price of copper would take our July contract to 68 cents, as shown on the top line of the chart. We are now long six and short six contracts. We have a paper profit of $6,000 in the six remaining longs, a realized profit of $1,500 in the two longs which we have sold, a paper loss of $4,500 in our short positions, and to date we have closed no short positions profitably. Combining those four entries gives us a profit of $3,000 in

COLUMN 8. Our margin requirement to hold the six spreads of $250 apiece is $1,500, which is easily covered by the $3,000 in COLUMN 8, so we have a surplus of $1,500 in COLUMN 10, which we may withdraw.

As stated previously, if the price continues to rally, we would eventually close out the six spreads.

If, however, the price declines from the 68 cent level to 66 cents, we would cover one of the shorts and add a long contract. The numbers on line 2 would be the same as before except for the realized profits under COLUMNS 5 and 7. We would be showing $1,000 in COLUMN 5 and $500 under COLUMN 7, which also changes the entries under COLUMNS 8 and 10. However, you should not bother to continually change those numbers; instead, you should leave your scale intact and merely deposit those profits in your total account.

If the price for July copper now drops to 64 cents, we cash another winner from the short positions and purchase another long, so that we are restored to our original holdings, as shown on line 3.

If at this time copper's price declines to 62 cents (or if it had happened originally), we go to line 4. We are obliged to purchase our ninth contract long, and we cover one of our four shorts, taking a $500 profit and reducing our shorts to three contracts. This gives us a net long position of six contracts.

At 56 cents we stop accumulating long contracts, and we have covered our last short position. We have a $19,000 paper loss in the longs and a realized gain of $5,000 in the shorts, for a net equity reduction of $14,000. Combining that with the margin requirement of $9,000 to hold the twelve contracts long, we have a total cash requirement of $23,000. That is after a decline of only 8 cents from our starting level, and our original assumption was that we feared a possible decline to 50 cents. If that were to occur, the 6 cent additional decline would be a loss of $1,500 per contract, or $18,000 more, for a total commitment of $41,000.

The ideal circumstance for two-sided scale trading, using the scale from Chart XVII would be for the price to oscillate between a low of 60 cents and a high of 68 cents; however, an 8 cent range for copper is small. Copper is more likely to swing through a range of 15 cents to 20 cents, and if that extra 12 cents appears on the *downside,* the results would be catastrophic.

One thing which makes two-sided scale trading hazardous is carrying charges. If, immediately after we commence a two-sided scale by purchasing eight contracts and shorting four others, the spot price of copper "locks" within a very narrow range, we would be hurt severely. Our example assumed a carrying charge of 1 cent per month, so by the time seven months had passed and our July contract had become the spot contract, we would have suffered a 7 cent decline due to carrying charges eroding the price. Referring again to Chart XVII, we can see that our July contract would now be down to 57 cents, at which point our net loss (COLUMN 8) would be $11,500, which is the $9,000 loss shown at 58 cents plus an additional loss of $2,500 for the 1 cent decline in our net long position of ten contracts. Spot copper is absolutely unchanged in price, but we have suffered an $11,500 loss.

Indeed, at this point we are extremely vulnerable, for we had originally embarked upon two-sided scaling because the price was oscillating in the 60's, but we also feared the possibility of a decline to 50 cents. If the price suddenly breaks to 50 cents, we suffer another 7 cent decline, or $19,250 in the eleven long contracts, plus a $1,500 loss in the single long contract which we would add at 56 cents, minus the $250 gain we would pick up from the 1 cent decline when we cover our last short at 56 cents. That means an additional total loss of $20,500. Spot copper is only 7 cents lower than it was when we commenced the scale, but we have accumulated a $32,200 loss.

If you will remember that July copper was trading at 72 cents when we wanted to commence the two-sided scale, you will see how dangerous it would have been if we had commenced our scale at that level. That was a full 8 cents above our assumed starting level of 64 cents. It is quite possible that the price would never have dropped to 64 cents until we started impatiently at 72 cents, and if copper prices then traded as described above — particularly with the price eventually dropping to 50 cents for spot copper — we would have absorbed another $24,000 loss from the 8 cent loss ($2,000 per contract) on twelve contracts. That would make the overall loss $56,000.

Obviously, the great hazard in two-sided scaling is the rapidity with which you accumulate contracts on the initial decline. By starting with a net long position of four contracts and then adding another long and simultaneously lifting one short, the net long position is being increased by two contracts with each 2 cent decline.

You might be thinking of varying my suggestions for a two-sided scaling plan by staggering the longs and shorts so that you are doing one leg on the odd pennies and the other leg on the even pennies, reasoning that this has the effect of increasing net longs only one contract each time, but it still has virtually the same result, for the single contracts are being added each penny instead of two contracts each 2 cents.

You may also have thought of starting with six longs and three shorts, or four longs and two shorts, but then your two-sided scale becomes ineffective because the first 2 cent rally puts you into a five-versus-four position or a three-versus-three, and you are out of action already.

Conversely, if you wanted to give yourself greater latitude on the upside, and you started with a position of long twelve versus short six contracts, you are only compounding the problem of holding too many long contracts if the price declines and you keep buying longs and covering shorts. If copper declines 12 cents, you would have covered all of your short positions and purchased six more longs, giving you a net holding of eighteen long contracts. Your exposure would be frightening.

Commissions can become a costly item in two-sided scaling. This is not because you are paying twice as many commissions, for you are still paying a commission only when you capture a winner, and you are capturing twice as many winners, but if you reach rollover time holding positions similar to those with which you started — long eight and short four — you will pay twelve commissions in doing the rollover.

It is also difficult to compensate for carrying charges when doing a two-sided scale. One technique for adjusting for carrying charges is to not reenter a buy order after a successful sale. However, what would you then do with the new short position? If you added or deleted longs or shorts, there would soon be no semblance of balance to the scale. If you start trying to guess whether to add or delete an extra long or short position, you are no longer trading a mechanical system and are merely trying to outguess the market. You might also have such large gaps between buy and sell orders that copper's price could swing through a relatively broad range without your making any trades. Meanwhile, the carrying charges would be steadily eroding the price so that you are steadily accumulating a growing long position and increasing your exposure.

Two-sided scaling, trading each 2 cents down and 2 cents up, is almost precisely the same as normal scale trading, but doing it each 1 cent down and 2 cents up. The only real differences are, 1) that you have started with a net long position of four contracts in inventory, and 2) that you will harvest a few profits from the initial short positions in the two-sided scale. Our Chart XVII showing the two-sided scale assumes a straight-line decline from 64 cents to 56 cents and requires $23,000 of capital. Chart XVIII shows the normal scale for copper, starting at 64 cents and buying each 1 cent on a straight-line decline to 56 cents.

CHART XVIII

EXAMPLE OF A NORMAL SCALE FOR COPPER

1	2	3	4	5	6	7	8
64	1	0	0	0	0	750	750
63	2	1	250	250	250	1,500	1,750
62	3	2	250	500	750	2,250	3,000
61	4	3	250	750	1,500	3,000	4,500
60	5	4	250	1,000	2,500	3,750	6,250
59	6	5	250	1,250	3,750	4,500	8,250
58	7	6	250	1,500	5,250	5,250	10,500
57	8	7	250	1,750	7,000	6,000	13,000
56	9	8	250	2,000	9,000	6,750	15,750

This scale requires only $15,750, and the risk is less because it holds only nine contracts instead of twelve. The two-sided scale would have the advantage if the price rose above 64 cents a few times, but carrying charges are likely to pull the price below 64 cents eventually, and as soon as the price begins to oscillate in that area, the two scales will produce identical results because the normal scale is buying one contract each 1 cent down while the two-sided scale is buying two contracts each 2 cents down.

Another alternative is the Chart XIX, which is a normal scale, nearly identical with Chart XVIII, except that it commences at 67 cents and carries down to 56 cents, for a holding of twelve contracts. The capital required is $25,500, which is not much greater than the $23,000 required for the two-sided scale which started at 64 cents. One important advantage to using this scale over the two-sided scale is that it permits you to start 3 cents higher. If you will remember that we assumed that July copper was trading at 72 cents in our early discussion, you will realize that we need only a 5 cent dip to commence trading with this normal scale rather than the 8 cent dip required for the two-sided scale.

CHART XIX

ANOTHER EXAMPLE OF A NORMAL SCALE FOR COPPER

1	2	3	4	5	6	7	8
67	1	0	0	0	0	750	750
66	2	1	250	250	250	1,500	1,750
65	3	2	250	500	750	2,250	3,000
64	4	3	250	750	1,500	3,000	4,500
63	5	4	250	1,000	2,500	3,750	6,250
62	6	5	250	1,250	3,750	4,500	8,250
61	7	6	250	1,500	5,250	5,250	10,500
60	8	7	250	1,750	7,000	6,000	13,000
59	9	8	250	2,000	9,000	6,750	15,750
58	10	9	250	2,250	11,250	7,500	18,750
57	11	10	250	2,500	13,750	8,250	22,000
56	12	11	250	2,750	16,500	9,000	25,000

For the sake of emphasis, I will repeat: Do *not* attempt to scale trade commodities from the short side. You cannot help but lose. The method I have offered is imperfect and only offers opportunity for profit if the commodity trades rapidly and with great volatility through a narrow range. If you insist upon scale trading from the short side *without offsetting long positions,* there will surely come the time when you will be handed your head in a basket.

Most important of all, please do not write me to say that you are commencing a naked scale on the short side. I'll know when I see your name in the obituaries showing "Cause of death: suicide." And your epitaph will read: "He made money for a while scaling from the short side, but soybeans went to $20."

XV

Starting Too High

Probably the most difficult aspect of scale trading is selecting the point at which to commence the scale. It is relatively easy to select the starting point after one or more commodities have experienced severe declines in price. You only need to compare the current price with the range of the last ten years and start somewhere in the lowest third of that range.

But what about a period following runaway prices? Perhaps prices cool a bit and return to something approximating normal levels, but the prices might still be above the desired range of the lowest one-third of the prior ten years. Inflation continuously pushes prices higher, and if an unexpected occurrence such as the Russian grain deals of 1973 happened again, we could see another temporary period of over-inflated prices. When they start to cool down again, at what point have they returned to "normal"? Do we wait for them to come all the way back to their former levels, or do we assume there is a new price plateau brought about by inflation and that these higher prices are the new norms?

First of all, I have never seen the time when *everything* sold at such a high level at once that *nothing* was available for scale trading, so this is probably nothing more than a chapter for academic discussion, but I will pursue the point.

Prior to 1973, soybeans had never traded above $5. All of a sudden, it was trading at $13. How far down did it have to come to reach a new plateau that could be considered normal? In retrospect we can say that the new plateau is around $6, but that price had never been seen before 1973. Today it is normal.

Let us say the next soybean spurt carries the price to $15 per bushel and then falls back to $8. Soybeans sold at the $8 level only seven times prior to the time this book is being written, and the soybeans price had never topped $13. Does this mean we will have $8 soybeans forever? Or is this just a level the soybeans must pass on the way back to $6?

There is one very simple way to handle that question. Use a complex buying scale. It really *makes no difference where you start* so long as you budget the bankroll to carry you back to a probable level and then to the possible level. Go ahead, buy a contract of soybeans at $8. Just be sure that you don't buy the second contract until the price hits $7.25. Then $6.75 and $6.50. Five more purchases at decrements of 10 cents each, and you are safely back to $6.00. Now you can get serious again about scale trading soybeans in their proper range. So far, the accumulated paper loss in MidAmerica contracts is only $5,500 if you never catch a single oscillation winner all the way down. The paper loss in the Chicago Board of Trade contracts is $27,500.

Don't forget that it is good practice to use an expanded selling scale whenever you use a complex scale for buying. The contract purchased at $8.00 might be offset with a 20 cent profit, while the contract purchased at $7.25 might seek a 17 cent gain. Those bought between $7.00 and $6.00 might seek 15 cents. It is natural that soybeans would be more volatile at the higher prices, and you should pick up enough oscillation profits in the upper ranges to cover losses accumulated on the highest priced contracts if the price declines.

Sugar is another example of how a person might have started buying too high on the return trip after a stratospheric price rise. Sugar always sold under 10 cents until 1974, and then it ran to 66 cents. It might have seemed logical to someone wanting to initiate a scale on sugar at 15 cents that it would never decline much lower.

That is all right as an assumption so long as the trader protects himself against the *possibility* that sugar might trade once again at 4 cents. Starting his scale at 15 cents, he should wait to make the next purchase at 12 cents. Then 10 cents. Then 9 cents, 8 cents, 7 cents, 6 cents, 5 cents and 4 cents. Sugar actually fell to about 7 cents in 1978, so the accumulated paper loss would have been $21,140. That amount assumes no profits from oscillations, but the truth is that that particular scale would have yielded oscillation profits substantially greater than $21,000. Furthermore, the price shot up to 45 cents in 1980, which would have provided far more than enough of a rise to sell this scale trader out of all of his sugar positions and leaving him with incredible profits and a newly installed pacemaker.

Let us now assume that he learned nothing from his first reckless selection of a starting point and that he starts again at 15 cents when sugar falls to that level in 1981. By 1985 sugar is trading around 2.5 cents, and this time his paper loss is $59,920. He lucks out; sugar trades at 16 cents in 1990. At $1,120 for each penny in sugar, if he sought 1 cent oscillation profits on the 15 cent contracts, 0.75 cents on the 12 cent and 10 cent contracts, 0.5 cents on everything down to 5 cents, and 0.3 on everything purchased under 5 cents, he has had a jillion oscillation profits and can afford numerous pacemaker replacements and the alimony he is paying to the wives he lost at the depths of the declines. Good for him, but that is not my cup of tea.

I certainly do not advocate that you carelessly jump into scale trading of any commodity that meets your fancy, feeling that the oscillation profits will protect you from your own foolishness. It is probable that these winners eventually will cover your mistakes when you discover that you have started a scale from too high a level, but it is more prudent to search a little longer and find something that fits the requisite of being in the lowest third of its recent range.

XVI

The Rollover

Each time I speak at a commodity seminar I open the session to questions, and one question which invariably is asked is about rollovers. The question itself is usually not about rollovers, but the answer always is. The questioner is usually concerned about the possibility of accumulating a large number of contracts of something just as that particular commodity is about to expire. I anticipated this problem of contract expiration a long time ago and not only made theoretical preparation for the circumstance but have made practical applications in actual trading accounts.

First of all, a properly conceived scale will usually be entirely liquidated before nearing the termination of the life of the contract, and, secondly, if unforeseen circumstances force the scale trader into a position where he holds some open positions as the contract nears expiration, it is relatively simple to roll the contracts over to a different delivery and continue the scale.

To substantiate my claim that the properly conceived scale should liquidate itself long before expiration of the contract, I will simply remind the reader that it takes a little more than blindly rushing into a commodity with a fat bankroll to assure success of scale trading. I would never start a scale unless I felt the commodity was near enough to its low that its chance for a rise in price was greater than its chance for a decline. It would not be sufficient cause for me to start scaling something just because it has a low price. I would want to study the fundamental situation and determine that this commodity is near to a low and potentially heading higher. I concede that the logical point for the turnaround is not always the point at which the price turns, but scale trading takes care of that problem for me. I make my first purchase only when I think the price shouldn't go any lower, and then if I find that I have started too early I just keep adding positions until the price turns. It isn't often that I (or anyone else who considers the supply/demand situation) am forced to accumulate a very large position, so it isn't often that I need a large price rise to sell me out. This is why rollovers are relatively rare occurrences.

However, there will be those inevitable occasions when unforeseen circumstances cause the scale trader to accumulate a relatively large position that is virtually impossible to liquidate on a normal selling scale, so he must do a little planning to accomplish his rollovers without problems.

There are several ways to resolve the matter. I will start with the ideal situation. This would be the condition where there is a relative tightness in the current supply of one physical commodity with prospects for ample supplies later, so the contracts trade without carrying charges or even in an inverted market. An example would be soybean oil during 1979; 1978 was a good year for soybean oil consumption, which supported prices slightly above average, but the abundant supply of 1979 soybean oil expected to be available from the 1978 crop should have held the 1979 futures contract prices slightly below average. The deferred contracts would be selling at a discount to the nearbys, but the addition of carrying charges to those contracts creates the uncommon situation of having all contracts trading at about the same price. In other words, when July trades at 24 cents, September trades at 24 cents, as do December, March, and May. Even the far July contract trades at 24 cents. In this situation, if a scale trader has begun scaling at 26 cents and presently holds three contracts bought at 26 cents, 25 cents and 24 cents, with resting sell orders at 25 cents, 26 cents and 27 cents, and if he has been unable to roll them before the delivery month is upon him, he need only sell the existing contracts at the 24 cent price (or thereabouts) and replace them with three contracts of a deferred delivery at approximately the same price. Then he cancels the original sell orders and reenters them to liquidate the new contracts at the old prices (25 cents, 26 cents, and 27 cents). He will pay three extra commissions, but if that is worrisome to the trader, he may add those extra amounts to his new sell orders.

In the above example he will be forced to convert paper losses to realized losses, but sooner or later the soybean oil price again will rise to 27 cents, and he will have sold all three contracts at prices which will recapture all the losses plus producing the three profits he originally sought.

Before going on to the next type of situation that forces a rollover, it is worth taking a pause here to point out that a situation such as that for soybean oil as described above presents a nearly perfect commodity in which to scale trade. The nearly identical across-the-board prices indicate a very close balance between supply and demand. That being the situation, it is likely that the price will oscillate with rumors, weather scares, political actions, etc., and at the end of the season it is likely that the price will be back where it started. Assuming — as in the case of 24 cent soybean oil — that the price of the commodity is sufficiently close to its probable bottom, and further assuming the scale trader has an adequate bankroll and sense enough to devise a scale which will guarantee protection of that bankroll, he can head for the golf course and just let the winners roll in. If he is buying each penny down and selling each penny up, he will receive another $600 paycheck each time a rumor comes along.

Back to rollovers. In the previous example I wrote about a market in which all delivery months were trading at approximately the same price. Every once in a while there will be a situation in which the deferred months trade at a *discount* to the nearbys. This is called an "inverted market." If the scale trader finds himself in the higher priced delivery month it probably means he selected the wrong contract in the first place, but it certainly presents no problem when forced into the rollover. As above, he closes out the existing positions, rolls forward to an equal number of contracts of a deferred delivery, and then reenters his sell orders at prices which will recapture the losses and produce the profits he originally sought. For example, if he has been scaling live cattle on a one-cent scale with a starting price of 46 cents, and the delivery month is approaching but the contract price is down to 44 cents so that he holds three contracts, it certainly is no problem to roll over if the deferred contract he chooses is currently trading at 40 cents. He cancels the sell orders he had in the expiring contract at 45 cents, 46 cents, and 47 cents, and he reenters those orders in the new contract to sell at 41 cents, 42 cents, and 43 cents. As before, he eventually recaptures the losses and realizes the gains he originally sought.

It is unlikely that the example in the previous paragraph will arise very often, for if the inverted market existed at the time the scale trader initiated his scale he probably chose the wrong delivery month. Since the success of any trading account depends upon minimizing risk, it is almost a cardinal rule of the scale trader that he start at the lowest possible price. If he elects to use a delivery month which is trading at a premium over a deferred contract his only rationalization can be that he expected more volatility — and therefore more winning trades — from the higher priced contract. But he must be willing to accept the greater risk. (It is also possible that a distant delivery — though lower priced — lacked liquidity.) Starting at the higher level, he must accept the possibility of the same ultimate low as the lower-priced contract, and, assuming the same amount of capital is available in either case, he must use a wider scale to preserve that capital. The wider scale might possibly result in fewer trades and thereby negate some of the anticipated benefits of the greater volatility. It is usually much wiser to trade the lower-priced contracts.

Another explanation for why it is unlikely that the scale trader will find himself in the situation where he is in an inverted market and faced with rollover problems lies in the probable cause of the inverted market's existence. Assuming that the market was a normal carrying charge market at the time the scaler initiated his position, but then it became inverted, the cause is almost invariably that a tight supply situation suddenly developed. This causes the nearby delivery months to rise to a premium over the deferreds. That being the case, it is likely that the scale trader has long since been sold out of all his positions with his upside selling scale. (An example of an unpredictable event which caused a tight supply situation might be an early freeze of the

Great Lakes which would prevent grains from reaching Chicago for delivery against expiring contracts. A rail strike has the same effect.)

The two previous rollover examples were ideal situations which offer no problem in resolution, but now we must consider the more normal situation where a rollover problem may actually exist. As an example, this situation could occur if the trader had begun scaling corn at $2.50 and found himself holding a substantial position when the crop turned out to be a bin-buster, resulting in the price of corn falling to — and hovering in — the area of $2.10 for a considerable period of time. If he had been buying each 10 cents down, he is holding five contracts. He has a problem, but it is not insurmountable.

First of all, if the trader has been involved in this particular scale for any length of time it is likely that there have been at least a few oscillations that have afforded him the opportunity to liquidate an occasional contract. If so, when he reinstates each buy order, he should enter that order to buy a deferred contract rather than the nearby contract which he has been trading. For example, when scaling corn as above, if he is able to sell at $2.20 the December contract which he purchased at $2.10, he enters a fresh buy order for the May contract 10 cents below the price which prevailed in the May contract at the time the December sale was executed. If, because of carrying charges, the May has been trading at about a 20 cent premium over December, it would be trading at $2.40 when the December is sold at $2.20. The new buy order would be entered for the May contract at $2.30, which would be equivalent to the December at $2.10. When his December contract bought at $2.20 sells at $2.30, he reinstates the buy order for a May contract at $2.40, which is equivalent to $2.20 in December, etc., etc.

If the price now oscillates in this range, he will be scale trading the May contract and holding the December contracts. When first notice day for the December contract nears, he has no choice but to sell them at a loss. He may reinstate those contracts by rolling over to May contracts and hoping to eventually recapture those losses by adding those amounts to the May contracts, or he may use this opportunity to take one or two carrying charge losses. It is a good time to take those losses, for they are almost unavoidable and are still relatively small at this time.

119

Obviously, this carrying charge rollover could eventually pose serious problems if the scale trader continuously rolled over into higher-priced positions, but this situation is exactly the same as described in Chapter XII, "Taking A Loss." If the scale trader finds he is accumulating more contracts than he can hold comfortably, he need only sell off one or two, accept the loss, and expect that the profits made on oscillations will more than overcome those minor losses. If he takes a 10 cent loss on one contract and a 20 cent loss on another, he recovers that as soon as he captures three 10 cent profits from oscillations. The properly conducted scale trading account should yield 95 or more winners out of each 100 trades, so if those five losers result in single- or double-increment losses, they will be covered more than adequately by the overwhelming profits from the 95 incremental winners.

So far, I have mentioned only those situations where it has been possible to roll out of one delivery month into another without any real problems. The situations described so far are the only ones you are really likely to encounter, but now I will present the hypothetical situation which will exist only rarely but must be described in case it ever happens to you. This would be the situation where you buy on a scale down and the price goes straight down and then just lies there, never rallying, right up to the day of first delivery notice. You were unable to ease out of the old contract and into the new one as sell orders were never executed in the old contract. If you have been accumulating on a tight scale, you might hold a considerable number of contracts. If you have been buying corn on a 5 cent scale down from $2.50 to $2.10, you hold nine contracts. If you plan to roll into a deferred contract which trades at a 20 cent premium to your contract, you run the risk of acquiring four more positions if the new contract sinks to the same price level as the one you are abandoning. (This is unlikely, for the carrying charge must be paid by someone, so the holder of the physical commodity is unlikely to sell without recapture of his carrying costs, but I am trying to create a hypothetical situation which probably will never exist but *could*.) The 20 cent premium is equal to four contracts on your 5 cent scale, so you might arbitrarily elect to roll over only six or seven of the nine contracts and accept the loss on the others. If you take three losses, they will be for a total of anywhere from 15 cents (if you elect to abandon the three lowest priced contracts which have zero, 5 cent, and 10 cent losses) to 105 cents (if you abandon the three highest priced contracts with 30 cent, 35 cent, and 40 cent losses). Even if you bite the bullet for the 105 cent loss, you will retrieve that with your next eleven 10 cent winners. I have never seen the situation where you could not have captured at least a few profits from oscillations, so I cannot conceive of your finding yourself in this hypothetical situation I just described, but if it should ever happen to you, I feel safe in saying that it would be unthinkable that the situation would continue for another entire year in the new contract. That would force you to buy four more contracts, but the chances of that happening are so remote as to be virtually nonexistent. The Law of Supply and Demand would take over, farmers would cut corn plantings to the absolute minimum, and prices would move up again.

In the hundreds of trades I have made during the nine years I have used the scale trading system I probably have never been forced into more than a few dozen rollovers, so the possibility of their encounter should not alarm you unduly; however, to prepare you properly for that eventuality I will give you some idea of the method I use to determine when I should begin the rollover procedure. Obviously, if you had begun a July scale in January, you would not begin to roll over to December contracts if you caught your first winner in February. But neither should you wait until the 20th of June to consider rolling over eight July contracts.

Sometimes I like to use a beta factor, which is a measurement of the volatility of each respective commodity. One of the attractive features of scale trading is that you never need to keep charts or moving averages, but if you enjoy using figures, you will keep them anyway. I keep a daily record of the high and low prices for the commodity I am following. Then, by isolating the highest price of the last ten days and also the lowest price of the last ten days, I am able to determine the maximum range for that period. I record it daily. Then I cumulate these volatility figures for the last ten days and divide by ten to determine the average daily volatility for that ten-day period. This figure is updated daily by dropping the tenth day back and substituting the current day, always using just the ten most recent days. This ten-day indicator of volatility will change only slightly on a day-to-day basis, and it gives me an excellent indication of the range through which the commodity I am scaling is likely to swing during the coming weeks.

It may require more of your time than you are willing to sacrifice to maintain statistics on each commodity you are trading, so after you have gained some experience an eyeball estimate should certainly prove nearly as reliable.

Let us assume that I am buying silver on a scale 10 cents down and selling it on a scale of 10 cents up. I have accumulated five contracts, and I have about two months to go until first notice day on my particular delivery month. I have done the volatility computation as described above, and I find that average volatility to be about 20 cents for any given two-week period. The 20 cent range indicates that I should be able to dispose of two contracts each ten days with my 10 cent selling scale. This would indicate that I probably should be sold out of my five contracts sometime within the next five weeks, which is sufficient time, since I have eight or nine weeks to go. However, I certainly would not want to buy any more contracts in my present delivery month because I could be put into the position of having six, seven, or eight contracts left with but five or six weeks to go. I begin the rollover immediately, and here is how I would do it:

Let's assume that I began buying the July silver contract at $4.70, and now it is hovering around $4.30. I would hold contracts purchased at $4.70, $4.60, $4.50, $4.40, and $4.30. I have sell orders scaled each 10 cents up from $4.40 to $4.80. I have also had resting buy orders at $4.20, $4.10, $4.00, $3.90, etc. I choose to begin a rollover into the December contract, which is trading at a 20 cent carrying charge premium to my July contract. That 20 cent premium will remain virtually constant and vary only slightly.

I may choose to roll over only four of the contracts and take a carrying charge loss on the other. Or, I may choose to not reenter a buy order if one contract is sold. Or, I may do any of the other rollover techniques previously described. But, for this illustration, let us assume that I will roll all of them.

The first step is to cancel all buy orders for the July contract and reenter them in the December contract *at a 20 cents advance from the July prices*. Thus, my new buy orders would be entered at $4.40, $4.30, $4.20, $4.10, etc. The July sell orders stay as they are. If the price rises 10 cents before I get to buy any December contracts, that would be fine, for I would be selling one of the July contracts at $4.40, and I would reenter the buy order for a December contract at $4.50 instead of a July contract at $4.30. That would have taken care of one of the July contracts, and I would have only four left to roll over.

If, instead of advancing 10 cents, the price declines 10 cents, I buy another contract, but it is the December at $4.40 instead of July at $4.20. Normally, I would be entering a sell order on the December contract at $4.50 to capture a 10 cent profit, but this is my first opportunity for a painless rollover. The July contract is now trading at $4.20, so I have a loss of 50 cents in the July contract which was purchased at $4.70, and I need a price advance of 60 cents to recapture that loss and give me my 10 cent profit. I will drop the sell price of that $4.70 July contract from $4.80 all the way down to $4.30, which is 50 cents less than I wanted. I then add the 50 cents (plus the additional 10 cent profit I am seeking on the new position) onto the $4.40 December contract and enter the sell order at $5.00.

If the price now advances 10 cents I am sold out of the July contract at $4.30 for a 40 cent loss (and without the 10 cent gain), but I will eventually recapture that when the December contract sells at $5.00. December is trading at $4.50, so I enter the new buy order at $4.40, and I repeat the entire process if the price declines again and another contract is purchased there. I roll over the July $4.60 contract by dropping its sell price to $4.30, adding that 30 cent loss and the 10 cent profit I did not get plus the new 10 cent profit I am seeking (total 50 cents) to the December $4.40 and enter the sell order at $4.90 to go with the one already resting at $5.00. I continue to repeat this process until all five contracts are rolled over, and then I have five December contracts, all purchased at $4.40. July is about to expire at $4.30, December is trading at $4.50, and my sell orders are entered at $4.60, $4.70, $4.80, $4.90, and $5.00.

While all this is going on, naturally, it is possible that silver may continue to decline instead of oscillating as I hypothesized. This changes nothing. I simply do the same type of calculation described in the previous paragraph and complete the rollover from the steadily decreasing price levels. I roll another contract each time a rally occurs, affording me the opportunity to sell another contract profitably.

All of this could have been accomplished without any calculations whatsoever by merely selling off all the July contracts and simultaneously buying December contracts to replace them, but then the question becomes, "When do you do it?" If you roll too early you are forever paying extra commissions. If you wait too long in a commodity which is thinly traded you may run into liquidity problems. Most important of all, if you attempt a gradual rollover as I have described you may find that the price advances enough for you to sell *all* the original contracts without the necessity for any rollovers or extra commissions whatsoever. Don't forget, you got into this scale in the first place because you expected a price advance rather than a substantial decline, so if you are stuck with a large position and you are forced into an extended rollover, it means you made some mistakes somewhere in your homework and probably started too high. If you actually started at a reasonable level there is always a good chance that the price will rally and bail you out. Except for the extra commissions, it can never hurt to wait too long to commence the rollover, because the worst that can happen is to be forced to roll all contracts in the final week prior to first notice day. The only penalty for that is that you pay some commissions that might have been avoided, but there is also the chance that you will catch the rally that takes you out of all positions without the need for any rollovers whatsoever. The reward potential frequently equals or outweighs the risk.

There are innumerable variations to the rollover method just described. You might elect to roll over the low-priced contracts first instead of last. You might choose to reduce the July selling price less than the full amount and thereby be required to add less to the December selling price. Most importantly, don't be ashamed to use rollovers to swallow some losses. It is ego-inflating to say you have never had a loser after the first one hundred trades, but because of carrying charges (See Chapter XII, "Taking A Loss") you might be accumulating a large position. Go ahead and take a few losses. There is nothing wrong with 95 winners out of 100 trades.

(Note: You may have been using a complex scale for buying, and that will require some adjusting if you use the beta factor method for determining when to begin your rollover. Suppose, for example, you had made the first few corn purchases on a 10 cent scale down, then some at 5 cents, some at 4 cents, 3 cents, and finally 2 cents. You have scaled to sell each 10 cents up. If you have calculated that corn has a volatility of 10 cents per two week period, and you hold twenty contracts, you would not allow a two-week increment for each contract. That would indicate forty weeks. Instead, you would count each five contracts bought on a 2 cent scale down as a single 10 cent increment; each three 3 cent contracts would be another increment; each two 4 cent contracts count as one increment; each two 5 cent contracts equal an increment. Thus, if you hold the initial contract plus one contract bought at a 10 cent decrement down, two contracts bought on a 5 cent scale down, four at 4 cents, six at 3 cents, and seven at 2 cents, you would possess only 8$^{1}/_{2}$ "increments," which would require about seventeen weeks of preparation for disposal rather than forty.)

The simplest illustration of a rollover would be the case of selling an expiring futures contract at a loss, immediately purchasing a deferred contract, and then adding the realized loss from the original contract plus the desired profit to the purchase price of the new contract to ascertain the price at which one would enter the sell order for the new contract. For example, if one has purchased a January Soybean contract at 560 and is forced to sell it in December at 555 to avoid delivery, he simultaneously purchases a July Soybean contract at the market," tacks on 5 cents to cover the loss on the December contract, and then adds 10 cents more to give himself the desired 10 cent profit on the trade. If the July contract is purchased at 590, the sell order is entered at 605.

Unfortunately, the rollover is usually more complex than that, for there may be several contracts which must be rolled simultaneously. In that event, I prepare a logsheet of the trades being closed out to assist me in computing the sell prices for the newly acquired positions. The logsheet becomes especially useful if it later becomes necessary to roll over some contracts a second time. My logsheet has nine columns, as follows:

COLUMN 1: "Trade Number." I number each trade to correlate the sold out positions with the newly acquired positions. The sold out "Trade #I" correlates with the new "#IA"; #2 correlates with #2A; etc. If it later becomes necessary to do a second rollover of a contract which had been rolled previously, 1 A will then correlate with 1 B. This correlation permits me to identify the exact amount of a cumulating loss on one or more contracts so that I will know the exact amount which I need to tack onto the new purchases to recapture all losses.

COLUMN 2: "Price Bought" is the scale level at which the contract was purchased. I prefer to ignore the bonus executions to keep the calculations as simple as possible. On some occasions, however, I will use actual execution prices. This would be when I have been locked into a scale for perhaps a year or more and am more interested in closing the scale than worrying about getting the last penny or two.

COLUMN 3: "Profit Goal." The profit I was seeking on the original trade. In the case of soybeans, my profit goal is 10 cents. Because the profit goal is included in the computation the first time the trade appears on the logsheet, it is unnecessary to repeat it on the rollover.

COLUMN 4: "Rollover Requirement." This is the amount of profit necessary from the newly acquired contract to complete the original trade, recapturing any loss and fulfilling the profit goal. You may add an extra increment to the "Rollover Requirement" to cover the extra commission, if you choose, but I will ignore that to keep the illustration as simple as possible. Column 4 comes from Column 8, as you will see later.

COLUMN 5: "Selling Goal." The price at which I must sell this contract to satisfy the "Rollover Requirement." Add Column 4 to Column 2 for entry under Column 5.

COLUMN 6: "Actual Sell." The price at which this \contract is actually sold. This column is left blank until the contract is sold. In the ideal circumstance, Column 6's "Actual Sell" is equal to Column 5's "Selling Goal," but if that were always the case, there would be no need for a rollover. As the contracts are sold one by one, you will list the actual selling prices under Column 6 and complete Columns 7, 8, and 9.

COLUMN 7: "Actual Profit." Subtract Column 2 from Column 6. Entries in this column will usually show a loss for the original trades, but they will show profits after they are rolled over, assuming the contracts are eventually sold at our target prices.

COLUMN 8: "Over/Under the Profit Goal." Subtract Column 3 from Column 7. If Column 7 shows a loss of, say, 10 cents, and if the "Profit Goal" of Column 3 is 10 cents, the entry under Column 8 is *minus* 20 cents.

COLUMN 9: "Cumulative Over/Under Profit Goal." Cumulate Column 8. This shows the amount of profit which we still must realize from the remaining contracts to recapture our losses and collect all of our desired profits.

For an illustration of how the logsheet appears in actual practice, let us assume that we hold four contracts of soybeans. They are January contracts bought at 550, 545, 540, and 535. We had wanted to sell them with 10 cents profit each, but the current market is only 540, and the contract is expiring. We choose to roll them over to July soybean contracts. We sell the Januarys at 540 and buy the Julys at 580. Here is how it would look:

Trade #	Price Bought	Profit Goal	Roll-over Over Reqmt.	Sell Goal	Actual Sell	Ov/Un Actual Profit	Profit Goal	Cumul. Ov/Un
1	2	3	4	5	6	7	8	9
1	550	10		560	540	-10	-20	-20
2	545	10		555	540	-5	-15	-35
3	540	10		550	540	0	-10	-45
4	535	10		545	540	+5	-5	-50
4A	580		5	585				
3A	580		10	585				
2A	580		15	595				
1A	580		20	600				

The entries under Column 4 on lines 4A, 3A, 2A, and 1A came from Column 8 on lines 4, 3, 2, and 1, respectively, except that the signs were changed from minus to plus. If we eventually sell the four contracts at our desired levels, the completed logsheet would appear thusly:

127

4A	580		5	585	585	+5	+5	-45
3A	580		10	590	590	+10	+10	-35
2A	580		15	595	595	+15	+15	-20
1A	580		20	600	600	+20	+20	0

It may appear that this is a lot of work for a simple rollover, and that is true; however, it could turn into a complex rollover if you are discounting for carrying charges (Chapter XVII, "Compensating for Carrying Charges") and find that you are stuck with two or three high-priced contracts which just won't sell. You may be forced to roll them over several times, and you certainly could lose track without a logsheet.

To carry the example a step further, let us assume that the contracts on lines 4A, 3A, and 2A sell at the proper levels, but 1A fails to sell at 600 and is trading at 596 near the end of June. We are obliged to liquidate that position to avoid delivery, so we sell it at 596. If we elect to roll it over to a November contract at 616, the logsheet would now have but two lines of entry, and they would appear thusly:

| 1A | 580 | | 20 | 600 | 596 | +16 | +16 | -4 |
| 1B | 616 | | 4 | 620 | | | | |

If the November soybeans price ever reaches 620 so that we may sell the final contract at that price, line 1B appears thusly:

| 1B | 616 | | 4 | 620 | 620 | +4 | +4 | 0 |

We finally have cleaned out the scale and sold the four problem contracts. We made only 10 cents profit on each of those four contracts, but along the way we may have had fifty interim profits from oscillations. Indeed, we might have recognized at some point during the long ordeal that we were repeatedly rolling over to higher-priced contracts and that the only way we would ever sell the final contracts would be for a huge rally to come into soybeans; therefore, we might have elected to absorb the loss of as much as 50 cents on one contract, 40 cents on another, 30 cents on another, 20 cents, and 10 cents. That is a total of 150 cents, but we have taken forty or fifty 10 cent winners and are far ahead of the game. This subject is covered completely in Chapter XVII, "Compensating for Carrying Charges."

It had long been the practice of the exchanges to wait until a delivery month of one year expired before it initiated trading in the corresponding delivery month of the next year. For example, the September 1984 contract would not commence trading until after the September 1983 contract expired around mid-September, 1983. In recent years, however, the exchanges have allowed trading of the new contracts a few weeks or even months before termination of the expiring contract. In the case of the metals and the financial contracts, they may go as far out as two years. This overlap can be very beneficial to the patient scale trader. Rather than commencing his rollovers too early, he may elect to await the availability of the new delivery contract before planning his rollover strategy. For example, if the scale trader is caught with a large position of accumulated corn contracts, that undoubtedly means a massive supply of corn has depressed the price and held it down. If the scaler has been trading the December contract and is faced with the prospect of rolling over to a delivery month which trades at a carrying charge premium to the expiring December contract, he might be pleasantly surprised to find that the new December contract starts trading at approximately the same price as the old December. The reason this can occur is that the huge supplies of old-crop corn being delivered against futures contracts have been stored for a year and someone needs to recapture those storage and other carrying costs, while the new December contract represents the first of the "new-crop" delivery months, and corn which is harvested in October may be delivered against the new December contract without built-in storage charges.

When I began this chapter I wondered if I really needed to include it in the book. I have had so little necessity for employment of rollovers during the years I have scale traded that I thought the subject could probably be omitted, but I included it to mitigate your fears if you are concerned about holding a large number of expiring contracts. I have had occasions where I had accumulated fifteen or twenty MidAmerica contracts but liquidated the entire position before having to do rollovers. That is because I had started my scale low enough to feel confident that there would be an eventual advance that would get the price 10 cents above my starting point long before I got into delivery considerations, so I merely waited and usually avoided the rollover. Besides, even if I had started buying corn, for example, at $2.50 and used a complex scale that gave me an inventory of thirty contracts with corn trading at $2.10, I wouldn't hesitate to roll over nearly the entire inventory. If, because of carrying charges, I pick up another ten contracts the next season, I would still roll over nearly all of them. The accumulated paper loss would be less than $10,000, and the oscillations that would have occurred during the year would have given me enough profits to absorb the few small losses as I rolled over most of the contracts. (Any time you are holding corn contracts at $2.10, should there be any doubt in your mind that corn will eventually reach $2.60 again?) That allows me to sell everything, to recapture all the losses, and to secure all the gains. With the "something for every-body" philosophy of both political parties and their blind devotion to the politically expedient policy of inflation for inflation's sake, I don't have to worry about whether or not we will see $2.60 corn. We might see $10.00 corn in my lifetime.

If math bothers you and you got a little nervous reading all of the calculations in this chapter, please be assured that I don't do all of those calculations each time. I had to show you the reasoning behind the calculations, but I pop them in a few seconds in my mind, and you can, too. Here is how you do it with one contract:

I bought January soybeans at 550 and had a sell order working at 560 when I was forced to roll to July. I sold the January at 546 and bought the July at 558, for a 12 cent premium. I just add the 12 cents to the 560 I was seeking on January , entering a sell in July at 572. I use Buy/Sell lines, so if I am able to sell the new July contract at 572, I know that I am to reenter a July buy at 562, which is 10 cents under my sell and 12 cents over the old January buy.

Ignore the calculation which says, "I need to get 4 cents to recover the loss I took by buying at 550 and selling at 546, plus I need 10 for my profit, so I must sell July at 14 cents over the 558 buy, or at 572." That is the mathematically correct way to do it, but I use the "shorthand" method and simply add on the premium.

It works the same if you hold six contracts or sixty. You can compute the entire new Buy/Sell line by adding the premium to *all* of the numbers in the old Buy/Sell line, and you can do it in seconds.

XVII

Compensating for Carrying Charges

All security and commodity trading systems undergo periodic changes and refinements to improve their effectiveness. Such is the case with our version of scale trading. We learned a lot from the Federal Reserve's experiment with double-digit interest rates, and because rates were pushed to levels which were more than double anything previously seen — and that was immediately after the Civil War — and triple any recent highs, we were forced to cope with an unknown quantity. This occurred after the original edition of this book was written, so this chapter has been added to inform you of what we learned from the Fed's "Great Experiment."

We have used the scale trading system very successfully since 1975, and we have made profits in eight of those nine years. The only year in which we did poorly was 1981. The cause of the problem was high interest rates. A review of the events of 1981 suggested the need for implementation of adjustments to buying scales to compensate for carrying charges during periods of high interest rates.

Carrying charges are defined as the cost of storing a commodity. Interest costs generally account for the bulk of the charges, but other expenses include space rental, insurance, transfer fees, and other incidentals. Carrying charges increase with higher interest rates and decrease with lower rates.

Prior to 1981, when interest rates seemed reasonable by today's standards, it was unnecessary to adjust scales for carrying charges. For example, a dozen years ago copper traded around 50 cents per pound, and interest rates averaged about 8%; thus, a full year's carrying charge was about 4 cents. In that circumstance, if the July 1972 contract of copper was trading at 50 cents, the July 1973 contract would be trading around 54 cents. A scale trader of copper could hold his ground if he captured two 2 cent winners per year, or one every six months. There was never a problem in realizing at least one 2 cent winner in each six months. The simplest way for the scale trader to compensate for carrying charges in 1972 was to buy the July contract at 50 cents, to eventually sell it at 52 cents, and then instead of reentering the buy order for a July contract at 50 cents, he jumped forward and entered a buy order in either the September or December contracts at 50 cents. This made the adjustments automatic, because the buying scale would not be reinstated until the deferred delivery fully discounted the carrying charges.

In actual practice, it worked like this: The cash price of copper would oscillate from a low of about 45 cents to a high of about 80 cents. To assure ample time to complete a scale without the necessity of paying frequent rollover commissions, but also to use a contract which was close enough to the spot contract to insure liquidity, the scale trader would select a futures contract about six months deferred. This contract would be trading at about a 2 cent to 3 cent premium over spot (cash). Therefore, the range for the futures contract which was about six months deferred from the spot contract might have been 47 cents on the low to 83 cents or 84 cents on the high. The rule of buying in the lowest third (Chapter XXVI, "Some Useful Guidelines") of the range would then dictate that purchases commencing at 59 cents or less would be proper. If the scale trader began at 52 cents, he could feel secure, for he was trading in the lowest *sixth* of the range of spot prices and the lowest *tenth* of futures prices.

If spot copper traded at about a nickel above its 45 cent low, or 50 cents, the futures contract for six month's deferred delivery would be around 52 cents, an excellent starting price. The scale trader needed only a 54 cent futures price to complete the scale. Even if he were forced to hold the full six months — by which time the futures price would have declined to the 50 cent spot price — his carrying charge loss would be a mere 2 cents. Meanwhile, if spot copper had declined to match the lowest price of the decade (45 cents), the total loss would be only 7 cents on the original contract, plus losses of 5 cents, 3 cents, and 1 cent on the subsequently-purchased contracts. This total 16 cent loss could be recovered with eight oscillation profits of 2 cents each. However, because the scale had been started so very close to the low, it is more likely that the price had rallied 2 cents above the starting level at least once during the six month trading period, allowing the trader to conclude his scale, to cancel all buy orders in the delivery month he had been using, and to reenter buy orders in a deferred contract at the same 52 cent level. This could go on for years with the 52 cent starting level always being used, thereby always compensating for carrying charges.

That was fine until we had runaway interest rates and $1.50 copper.

With interest rates topping 20%, and with copper priced at $1.50, the annual carrying charge on a contract of copper would exceed 30 cents. If the scale trader used a delivery option which was one-year deferred from the spot contract, and if copper held virtually unchanged for that year, the scaler would have purchased sixteen contracts with paper losses running from 30 cents down to 28 cents, 26 cents, etc., to the final contract with 0 cents loss. The cumulative loss would be 240 cents, or $60,000. It would have required 120 oscillation profits of 2 cents each to merely overcome the carrying charges and stay even. That is possible, but highly unlikely.

$1.50 would have been too high a level from which to commence a scale in copper, but when the price fell back to less than $1.00 and interest rates declined to about 17%, the carrying charge burden was only 17 cents instead of 30 cents and made copper a commodity to watch for further declines and commencement of a scale. Copper's price continued its slide, eventually trading in the low 80's, which qualified copper as a reasonable candidate for scaling according to the "lowest third" rule. Interest rates were still around 17%, and the annual carrying charge was about 14 cents, or slightly over a penny per month. It was impossible to foretell at that time whether copper prices would decline or would hold this level, sustained by the new inflation plateau. Most analysts were saying copper prices would hold at that level, citing the 85 cent to 90 cent production cost as their basic reason. Interest rates were also expected to decline, allowing for increased consumption of copper through higher auto and home sales. Lower interest rates would have reduced carrying charges, mitigating the need for carrying charge adjustments to the scales.

Unfortunately, interest rates did not come down, the economy went into a tailspin, commodity prices — including copper — collapsed, and scale traders who had not made carrying charge adjustments took severe losses. These losses could have been mitigated by adjusting buy orders when reentering them after a profitable sale.

This may be accomplished in several ways: One might trade very aggressively with a large amount of capital and a tight scale, assuring enough oscillation profits to offset the carrying charges, but running the risk of accumulating a large position and resultant substantial loss if the recession persists; or one might absorb an occasional loss if that loss can be held to a minimum and the realized profits from the other trades are sufficient to yield an overall profit; or one may discount the price on buy orders when they are reentered following successful sales.

Few people have the capital available to utilize the first method, and even those who have the capital would probably be unwilling to trade as aggressively as required, for it would be necessary to buy each 1 cent down and to sell each 2 cents up. Using today's prices as an example, spot copper is trading around 70 cents, and the annual carrying charge is 8 cents; if copper slipped 4 cents and hovered there for a year while the carrying charge forced an additional 8 cent decline, this would force the scale trader buying each penny down to accumulate thirteen contracts with a combined paper loss of $19,500, plus the $9,750 margin requirement.

The second method is simple, for it requires only that the trader arbitrarily dispose of an occasional contract after he has been forced to accumulate several contracts on a decline, but the price subsequently rallies enough to allow him to cash a few profits and to dispose of one or more surplus contracts if the resulting loss is less than the cumulative profits from the winners. For example, and again using today's 70 cent price and 8 cent annual carrying charge, let us assume he commences a scale buying each 2 cents down and selling

134

each 2 cents up. If copper goes into a sustained but slow downward drift lasting six months which results in a 6 cent decline in the *spot* price of copper, he will have seen his *futures* contract price decline 10 cents (6 cents from the decline in copper and 4 cents from half of one year's carrying charges), and he would have accumulated six contracts. If copper then makes a quick spurt which rallies the price 10 cents in three months, the scale trader would be able to sell four contracts profitably. (He cannot sell five because the carrying charge during that three months would have depressed the price of his futures contracts approximately 2 cents each.) This gives him 8 cents of profit from the four 2 cent winners and permits him to dispose of the last two contracts with a zero loss on one and a 2 cent loss on the other. That nets him 6 cents ($1,500), which seems hardly worth the risk, but if there had been a few oscillation profits during that nine month period, the effort was worthwhile. It would be normal to expect about one oscillation profit per month from a 2-cent-down 2-cent-up scale, so there should be 18 cents of additional profit from those nine monthly winners to go with the 6 cents, or a total of 24 cents, which is worth $6,000. In my opinion, it is mandatory for the scale trader to accept those two minor losses, for he must recognize that he was fortunate to catch a 10 cent rally and that spot copper is now 4 cents higher than when he began and must advance another 4 cents if he is going to insist upon profits from those last two contracts; furthermore, while he is waiting to cash those last two, carrying charges are still working against him at the rate of 2 cents each three months.

To be more specific, here is the example using actual numbers: Let us assume that spot copper in September 1983 is trading at 70 cents. We want to scale copper, so we select the September 1984 contract. It is selling at 78 cents because of the 8 cent annual carrying charge. If spot copper absolutely locked at 70 cents for six months our September 1984 contract would slip 4 cents to 74 cents because of the carrying charges. However, we have assumed that spot copper has declined 6 cents, so with copper down to 64 cents, our September 1984 contract is down to 68 cents. We have purchased at 78 cents, 76 cents, 74 cents, 72 cents, 70 cents, and 68 cents. The 10 cent rally carries spot copper up to 74 cents, but it takes our futures contract only up to 76 cents instead of 78 cents because of the 2 cent carrying charge erosion. We have sold contracts at 70 cents, 72 cents, 74 cents, and 76 cents, netting 2 cents ($500) on each, but we still hold a contract bought at 76 cents and one at 78 cents. By selling those last two contracts at the current 76 cent price we break even on one and lose $500 on the other. We net $1,500, plus oscillation profits.

The third method is the best because it automatically compensates for carrying charges. It merely requires that the scale trader discount the price on his buy tickets when he reenters them after a profitable sale. For example, he starts a copper scale at 70 cents in the September 1984 contract and purchases each 2 cents down while selling each 2 cents up. He buys at 70 cents, 68 cents and 66 cents. He sells his first winner on a rally to 68 cents. When reentering the buy order, he places it at 65 cents instead of 66 cents, and he reduces all resting buy orders 1 cent so that the other buy orders are still scaled 2 cents apart, now at 63 cents, 61 cents, etc., instead of 64 cents, 62 cents, etc. If he makes the purchase at 65 cents, he will enter that sell order at 67 cents. If he makes that sale at 67 cents, he will enter the repurchase order at 64 cents instead of 65 cents, and he will again reduce all the lower buy orders by 1 cent. This method is a "pay as you go" plan making adjustments on a regular basis.

The amount of reduction of repurchase orders must be determined by the trader and should be a function of his scale. If he is buying each 1 cent down, he will have twice as many trades and therefore will reduce the repurchase orders only $1/2$ cent; if he is buying each 3 cents down, he will have considerably fewer trades (because the carrying charges become significant in such an inactive account), and he would have to discount his repurchase orders at least 2 cents.

One problem with method #3 is that the price may start with a modest decline and then oscillate at a price slightly below the top one or two buy prices. Because you are continually reducing the repurchase orders, this has the effect of widening the gap between the top one or two contracts and all contracts below. In that circumstance, it eventually becomes necessary for copper to make a large price advance to dispose of those top contracts. Instead of waiting endlessly for that rally and allowing the carrying charge loss to increase, the trader would be wiser to sell the top contracts, absorb the losses, and use the released capital as part of the scale at lower prices where he may pick up some oscillation profits to offset those losses.

A trader who refuses to take an occasional carrying charge loss has an ego problem. He wants 100% winners, but this system is not designed to produce more than 90% to 95% winners. Occasional carrying charge losses are mandatory for success in scale trading.

* * *

The foregoing part of this chapter was copied verbatim from the previous editions of this book. Interest rates at the time of that writing were over 10%, while they are closer to 3% today. I felt it was more informative for you if I stayed with the 10% rate in the example because if interest rates stay around 3% you will rarely have to do a rollover calculation; instead, you merely sell all of your longs and roll forward to a delivery month about six months deferred by buying the same number of longs. You then add the small rollover premium to your new purchase prices, as described earlier in this chapter.

For example, if you had purchased July copper at 76, 74, 72, and 70, and July copper is currently hovering at 70 cents, you sell the four Julys at 70, purchase four Decembers at 71 (the *true* premium in 1994 prices with 3% interest rates). Your July sell orders had been entered at 72, 74, 76, and 78. Merely add 1 cent to each of these and enter your December sell orders at 73, 75, 77, and 79.

I fear that the Federal Reserve will touch off another round of inflation when it starts to raise interest rates soon — probably before this book comes off of the presses — and the illustration of compensating for 10% carrying charges will be more meaningful than if I demonstrated the 3% calculations.

Note: I am probably the *only* person in the world who thinks raising interest rates *increases* inflation, but I will present my case in Chapter XXIX, "Interest Rates and the Federal Reserve."

XVIII

Selecting a Broker

It may not be as easy as you might think to find a broker who will cooperate with you in the operation of your scale trading account. First of all, it involves a lot of work for the broker to monitor all your positions, and the scale trading account just will not generate the total amount of commissions that the broker is accustomed to generating with the typical commodity account. If you attempt to get your regular broker to handle your scale trading account he probably will recognize that it will result in a lot more work for him and less commissions, and he will try to dissuade you from using the system. Don't accept that. Get a new broker.

I am appalled at the many clients I see who trade with brokers who know little or nothing about commodities. The client may have a satisfactory relationship with his stockbroker, a trust solidified by many years of compatible and mutually profitable dealing in stocks. However, that particular broker may be a stock specialist who doesn't know the first thing about commodities. Yet, when the client gets a hunch on silver and makes an impulsive decision to purchase a commodity futures contract in silver because of something he read or saw on television, he has his trusted stockbroker handle the transaction. That is a case of the blind leading the blind. This broker who specializes in stocks may have such a problem in writing the order that he may be forced to seek the aid of a commodity broker within the same office simply to enter the order Can you imagine what it would be like if this same customer deposited $50,000 with this stock specialist and sought his assistance in conducting a scale trading account in four or five commodities? They would go absolutely whacky together.

On the other hand, the fact that a man is a commodity specialist does not guarantee his competence as a commodity broker. It may have been nothing more than the enormous percentage of commissions he takes from his commodity accounts as compared to the relatively low percentage that he earned from his former stock accounts which caused him to begin to devote his time exclusively to commodity accounts. Because of the leverage being ten times greater in commodity accounts than in stock accounts, commodity brokers may glean ten times the commissions from commodity accounts as stockbrokers will earn from stock accounts of similar size.

It is not that brokers are basically dishonest or particularly incompetent; it is more that they are naive. They accept as truth that which is told to them by their superiors, and they rarely challenge the gospel. It is possible that brokers actually doubt some of what they have been told, but usually it is simpler to take the course of least resistance, to accept the company propaganda, and to pass that information along to clients without question. A perfect example of this is how brokers blindly accept their firm's claimed performance records in theoretical commodity accounts. Based upon these records which frequently ignore commission costs, which assume executions that are impossible because of gap openings or limit moves, and which quote percentage returns based upon small initial cash commitments when the actual amount of cash required would eventually have been much greater because of margin calls for additional capital, brokers naively solicit clients to invest capital in the firm's managed commodity account programs, only to discover later that the results when using real money never match the results in the theoretical accounts.

Another example of the misguided broker is the one who gives seminars on charting techniques, claiming that charts may be used as a guide to stock and commodity trading profits. The typical rookie broker has had some experience in trading before he becomes a broker, and chances are he used charts. He probably made profits with his charts, but usually he has not realized that the primary reason for his profits is that he — like most traders — did most of his stock trading from the long side and that the stock market went up during the time he held positions. His stocks simply rose with the rest of the market. Once he becomes a broker, the only tools handed to him are a desk and a telephone, so he decides to conduct charting seminars to build a clientele as rapidly as possible.

Before the first meeting, he pores over the chartbooks and selects perfect examples of double and triple tops and bottoms, flags, pennants, key reversals, head and shoulders patterns, and all the other classic patterns which technicians seek. He photocopies an example of each of the patterns and distributes copies to each person in attendance that evening. The student has to be impressed by the uncanny accuracy with which these charts foretold the direction of the next movement in price. Unfortunately, the student doesn't realize that the broker selected a *classic* example in each case to demonstrate a pattern which worked. Take head and shoulders patterns as an example: it is almost impossible to find a chart of *anything*, be it a stock or a commodity, which does not have at least one head and shoulders pattern in it. Indeed, the charts of some may contain two or three such patterns. From the thousands of these head and shoulders patterns which appeared in the chartbook, the broker has selected the perfect example for reference. Certainly this one worked; in fact, half of them worked, but the other half failed. The student can't know this. He is a neophyte receiving his introduction to the world of technical analysis.

This does not mean that the broker is deliberately trying to deceive prospective clients; it is only that he believes that he made money with charts and is trying to teach the technique in an effort to build a book of clients. Nor is the seminar method of acquiring new clients limited to rookies. Many of the brokers giving technical seminars are thoroughly experienced veterans who continually conduct seminars to replace the disenchanted clients who have drifted away.

One of my best examples of the futility of trying to predict commodity price movements from charts is based upon the results in the account of a former client who was the president of a club which met weekly to discuss charting techniques. The members were employees of one of Southern California's large aerospace firms. One member had purchased a copy of this book, and he arranged for me to be their guest speaker one week. I might as well have saved my time and breath, for these men were all engineers — mostly Ph.D.'s — who lived and died by the computer and refused to believe that a person could beat the commodities markets with a method such as scale trading which did not require the use of a computer. After delivering a brief talk outlining the basic concept of scale trading, I spent the balance of my allotted time defending scale trading against the attacks of these engineers who were more interested in arguing for their respective trading methods than in learning about mine. Obviously, I obtained no business from that group.

However, the president of the group was probably embarrassed by the rough treatment I had received, so he opened a regular trading account with me, on the understanding that I would not try to convert him to scaling and that I would never make recommendations. I was only to be an order-taker. I agreed.

During the several months that I had this chap as an account he made twelve roundturn trades. On occasion, I would call him to confirm that he had established a new position through the execution of an open order which might have been entered two weeks previously. Sometimes I would be told that he was away from his desk but could be reached in the research lab. When I called the lab, he would say he did not have his charts with him and therefore did not know exactly where he wanted to enter his stop. He would offer to call me as soon as he returned to his office and could consult his charts. I had my charts on my desk, so I would tell him that I knew exactly where he would be entering the stop. He always accepted my figure, then confirmed it when he checked his own charts, and then asked how I knew where he had wanted the stop.

Knowing where he wanted his stops was so easy it was ludicrous. He always placed sell stops just under the last support level and buy stops just above the last resistance level. Unfortunately for this client and thousands of people like him, professional traders watch charts too, looking for this very thing. If they think they can drop a commodity's price a few cents to force the execution of the stops which have been entered by all the world's chartists, they will do it in an instant. They sell just enough to hit the stops, and once the stop level is reached and all the stop orders become market orders to sell, the professionals buy to cover their short positions. Because the market is breaking as the mass of stop orders is being executed, the professionals buy to capture their profits. Their execution costs are minimal, so they reap substantial profits from very modest moves. It may seem unfair — and it probably is — but it is legal, and it is part of the shearing of the lambs which goes on every day at the commodities exchanges.

One would think that experienced and intelligent traders — remember, he holds a Ph.D. — such as this man should recognize that this is common practice on the commodities exchanges, but he and the others go on providing the fodder for the voracious appetites of the professional traders. While he traded with me his record was twelve trades, eleven losers, one winner. Eleven times he was stopped out with a loss and one time he made a profit. You may ask, "How did that profit happen?" He was long a Deutschemark contract when that currency was revalued, and he fell into a profit. The revaluation of a currency happens about once every five years, and since it has been nearly five years since I lost that client, I presume he has had one more winner.

Another example of the naivete of stock brokers is the manner in which they all seem to follow a single economist, analyst, or market letter writer because he has been absolutely correct in calling the last ten turns in the stock market. They fail to realize that it is all a numbers game, and that through the process of elimination and pure statistics, out of 1,024 analysts, one will have to be right ten consecutive times. If each of the 1,024 persons makes a recommendation, 512 will be right, and 512 will be wrong. If those 512 who were right make a second recommendation, 256 will be right the second time, and the other 256 will be wrong. After the third recommendation, 128 will have been right three consecutive times. Eventually, after ten recommendations, only one person has been correct all ten times. But that doesn't make him a guru. In the next ten recommendations, it may be his turn to be wrong all ten times.

This is like 50,000 people picking the Thoroughbred races at Hollywood Park in what they call the Pic-Six, in which the bettors try to pick the winners of six consecutive races. There may be 50,000 possible combinations, but a grandmother using a hatpin to make her selections has as much chance of winning as experienced handicappers. It is sheer chance which determines the selector of six consecutive winning horse races, and it is pure chance if an analyst calls the turn of the market ten consecutive times.

I know of no ideal method of selecting a commodity broker, but I can suggest several pitfalls to avoid in seeking a broker. These suggestions apply when selecting a broker for any type of commodity trading, but they are especially apt when seeking a broker to assist in scale trading: (1) Never select a part-time commodity broker who devotes the other portion of his time to stocks, bonds, options, etc. (2) Do not fall into the trap of believing the commodity broker (or stockbroker) who says that he can produce winners by interpreting chart patterns. Charts are the road map to the poorhouse. They are right 50% of the time and wrong 50%. So is coin-flipping. (3) Stay away from trend-followers. They score huge profits occasionally, but over the long haul they suffer net losses. (4) Avoid commodity brokers who specialize in spread trading. Because spread margins are only one-fifth the regular margins, spread brokers will induce you to trade five times as many positions as you would otherwise trade. Since spread commissions are half-again as much as regular commissions, you will pay 7.5 times as much in commissions and go broke 7.5 times faster.

In case you doubt my contention that chart signals work half the time and fail half the time, I offer the following: Charles Dow was the first publisher of "The Wall Street Journal," and he was the editorial writer for that paper. Over the years of his editorial writing he proffered his thoughts on stock market strategy. He published these editorials until his death in 1904.

William Peter Hamilton then became the editor of the paper, and he took over the task of writing the editorials. Among his writings he frequently referred to the prior editorials of Dow, and the compilation of these writings came to be known as "The Dow Theory." (Thus, it was actually Hamilton who was more responsible for the Dow Theory than Dow, himself.) During the span from 1904 to 1929, the period during which Hamilton wrote the editorials, Hamilton announced ninety Dow Theory signals which — according to the Theory — presaged a turn in the market. The Dow

Theory is probably the most hallowed of all technical indicators known, but it was right precisely 45 times and wrong precisely 45 times.

To protect against chart pattern failures the broker recommends that the client use stop orders* to immediately close out losing positions. Stops don't benefit the client. They only benefit the broker. He can put the client into cattle on Monday, stop him out on Tuesday. Put him in silver on Wednesday, stop him out on Thursday. He puts him into cotton on Friday, and they finally get a winner. Cotton makes enough profit to offset the cattle and silver losses, and the account is still breathing. Barely.

This goes on until the client gets stopped out about six consecutive times, and he closes the account with whatever remains of his capital. He usually finds he started the account with $8,000, salvaged $1,400, and paid $5,000 in commissions. The undaunted broker schedules another charting seminar and finds more lambs for the slaughter. It never ends.

Some brokers try to take advantage of your emotions when you have accumulated an uncomfortable number of contracts in a scale and are wondering whether to continue the scale or to give up and liquidate all of the contracts. They will suggest that instead of liquidating the position you short an equal number of contracts of a different delivery month. They rationalize that stupid advice by saying that you are still holding your original contracts, but if the price goes lower you can cover the shorts and pick up a profit. That is absolutely untrue, because the profit you are accumulating on the shorts is being offset by an exactly equal further loss in your original longs. Assuming you have made an irreversible decision to terminate the scale, the broker who dissuades you from selling out and recommends the tactic of shorting an equal number of contracts of another delivery month is nothing short of a thief. Nothing can be accomplished by this tactic except for the broker earning a double set of commissions.

---

* A stop order" is an order which instructs the broker to buy (or sell) at the next available price the instant a particular price is touched or penetrated. These orders are sometimes erroneously called "stop-loss orders" because it is claimed that they will limit the amount of loss. This is untrue.

Among the biggest deceptions of all are the computerized trading systems. The people who use these methods have taken all of the conditions which existed in prior years and programmed this information into a computer. They use statistics for crop production, carryover, exports; anticipated consumption for food, feed, seed; government policy for the next year, such as loan, support, target, and parity levels, etc.; and all kinds of technical statistics such as volume, open interest, positions of large traders, positions of small traders, etc. After thousands of dry runs with the computer they feel they are prepared to offer their management capabilities to the public, so they show their theoretical performance records and extract substantial amounts of capital from these innocents. Somehow the hocus-pocus rarely works with real money. The problem is that the computer correctly predicted a substantial increase in the soybean price the theoretical year of the drought, but once the real money is laid on the line it rains all summer and the computer drowns — along with the customers. The computer cannot predict Acts of God. The computer is simply outclassed when it competes with the Deity.

Think about it — how can the computer anticipate rain? The Council of the American Meteorological Society on Weather Forecasting in its policy statement of 1976 stated, "For periods from 5 days to one-month coverage, temperature conditions can be predicted with some slight skill. Day-to-day or week-to-week forecasts within this time range have not demonstrated skill. There is some skill in prediction of total precipitation amounts for periods of 5-7 days in advance; skills for longer periods are marginal. For periods of more than one month — skill in day-to-day forecasts is minimal at the present time."

Knowing who *not* to go to may be of some help to you, but knowing the right broker to go to is a tougher problem to solve. The greatest difficulty you will have will be in finding a broker willing to devote all the time and attention required of a scale trading account. He will be required to learn something about the operation of the system, but he may be reluctant to do this when he realizes that he will earn far fewer commissions than he is accustomed to. He has been making a good living by convincing people they can make money with three winners out of ten trades — just as long as the customer "cuts his losses short (with stop orders) and lets his profits run." The typical commodity account generates 30% to 50% commissions per year, with many generating 100% or more. In other words, a $10,000 commodity account using stop orders and probing for the occasional home run, will crank out $3,000 to $5,000 in commissions for the broker, and if the customer is aggressive enough, using lots of spreads and trading oversized positions, the account may generate $10,000 or more in commissions. The scale trading account will never do this well for the broker. It should generate no more than 10% annually, or $1,000 in commissions in a $10,000 account. Not many brokers are going to be willing to give up those juicy commissions to allow the customer to convert his trading account to an investment account.

It never ceases to amaze me that clients ask their commodity brokers if it is a good idea to switch to scale trading. Can they really get an unbiased answer? You don't *ask* him; you *tell* him. Asking the broker is like asking your banker if he thinks it is a good idea for you to withdraw $10,000 from your savings account to invest in a mutual fund. Do you really believe he is going to say yes?

There is a standing joke within the commodity brokerage fraternity which says all commodity brokers should gather on January 1 and throw their account books into a pile and then everyone reaches in and selects a new book. Very few commodity trading accounts survive as long as a year, so no one would be giving up much, and the brokers could all begin anew. If the brokers would only recognize that they could have highly successful accounts which would last for years and bring in referral business, they might be willing to forego the liberal commissions of the typical trading account and switch their clients to scale trading. The first requisite for finding a cooperative broker to work with you on a scale trading account is to find one who is willing to waive high commissions and accept low commissions while the account grows. Unselfish commodity brokers are hard to find.

The second requisite is that he have enough patience to refrain from trying to induce you to overtrade, or to start a scale too high just to get action, or to encourage you to use scales which are designed to make a substantial number of profits so long as the commodity stays in a relatively narrow range but will bankrupt the account if the price drops to an unexpected low. Properly managed scale trading accounts never even receive margin calls — much less bankruptcy. I suppose the second requisite actually comes under the heading of unselfishness, but I prefer to label it "patience." A scale trading account may lie virtually dormant for weeks or even months and then yield numerous trades in a few days, but commodity clients and brokers are accustomed to daily trading — even hourly. Yes, patience is an absolutely essential quality in a broker who will be of assistance to a scale trading client.

The third requisite would be an understanding of the system. That seems too obvious to require comment, but if the broker does not have an implicit understanding of the system, he can bury the client. I have seen brokers encourage clients to add to positions "on a scale down," suggesting that this is scale trading. They have the client take a long position in silver at $5.50, and when it starts to fall they have the client add positions at $5.40 and $5.30. Then the price rallies, and they hold all three contracts, following the advance with a trailing sell stop order 12 cents under the highest price attained during the rally. They finally are stopped out when silver hits $5.87 and falls back to $5.75. That is not scale trading — that is pure luck. What if silver had fallen to $3.50? The client probably had $6,000 in the account. At $5.30 the account held three contracts with margin requirements of $1,250 per contract, or $3,750, plus a paper loss of $1,500, or a total of $5,250, and the account is barely breathing. At $5.20 the margin requirement for the four contracts is $5,000 plus $3,000 to cover the paper losses, or a total of $8,000. That's $2,000 more than the account had. Margin call!

It requires $30,000 to scale silver, not $8,000. The only way the broker can properly refer to the account as a scale trading account is to predetermine the scale within the limits of the bankroll, with a projected bottom for silver at $3.50 instead of $5.30.

You may find it hard to believe, but the greatest challenge to the broker who is inexperienced in scale trading may well be the entering of the orders. Setting scales is simple enough, because that is done long before the first order is entered or the first trade executed, but entering offset orders may prove confusing for him. It seems simple enough to say you merely want to buy each 10 cents down and sell each 10 cents up, but because of the brokerage firm's accounting computer being programmed to do First In-First Out (FIFO), the broker may become confused. For example, you might start a silver scale buying first at $4.80, then at $4.70, $4.60, $4.50, and $4.40. Silver then oscillates between $4.40 and $4.50 so that you are cashing repeated 10 cent winners. With the first winner the computer offsets the $4.80 position. Next goes the $4.70. Then the $4.60 and $4.50. When the price dips again to $4.40, the account will show five contracts in position, all bought at $4.40. The inexperienced or inept broker might think he is supposed to have resting orders entered for you to sell all five contracts at $4.50 instead of $4.50, $4.60, $4.70, $4.80, and $4.90. Don't laugh. I have seen it happen with the most experienced brokers. One reason why it happens so easily is that many brokerage firms automatically cancel all open orders on the last day of the month (as a precaution to erase forgotten orders from the books), and it is easy for the broker to commit the error of reentering the orders 10 cents above their actual acquisition levels rather than 10 cents above the scale prices. This can confuse a broker who is handling several scale accounts, each using a different scale, particularly after months of trading when, because of FIFO, the contracts still in the account bear no relationship to the scale.

Another consideration is whether the broker will take the time to monitor your positions during the trading day. If he is primarily a stockbroker and pays little attention to the commodity market he may not even be aware that soybeans opened down the 30 cent limit, giving you three purchases on your 10 cent scale, but requiring immediate entry of offsetting orders in case the soybean price rallies before the broker receives confirmation of execution of the buy orders. I have seen accounts scale trade pork bellies on a *halfpenny* (!) scale, buying each 1/2 cent down and selling each 1 cent up. If you have followed commodities you know that bellies can open down the 2 cent limit, run 4 cents to be up the limit an hour later, and then drop 2 cents to close unchanged for the day. Your broker must be alert to these price changes so that he may enter the offsetting orders very quickly, for many times the volume will be so great at the exchange that they are unable to confirm trades for many minutes — even as much as an hour or more — which would be long after offsetting orders should have been entered and possibly executed. In the case just cited, there might have been four missed trades, which means the client has missed a profit of $1,200 to $2,000 depending upon the bonuses he would have received on the downward gap opening. That is a very expensive premium to pay simply to do business with a broker who doesn't have the time, the inclination, or the desire to monitor your account. Keep him as a friend, but get yourself a different broker to handle your scale trading.

You should be aware that commodity trading differs from stock trading in that there is no specialist keeping a book which guarantees that you will receive execution of your order if the price penetrates your limit. In the hectic action of commodity trading it is possible for a commodity to be trading at one price on one side of the pit and at a totally different price on the other side of the same pit. Therefore, you have very little chance of demanding an execution by pointing out that your limit was penetrated. Your broker may always use the excuse that his floor trader was unable to execute when the truth may be that he simply forgot to enter the order. This is especially prone to happen when commodity prices fluctuate rapidly as mentioned above and the broker is not aware that an order of yours has been executed and should have an offsetting order entered. How would he know if he is not monitoring your positions?

The most egregious case I ever witnessed of an incompetent broker bungling a client's account occurred on June 1, 1983. (I am citing the specific date so that you may check the record for the accuracy of my tale.)

The stockbroker who is the culprit in this story is what is known as a very large producer with a major wire house, meaning that he generates substantial commissions from his stock brokerage accounts. For this, he has been given the title of "Vice President, Investments." Too many people assume that a title in the brokerage business indicates knowledge or experience; frequently, it only indicates large production, as in this case. Indeed, this broker generates so much in commissions that he rarely bothers to arrive at the office by the 7 a.m. (California) opening of the stock market, usually arriving around 7:30. (Today the stock market opens in California at 6:30 a.m., and that stock broker comes in at 7:00.)

This broker executes occasional commodity orders for his clients, but these orders are generally unsolicited and done only as a convenience for clients.

149

He came to me after the close of commodity trading on Tuesday, May 31, and asked me to show him how to write a commodity ticket to purchase ten contracts of sugar. He admitted he didn't even know whether he was buying the # 11 world contract or the # 12 domestic contract for sugar. I showed him how to write the ticket, but before allowing him to place the order in the wire room for transmission the following morning prior to the New York opening, I advised him of some events which had occurred that day and which could have a bearing on the opening price for sugar Wednesday morning. There had been a recent sharp advance in a number of international commodities, including cocoa, coffee, and cotton, which had made life-of-contract highs; platinum and palladium which were near to contract highs; and gold, silver, and heating oil which, although not at contract highs, were near their highest levels in months. Sugar had had the most dramatic move, doubling in price in just the last fourteen weeks.

I pointed out to him that the 10:43 a.m. closing time for sugar was the earliest of all these commodities and that there had been as much as three quarters of an hour to a full hour and a quarter of trading time remaining in these other commodities after sugar closed that day. Although sugar had closed up the fifty point limit that day, prices for international commodities had broken in the hour after sugar's close, and these other commodities had suffered very sharp declines. Gold, for example, had dropped $30 in that hour, silver had dropped 70 cents. I suggested that the collapse in these other international commodities would probably be reflected in sugar's price in the morning, and that it could open sharply lower. I informed him that we receive a pre-opening call each morning which gives a usually accurate indication of the expected amount of change in price from the previous night's close for each commodity, and I urged him to hold back his order and come in early enough Wednesday morning to see what the indication might be for sugar's probable opening price. The limit for Wednesday had been expanded to 100 points because of repeated limit moves, but there is never a limit on the two nearest options of sugar, so I advised him that if the pre-opening call for sugar was for a decline of more than 100 points, he would be the only broker in the country executing a buy order while the floor brokers would be thrilled to take his money. Sugar opens at 7:00 a.m., and this stockbroker insisted that he just was not going to bother to come in that early; "Besides," he said, "my customer will be pleased if he saves 100 points on ten contracts, which would be $11,200."

I came in at my usual early time Wednesday, and I was sick when I saw the pre-opening call indicated an expected drop of 130-150 points for sugar. There was nothing I could do to prevent this arrogant stockbroker from injuring his client.

Sure enough, the spot (July) contract opened down 136 points, and the unsuspecting client bought the deferred March contract only 100 points down. He was already thirty-six points losers, with no chance to improve upon that, and with only the chance that it could get worse. He cannot recover any part of his loss until the price of the spot contract has rallied at least 36 points; above that, he will finally enter the profit column. On the other hand, if the spot price continues to decline, his loss only increases without his being able to do anything about it. He can't sell, for it is locked limit down. It was a no-win proposition.

If the broker had not entered the order, he would have been aware that he had 36 points "with which to play." As long as the spot price stayed down more than 100 points, the order should not have been entered. If the price rallied 36 points so that the spot and the deferred March contracts were in parity, then the buy order could have been entered for March, and the client would have had his ten contracts without any unnecessary penalty. He would have had exactly what he wanted at the price which he was willing to pay.

As it developed, the spot contract hovered briefly and then plunged to close the day down a total 220 points. The poor client was faced with a downward adjustment of 120 points before March could reach parity with spot July. That 120 points gave the client a $13,440 loss in a position which he should never have held.

After the close of trading, I explained to the broker what he had done to his client, and his only response was: "He can afford it."

The following morning, Thursday, the spot July contract was indicated to open higher according to the pre-opening call. It actually opened with a modest rally of 24 points. This made the net decline for the two days 196 points (220 minus 24). The March contract had already dropped 100 points on Wednesday, so it needed to drop 96 more on Thursday to reach parity with July. It opened 83 points lower instead of 96 because computerized traders were hammering the July. It would now have been proper for the ten March contract buy order to have been entered, for the July and March contracts were adjusted to near-parity. It is impossible to state the exact price at which the ten March contracts would have been purchased, but it would obviously have been somewhere in the range of Thursday's trading instead of Wednesday's. The logical price would have been at Thursday's opening. The price of the spot contract subsequently broke 80 more points during the day before rallying to close with a 32 point gain on the day. That subsequent action is of no consequence, for we are only concerned with the *logical* point of entry, and that was at the opening. The March contract declined 17 points to lock limit down (100 points) while the July was down 80, but it also rallied with the comeback of the July contract, and March closed the day with a decline of only 68 points, or what should have been a 15 point gain instead of a 68 point loss.

The arrogance of this broker had caused the client to accept a $7,616 loss in a position which should have been a $1,680 gain. I don't know if "he can afford it," but I do know he can afford a new broker. That is one devil of a lot of money for a client to lose simply because his broker is a prima donna who doesn't like to get up early!

Incidentally, that client would win an arbitration hearing and get his money back immediately, but I suspect he doesn't even know what happened.

Perhaps the only practical way to select a commodity broker who can properly service a scale trading account is to sit down with him and have a long talk. It would be easy enough to determine his willingness to devote time to such an account. You might even be well advised to select a comparatively inexperienced man who has chosen to devote full time to commodities but as yet has not built up a large clientele with its corresponding demands upon his time. If you would like some advice on selection of a broker equipped to handle scale trading accounts, please write me at P.O. Box 3882, Westlake Village, California 91359-0882.

XIX

Selecting a Brokerage House

Just as it is important to select a compatible individual commodity broker with whom to trade, it is equally important to select the proper brokerage firm with which to trade. The differences between firms may be subtle, but they may also represent the difference between mediocre and outstanding performance in your account.

The most obvious difference will be in the area of commissions. Some brokerage companies charge their customers absolute minimum commissions while others charge "standard" commission rates which may run as high as 50% above those charged by other firms. The firms charging the higher rates may try to rationalize their high fees by pointing to their research, their electronic equipment which is claimed to produce faster executions, or their computers which are supposed to produce faster confirmations and more accurate accounting results, etc. I don't buy that.

As for the confirmations and accounting, there is little — if any — difference among firms, for all are required to make "same day" reports to clients. Also, I am not particularly impressed by electronic equipment, for I have had occasional dealings with small firms which have produced far more accurate statements by hand than the large firms with their computers. As for the research, I will comment on that presently, but for now suffice to say that I personally would select a firm with lower commissions virtually every time over the firm which charges higher commissions. This is especially true when scale trading, for there is very little that the *firm* may provide in the way of services to the individual. The *broker* must provide service, but not his firm.

A second major consideration is margin requirements. Most firms require the customers to meet minimum requirements only, but some firms treat commodities trading as a sideline and require margin deposits which are substantially above minimums. If, for example, you are trading wheat and have the choice of depositing $1,000 margin per contract at one house or $2,000 at another, it is obvious that your percentage return will be twice as great at the one house as at the other. You might be inclined to conclude that this is not so because you do not expect to ever make a total commitment of your bankroll under the worst possible conditions (which is how successful scale traders should calculate scales in advance), but you must also admit to the possibility that your estimates of potential lows may turn out to be erroneous, and that you may find it necessary to have a greater amount of margin available than you had expected. If you are carrying your positions with a firm that requires double margins, you may be forced right out of the market at the very bottom. I would only trade with a firm that grants margin requirements which are consistently among the industry's lowest.

It is particularly important that you use a firm with low margin requirements if you are trading with a bankroll that is too small to permit the purchase of U.S. Treasury bills to be used as collateral for your commodity trading. If you are permitted to deposit minimum amounts, the surplus may be held in interest-bearing reserves. Thus, that surplus margin would be earning interest in the low margin account but not in the high margin account.

Some firms will allow you to deposit T-bills as collateral for your entire account, requiring only that you cover your paper losses on open positions with cash. Other firms may deposit your capital in an omnibus T-bill account, paying you the equivalent of T-bill interest on the entire account, but these firms usually segregate the amount you need for your margin and pay you nothing on that. It depends upon whether your margin requirements or your paper losses are greater if you want to determine which of these two methods will produce the greater interest return on your reserves.

Some firms will impose charges for services they perform. Most firms charge only the standard commission charges, so I would not deal with a firm that charged any fees which I considered significant and for which I would not be charged at another firm.

Now, for the matter of research. Most of the major commodity firms pride themselves on the size of their research departments and spend a great deal of money advertising their research, but I have never been impressed with any commodity firm's research. That is not intended as a rap against the firms; it is merely a statement of an opinion. It seems to me that mere chance plays as important a part in commodity research as all the hard work of the researchers. After reams of statistics have been collected, it rains — or it doesn't rain — and all the figures are out the window. Or it's a change in government policy, a new tariff, a currency devaluation, the overthrow of a government, an early freeze, or any one of a million other things that can upset the applecart.

I consider it absolutely essential for scale traders to work directly with commodity brokers. The only exception would be if the client has given discretionary authority to the broker, otherwise, the counsel of a broker is indispensable.

The area in which the broker may offer the greatest help is in research. Unless the client is a retired commodity analyst, he cannot possibly interpret all the commodity news he reads. Even if he has his own commodity news printer in his office, he still will need the assistance of a commodity research team to help him to analyze government reports, complicated farm price support programs, the effect of subsidy programs in other nations, exports, imports, currency devaluations and revaluations, embargoes, and a myriad of other items which may affect commodity prices. The major commodity houses have a complete staff of research analysts who will not only make daily comments of a general nature relative to the commodities in which they specialize, but they also offer nearly instantaneous commentary relative to newsbreaks. This commentary usually is delivered by speaker phones on the desks of the commodity brokers throughout the branch offices, and then it is followed by hard copy printouts on the house's private wire system. It seems to me that the availability of such commentary as well as the broker's ability to make a direct call to that analyst for amplification of that commentary are invaluable to the client.

Unfortunately, analysts frequently commingle interpretive commentary and prognostication. Too frequently, it is impossible to separate the two, and the broker and client are overly influenced by the analyst. This may prove very costly for the client.

A typical example of an analyst allowing his commentary to become tainted by his personal prejudice is when he is a technician and has become a trend-follower. When asked how much further negative effect a flash of bad news will have on an already declining commodity (or the positive effect on a rising commodity due to good news), he may suggest a likely continuation of the trend. He may have overlooked the fact that the news may have been anticipated to a certain degree, and that the price movement may already have discounted the news. He doesn't realize it, but his devotion to trend-following prevents him from giving an unbiased opinion.

This is not to say that analysts will deliberately attempt to deceive you; it's just that they allow their analysis to be influenced by extraneous personal prejudices, and it is difficult, if not impossible, for the broker and client to recognize when that situation exists.

A perfect example of such a condition occurred in late 1982 and into 1983 with an analyst at one of the major commodity houses. This livestock analyst is reputed to be one of the best in the industry in his area of specialization. He is a superb fundamental analyst, but he is also a trend-follower, and he buried his firm's clients in 1983 with his recommendation to buy hogs and pork bellies.

Hog and pork belly prices had advanced in a virtually straight-line upside configuration for three years. This was because livestock raisers had reduced the size of their herds following the 1979 disaster in hog and pork belly prices. By 1982, hog prices had increased 100% and pork bellies 300% from their 1979 lows. Being a trend-follower, this analyst predicted that prices would continue to rise well into 1983. He predicted that the hog price which had already advanced from 30 cents to 60 cents would top 80 cents. Pork belly prices had risen from 26 cents to above $1.00 before settling back to 80 cents in late 1982: he confidently predicted that the pork belly price would exceed $1.00 in 1983.

This analyst's belief in pending higher prices was based upon his theory that hog raisers would soon begin to expand their herds through an increase in breedings and that the withholding of the sows from slaughter would create a temporary shortage of pork, which would send hog and belly prices into an explosive upside move. The theory seemed plausible enough, but he had become so hypnotized by the rising trend in prices that he was no longer objective. He seemed to expect these two trees to grow to the sky.

He had overlooked the simple fact that the hog/feed ratio had risen to record levels and had been there for months. It is normal for 100 pounds of hogs to sell at 10 to 15 times the value of a bushel of corn, meaning that the normal ratio ranges from a low of 10:1 to a high of 15:1, but it had exceeded 20:1 and was nearing 25:1. Instead of relying on common sense to tell him that farmers probably had already started expanding their breedings, he relied upon the USDA estimates of breeding intentions. The problem with using these numbers is that they come directly from a census taken among farmers. Obviously, farmers lie when giving out such information, for they are engaged in a giant poker game with commodity traders. By giving the USDA lowball numbers on their breeding intentions, the farmers are helping to create the *impression* of a hog shortage which does not exist; this keeps prices high and allows the hog farmer to hedge his increasing hog numbers at inflated prices. The low numbers of hogs thought to be available kept prices up and kept this analyst predicting higher prices yet to come. It was not until well into 1983 when *slaughter* numbers began to replace farrowing numbers that it became obvious that the farmers had lied. Slaughter numbers should have been coming down because of the supposed hog shortage, but slaughter numbers stayed very high. By this time it was too late. Prices were down substantially, and the clients had taken a merciless beating.

This analyst was quoted in a February edition of a national business weekly as predicting there would be "an explosive upside move in hogs and pork bellies." Three months later, with the hog and belly prices down 6 cents and 16 cents respectively, this analyst was quoted again in the same periodical. I am sure you have guessed that he was still saying, "There will be an explosive upside move in hogs and bellies." The price exploded all right, only it was to the downside. Hogs and pork bellies dropped a total of 13 cents and 31 cents respectively.

Don't be too harsh on this analyst. He is no worse than the rest. I only cited his example because the documentation of his exact quotes appeared in print in a popular periodical. Most other analysts do the same. They get carried away with a theory and lock into it until it is too late to change.

The point is, you must use the assistance of a broker and his research department, but you must also temper their enthusiasm with some interpretation — or common sense — of your own.

One of the things I have seen in my years in the investment business which has been particularly bothersome to me is the penchant people have for claiming all their winners were their own ideas while all their losers were their broker's (or his firm's) ideas, so I do not intend to imply that commodity research is worthless, only that I am saying that research should be used as nothing more than a guide to set parameters for scale trading. If the research department thinks wheat should range between a low of $3.40 and a high of $4.20 for the next twelve months, use that as a guide for setting your scale. You might set up a scale which starts buying at $3.80 and goes to a *probable* low of $3.40 (at which point you should still have 50% of the bankroll intact), but your own common sense should tell you that the research department's parameters may be upset by a bumper crop from the Southern Hemisphere, a reduction in consumption because of worldwide depression, or any one of dozens of other unexpected events which might occur. Therefore, you should allow for the *possibility* that wheat might sell as low as $2.80 under those conditions and set your scale to accommodate that low price and have 30% still in reserve at that level.

If your account is large enough, it might be wise to use two or more brokers so that you get differing opinions and may make your own determinations of price parameters based upon a consensus of opinions.

Most important of all, you should avoid the trap of listening to short-term projections which come either from research or from your broker. The person whose job it is to give day-to-day opinions may actually be too close to give objective opinions. Like all the rest of us, that person must, at times, become emotional and give opinions which are tainted by emotions. For example, he may be expecting a rise in the price of wheat, based upon his studies of supply and demand. However, the price of wheat declines immediately after his buy recommendation. For the first few days of the decline he encourages adding to positions, but as the decline continues, he begins to find reason for doubting his original analysis. He is influenced by the day-to day events which have caused the price to decline temporarily. His job depends upon the accuracy of his recommendations, so he begins to become emotionally involved. His doubts turn to apprehension, then fear. The short-term news overwhelms long-term considerations, and the analyst reverses his original opinion, now recommending that clients liquidate their long positions and go short. This is usually the precise point when he should be recommending buying, but his emotions get the better of him, and he is recommending selling.

For the first few days after his new recommendation the price may rally, but he labels it nothing more than a technical rally in a market which has reversed its major trend from rising to falling. After a week or two of a generally rising price, he begins to wonder again about his reversal, for now he realizes that the factors which brought about the brief decline were short-term influences and may not have a lasting effect. As the price continues to rise his doubts again turn to apprehension and ultimately to fear as he becomes emotionally involved. Again, he reverses. He has returned to his original position — long wheat — which was based upon his overall view of the market for the year, but he made two very bad recommendations between, and these losses may be impossible for the client to overcome. If the first loss was 20 cents and the second was 30 cents, the client must now realize a gain of 50 cents just to get even, plus commissions. Not only is that difficult, but he is starting from a level 10 cents higher than the point at which the original buy recommendation was made, so it may be impossible to recoup the loss on this trade.

This example I have just given demonstrates the emotional involvement of an analyst (or broker, or client) where fear is dominant. Greed is the other emotional factor which will dominate those who speculate. When prices are running to the upside, it is difficult to ignore the opportunity to climb aboard the gravy train, so you must steel yourself and ignore the recommendation of an analyst who suggests that you buy something that is moving rapidly to the upside. That would be inconsistent with the principles of scale trading. It may be fine for commodity speculators, but I insist that scale trading is more akin to investing, so it would be imprudent for a scale trader to commence a scale in a commodity which is presently undergoing a rapid price increase.

Lastly, but very importantly, do not select a brokerage firm to assist you in scale trading if its research is based to any major degree upon technical considerations (charts). I am adamant in my insistence that charts are absolutely useless, that coin-flipping is as reliable. Furthermore, scale trading is usually done in direct contravention to chart signals and trend-following. At the point where chartists and trend-followers are selling, we are buying, and at the point where they are buying we are selling.

It is probably a good idea for you to read the fine print when you sign your Commodity Account Agreement at the time you open the account. This would be true regardless of whether you opened your account with a full-service broker or a discount house. The important section is the one about "Arbitration." Again, without giving legal advice, it is my understanding that if you agree to arbitration you waive your right to a court trial at any later date if there is a dispute over your account. You cannot be forced to sign the arbitration portion of the Agreement, and I am told that if you do not sign it you still may choose arbitration, but you may also choose a trial in court. You might want to ask your attorney about this.

XX

Discount Commissions

Most of the foregoing chapters of this book have been repeated verbatim from previous editions because the text described the scale trading system. A few words were altered for the sake of clarity, and a couple of anecdotes were added, but the only real change in all of those chapters was the suggestion that you use the bottom third of the range of the last ten years — instead of the previously suggested five — in determining the starting points for your scales. Because the scale trading system is based upon the immutable Law of Supply and Demand, the system will remain unchanged for 1,000 years.

In the earlier editions of this book in this chapter, "Discount Commissions," I presented what I considered to be all of the arguments pro and con relative to using a discount broker or a full-service broker. I tried to leave the reader with the conclusion that it was pretty much personal preference, that dealing with a discount house might save you a little in commissions, but you might consider it worth the extra cost to receive full service. Flip a coin. Take your pick.

Today, however, I say *a trader has to be out of his mind to do business with a discount house!* There is a mountain of evidence

161

which has come to light since previous editions of this book were written, and you may not be aware of these problems, so I will inform you of the things I have observed and let you decide whether you want to risk throwing your money away with a discount house.

For the benefit of those who never read an earlier edition of this book I will repeat all that was said previously. Again, things will be repeated verbatim. The only things which will be changed will be some words for clarity and interest rates and commission rates to adjust to normal conditions. For example, I previously used 10% interest earnings on U.S. Treasury bills and money market accounts. We were on the way down from 17.5% at the time that was written. Today we are at 3%. Neither is realistic. Over the years, T-bill rates should stay around 6%, so I will use that number in the interest income illustrations.

Also, in previous editions I used $30 as the commission rate for discount brokerage houses, and that is accurate today; however, I used $70 as the typical rate among full-service brokerage houses, but that is too high today. Over the years the full-service firms have felt the pressure from the discount houses, and they have been forced to lower their commissions. This does not mean that discount houses have taken business away from full-service houses; it simply means that customers are aware that full-service houses grant discounts off of their published rates to keep from losing business, and *every* client can receive discount commissions *everywhere.* If you are not receiving discount commissions from your full-service broker it is only because you failed to ask. One major brokerage firm spends hundreds of millions of dollars per year on its advertising campaign with the central theme: "Because he asked!" Take their advice and *ask* your broker for the discount. You will get it! You should not pay more than $50 *anywhere* for a roundturn commodity trade.

Major wire houses charge roundturn commodity commissions which may range from a low of about $50 for a Chicago Board of Trade oats contract to a high of about $125 for the 5,000 ounce Comex silver contract. Although there is no set rate established by the various exchanges, competition has forced the wire houses to be relatively consistent in their charges. One house may charge $5 more for roundturn commissions on one commodity but charge $5 less for another. Discount commission brokers charge $25 to $30 per roundturn for the same trades. It might appear patently obvious that there is an advantage in dealing with the discount brokers rather than wire houses. (Note: For the sake of this discussion, the term "discount broker" means the firms which execute your commodity transactions for approximately $30 per roundturn while providing no research, and the term "wire house" describes the full-service brokerage houses which offer research, assign a broker to assist you, and charge approximately $50 per roundturn transaction.) This, however, is not the case. In fact, I have considered what I deem to be the advantages and disadvantages for both sides, and I am unable to draw a conclusion which I would consider unarguable based solely on costs. (The overwhelming arguments in favor of the wire houses will come at the end of this chapter.)

There is no question that the trader with $25,000 who simply wants to jump in and out of five or ten contracts at a time, trying to outguess the market, will save money with the discounter, for he may trade fifty times before going broke instead of forty. After all, a person who tries to outguess the market can't possibly win. It is not a matter of *if* he is going to go broke but *when.* If he is paying an average of $30 commission per contract per roundturn instead of $50, he saves $20 per contract per roundturn, or $100 on a roundturn of five contracts. His saving would be $200 on a ten-contract roundturn trade. If he can save an average of $150 per trade, and if he executes fifty trades, he will have saved himself $7,500 in commission costs, or 30% of his original capital. It would be foolish for this type of trader not to deal with the discount house.

However, this book deals with scale trading, a systematic trading method which seeks to grind out a very modest percentage profit and which guarantees very few trades over any period of time. Statistics show that an average commodity trading account will generate 40% to 50% commissions (as a percentage of starting equity) annually, but scale trading accounts generate only 8% to 10%. This very low level of commission generation should cause the prospective scale trader to consider whether there is sufficient reason to abandon the traditional wire house brokers to trade with the discounters.

While working as a commodity broker with a major wire house, I had five professional managers who executed their scale trades through me and insisted that they had never used a discount broker.

It was basically a case of the tangible benefits of the commission discounts failing to outweigh the intangible benefits of having access to our research and other services. Our firm charged commissions which were considerably higher than those charged by the discount houses but which were competitive with other major wire houses. I had very frank discussions with these managers as we weighed the pros and cons, and their ultimate decisions were to go with the wire house. I will now relate some of the items which entered our conversations and allow you to make your own decision as to what was most influential in the decisions of these professionals:

As stated previously, if you plan to open a $25,000 account and just slug it out with the big boys, trading several contracts at a time, you will do well to have your account with a discount broker. This is especially true if you make all your own decisions and don't want to pay for research which you may never use. You will save about $20 per contract per roundturn transaction, or a saving of $50 to $60 per week if you make as few as two or three trades per week of single contracts. If you trade that frequently and trade multiple contracts, your savings will be even greater. That saving will keep you alive through a couple of extra trades before you join the other commodity losers, but that is the only benefit you will gain.

If, instead, you plan to be serious about commodity trading and you use scale trading to at least give yourself a chance to succeed, there are numerous considerations for you to contemplate. Let us first consider the pure economics of the matter:

Before offering the arguments pro and con for discount houses and wire houses, I must first explain something about the operating techniques of the discounters. It is about their margin requirements and the manner in which you must maintain your account.

They advertise that you may deposit as little as $10,000 worth of U.S. Treasury bills as collateral for your commodity trading, but they also require that you deposit an additional 10% in cash to meet their margin requirements. Thus, if you opened an account with a discount house by depositing a $10,000 T-bill, and if you then purchased commodity futures contracts with margin requirements of $5,000, your T-bills would cover only 90% of the margin requirement, and you would be required to deposit an extra $500 in cash. Even if you had a million dollars of T-bills in your account with the discount house, that would only cover $4,500 of the margin requirement and you would be obliged to deposit $500 in cash. The wire house would allow you to cover the entire $5,000 with your T-bill, and they would require no further cash.

Wire houses usually have their own money market funds which you may use as a repository for surplus cash, but I am unaware of any discount broker offering this service. This is a very important point in favor of the wire house, for surplus cash in your account with the discounter earns no interest, while surplus cash in a wire house account is immediately swept into the money market account to earn interest for you. As you will see, the interest earned at the wire house may be sufficient to overcome the commission difference.

You should also be aware that it is impractical to say that the discounter requires only an extra 10% in cash in your account for margin purposes, for your equity will oscillate substantially when scale trading (or with any kind of commodity trading), and if you withdrew your surplus equity each day that it exceeded your margin requirements, you would be facing the possibility of a margin call the following day if the equity fell below margin maintenance levels. If you were to attempt to have the discount house wire the surplus to your bank each time you were in surplus, and if you wired the money back to the discounter each time you were in deficit, the bank wire charges could be substantial. Furthermore, if you hold your equity to an absolute minimum with the discount house, you run the risk of a sellout if you are out of touch with them for a day or two. This is because they have no personal contact with you — you are just a name, living 2,000 miles away — and sound business practice dictates that they liquidate all or a part of your account to meet the calls. For these reasons it is virtually mandatory that you maintain about 25% cash in your account at the discount house rather than the 10% advertised. The interest lost on such a substantial amount of equity would probably equal any commission savings.

Let us now consider two $10,000 accounts, one opened at the wire house and the other opened at the discount house. In either case, the $10,000 is inadequate to purchase T-bills and to have sufficient cash remaining in the account to cover possible paper losses, so we will assume that both accounts stay fully in cash.

The $10,000 deposited with the wire house would go immediately into their money market fund to start earning interest. As soon as a commodity trade is executed, a portion of the $10,000 is transferred to the commodity account to cover the margin requirement. The balance remains in the money market fund. When the futures contract is finally liquidated, the margin deposit — plus or minus profit or loss — is returned to the money market fund to earn interest again. It is impossible to guess how much the average balance would be during the year, but I think it would be fair to estimate that an average of $3,000 would be in the commodity account and $7,000 would be in the money market fund. At money market rates of about 6%, the interest earned on that $7,000 would be $420 which the wire house account receives while the discount house account earns no interest.

That $420 of interest forfeiture is an enormous amount of money to throw away, and there is no way in the world that a properly managed $10,000 scale trading account can overcome penalties of that magnitude simply through commission savings. At $20 per round-turn, it would require twenty-one trades in a single year, and that is far too aggressive for a $10,000 account.

You must remember that a properly managed scale trading account strives to produce only a 40% annual profit, or $400 for each $1,000 in the account. Because we usually trade with scales which average around $400 profit per trade, we seek a single winning trade for each $1,000 of account size. Thus, a $10,000 account should average one $400 winner each five weeks, while a $50,000 account should average one winning trade each week. Now you will recognize why I say it is to the scale trader's disadvantage to deal with the discounter if his is a $10,000 account. If the wire house charges an average of $50 per trade, which is about $20 over the average of about $30 per trade charged by the discount house, the scale trader would save $200 by executing his ten trades with the discount house, but the net *loss* to him is $220 when the $420 of unearned interest is taken into consideration.

There was a time when wire houses required a minimum deposit of $50,000 in an account before they would permit you to purchase U.S. Treasury bills for commodity collateral in lieu of cash, but the discount houses took the lead and began permitting the deposit of as

166

little as $10,000 in T-bills. Many of the major wire houses now accept $10,000 T-bill accounts because of that competition. There must also be some cash in the account. The cash serves a single purpose with the wire houses and a dual purpose with the discounter. The primary purpose is to cover paper losses, and that is required at both houses. For example, at either house, if you open an account with the deposit of $10,000 cash and request that they purchase $10,000 worth of ninety-day T-bills for your account, the cost of the bills would be about $9,850*, and you would have $150 in cash remaining in the account. Although you have $10,000 worth of T-bills in the account, both houses will compute the collateral value at only 90%; thus, you actually have only $9,000 of margin buying power available. The discounter gives your purchasing power a slight additional haircut by allowing only 90% of your margin requirements to be covered by the discounted T-bills and requiring that the other 10% be covered with cash. Thus, the margin purchasing power of each $1,000 worth of T-bills is $900 at the wire house and only $810 at the discounter, with the additional $90 requirement being covered by the deposit of cash which earns no interest. I would like to make a few comparisons between the dollar outcome of similar accounts at discount houses and wire houses, but it gets rather complicated if haircuts are imposed on top of haircuts, so the only one I will use is the discount house's 90% T-bill coverage and their 10% cash requirement

Assuming you have purchased your $10,000 worth of T-bills at the discount house for a cost of $9,850 and that the $150 difference remains in cash, if you were to choose to commit the entire $10,000 on your first trade and purchase ten contracts of cattle, for which the margin requirement is $1,000 per contract, the T-bills would cover the first $9,000, but the $150 cash would be insufficient to cover the $1,000 cash requirement. You would be obliged to deposit another $850 immediately. With the wire house, the $150 (plus the extra $850) would remain in the money market fund earning interest, for your T-bills met the entire margin requirement.

---

* In purchasing U.S. Treasury bills, you do not pay the face amount. Instead they are purchased at a discount from face value, and upon maturity you receive the full face value. The discounted portion is your earned interest.

If the price of cattle drops a penny, your loss would be $400 per contract, or $4,000 total on the ten contracts, and you would be obliged to deposit another $4,000 to cover that paper loss. The rule is the same at both houses: T-bills may not be used to cover paper losses. Only cash.

The foregoing is an extreme example of an all-out trader's account, but the principle is the same for traders who employ methods as conservative as scale trading. Although you might scale trade only a single commodity and accumulate single contracts, you would be subject to a margin call almost immediately if you tried to use T-bills in your $10,000 account. If you bought only a single contract of cattle, the T-bill would cover the first $900 of the margin requirement, and the $150 cash surplus would cover the other $100 requirement, but that would leave a mere $50 surplus in the account, which would be erased by the paper loss from the first quarter-cent decline in cattle's price. If you run into any kind of serious decline, you will be forced to either liquidate the T-bills or to deposit additional cash margin. Most brokers (both discount and wire) levy a service fee of about $35 to $55 each time they buy or sell T-bills for you, so if you start liquidating your T-bills and repurchasing them each time you are in and out of trouble with your scales, you will have dissipated your commission savings in short order.

It is impractical to discuss opening a $10,000 T-bill account with either house because of the very high probability that you will be called upon immediately for additional cash. In either case, a cash reserve would be essential, so we might as well compare $15,000 accounts.

I prefer to buy one-year T-bills instead of ninety-day so that I don't have to pay another commission three extra times a year. A one-year $10,000 T-bill yielding 6% would cost about $9,400. I will use the same cost for both the discounter and the wire house, so the illustration is consistent.

The $15,000 account at the discount house uses $9,400 to purchase its $10,000 T-bill, and the other $6,600 sits in cash earning no interest. The T-bill earns $600 of interest. We want this account to complete fifteen roundturn trades during the year, which gives us a total commission cost of $450 at $30 per roundturn. The net difference between the $600 of interest earned and the $450 of commissions paid is $150.

An identical account at a wire house would earn $600 of interest on the T-bill and $396 on the $6,600 cash surplus which is held in a money market fund earning 6%. The total interest income is $996. This account also completes fifteen roundturn trades during the year, and with the commission per trade at $50, the total commission expense is $750. The net difference between the $996 of interest earned and the $750 of commissions paid is $246, or $96 in favor of the wire house. That should not be enough to sway your thinking either way.

I recognize that I am being quite cavalier in my illustration of how the money is deployed. I have assumed that the entire cash amount is deposited in advance with the discount broker, when it actually could be held in one's own money market account until needed, but it could be debated whether this is practical because of the danger of a sellout at the discount house.

One might even say that during the periods when the account is flat, all but a token amount (to keep the account open) may be withdrawn from the discount house and deposited in a money market account. This is also an arguable point, for it is not entirely true:

The discounter will not permit you to enter an order unless there is an adequate balance resting in your account to cover the entire margin requirement for the transaction. If news should break suddenly, causing a sharp break in the price of a commodity which you are considering scaling, you would miss a buying opportunity if you have emptied your account and have only a token amount of cash on deposit. By the time you could wire funds to the discount house, the price might already have rebounded to the level at which you would have been cashing your winner, and you have missed the trade entirely. One such missed trade at $400 would have cost you approximately the amount of your commission savings for a full year. That is false economy.

If you maintain only a partial credit balance in your account with the discount house and shuttle cash back and forth between the broker and your bank, the wire charges can become costly.

I suggested that you could miss a trade when there was sudden and sharp-breaking news, but it could also happen if you were merely out of touch with commodities temporarily. You might be on vacation, or away on a business trip, or involved in a project which requires your total attention and keeps you from monitoring the commodities markets daily. The discount house will not accept your open orders if you do not have adequate margin on deposit with them, but you will be assured of entry if you are dealing with a wire house, for they have your entire capital on deposit in their money market account and will accept your open orders.

The pendulum begins to swing slightly in favor of the discount house as the account size increases. A $25,000 account at a discount house would hold $20,000 of T-bills, at a cost of $18,800, with the surplus $6,200 earning nothing, while that $6,200 surplus would earn $372 of interest at the wire house. Both accounts execute 25 trades, with the $20 higher commission at the wire house costing the trader an extra $500. The $372 of extra interest earnings with the wire house is insufficient to cover the $500 of extra commissions, so the discount house has a $128 advantage in the $25,000 account. Again, that is hardly enough to sway your thinking either way.

The numbers in a comparison of two $50,000 accounts would exactly double. This would make the advantage for the discount house $256 over the wire house. However, a $50,000 account might be able to negotiate some form of discount on the commissions at the wire house. If it were granted $45 commissions instead of $50, the $5 savings on 50 roundturn trades would equal $250, or almost exactly enough to overcome the discounter's previous $256 advantage.

The percentage of capital divided between T-bills and the cash surplus changes slightly in the $100,000 account. In the examples for the smaller accounts, I had allocated about 75% to T-bills and 25% to cash at the discount house, and then I assumed identical numbers for the wire house. The 75-25 split is about correct when you realize that the discounter requires 10% in cash right off the top. Another 15% in cash to cover price fluctuations would be about right, for paper losses in a scale trading account could fluctuate by that much in a short time in a volatile market. It would be imprudent to keep less than 25% in cash with a discount house until your account is sufficiently large to allow proper diversification. I suggest that this would mean that you should have $100,000 or more in your account before reducing your cash percentage below 25%.

A $100,000 account could hold $80,000 worth of T-bills (at a cost of $75,200) and $24,800 in cash, but I would not try to get it any tighter than that. With $80,000 of T-bills, the two accounts would each earn $4,800 of interest, but the wire house account would earn an extra $1,488 of interest on the $24,800 of cash in the money market fund, for total interest income of $6,288. At $30 per roundturn on the 100 trades, the commission cost with the discounter would be $3,000, or a net difference of $1,800 between the $4,800 of interest earnings and $3,000 of commission costs. The account at the wire house might now have earned an even larger discount, so it would be paying a $40 commission per roundturn, or $4,000 for 100 trades. That leaves $2,288 of net income after deducting the $4,000 of commission costs from the $6,288 of interest income. Again, the $488 advantage to the wire house ($2,288 less $1,800) is inconsequential in an account of this size.

The very large client at the wire house may request — and probably will receive — the house's ultimate discount rates. These rates are called "hedge rates," and they are equal to those charged to the corporations which do their commodity hedging through these firms. An average hedge commission rate might approximate $20 per roundturn (even as low as $8 in some cases), or $10 *less* than the commissions charged by the discount house. The commission saving to a $200,000 account making 200 trades and saving $10 per roundturn would be $2,000 to go with the $12,576 (twice $6,288 shown above), or $14,576, compared with $3,600 (twice the $1,800 shown above) at the discount house. That's nearly $11,000 in favor of the wire house.

The amount of commission you will pay with a full-service broker depends upon your ability to negotiate. I have negotiated $20 to $25 rates for the accounts I manage. (One wire house broker offered me $12 rates, but I refused, saying that he could not afford to keep an eye on my clients' accounts if he didn't earn any money. It was worth it to pay more to insure that he was watching the accounts with me.)

In all of these illustrations, I used a 6% interest rate for the calculations, and it was the interest earned on the money market account which allowed the wire house account to compete evenly with the discount house. If interest rates fall, the earnings from the money market fund will decrease, swinging the advantage slightly toward the discount house; however, if we start to see double-digit interest rates again, the advantage will swing dramatically in favor of the wire houses. Not only would the interest paid on the money market reserves increase over the zero interest rate earnings of the cash reserves held with the discount broker, but it is likely that commodity prices would again start oscillating through wider ranges, necessitating that margin requirements be increased. This would force the discount houses to require you to maintain an even larger cash reserve to cover their 10% cash-margin requirements. This would impose an additional interest forfeiture penalty upon your account.

The foregoing examples of interest earnings approximately equaling the spread between discount and full-service commissions in accounts under $100,000 in size represent tangible evidence that there is neither an advantage nor a disadvantage in dealing with either discount brokers or wire houses. On the other hand, there are various intangible factors which each individual trader must assess for himself before determining which type of broker he will choose.

The most obvious of the intangibles is research. How much is research worth to you? The discount houses plainly say that they are there only to execute orders and do not provide research. This is precisely why they can offer the discount commissions. They do not employ a staff of analysts earning six-figure incomes. Personally, I want access to those analysts, and I am willing to pay the higher commissions to be able to reach them.

A scale trader is very much like a long-term stock buyer or a commodity "position trader." All three are taking the long-range approach, willing to hold a position until it eventually rises in price. In my opinion, all three need periodic commentary from an expert stock or commodity analyst. The stock buyer and the commodity position trader can use the advice which may help them to decide how long to hold a position before finally liquidating it. The scale trader hasn't much choice but to stay with a position once a scale has been commenced, but advice from his firm's research staff may help him to determine the best level from which to start. Unless a trader is thoroughly experienced and has the ability to interpret crop reports, weather data, international events, political actions, and the myriad of other factors which may influence commodity prices, he has no alternative but to deal with the wire house to take advantage of their research. If he prefers to rely on his hunches, he will probably do very poorly.

A second intangible item to be contemplated is the difference in margin requirements between discounters and wire houses and in their rules relative to your meeting their margin calls.

Minimum margin requirements are set by the respective exchanges for each of the commodity futures contracts which they trade. These minimums are subject to review by the CFTC, but the exchanges set the requirements as they determine appropriate according to volatility and liquidity. Minimum requirements may be raised or lowered as market conditions dictate, and the new minimums become retroactive to include all open contracts on the books at the various brokerage houses.

The brokerage houses are obliged to require that customers meet the minimum margin requirements, but if the house deems it advisable to ask for higher margins, it may. Very few houses which deal with the public keep their margin requirements at exchange minimums.

If the exchange minimum for a particular futures contract is $1,000, a typical discount broker may require $1,500, while a wire house may require only $1,300 to small accounts and $1,200 to large accounts. The reason why the discounter sets its requirements so high is to reduce the necessity for frequent margin calls. Employees of the discount firm are primarily order-takers and do not have the broker/client relationships which Account Executives have at wire houses. Therefore, it is more difficult for discount brokers to enforce margin calls.

There are three types of margin calls: margin calls, T-bill calls, and cash deficit T-bill calls.

The most familiar is the margin call. It is issued when an account which uses only cash for margin deposits has its equity fall below the margin amount required to hold all its positions. For example, an account which starts with $5,000 might purchase four contracts of a commodity for which the margin requirement is $1,000 per contract, or $4.000. This account has excess equity of $1.000. However, if the commodity declines in price so that there is a paper loss of $300 per contract, or a total of $1,200, the excess has been consumed, the equity has been reduced to $3,800, and a margin call for $200 is issued for the purpose of restoring the equity to the required $4,000. Most houses will give you two days to meet the call. If it is not met within the allotted time, the brokerage house has the right to liquidate sufficient contracts from the account to reduce the margin requirement to a level which is covered by the remaining equity.

Incidentally, one of the advantages in dealing with a wire house as opposed to a discount house is the manner in which you are permitted to meet margin calls. The discount house cannot accept your statement that the check is in the mail if it is late in arriving, for they don't know you personally. It may be true that you did mail a check but as a matter of sound business practice they must adhere firmly to their rules and insist that you meet your calls promptly, or they will sell you out. The only way for you to counter that problem is to either maintain surplus equity (earning no interest) in your account or to be available for a telephone call at all times and to be prepared to wire funds. The bank charges for wiring funds can become a costly item for a small account. If you are dealing with a wire house, it is likely that your broker knows you well enough to vouch for your veracity and delay his margin department for a day or two if there is a problem with the mail. In that case, you or your spouse could drop off a check on the way to work and avoid being sold out.

The T-bill call is issued to accounts which have U.S. Treasury bills and cash on deposit for margin, but the cash portion of the account is inadequate to meet the house's margin requirements. For example, an account might be opened with $50,000 cash, and the client instructs the house to purchase $50,000 worth of one-year T-bills to be used as collateral for margin. The T-bills might cost about $45,000, so there is $5,000 of cash surplus remaining in the account. The discount broker requires that accounts which use T-bills for margin may meet the margin requirements 90% with T-bills and 10% with cash; thus, if this account immediately purchased commodities futures contracts requiring $40,000 margin, it would need $36,000 worth of T-bills and $4,000 in cash, which it has, along with a $1,000 cash surplus. If the commodities decline $2,000 in value, that loss is deducted from the cash portion of the equity, reducing the cash to only $3,000 instead of the $4,000 required. The house will not be too concerned about this account, for it still has the $50,000 of T-bills and $3,000 of cash. The house will again grant two days for you to meet a T-bill call, which may be met by mailing a check if it can arrive in two days, by restoration of equity through price improvement within those two days, or by wiring funds on the second day. If the T-bill call is not met, the house will liquidate a portion of the T-bills to put enough cash into the account to bring the T-bills and cash into proper balance.

The cash deficit T-bill call is similar to the T-bill call. Using the same example as the preceding paragraph, if a sudden break in prices causes a large paper loss of, say, $8,000, the entire cash equity has been consumed, and the account is subject to a cash deficit T-bill call of $3,000. Because the house has been obliged to cover your paper losses with $3,000 of its own capital, it will require that you meet a cash deficit T-bill call immediately. It must be met by bank wire the same day. If it is not met, the house will redeem a portion of your T-bills immediately. If necessary, the house may also liquidate some commodity contracts.

I have previously mentioned the necessity of discount brokers keeping margin requirements high for self-protection, but further elaboration is in order here. They say in their literature that you have two days in which to meet margin calls, but that is not true. Cash deficit T-bill calls are due instantly, and when you tell them that you have arranged for your bank to wire funds, they will call the bank to verify it. If you have not wired the funds, you will be sold out immediately. The reasons the discounter must keep a hair trigger on margin calls while the wire house has some flexibility are two: 1) a renege at a discount house is almost uncollectable, and 2) the discount house has no Account Executive to hold responsible for a renege. At the wire house, if the customer reneges, the loss is usually deducted from the Account Executive's paycheck.

If a customer of a major wire house reneges, it is relatively easy for the house to sue him, for he probably has been doing business with a branch office in his hometown, and they have an attorney on retainer in that town who has the specific responsibility of handling these cases. As long as he is on retainer, it costs them nothing to sue. With the discounter, however, the story is different, for their clients are scattered all over the country and they may maintain only the single home office and transact all of their business by toll-free telephone lines. If they are hit with a renege, it would be very difficult to sue because of the expense.

A secondary reason for both types of firms to set higher than minimum margin requirements is to obtain the float on your capital. After the wire house has paid 40% of your commissions to your Account Executive, and after allocating another large percentage amount to the costs of maintaining a large research staff, their gross income per trade is probably not much different from that of the discounter. After each has deducted processing charges for executing the trades, wire charges, computerized confirmations, stationery and postage charges, rents and salaries, etc., there is very little net profit left from each execution. Where both firms earn the major portion of their incomes is from the interest on the cash credit balance in your account. When you and thousands of other people like you open an account and deposit cash for margin, the excess cash above that portion which is committed to your T-bills is ostensibly held in cash by the firm for your account; however, they take these multitudinous sums and invest the total in T-bills, keeping the interest for the house. This is why both types of firms will discourage you from using T-bills for margin, for if you do, you keep the interest, thereby depriving them of their primary source of income.

To illustrate how lucrative this T-bill income can be, consider the float carried by a medium-sized brokerage house. Large houses may have 100,000 or more commodity accounts, but consider a smaller firm with only 10,000 accounts holding free credit balances of an average of $20,000 in cash above its T-bill holdings, if any. That is $200,000,000 which the firm may put into T-bills, and if the current yield is 6%, that is a $12,000,000 profit for the firm. It is no wonder that they are satisfied to break even on commissions.

Your broker may dispute this and claim that customers' margin funds must be deposited with the clearing house for each respective exchange and for the full amount of the required margin. That is not true. The house is required to deposit only enough margin to cover the *net difference* between its customers' long and short positions; thus, if the firm has customers holding 100 contracts long and other customers holding 102 contracts short in a commodity for which the exchange's margin requirement is $1,000 per contract, the total amount which the house must deposit is not $202,000, but only $2,000. It has collected $202,000 from the clients, but it is unnecessary to deposit more than $2,000, so they put the balance into T-bills and keep the interest.

Among the advantages of dealing with discount houses is the ability to trade nearby contracts when scaling in small accounts which earn no interest to offset the commission difference. In selecting delivery months to trade, I have suggested that you compromise between trading the nearbys which are more active and therefore more liquid and the distant contracts which would save you rollover commissions but are illiquid. This decision is obviated if you use the discount house, because you can afford to pay those few small extra commissions which will probably be more than covered by the extra trades which you will realize in the more volatile nearby contracts. However, the discount house loses this edge as soon as your account is large enough to earn interest.

Another advantage in dealing with the discount brokers is that they may allow you a commission rebate which may be applied against the cost of having your own quote machine. However, if your trading volume is large enough to warrant having a quote machine, you already qualify for very deep discounts at a wire house, and the savings would cover the cost of the quote machine and probably a part-time secretary.

The discount brokers claim in their advertising that they are fast in reporting trades back to you. I have found that to be untrue. I opened an account with a discount house to test their claims, and I found their confirmations of executions to be much slower than those of a wire house. I have my own quote machine, so I could see when I was entitled to a fill, and after allowing a reasonable period of time, I would call to inquire. A startling high percentage of the time the trades had not been reported — even after an hour or two of waiting. I suspect that this is because the discount broker probably did not have its own traders on the floor of the exchange and had to farm out orders. The floor broker who handled the order was probably employed by another firm and gave more attention to orders from his primary employer.

The same might be said for prices on executions. I never got the feeling that I was getting the best possible executions at all times with the discounter. It is impossible to ascertain the truth, but I liked my executions with the wire houses better.

One compelling reason for trading with a wire house is that you will have your own Account Executive who will not only pass along the firm's research, but can also assist you in ways upon which no tangible value may be placed. Once a good rapport is established with the Account Executive, his opportunities to assist you become limitless. An excellent example would be if you were scale trading orange juice and held four contracts when a sudden over-night freeze hit Florida. The Account Executive is in the office probably before you are out of bed (at least in California), and he reads that the freeze is so severe that orange juice may lock limit up for five consecutive days. Without even calling you, he will cancel your sell orders, thereby giving you $4,000 profit per contract instead of $400. Discount houses can't do this, for there is no Account Executive assigned to your account.

A similar situation could exist on a morning following a pig crop report. Pork bellies could open limit down, rally to trade limit up, and then collapse to close limit down. Unless you are monitoring the pork belly market closely, you might not be aware that you have purchased one or two contracts. You are out of luck with the discount house, but your Account Executive at the wire house has entered your offsets and cashed your winners. How much is that worth in discount commissions?

The discount house has a pool of order-takers handling your account, and they have your open orders commingled with those of many other customers. This makes it difficult for the customer to ascertain whether he has a particular order entered. As an example, I was entering a series of scale orders one time when I was distracted by another phone call. The orders I was entering were sufficiently far away from the market that I was able to hang up the phone with the expectation of calling back to complete entry of the orders. I was certain exactly where I was on the scale at the time of the interruption, but I asked the order-taker for confirmation. He said that information would not be available until the following day. That could never happen with an Account Executive at a wire house. That is because you work with a single Account Executive instead of a team of order-takers. I absolutely could not believe that the person to whom I was talking had no way to check my open orders until they were filed the following morning. They make you dictate all your orders into a recorder for their protection, but the client appears to have little protection.

The wire house Account Executive can help you in another way. Let us say you are considering scaling copper and cotton. Your capital is adequate for trading only one of these commodities. You cannot instruct the order-taker at the discount house to enter scale orders for both commodities and then cancel the second scale as soon as the top order is executed in the first. There is no way they could monitor such an order. However, the wire house Account Executive could. Your alternative with the discounter is to try to guess which of the two will drop to your desired level first and enter buy orders only in that one, but the other could drop and rally intra-day, causing you to miss an opportunity of cashing a winner. If that happens only once a year, it would pay the commission difference.

I have tried to give you some of the tangible and intangible items which you should consider in determining whether you want to deal with discount houses, and to this point I consider the matter pretty much a choice of personal preference. At certain size levels there might be a slight advantage one way or the other in commissions. Having an empathetic account broker and having his firm's research available may be arguments in favor of the wire house. However, there is one overwhelming factor for you to consider, and that might swing you to the wire houses.

Your most important consideration when weighing whether to do business with a discount commission broker should be protection of your capital from loss through malfeasance, misfeasance, or fraud perpetrated by the brokerage firm or its employees. There is no such thing yet as the Securities Investors Protection Corporation which protects stock and bond investors; therefore, it is mandatory that you do everything you can to protect yourself. In my opinion, this means dealing only with firms which are *clearing* members of *all* of the commodity exchanges.

When the silver market collapsed following the Texans' unsuccessful effort to corner the market, it was reported that one major wire house was on the brink of collapse because of an overextension of credit to the conspirators. The failure of this house would have had a temporarily devastating effect on the clients of the firm, but they would have survived. That is because the house was a clearing member of all principal commodity exchanges. All open commodity futures contracts would have been transferred out to other clearing member firms, and they could have been liquidated smoothly. Cash credit balances in the accounts of the clients of the firm would have been subject to the bankruptcy laws, but any client loss there would have been minimal when compared to the problems which would

179

have arisen with the futures contracts if they could not have been transferred to other firms.

If a non-clearing firm is forced into bankruptcy, all open futures contracts become a part of the bankruptcy proceeding and are frozen until the bankruptcy action is resolved. This can take a year or two, during which time futures contracts are expiring, thereby necessitating receipt or delivery of the commodity. Can you imagine the problems a person would have if he is tendered (delivered) ten contracts of pork bellies against the long position he held at the time of the declaration of bankruptcy? The pork bellies might be deemed not retenderable because of undefined ownership, and the confusion would only increase while this perishable commodity goes unclaimed.

Under the best of circumstances, it would require a month or two for a non-clearing firm under Chapter 11 to get its affairs sufficiently in order to reopen trading for its customers. Those customers would have been locked into their positions during that time, unable to buy or sell. It could be catastrophic for a person who is long a sizable number of contracts and cannot sell them in a collapsing market. By the time the firm is able to resume trading, his losses could total tens of thousands of dollars or more.

It is inadequate to say that a person could take an offsetting short position at another house until the bankruptcy freeze is lifted, because the contracts could expire during an extended proceeding. Furthermore, the client might have insufficient capital to deposit the required margin at the second house. It is also possible that he had an open order which *might* have been executed on the fateful day that the firm suspended operations, and he doesn't know whether he is still holding that position, a part of it, or none at all.

As with the clearing member firm, cash in the accounts of clients of a bankrupt non-clearing firm become a part of the bankruptcy proceeding and might be repaid at a small fraction of the original value. Each account owner becomes a "general unsecured creditor" and receives settlement along with all the other creditors of the company. After the enormous legal fees are deducted, creditors are usually lucky to receive ten cents on the dollar. However, it is likely that the clearing member is a division of a major firm, and the parent firm probably would make full restitution to prevent tarnishing the image of the entire firm. If the losses from the collapse of the commodity division are greater than the parent chooses to cover, it is possible that the division — and all its cash debits — could be sold to another major wire house which is effectively purchasing all the commodity accounts and commodity business of the firm. The new firm might possibly make restitution of the deficient cash balances.

This type of bailout is unlikely at the discount houses, for it is probable that only a wire house would have sufficient capital to assume the debits of another firm, and it is improbable that a wire house would be willing to buy accounts which have been dealing for discount commissions. There is too much risk that as soon as the wire house has paid off the debits and the clients have received their cash, that the clients might then transfer away to another discounter.

I suspect that in the event of the collapse of a commodity house, you would have very little chance of avoiding a chaotic problem unless your broker is a clearing member of all of the commodity exchanges. Remember what I said earlier: No customer has ever lost a single cent as the result of the failure of any commodity clearing house.

The demise of a commodity firm need not come from external forces; it could happen internally. We recently witnessed the failure of a huge commodity dealer in Florida. Their sales were reputed to be $140 million, but much of that money was never invested for the customers' accounts, and instead was misappropriated for the use of the owners of the firm. Although their business was primarily gold and silver bullion, there was no gold, and court officers found only fifty blocks of wood painted to resemble gold bars in the firm's huge vault.

Times are good for commodity brokerage firms today, and to say they are proliferating is an understatement; they are springing up like weeds everywhere. Especially the discount houses. It is difficult to foretell how well they will do if commodity trading volume declines. As long as volume stays high, these new operators will probably stick around, but if volume declines, they might fold their tents and disappear in the night. One particular problem is the temptation which is there for dealers to begin to use customers' funds for speculating in commodities for the house. We saw this when gold and silver had the big run in 1979-80. Many new dealers came into the business at that time and got carried away with the apparently easy profits available in the precious metals. They used customer funds to buy gold and silver for their own accounts, and when prices collapsed, so did the firms. Clients who had bought low and sold higher expected to receive their profits, but instead received only a bankruptcy court's notice that they had lost everything, including the original investment.

I can't help but notice the ads which discount brokers have been running, undercutting each other to expand their client lists. I suppose this is all right during a rising market, but if volume recedes and they continue this fierce competition, they may pull each other down.

Because each exchange guarantees through its clearing house that accounts will be transferred away from problem firms to financially responsible firms, the exchanges set fairly high financial requirements on clearing member firms to insure that the accounts will be acceptable to the new firm. Each clearing member firm is subjected to fairly strict quarterly audits (as well as spot audits by the CFTC). They are required to maintain 6% of their assets in cash, and if that percentage declines to 4%, they are subjected to monthly audits. If that figure falls below 4%, the accounts are transferred to other clearing members.

In summary, I would say that the financial integrity of the broker should be paramount in your selection of the firm with which to do your trading The availability of research and the services of an Account Executive should also be worthy of consideration. Interest earnings from a money market account is important. Margin requirements, executions, reporting time, etc., are minor considerations. After all of these considerations then one may consider the advantages of reduced commissions.

I have presented the evidence. Now you must make the judgment.

* * *

All of the foregoing text in this chapter was repeated verbatim from earlier editions of this book, with minor changes for clarity or a few sentences added to bring comments current with today's conditions. Now I will present the new evidence which tells me that a person should *never* — *repeat NEVER* — do business with a discount house under any circumstances. I will start slowly and conclude with the blockbuster.

One of the most annoying things about dealing with discount houses is that they are so understaffed that they are very slow in reporting trades — *if they report them at all!* I still have one managed account with a discount house, and I swear that they do not report four out of five trades. I have quarreled with them countless times about the problem, and they have a standard answer: "We called and got a busy signal, so we didn't try again." (When my full-service brokers get a busy signal they call until they reach me or enter the offsets for me.) I reminded the supervisor on the desk at the discount house that they are *obliged under the law* to report those trades. He demonstrated the caliber of people they hire by telling me, "We meet that legal obligation by *mailing* you a confirmation." It takes three or four days for mail to go from Chicago to California — probably with a weekend thrown in. Six days without notice is ridiculous!

In case you are wondering why I sometimes don't know when I am entitled to an execution, please remember that I have hundreds of open orders working at most times, and I cannot take the time each morning to check several hundred open orders — all entered at different levels because of differing sizes in different accounts.

That is a minor problem, but it occurs only with discount brokers. It never happens with full-service brokers.

Another problem with dealing with discounters which is NOT minor but which could cost you tons of money is their penchant for changing margin requirements *without notice.* I'll give you an example of what a discounter did to me: I was scale trading a very large partnership account, and among the things we were buying were the grains and the meats. A USDA Grain Crop Report was issued one Thursday after the close. It was devastating, and all of the grains were down sharply on Friday. After the close on Friday the USDA released the Pig Crop Report, which was just as devastating. Monday morning the hogs and pork bellies were nearly limit down, and the grains continued their tumble. I have more guts than Dick Tracy, so I continued buying aggressively. Tuesday the discount house lost *ITS* nerve and raised margin requirements by 81% (!). I was so angry with the desk supervisor who was making the demand that I hung up on him. Three minutes later my phone rang, and it was the president of the discount firm saying, "You will have that $150,000 here *IN ONE HOUR,* or we will liquidate the account!"

I was livid, but he had our money, so there was nothing I could do but to start selling contracts to meet the call. I could see the prices rallying smartly — as they usually do after such a sharp break — so I tried to stall and sell only three, four, or five contracts at a time. They hounded me all day to sell more, but prices were still rallying, so I took the phone off the hook. By the end of the day most of the prices had recovered fully, but we had been *forced* to liquidate one-third of the account near the lows of the break. We would never have had a problem if they had not practically doubled the margin requirements, but *they* lost their nerve and crushed us

By the end of the month the grains and meats were making new contract highs, but we had lost money by being sold out forcibly. Most of the partners were unaware of what happened, so they couldn't understand why we had failed to make huge profits under those ideal conditions of a sharply breaking market followed by a smart rally. They probably thought I had lost *my* nerve. Fortunately for the owner of that firm, I calmed down, and what I really lost was the urge to kill.

That is a hair-raising tale, but it is penny ante compared with what they pulled at another discount house which lost its nerve. (I was not involved with this one, but everything I am about to tell you is not hearsay; it was reported widely in the media.) This story has nothing to do with scale trading, but it is frightening, and it is absolutely true:

Do you remember the October day in 1987 when the stock market dropped 508 points? The Dow Jones Industrial Average had already fallen about 26% before that day, so many speculators were trading the Standard & Poor's 500 Stock Index from the long side (betting on a rally).

The margin requirement on an S&P 500 futures contract was $40,000. Some speculators at this infamous discount house held ten, twenty, or fifty or more of the S&P contracts. The 508 point collapse came close to wiping out the entire margin on each of these contracts. As with the other discount house, this discounter lost its nerve and *raised the margin __500%__!* They also gave *all* of their clients one hour to get the money in. $200,000 cash in one hour *per contract*!

I don't care how rich a person is, not many people keep $200,000 in a checking account. Those trading ten contracts were called upon to produce $2,000,000 in cash in one hour. Obviously, not one person met the call, and they were all sold out. The market rallied 250 points that first day, although it retained only about 150 of that. It regained the other 100 points the next day, and it hasn't looked back since. Early in 1994 we have seen the market rally for six straight years since that infamous day.

The people who were sold out formed a group, hired an attorney, and brought a class action against the firm. The judge threw the case out, stating that when the people signed the Commodity Account Agreement form at the time they opened their accounts they agreed to allow the brokerage house the right to raise margins by any amount it chose *without notice* and without consideration for time.

The irony of that story is that the head of that firm goes on advertising on TV, "We give ALL of our accounts exchange minimum margin requirements." Then in the fine print he mumbles, "Of course, we reserve the right to raise margins under unusual conditions." He cost his clients millions upon millions of dollars, and yet he is able to continue to run that ad. Why? Because that kind of advertising is not regulated!

That is not the only time that margins were raised 500% and the customers were given one hour to submit the cash. It had happened at least once before, but the number of people involved was smaller, and the case drew less publicity; however, every client of that firm trading a particular commodity options contract defaulted, and the loss was in the millions.

You may ask if this couldn't happen with a full-service firm. Yes it could, but it is unlikely to happen because the full-service firm's commodity business is probably only a minor portion of their total business. If they lose heavily the next time the stock market collapses — which it will do again — because speculators trading the S&P walk away from $50 million in losses, leaving the commodity department holding the bag, the full-service firm will simply take that amount out of petty cash to save the commodity department.

Most of the full-service commodity houses are subsidiaries of major investment banking firms which also do stocks, bonds, mutual funds, underwritings, etc. The parent would do everything in its power to avoid a problem in the commodities subsidiary to protect the reputation of the other parts of the firm. Furthermore, many of the giant investment bankers are owned by an insurance company or some similar investment giant with separate subsidiaries doing real estate, credit cards, or similar high-profile dealings with the public. If the stock market collapse took the securities firm which is the parent of the commodities firm down the tubes also, the insurance company probably would put up a billion or so dollars to save all of the subsidiaries to preserve the reputation of the insurance firm and its other famous subsidiaries.

Commodities is 100% of the business with the discounters, and there isn't a one which could take a hit of more than a few million dollars.

Now the biggie: There was a time when I did a lot of business with discounters. Naturally, I was concerned about the financial integrity of the firm, so one day I called the house counsel for the firm. I said, "When I opened my first account with you it was only $10,000, and I appreciate all of the things that you did to help me get started. Now I have over $1 million with your firm, and I need to know the straight story. What happens to my clients' money if your firm goes belly up?" His answer: *"I don't know."* He wasn't saying that he did not know the law. He explained that the law was being interpreted two different ways, and since the two interpretations had never been tested in court, it was impossible to determine at this time which interpretation would prevail in court. I'll try to explain:

The law with which we are concerned is the one about your account being transferred overnight from your clearing member firm to another clearing member firm if the first clearing member firm goes broke. The exchanges like to claim that (in their interpretation) your account will be transferred, but the Commodity Futures Trading Commission says they interpret the law to say that you become an unsecured creditor in a bankruptcy and that your account *will not* be transferred out. I mentioned this briefly earlier in this chapter, but only in the context that it could happen to you if you were not with a *clearing member.* In the ten years since that was written I have discovered — because of this conversation with the house counsel for a giant discount firm which is a clearing member of all of the major exchange clearing houses — that no one knows for certain just what would happen.

I will give you the scenario in which I think it would be a cinch that you would never get your money back from a discount house which might be a clearing member of all of the exchanges' clearing houses: In the past when we have had a clearing member firm go bankrupt, it has always been an isolated single case. No problem. Transfer the accounts overnight. But if we get the kind of smash that I think the stock market is going to take, we could see massive numbers of brokerage firms going down together. The collapse of one giant could take ten other firms with it because of the huge amounts of stock owed by all firms to countless other firms on a daily basis in just the normal transfer of stock from the selling firm to the buying firm. The collapse of those ten firms could take ten more with each of them. There could be chaos in Wall Street. If that happens, it is a safe bet that commodity brokerage houses would be collapsing, too, and I have to believe that it would be impossible to transfer your account to another brokerage firm overnight. Because the discount houses are tiny in comparison to the full-service firms, they would be the first to go. Surely the CFTC would step in and lock your account into the bankruptcy proceedings of the discounter. Probably all that you would get back from an account with a discounter would be carfare to the poorhouse.

I have described a worst case scenario in which hundreds of brokerage houses go down together. Perhaps that is extreme. But what would it take for the CFTC to step in? Five going broke together? Ten? Twenty? Nobody knows. But I don't want to have to guess. I have an account with a full-service broker, and it pays $20 per roundturn. Just recently I received that house's audited annual statement. It showed that they had $13 billion in assets. Of course, most of that belonged to the customers, but after deducting the clients' $11.7 billion, the firm's net capital is $1.3 billion — with a "B". One "giant" discounter advertises that it has $400 million in customer accounts. After deducting the customers' holdings, this discount house's net worth is a mere $20 million! With an "M".

187

If that firm has a lot of S&P index futures traders, and if the stock market takes a dive, the firm's paltry $20 million of equity could vanish in a day.

A minor item which is not of earth shaking proportions but which could come into play if a discount firm goes under and the accounts are *safely* transferred to another clearing member without delay, is the matter of the commissions which the new house charges. Nothing says they must give you the same low rate you got before. Nor does anything say there is a limit to what they can charge you. Remember, the clearing house wants to place your account with another clearing member which has unquestionable financial resources. You may have been doing very well with your scale trading while paying $30 roundturn commissions, but the new house could be an industry giant which tries to discourage one-contract traders, so they may charge a minimum of $130 per roundturn. If yours was a small account with as few as ten open positions, the new higher rate is at least a $1,000 penalty when those contracts are sold or *transferred* (in case you think you have been shafted and elect to transfer your account to a firm which charges only $50 roundturn) to a third firm, in which case you will pay the $130 commissions *at the time of transfer* at the brokerage house to which your account has been assigned and then $50 more as the contracts are sold at the third firm. Now your undeserved penalty is $1,500. It may never happen, but why risk it?

The firm to which your account has been transferred may also have a policy of setting extremely high minimum margin requirements to discourage one-contract traders from doing business with them. If their margin requirement for accounts of your size are double what you had at the previous firm, you may find yourself getting an immediate margin call. If you are unable to meet the call, contracts will be sold out of your account. They couldn't care less about you. They inherited your account along with several thousands of others, some of which were very large and worth keeping. The brokerage firm would probably grant those large accounts exchange minimum margins and their very lowest commission rates.

Keep in mind that wire houses are called "full-service," and that is exactly what you get. I try to make *The Scale Trader* a teaching letter, and there is an item which I failed to cover in earlier editions of the book that I repeat each few months in the newsletter. It has to do with "full-service," so this is the perfect spot to cover it:

The commodity research which is available from full-service brokers is indispensable. I can't imagine anyone trying to trade any commodity system without research and an occasional call from your broker to alert you to the latest news development. In the case of a Pig Crop Report, you may not even be aware that a report has been released, and it is a cinch that your discount broker — the clerk on the order desk — knows nothing about it and wouldn't call you if he did. But Pig Crop Reports are notorious for being other than what was expected, and the morning after the release of the report the hogs and pork bellies may open up or down the limit. Indeed, it is not unusual for them to lock limit up or down for two or three days after the release of a shocking report. If you are scaling pork bellies, buying each penny down and selling each penny up, you *must* be made aware by your broker of the expected price movement due the following morning. A discount broker is not going to call you, but a full-service broker is going to call you immediately upon release of the report. He might save you thousands of dollars, which will pay the difference in commissions for the next five years.

For example, you are buying bellies at 5000, 4900, 4800, 4700, etc., and you already own the top three contracts. They closed this day at 4725. The report is released, and it is shocking because production number are 4% over last year instead of the 2% under everyone had been expecting. Floor traders react to the report by saying they expect bellies to lock limit down (2 cents) at least three days, and maybe four. You are unavailable by phone for a few days, and when you finally speak to your discount broker, he informs you that they bought two contracts for you at 4525, two more at 4325, two more at 4125, and one more each at 4030 and 4000 (because the first trade the fourth day was at 4030, followed by a slightly lower dip to 3980 before closing at 4000). The current price is 4000, so you have a 1950-point loss in those eight contracts, which is $7,800. (I am ignoring the first three contracts because the loss would be the same at the discounter or the full-service firm in those three contracts.)

If you have your account with a full-service house, and if you have signed the limited-power-of-attorney form (which I recommend that you do), your broker was fully aware of the results of the Pig Crop

189

Report, and if he was unable to reach you to tell you the news, he has gone ahead and cancelled your open buy orders until there is free trading again, in which case he buys seven contracts at 4030 and one at 4000. He saved you $7,080. That is worth a lifetime of commissions.

This is the advice I give in the newsletter: In case you were actually in touch with your full-service broker, and he informed you immediately after the release of the report that the bellies were going to be sharply lower for a few days, you would simply check with him the next morning to ascertain the "pre-opening call," which is an indication derived from a poll taken among floor brokers, that the bellies are expected to open limit down the first day, you cancel your buy orders and wait for the market to open. If the bellies actually open limit down at 4525, you avoided buying the 4700 and 4600 contracts at 4525, but in case something happens which might send the price racing upward, you enter a buy stop order for two contracts about 30 points above "limit down," or 4555. The price does not come off of limit all day, so your day order expires.

You check with your broker again the next day for the pre-opening call, and you are told the price is expected to drop another limit, to 4325. After the market opens limit down at 4325, you enter a buy stop for four contracts at 4355. Again, the price stays limit down all day, so this day's stop order expires.

You do the same thing again the next day, except that you now want to buy six contracts at 4155 stop. Again, no action, and the day order expires.

The fourth day the pre-opening call is for the price to open "50 to 150 lower." You are on the phone with your broker at the precise moment that the bellies market opens, and if it opens limit down, you use the buy stop again; however, if the pre-opening call was accurate and there is active trading, you give your broker a market order to buy the six contracts you have not purchased, plus you reinstate your scale to buy at 4100, 4000, 3900, etc. You buy seven contracts when the price opens at 4030, plus one more when the price drifts below 4000.

The reverse of all of this would be true if you are selling into a very bullish Pig Crop Report. As long as the pre-opening call indicates a limit up opening, you cancel your sell orders and enter sell stop day orders 30 points under the limit up opening. You repeat the action daily until there is an indication of less than a limit up move, and you are on the phone with your broker to monitor the opening. If the opening surprises with another limit up move, you enter the sell stops. If, instead, there is free trading, you immediately enter a market order to sell all of the contracts which would have been sold on your cancelled scale, plus you reenter the scale orders to sell the contracts whose prices are still above the current trading price. (This would happen if you had held, say, a dozen contracts and the limit moves took the price up only 8 or 9 cents instead of the 12 cents you needed to complete the scale.) By cancelling ahead of limit moves, you either save bundles on the buy side or reap huge bonuses on the sell side.

This technique is especially handy if the price locks limit down the first two days but opens limit down the third day and then puts on a big rally to actually close higher the third day. You bought all six of your contracts (4700 to 4200) on the stop at 4155, and if the price closes the day at 4350, you cash the 4200 contract (which you bought at 4155) at 4300.

You may be able to get the Pig Crop numbers and the pre-opening call numbers from a discounter, but that is on the assumption that you were aware that a report was due and that you took the initiative to call. It's all automatic if you are dealing with a full-service broker.

I used pork bellies for this illustration, but you would follow the same technique after an Orange Crop Report, or a Grain Crop Report, or any one of the numerous USDA or other government agency reports which can be very shocking and which can produce limit moves. Similar action may be expected following a weather report indicating an Arctic Express is moving into New England and is expected to cover an area all of the way to the Ohio Valley and possibly as far south as Florida. That could send heating oil scooting upward, and it almost surely would send orange juice limit up.

I repeat, one has to be out of his mind to have a commodity account with a discount house. Because of the low commissions available at full-service houses, the interest which may be earned on cash in the account, the oversight and protection which the broker gives to your account, and especially because of the financial integrity of the firms. I submit that you are depriving yourself of essential services, and you may be foolishly risking every penny in your account if it is with a discount commodity broker.

XXI

The Managed Account

There aren't too many people who would consider removing their own tonsils, and I question the wisdom of the person who writes his own will. The person who prepares his own income tax return in this age of increasingly complex tax laws is probably throwing money away if he doesn't enlist the aid of a qualified tax attorney or accountant who can apprise him of all the deductions and write-offs available. A person pays thousands of dollars in fees to an architect and interior decorator to design and furnish a home or office according to the designer's taste because he considers the professional to be better qualified than himself. This is because we respect the skill of these professionals, skill acquired through years of training and experience. We pay dearly for their advice on nearly everything. Nearly everything, that is, except investing. Investing seems to be the one area in which virtually every person considers himself to be expertly qualified. There are fewer do-it-yourselfers at the lumber yard than in the boardrooms of brokerage offices.

One thing I have never been able to fathom is the fetish people have for managing the investment of their own money. The only possible explanation that I can think of is that they want to be able to go to cocktail parties and brag about their winners — they never mention the losers. Either that, or it is the thrill they feel when cashing a winner, knowing they acquired additional resources without labor. Something for nothing. Psychologists must love this subject. I think it must be a strawberry patch for behavioral research and analysis.

Perhaps one reason why people try to do their own investing is the frightful record of the majority of professional money managers. It can hardly foster faith in professional managers to read that one of the major New York banking trusts which employs numerous trust account managers bought IBM stock on 236 different days and sold IBM stock on 125 days during 1977. Since 1977 had only 253 trading days it is apparent that this trust department frequently was both buying and selling IBM stock on the same day. It is probable that on some occasions one of the trust's managers was selling while another was buying simultaneously. When queried about this, the bank explained, ". . . securities may be bought to serve investment objectives of certain clients at times when reasons unrelated to investment judgment — need for cash for taxes or other disbursements, for instance — make it advantageous for other accounts to sell them." Hogwash. Each portfolio manager has the fiduciary obligation to get every eighth-point possible for his client, so when he buys he is saying the stock has absolutely no chance to fall as much as another eighth, and when he sells he is saying there is no chance for the stock to rise another eighth. There is something wrong with the system when two managers working within a single trust department, having identical information available, draw exactly opposite conclusions and buy from or sell to each other.

The economy went through a recession in 1957, and there was a great campaign waged to stimulate the economy. It was called "You Auto Buy Now." American Motors and Studebaker introduced a line of compact cars that sold rapidly in that depressed economy. In 1958 their two stocks soared on the New York Stock Exchange. Near the end of that year one of the major New York Stock Exchange houses conducted a poll among its brokers, asking for nominations for the three best and the three worst stock investments for the coming year of 1959 from the 1,200 listed at that time. The three stocks which drew the most votes for the probable best performance for the coming year were American Motors, Studebaker, and one other. The brokers of that same firm also voted for American Motors, Studebaker, and one other as the probable three worst performers for the coming year. How should that make an investor feel? All these brokers with the same information available picked the same two stocks for both the best and worst. That is incredible. They had 1,200 stocks from which to choose. It might have made sense if they had selected, say, an airline, a utility, and a steel stock for the best, and a railroad, an oil company, and a department store chain for the worst, but out of 1,200 stocks they picked the same two for both best and worst. Unfortunately, if you had walked into one of their offices seeking investment advice and planning to open an account, it was just a question of whether you turned left or right after entering the front door. One way you win; the other way you lose. Flip a coin. But if you are going to flip a coin to determine which broker to use, you might as well flip coins to determine which stocks to buy.

What about mutual fund managers? Their record is about as visible as possible for managed accounts. Mutual fund managers make all the same mistakes the public makes. In fact, they sometimes do worse for a reason which has nothing to do with investment judgment. They sell in a panic — like everyone else — because they don't want that next quarterly report to the fund's stockholders to show that they failed to anticipate the decline. Then they turn around and buy it all back *after* stocks have begun to soar. Their buying is also of panic proportions as they fear issuing another quarterly report which might indicate they failed to anticipate the turnaround. This practice is called "window dressing."

I have seen the sales kit distributed among the commodity brokers of one of the largest brokerage houses. It extols the virtues of the nine types of managed accounts the firm offers in commodities, intending that the salesmen bring managed accounts into the firm. Some of the information contained therein defies belief. "The results given are hypothetical rather than actual," it begins. "Actual executions may not have been comparable to those used in hypothetical results because of range of opening and impact of resting orders on opening. Limit moves must be considered, for executions may not be possible on such days. In certain programs, commissions and additional charges have been deducted, while in other programs they may not have been deducted." Remarkably, they choose to ignore the commissions on the hundreds of trades — that amount is only equal to about 50% of your committed capital. Worse yet, they ignore conditions which would make it impossible for you to trade — such as limit moves. They are saying that they accept all the benefits of the limit move when it goes their way, but they refuse to accept the liability to their record when it goes against them. In other words, when the computer gives a buy signal on a breakout, they automatically assume they are in, even though it may have been impossible to buy as five consecutive upside limit moves may have occurred. This type of thing happens when an overnight freeze hits Brazil and decimates the coffee crop. You can't get into a trade for a week as prices are locked limit up with no trading, but the computer says *it* got in.

Several consecutive limit moves in one direction are frequently followed by a sudden reversal and a series of limit moves in the opposite direction. The price pauses at the turnaround point only long enough to allow the pigeons into the roost, and then the trap slams shut. Following the computer's buy and sell recommendations, the only executions you could get would be at the extremities of the move, which would be a catastrophic whipsaw. And yet, the computer says it went long at the bottom, sold out and went short at the top. Nonsense. That is hypothetical. Try it with real money. Just be sure your passport is in order in case you get locked into a position with ten contracts going limit against you for seven consecutive days.

This firm's material goes on to make some more interesting statements. "Ninety percent of those trading commodities lose money . . . It is possible and should be expected that as many as seven of every ten trades will be losses . . . Because of those two statements, odds are that an initial equity will show a loss before showing a profit . . . Since it is necessary in an active commodity account to continually probe the market, total commission costs can be very high in relation to equity." Those four statements are absolutely true — about the only truth in the kit. They negate whatever credibility they had acquired with those four statements by offering the following: "In commodity trading, for every dollar of loss there is a dollar of profit. Odds are that if as many as 90% of the people who trade will be losers, the remaining percentage will receive all the profits." That is a deliberate misstatement of fact. What about the commissions? The truth is that every time there is a commodity trade someone *may* win, but someone *must* lose, and they both will pay a commission. If the trade is a break-even trade they *both* lose, for both paid a commission. As traders take turns having winning and losing trades, the money passes back and forth, and the payment of commissions is to both traders like the action of a grater on a block of cheese. Just as surely as the grater consumes the block, so, too, will the commissions consume the two bankrolls.

One of the kit's hypothetical accounts shows a $4,500 loss for 1976 and an $11,500 gain for 1977, or a combined gain of $7,000 before commissions, making no allowance for limit moves which might have altered the record dramatically, and ignoring the possible effect upon price executions which would have resulted from this very large house making *actual* recommendations to its very large sales staff and huge clientele. In a classical contribution to history's understatements, they estimate commissions at $4,200 on the account's 140 trades, which equals $30 per trade. How can they get away with that? This firm doesn't have a single commodity which may be traded for a commission as small as $30. Their minimum commission is $50, and the average would be about $60, for a total of about $8,400 on 140 trades. Those commissions would have turned their hypothetical gross profit of $7,000 into a real net loss of $1,400.

It is very difficult to determine whether a private manager's claims of performance are accurate, for he may be showing only his best accounts, but you may have a clue when it comes to publicly offered commodity pools. They are required to publish a prospectus, and you may learn a lot by studying this document. If a footnote says the performance record is for this one account under this manager's control and does not include others because they were not operated under the same technique, you can probably assume that he ran a dozen accounts simultaneously with only minor variations in technique, and then he published the record of the best one. Those minor variations were enough to allow him to exempt them from inclusion in his overall record. Eleven of the twelve might have done poorly, but as long as one did well, that is the one he will claim demonstrates his management ability. Unfortunately, the practice is legal.

Another footnote to watch for in the prospectus of a publicly offered pool is the notation that the manager's accounts of less than a year of longevity are excluded from the record. The impression which that manager is trying to create is that it takes a year or more of faithful adherence to his trading method to accomplish the desired results. That may possibly be true, but it can also mean that a great many of his former accounts lost so much money during the first year of trading that they quit. Those who have stayed longer have been fortunate enough to catch one of the big moves, which gave them the extra capital to withstand the bombing which destroyed the new accounts.

A perfect example of this type of unethical deception occurred in the 1979-80 silver runup and collapse. This firm uses trend-following for their managed accounts, so it is accurate for them to claim that they became buyers of silver when the price moved to a new all-time high in late 1979 when the massive manipulation began. Their method would have cost them a whipsaw or two during the final quarter of 1979, but they would have been comfortably on the long side during December and the first half of January; however, it is a blatant lie for them to claim that they sold out, went short, and made another huge gain as the price retreated from the $50 high to about $10. The reason for this is simple: It was *impossible* to get short, for trading had been restricted to "for liquidation only" transactions. When panic buying of silver got out of hand, the exchanges raised margin requirements to $75,000 per contract and banned new trades by permitting only those traders who currently held positions, whether long or short, merely to liquidate without establishing new positions; therefore, it was impossible for traders who held long positions to liquidate them and simultaneously take short positions. Indeed, it was the very action of the exchanges raising the margins and restricting trading which probably precipitated the collapse. Whatever the cause, when the price of silver broke, it was down the limit twenty-two consecutive days. Many managers who publish hypothetical performance records claim to have been short during this period, but that is a false claim. That is a distortion of $100,000 in the claimed profits, which is enough to make any hypothetical account profitable.

Performance records published by managers and by the rating services which compare records of public funds (partnerships) usually contain a tainted number as part of the record. Most of these funds were offered to the public at $1,000 per unit, with about a 5% sales charge going to the salesperson who solicited the investment.

Thus, each $1,000 unit had an immediate value of only $950. The managers like to quote their records from the level of $950 rather than the proper level of $1,000. If that initial $50 is recovered, the manager claims he is 5.26% ahead, but the investor has only returned to his starting level and has a 0% gain.

It is obvious why the managers use this type of "creative accounting," but you may question why the rating service publishers participate in this self-serving scheme. The reason is that most of the public funds are trend-followers, and thus are subject to going broke (four more already this year). The publishers have an ulterior motive in perpetuating the industry to thereby keep their own publication alive, so they abet the crime in every possible way.

Similar tactics are used by publishers of services which rate newsletters. It behooves these publishers to give the letter writers every possible break; otherwise, if subscribers to the rating service realized how really bad the records of the newsletter publishers were the publisher of the rating service would run out of subscribers and be out of business. Here is an example of the egregious distortions which one rating service does for the benefit of selected newsletter publishers: Under one column he estimates the margin required to hold all of the open positions currently recommended by the newsletter. Let's say it is $8,000. Under another column he shows the gain for the year as $4,000. Under the "percentage gain for the year" he shows that as 50%. *However,* he has chosen to ignore the column which shows the deepest drawdown in a *single month* during the year, which might have been $24,000. If you had followed that writer's advice you would have lost your entire $8,000 three times over and could only now show a current gain of $4,000 if you had deposited another $8,000 (total: $32,000) in the account. There is no telling how many other months showed drawdowns of $5,000, $10,000, or $20,000 because he shows only that single worst month. Even without allowing for any other poor months, the gain is only $4,000 on $32,000, or 12.5% instead of 50%.

The reason this one rating service publisher does this is to insure that his subscriber list stays large. Suckers think they are getting a good comparison of different newsletters, but the figures are deliberately distorted. His motive behind the chicanery is that the rating service offers for sale a new trading method in every one of its publications. If the rating service had no subscribers, it could not sell these trading systems.

The publisher of the rating service got his comeuppance in 1993 when he wrote a derogatory review of a trading system being offered by a competitor. The competitor retaliated by computerizing a one-contract trade for all 32 of the systems the rating service had published during the years of its existence. Not one of the 32 systems had produced a profit, and the cumulative loss was $2 million! The retaliating competitor mailed the results of his empirical study to everyone registered as a commodities professional, demanding that the publisher of the rating service either resign from the business or at least go back to merely publishing the rating service without hawking his worthless systems. The publisher of the rating service ignored him.

Just as there are with stock mutual funds, there are commodity funds which sell with and without sales commissions. They are called "load" and "no-load" funds. Stock investors learned long ago that the sales charge goes only to a salesperson and cannot possibly affect the performance of the fund. The same is true of commodity funds, so managers and publishers who want to present the truth should start performance records from $1,000, not $950.

Another confusing factor about performance records is starting dates. A four year old fund may have a marvelous record while a three year old fund may appear to have done poorly. The explanation could be that the older fund caught the fantastic gold and silver market of 1979-80 while the second fund barely missed it. The gains made during that big move should have given the older fund a huge gain, or enough of a cushion to be able to publish an acceptable long-term record despite poor performance thereafter. Starting dates only a few months apart can produce dramatically different records; once again, referring to the 1979-80 gold and silver run, nearly all of the action occurred in just four months.

Even if professional managers could produce a creditable performance record, in many cases their management is not worth their fee. Frequently, the fees are downright confiscatory. I am aware of at least six types of fees that they charge, but I am sure there must be some innovative minds that have dreamed up exotic additional fees. For independent managers who are unaffiliated with a brokerage house, the three basic fees are: (1) a sign-up fee of about 5%, which goes to the salesman who solicited the account; (2) an annual percentage (usually charged monthly or quarterly) of assets under management, a fee which may range from 6% annually to 18%; and (3) an incentive arrangement which awards the manager as much as 33% of the profits.

Brokerage houses generally are not permitted to participate in the profits of the accounts nor to charge any management fee other than commissions and costs, so they have had to invent some novel methods to increase their "take" from clients. They have these three additional means of extracting fees from managed accounts: (4) increasing commission rates beyond the normal minimums to as much as double the rates charged non-managed accounts; (5) tacking a service charge onto each confirmation of an executed trade; and (6) holding all margin deposits in U.S. Treasury bills in the manager's name rather than in the name of the managed account so that the manager receives the interest instead of passing it along to the client.

A brokerage house may circumvent the rules prohibiting it from acting both as a fee-earning manager and commission-earning broker simultaneously by simply forming a subsidiary division to "independently" manage commodity accounts. This way they may collect all six of the fees described in the two previous paragraphs. One major commodity house formed a subsidiary to manage a huge limited partnership it had formed. They charged a basic 6% annual fee plus retaining the 6% T-bill interest. That is a guaranteed 12% annually for the firm before the first trade is executed. In the management contracts between the subsidiary and its parent the manager had to *guarantee* commissions equal to at least 1% of the partnership's assets monthly. If the manager failed to generate a minimum of 1% brokerage commissions monthly it had to forfeit the difference to the parent from its own management fee. (Talk about a conflict of interest!) That was another minimum 12% expense, so the subsidiary and the parent were guaranteed 24% income per year right off the top. After all that, if they earned a profit from trading, the manager received 20% of that. Last I heard, the asset value of that fund had declined 50% in six months. Small wonder.

Another giant firm had a contractual arrangement with an outside manager to charge a basic 9% annually and to take 25% of the profits. It was never made clear to me who got the T-bill interest. To encourage investors to enter the pool that was formed in 1975 as the trading vehicle, the brokerage house drew a commitment from the manager that no more than 15% of the assets would ever be employed in commodities and the other 85% would be held in reserve. I still marvel at the fact that the firm was able to attract about $1.5 million into this pool, for it had to be obvious to anyone who gave the least consideration to the proposition that it would be almost impossible for it to be a winner. Giving the manager the benefit of the doubt by assuming the then 9.5% T-bill interest (which is being earned on only 85% of the assets and therefore is actually only an 8% return on the total assets) goes to the pool's partners, and giving the manager further benefit by assuming that he has the fantastic good fortune to make a 100% profit (highly unlikely) on the 15% which is in commodities trading, the overall gain is 8% plus 15%, or 23%. After deducting the basic fee of 9% and the incentive fee of 5.75%, the net return to the investors is 8.25%. That is less than they could have earned in a savings account — and without the risk.

In 1975, when I was forming the previously mentioned commodity trading partnership which was to be offered publicly to California residents, I went before the Department of Corporations, State of California, and requested that I be allowed to charge a simple basic fee without the incentive fee. I argued that incentive fees tend to work to the detriment of the client, for they encourage the manager to trade his accounts aggressively and imprudently in the hope of earning larger fees. It amounts to having the manager taking extra risks with the client's money with the result that the client takes 100% of the losses but realizes only 75% of the profits after the 25% incentive fee is deducted. I further argued that there was already an incentive for the advisor to make the accounts grow because his fee — which was a fixed percentage of assets under management — could only increase if the accounts appreciated in value; conversely, he was subject to penalty because his fee would diminish if his accounts decreased in value. Good performance could also bring rewards as new accounts were referred by satisfied clients.

Commodity partnerships were too new at that time to have established a history of performance under incentive fees, but I pointed to the abysmal record of the few *stock* mutual funds with incentive fees. It was all to no avail, and the Department insisted that all commodity funds in California earn incentives as part of their fees. However, they have since relented, for the performance records of managers operating under incentive arrangements have been terrible, and now incentive fees are prohibited in California.

A flat fee of 1/2 of 1% per month, or 6% annually, seems adequate, for that charge will be covered by the interest earned on the U.S. Treasury bills in the account — the interest from which should definitely go to the client. Anything above 6% seems excessive, and incentive fees should be barred altogether. The client has a chance to make a profit with my suggested fee, but a fee greater than 6% seems too great a burden for the client to shoulder. The reader should also be aware of the unscrupulous practices of some of the people who represent themselves to be commodity advisors. The CFTC hasn't the size of staff necessary for complete regulation of the commodity trading industry, and this has permitted a few unethical operators to enter the business.

Someone once said that actions taken by politicians to cause a certain action to happen invariably have the exact opposite effect. I will give you an example of something the CFTC has done for the purpose of protecting potential investors seeking management of their commodity investments but which opens the door for total deception and thievery: When I wrote my standard Managed Account Agreement to be used with the commodity accounts which I manage, I inserted wording which said the owner of the account could not trade in the account while it is under my management. My purpose was to keep the owner from using some of the cash reserve which is so important to a scale trading account and perhaps forcing me to liquidate positions while prices are down. The CFTC rejected that clause from my contract, saying that it was not right to bar a person from trading his own money.

I protested that if the owner of the account made some crazy trade that lost a lot of money, my "track record" would suffer because it would appear that I had made that trade. The CFTC's answer was that any trades made by persons other than the manager could be *deleted* from the account's record.

They thought that they were protecting the investor, but they opened a potential can of worms. Two unscrupulous schemers could use the CFTC's intended protective action to fleece the world by creating an incredible — but phony — track record which could never be replicated in real life. All that the conspirators would have to do is to set up an account, make 100 trades with fifty winners and fifty losers, say that the manager selected the winners and that the account owner selected the losers. The manager then runs ads claiming gains in the hundreds of percent and brings in millions of dollars to manage. I suspect that this is done regularly.

One clever stock trading advisor recently concocted a scheme which was designed to bring large sums of money under his management. He advertised that he would give $10,000 cash to the first person who could match his trading record for the last ten years. He was claiming to have made several thousands of percent gains. He expected that no one would be able to match his record, but one person claimed the prize. The trading advisor refused to award the prize, so they went to court. Because no prize had been awarded, another person stepped forward to claim the prize, saying he was the first to do so. The trading advisor finally awarded one $10,000 prize to stem the tide of claims. Then the truth came out:

This well-known trading advisor who does a weekly investment show on national TV was claiming a record based solely upon theoretical performance from back-dated work done from known results. Not only had he designed a system around *known* results, but — get a load of this — he changed his system *three times* during the theoretical ten years! Although margin on stock purchases is limited to 50%, this chap arbitrarily assumed that he was using 500% at the critical points each time the stock market reversed. His ads claimed that he had turned $10,000 into $40,000,000 in ten years. By the time the regulators caught up with him he had brought in millions of dollars for managed accounts. They made him stop running the ads, but they did not require that he return the money. Despite this conniving, at least two other people had sharper pencils (or faster computers) and beat his concocted record.

Evidently no one was disturbed by his actions because he is still doing his weekly TV show and still attracting investment accounts to manage.

The "track record" scams are endless. Here is another true story: One brokerage firm does a regular TV show in which they invite commodity newsletter publishers to be guests on the show. The host of the show always praises today's guest publisher in such a way that viewers get the impression that the host has done a lot of digging before discovering this unknown writer with a remarkable new trading method. Baloney! The writer *paid to* get on the show. Obviously, the publisher — who is not identified as an advertiser — asks to go on the show the week after he has his only big winner of the year. Viewers are offered a free copy of this writer's newsletter, and they receive the one with the single humongous winner of the year. It works for the host because he was paid, and it works for the writer because he sells subscriptions, but it is the public which pays the bill.

Here's another: A newsletter publisher goes for a couple of years with totally undistinguished performance and then he has a six week period during which he has been long T-bonds as they roared straight up for the entire six weeks. That is his first decent winner in two years, giving him a 387% profit on the T-bond margin, so he advertises, "387% in six weeks!" Like he does it every six weeks.

Falling for that deceptive ad is no worse than sending money to purchase the trading secrets of the person who won this year's trading contest sponsored by a brokerage house. Remember, commodity trading is heads or tails, a winner and a loser on every trade. There are thousands of entrants in that type of contest because they all hope to be the top gun of the year and to attract millions of dollars to manage. The guy who won simply caught "heads" more times than anyone else. He may advertise, "I won this year's trading contest; send $295, and I'll send you my secrets on trading." What if he ran a truthful ad saying, "I won this year's coin flipping contest; send $295 and I'll send you my secrets on coin flipping." If you send $295, you should be prepared for the coins to come up tails next year.

If you don't believe my claims that last year's winning coin flippers will probably be this year's losers, consider the following: One giant Wall Street brokerage house assembled a stable of "eleven traders with a dazzling collective track record, returning 31.2% a year over five years." With that kind of sizzle they were able to raise $252 million for the biggest commodity pool of the time. Over the next four years they averaged gains of a mere 1.2%.

Another commodity pool operation formed by a Nobel Prize-winning economist put together a stable of computer jocks who had track records with annual gains as high as 165%. With that kind of record they attracted over $1 billion in four pools. Over the next four years the funds gained an average of 1.2%, zero, 4%, and 7.2%. The heavy withdrawals by disappointed investors has reduced the combined total in the four pools to $175 million.

One commodity fund management company managed four offshore funds which claimed three-year gains ranging from 173% to 288%, compared with only 76% for the next-best fund, and claimed to have $270 million in the four funds combined. They got away with these apparently phony claims because there is no regulation of offshore funds. No one has ever been able to verify either the claims for performance or for size, but money keeps pouring in because their claims are unregulated. Most professionals doubt the veracity of their claims, but the head of the firm refuses to produce proof of the claims on the basis of protecting trade secrets.

One of the simplest scams was recently repeated by one of the major mutual fund management companies. They managed a $334 million stock mutual fund which had a lousy record. They also had a fund with less than $1 million in it, but which had an excellent record. The $334 million fund was absorbed by the $1 million dollar fund, and because the track record now is only that of the former $1 million fund, we now have a $335 million fund with an excellent record. Figures don't lie, but liars figure.

There are frequent stock market trading contests in which contestants pay $100 to enter and are given $10,000 of paper money to invest for three months. The legitimate contestants select about five stocks and "invest" $2,000 in each. The sly guys take a shot for a lousy hundred bucks and buy 20,000 options at 50 cents apiece. They might enter the contest ten times, for a total cost of $1,000, and they buy 10,000 to 20,000 of each of ten different cheap options. One of the stocks turns out to be a big mover, and the options go bonkers. The legitimate contestants show a 57% gain in three months (a remarkable performance in itself), but five or six of the sly guys have turned their $10,000 into millions. Then they advertise their incredible records and go into business as money managers. It is impossible for them to replicate their performance because you can't buy 10,000 or 20,000 of most options; you might be lucky to buy 5. The contest manager doesn't care because he has a bushel basket full of hundred dollar bills, and he is already preparing for the next contest and another bushel basket full of hundred dollar bills.

It is common practice for advisors to arrange a kickback scheme with a cooperating commodity broker. The prospective investor consults a broker for the recommendation of a good commodity advisor, and the broker — quite naturally — recommends the advisor who is his confederate in the kickbacks. When the unsuspecting client accepts the recommendation and opens an account with the advisor, he has exposed himself to risk above and beyond that which is inherent to commodity trading. The advisor overtrades the account, generating excessive commissions for the broker. The broker, in turn, kicks back a portion of those commissions to the advisor, and the client is caught in the middle.

This cooperation between a broker and an agent can be made to work in the opposite direction. Here's how:

In the commodities business there are people known as Introducing Brokers. That term generally refers to small brokerage firms which are not large enough to have their own accounting departments, so they clear through a large firm which may do the accounting for many IB's. A very high percentage of small brokerage firms are IB's, and there is nothing wrong with that.

Another kind of IB, though, is one who solicits managed account business for commodity trading advisors. Most of these IB types are real scoundrels. They have no regard for the clients; their only regard is for the commissions which can be created by the advisor to whom they steer money because the IB — legally — receives a percentage of the commissions generated in the managed accounts.

There are thousands of trading advisors at work at all times, trying to generate a good track record. As discussed earlier in this book, your bell curve dictates that a few of those thousands of advisors will have a good record in a given year. These unscrupulous IB's will contact the hot trader and offer to raise money for him to manage on the condition that the advisor guarantees a certain high dollar amount of generated commissions. If the advisor fails to produce the stated commission amount during the first year, the IB steers the account to the current year's hot trader. That is easy for him to do because it is unlikely that the first advisor was the top trader two consecutive years, and he convinces his investor-client that the first trader has lost his touch and the new top gun can perform miracles.

I received a call one time from an IB who had just read this book, and he was bubbling with enthusiasm as he claimed that he could raise $3 to $5 million for me to manage. I tried to temper his enthusiasm by explaining that scale trading could not generate the 50% annual trading commissions to which he was accustomed, but that it would produce only 8% to 10%. Click! He hung up. He didn't even say good-bye, and I never heard from him again.

A less common — but no less detestable — form of thievery which advisors and brokers can perpetrate upon their unsuspecting clients is the switching of account numbers on winning trades. To accomplish this, the advisor instructs the broker, for example, to buy cotton at the morning's opening price for Client A. If, during the day, the price of cotton declines, the position is allowed to remain in Client A's account; however, if the price rises, the advisor informs the broker that he has given him the wrong account number on the purchase and requests that the broker change the account number to move the cotton position to Client B's account. The winning cotton position is liquidated from Client B's account the same day. Obviously, Client B is the advisor's confederate, and they split the profit. The broker is usually a partner of the confederation, but that is not essential.

The most common type of rip-off which advisors and brokers use is the preferential allocation of order executions. This is accomplished by entering one market order for a large number of contracts of a single commodity; the order ticket has no account number on it, but it bears the notation "account numbers to follow." The ostensible reason for the entry of such an order is that the advisor may be intending to make simultaneous purchases of the commodity for a large number of his clients, and in a fast moving market he fears that it would be disadvantageous to some of the clients to attempt to enter the orders individually. If the advisor must go through the time-consuming process of reciting each order separately as the broker writes them and enters them, the execution price on the last order may be substantially different from that on the first order. Batching of orders without account numbers is a common practice in both the stock and commodities markets. Unfortunately, the practice provides an ideal vehicle for skimming funds from clients' accounts.

After the large order is executed, the advisor must submit the account numbers so that the contracts purchased may be allocated to the proper accounts. It is probable that the large order was executed in numerous segments at varying prices; e.g., an order for twenty-five contracts of pork bellies might be executed with a range of twenty to thirty points separating the lowest and highest executions. That is normal, for pork belly prices change ten or fifteen points in the blink of an eye and may run fifty points in less than a minute. So, how does the advisor allocate the executions? Obviously the best execution prices go into his wife's account, the next best into his brother-in-law's account, the next best in the account of his largest client, etc. By the time it comes to allocation to his smallest account, only the poorest execution price remains. It may not seem important, but the difference of a mere twenty points on a two contract order in pork bellies is $160. For the large trader, the difference of twenty points on a twenty-contract order is worth $1,600. How long can the small traders go on forfeiting $160 per trade to subsidize the advisor's large accounts?

The pork belly market is an extremely active and fluid market wherein good executions are commonplace, but take the above situation and substitute the terribly volatile lumber, heating oil, unleaded gasoline, or coffee markets. Think of the opportunities for abuses there.

By now, you must be wondering what option remains if you should not manage your own money but also must be wary of others who would manage it for you. There is an alternative. It is scale trading. It requires so little skill to scale trade that any individual can do it. Its simplicity makes it an ideal vehicle for the employment of speculative capital. However, no matter how much capital you have available, you must also have the proper temperament to wait patiently during the accumulation of paper losses throughout extended declines and the discipline to avoid the temptation to deviate from scale trading tenets. If you lack the patience and discipline, you should seek out a professional manager who will do your scale trading for you.

The commodity clients who most need to scale trade are those who are frequently unavailable for calls from the broker: business executives who are in day-long closed-door meetings, outside sales-people who travel, doctors who spend long hours in surgery, to name a few. These people are also the ones who should have advisors managing their accounts, for it is likely that the demands of their professions upon their time make it more profitable for them to devote full time to their own work while allowing a professional advisor to supervise their commodity investments. At 6%, the fee on a $50,000 account is only $250 per month, and that is but a token amount for a professional person who is more successful in his own work than he has been at commodity trading.

You might want to talk to an advisor about the many advantages of a partnership. You, as an individual, might have inadequate capital for proper diversification. Your capital also might be insufficient to meet the minimum requirements for the purchase and deposit of U.S. Treasury bills as margin in lieu of cash. However, if several individuals form a partnership, they may obtain these advantages, and more. Best of all, the interest earned on the T-bills will equal the management fee, giving the partnership professional management literally without cost. The subject of partnerships is covered more completely in Chapter XXIII.

If you are interested in talking with an advisor who is an experienced scale trader, please write me at P.O. Box 3882, Westlake Village, California 91359-0882, and I will furnish the names of a few advisors besides myself who use scale trading.

XXII

Accounting and Tax Considerations

I have already mentioned that in commodities trading the brokerage firm's accounting department will use FIFO (First In, First Out) for offsetting trades; thus, you may have wondered how I can claim that a scale trading account will show a very high percentage of winners when it is obvious that there will be times when an account will accumulate a great many positions on a scale down before it begins to sell any of the positions on a scale up. If the account starts buying soybeans at $6.50, buys each 10 cents down to $5.90, and then takes its first profit by selling a contract on a rally to $6.00, how can this be called a 10 cent winner instead of a 50 cent loser?

The answer is simple. The owner of an account has the right to inform his broker that he will designate the specific contract to be offset each time a position is liquidated. In the above example, seven contracts were put into the account before the first sale was made at $6.00; if the trader does not designate a specific contract to be offset against that sale, the computer will automatically offset the first trade that went into the account. That would be the purchase at $6.50, resulting in an apparent loss of 50 cents; however, if the trader instructs the broker to offset the $5.90 purchase, the sale at $6.00 will result in a 10 cent profit.

I wanted to have a performance record of an actual account to refer to in this book to demonstrate the efficacy of scale trading; therefore, during the year I wrote the original edition of this book I used specific offsets in one of the partnerships I advise. My secondary purpose was to obviate any possible contentious action by regulators who might dispute my claim of 95% winners when FIFO accounting would probably have produced P&S statements showing only about 60% winners. That account had 130 trades, 130 winners. There were some open contracts in the account at year-end which had paper losses, but after deducting those losses the account showed a net gain of 74% for the year.*

Because there are few reasons for using any method other than FIFO accounting, that was the only account in which I used specific offsets. Indeed, there are probably more reasons for *not* using them.

Commodity accounts are equity accounts, which means that a computation is done daily by the computer to determine the total equity in the account for margin purposes. The cash in the account, plus or minus open-trade gains or losses, determines the total equity. Therefore, it matters not to the computer whether you close out a winning, losing, or break-even position, the equity remains the same. As equity increases in the account, the client has the right to withdraw any excess over his margin requirements regardless of whether that excess came about as a result of closed out profitable trades or paper profits still retained within the account; conversely, the account is subject to margin calls when the equity falls below margin requirements, regardless of whether the deficiency was caused by realized or unrealized losses.

The reason it is customary for the brokerage house to close out your oldest positions first is that the oldest positions on the books are the ones targeted for first delivery notice when that time comes. The house has a better chance of avoiding a delivery problem for you if you accidentally (or deliberately) hold an open long position into the delivery month if it has used FIFO and closed your oldest

---

* A copy of the auditor's report is available upon request.

positions first to keep the remaining positions as near-term as possible, placing your contracts lower in delivery order and putting contracts held by other traders at other firms ahead of yours in the delivery order. The actual dollar results in the account will always be the same in the long run no matter whether the house's computer uses FIFO, LIFO (Last In, First Out), specific offsets, or any random selection process.

To illustrate: Let us say that you have bought three contracts of cattle in an uninterrupted decline from 46 cents to 44 cents. You hope to cash a 1 cent profit on each contract. If the price rises in a straight line you will be selling at 45 cents, 46 cents, and 47 cents. The FIFO method will show a I cent loss on the first sale, buying at 46 cents and selling at 45 cents; a I cent gain on the second sale, buying at 45 cents and selling at 46 cents; and a 3 cent gain on the final sale, buying at 44 cents and selling at 47 cents. The net profit is 3 cents, excluding commissions. The identical result would have been achieved by specifically offsetting the first sale at 45 cents against the 44 cent buy; the second sale at 46 cents against the 45 cent buy; and the third sale at 47 cents against the 46 cent buy. You need only remember that each sale is being executed one increment above a corresponding purchase to realize that it makes no difference which method is used to offset the positions.

Prior to 1976 it was necessary to hold security and commodity investments for at least six months to obtain long-term capital gains treatment, but Congress altered that in that year. However, commodity trading was somehow overlooked by the Congress, and when the holding period was increased to twelve months for securities it remained at six months for commodities. This led to the development of an entire industry within an industry. The new industry used commodities as the vehicle to create fictitious (but legal) commodity trading losses. Some commodity brokers earned a substantial income doing nothing other than "commodity tax straddles."

The customary method was for the client to enter a commodity straddle position during the summertime. It was considered best to use a volatile commodity such as silver. The client would assume a long position in March silver and straddle it with a short position of an equal number of contracts of May silver. The size of the fictitious loss which the client hoped to create would determine the number of contracts he would straddle. Let us assume for the purpose of this illustration that the client wanted to create a $100,000 loss to offset $100,000 of gains previously realized from stock, real estate, or commodities trading. He probably would use 100 straddles, long 100 March silvers against short 100 Mays. The contracts would have parallel movement so that any loss in one leg of the straddle would be offset by an identical gain in the other leg; he had no risk other than a possible change in the spread between the prices of the two contracts due to a change in carrying charges which might result if there were a change in interest rates, but any change between March and May contracts would be so minuscule as to be meaningless in the overall scheme. The straddle position was held until silver moved 20 cents in either direction. A 20 cent move in the Comex 5,000 ounce silver contract is equal to $1,000 in each contract; thus, one leg of the straddle had a $100,000 loss and the other had an offsetting $100,000 gain. Continuing our assumptions, let us say that it had required three months for silver to decline 20 cents (it was not as volatile in those days). The client would immediately close out his March long position by selling the 100 contracts. He had realized a short-term loss of $100,000 which was offset by the $100,000 gain in his short position in the May contracts. By lifting one leg of the straddle he left himself vulnerable to an actual loss of sizable proportions in the May short position which he still retained, so he would purchase 100 contracts of July silver concomitantly with the selling of the March contracts. He had returned to his straddle position, short 100 May contracts and long 100 Julys.

He would continue to hold the straddle until at least January of the new year. That assured him of showing the $100,000 loss in the old year. Then he would close the May-July straddle, resulting in a $100,000 taxable gain in the new year. He had gained nothing as far as capital gains and losses were concerned, but he had delayed the payment of the taxes on his $100,000 real estate profit for a year. If his highest tax bracket was 40%, he had delayed the payment of $40,000 of taxes for a year, which gave him the use of that money for an extra year.

No matter what happened to the price of silver while he held the May-July straddle, his $100,000 gain would remain intact, for any profit or loss on one leg of the straddle would be offset by an identical loss or profit on the other leg.

The primary objective of this tax gimmick was merely to defer payment of taxes for a year, but sometimes the client reaped an unexpected bonus. This would occur if his long position was a winning position and was held at least six months. This resulted in a $100,000 short-term loss being realized but being offset by a $100,000 long-term gain. Because long-term gains are taxed at one-half the rate of short-term, it resulted in a windfall for the client. Indeed, brokers began to encourage clients to trade in distant contracts to assure there would be time enough for the long leg of the straddle to show a gain at some time during the life of the trade. By that time brokers were making incredible commissions from an obvious loophole which required plugging by the Congress.

The change came with the 1981 Tax Reform Act. However, the commodity industry performed one of the greatest con jobs of all time when it convinced Congress that speculators would no longer trade commodities if commodity tax straddles were eliminated. Congress bought that ludicrous plea and offered a compromise. THAT COMPROMISE MADE COMMODITIES THE MOST TAX-ADVANTAGED INVESTMENT AVAILABLE TODAY.

The compromise simply said that all open positions must be "marked to the market" at year-end, in return for which all commodity transactions would be treated as 60% long-term and 40% short-term *regardless of the holding period*. Mark to the market means that all profits and losses from open positions in one's account at year-end will be treated the same as closed positions so that commodity tax straddles become impossible. However, the commodities industry traded a mule for a race horse, because the old tax straddles merely deferred payment of taxes and did not avoid them, whereas the 60%/40% treatment is of enormous advantage, because a profitable trade may now be 60% long-term even if held for only a matter of days or hours. One objection which high bracket traders had previously lodged against scale trading was the short-term tax treatment which the profits received, but that is no longer true.

Under the new tax law, a trader with $30,000 of realized gains during the year who also holds $10,000 of unrealized losses at year-end would be taxed only on the $20,000 of net gain; similarly, a trader who has $8,000 of realized gains against $10,000 of unrealized losses

214

in his account at year-end would be allowed to declare a $2,000 net trading loss for the year, and a trader showing $5,000 of realized gains plus $4,000 of unrealized gains must declare net gains of $9.000 for the year. In all cases, the meter is returned to "zero" after being marked to the market so that tax treatment for the new year is based only upon the change in value subsequent to December 31.

Returning to our illustration of the account with $30,000 of realized gains and $10,000 of unrealized losses at year-end, his profit would be treated as 60% long-term and 40% short-term on his $20,000 net gain. The maximum tax rate for both short-term and long-term capital gains is 28%, so he would pay a maximum tax of $5,600 and keep the other 72%, or $14,400.

Continuing the same illustration, this trader had $10,000 of unrealized losses in the open positions in his account at year-end, which now becomes a zero loss for the new tax year. If prices move favorably, so that he is able to recoup those losses to break even on those trades, he has a $10,000 taxable gain for the new year. That is because he marked to the market and deducted those losses in the old year. At no time did he suffer any disadvantage, for all trades were subject to the same 60%/40% treatment, regardless of the holding period.

Tax laws still require that securities and real estate be held for a minimum of twelve months to qualify for long-term capital gains treatment; thus, scale trading of commodities futures contracts becomes more attractive than ever. A conservatively managed scale trading account could average 40% per year profit, and a trader in the highest income tax bracket would net 72% after payment of the maximum 28% capital gains tax.

There are so many contingencies and variables in the tax codes, and the Clinton Administration has promised to make many new changes, so please do not rely on the above as the current status of the tax laws. I am not a tax advisor, nor do I give legal advice. I believe the comments in this chapter about tax treatment of commodities trading is accurate as of the time this book is written, but the drive by federal, state, county, and city governments to generate new tax revenues could cause the above tax advantages to be cancelled at any time. I urge you to check with your tax accountant or attorney before assuming anything about the tax treatment for commodity trading.

Before closing this chapter on accounting procedures, I should call attention to an unethical practice which advisors have used to deceive unsophisticated clients: A few years ago there was a commodity advisor in Los Angeles who ran a boiler room type of operation, with hard-sell advertising on local television. He catered to inexperienced people instead of knowledgeable investors; this was essential to his scheme. Most of the trades he executed for his managed accounts were spreads. When a spread moved favorably, the entire position was liquidated by closing out *both* legs — the long and the short — simultaneously. When the spread moved unfavorably, only the profitable leg was liquidated — *either* the long or the short — and the unprofitable leg was retained. Thus, all P&S statements showed profits, creating the impression that the advisor was extraordinarily successful in his management of clients' accounts; however, few of the customers realized that most of the apparent profits were nullified by unrealized losses which were still in the account. Had the clients been more familiar with commodity accounting methods they would have better understood their monthly statements which showed the unrealized losses. Some customers who had started with the initial $10,000 minimum were so impressed that they deposited additional tens of thousands of dollars to their accounts. Eventually, of course, the losing legs of the spreads expired and had to be liquidated with shocking losses. It was only then that the customers came to realize that they had huge overall losses in their accounts. The CFTC received numerous complaints about the advisor, and he was subsequently put out of business.

From the above, it should be clear that advisors can use devious methods — including specific offset accounting — to confuse clients. For his own protection, the intelligent investor who seeks help from a professional advisor should be alert to these deceptive practices. Likewise, advisors should avoid deviating from the commonly accepted accounting procedures to avoid being accused of attempting a deception.

Over the years I have received many calls from new scale traders who were disappointed to be informed by their brokers that the firm would not allow specific offsets (LIFO) and insisted that the client accept the house computer's FIFO accounting. If they had purchased several contracts on an initial decline and then had cashed the first winner on a slight rally, the client was shocked to find that the computer gave him a "loser." If this has confused you also, please again read the earlier example in this chapter about trading cattle wherein FIFO gave a - 1 penny, + 1 penny, and then + 3 penny result as compared with LIFO which gave a + 1 penny, +1 penny, and +1 penny result. The results are identical.

It is a pain in the neck for the broker to have to contact his accounting office at the end of each trading day to do all of the specific offsets if he has a large clientele doing scale trading. Furthermore, some houses fear — rightfully — that any gimmick accounting method might someday be used by the client who has lost money to claim that he thought that his account was having nothing but consecutive winners. Clients have a knack for pleading ignorance when they get into a courtroom, and sympathetic judges usually favor the client over the brokerage house, so you can't blame the house for refusing to use specific offsets (LIFO).

You will never have a problem if you use the Buy/Sell lines shown earlier in Chapter XIII, "The Complex Scale."

I *never* request LIFO accounting in my managed accounts for the very reason that I don't want to be accused of showing virtually all winners. But in issuing my monthly statements I send clients a list of trades on a FIFO basis so that they may reconcile to the broker's monthly statement *plus* a list of trades on a LIFO basis so that they may see how we are doing from the scale trader's point of view.

217

XXIII

Partnerships

Some very revealing information has come from an analysis of the performance records of commodity trading accounts with limited resources. Researchers visited a branch office of each of three different commodity firms. In each of the three offices, they randomly selected one hundred accounts which had an equity of $5,000 or less. They returned a year later to ascertain the success of these accounts. Not a single one of the three hundred accounts had a profit for the year.

Commodity Futures Trading Commission statistics show that 60% of all commodity accounts have less than $5,000 equity. From the above paragraph it is safe to conclude that at least 60% of commodity traders lose. But the CFTC also tells us that 85% of commodity accounts have equities of less than $10,000, so it is probably a safe assumption that a major portion of these accounts eventually fall below the $5,000 mark, and then they also disappear.

Generally accepted theory is that more than 90% of commodity traders lose.

Why?

The probable answer is that individuals with limited resources try to trade against others with virtually unlimited resources. Trading in commodities with $5,000 of capital against individuals — in some cases corporations — with assets in the hundreds of millions of dollars is tantamount to playing in a no limit poker game with a $50 bankroll against an opponent with millions of dollars. The person with the $50 bankroll might win a few modest pots and stay alive awhile, but sooner or later the player with the unlimited bankroll will eradicate the player who started with $50, and then the game ends. It is simply a matter of staying power.

Actually, it is more like flipping coins with a modest number of coins against someone with a sackful of coins. For example, a person with ten coins could continue in action as long as he is ahead by five, ten, or twenty winners, but the instant that he falls ten behind the game is over. Although the individual with the sackful of coins might fall behind by a considerable number of coins, he can play with complete confidence that the pendulum will eventually swing his way. When it does, he will bury his opponent. He can afford to fall behind by ten, twenty, or even fifty losers, but he need get ahead by only ten winners to annihilate his opponent. The commodity trader with but $5,000 of capital seeking a $500 profit or loss on each trade faces obliteration as he approaches ten losers. What chance has he against traders with assets in the hundreds of thousands or millions of dollars?

Without staying power, a commodity trader hasn't a chance.

If you think I am incorrect in this thinking, simply consider the following: A person is a floor trader on one of the exchanges in Chicago. He wants to buy a lovely home on Sheridan Road, north of Chicago, with a view of Lake Michigan. Although he has plenty of capital with which to make the purchase, he wants to keep the cash available for commodities futures trading. He goes to the bank for a million dollar loan. Meantime, you are a corporate executive with twenty years of employment with your company who has recently received a significant promotion to a division management position, an increase in salary to $200,000 per year, and has been transferred to Chicago. You wish to purchase a similar home. You apply for a loan at the same bank.

You have a guaranteed paycheck because you have a *contract*. The floor trader has nothing. He doesn't have a guaranteed paycheck because he doesn't even have a job. Your loan application is refused; his is accepted. Why?

The bank considers you to be too great a risk because your corporation is doing some restructuring, and they fear that you may be terminated because of the buyout clause in your contract. However, in Chicago a well-heeled floor trader is considered to have a license to steal. And as long as the commodity exchanges stay open, floor brokers have a greater "guarantee" of a steady income than does a corporate executive.

The bank returns your rejected loan application with a note of remorse attached. The floor trader's approved application is returned with a note saying, "Will *one* million be enough?"

The following anecdote will give you an example of what the floor traders do to insure profits: (This is a true story.) A young man began a career as a floor trader with a fair amount of borrowed capital. His early trades were successful enough to earn a following among investors who gave him large amounts of money to manage for them. With the large amount of capital he had under his control he was able to move markets in the direction he chose. As an example, if wheat had hovered for a while barely above $3.00, always managing to bounce upward each time the price dipped to $3.00, he — *and all of the rest of the world* — knew that all of the sell stops were located at $2.99 or $2.98.

The next time the price of wheat dipped to $3.02 he slammed the market by selling (short) huge quantities of contracts of wheat. This is called "gunning the stops." The price would break, quickly falling below $3.00, electing the stops, and sending a wave of sell orders onto the floor. In a matter of minutes the price would be $2.92, and this floor trader would step in, buy back (cover) his shorts, and take home a 10 cent profit per bushel. Because he had done it on ten million bushels, he had made $1 million in a matter of minutes. (Rock musicians, eat your hearts out.) All he had to do now was to watch the charts until he saw another opportunity to gun the stops.

Unfortunately for him, some people with bigger bags of coins came along and spoiled his game — temporarily. The people with the bigger bags of coins were the giant public pools (partnerships). This highly successful floor trader had hundreds of millions of dollars with which to move markets, but he met his match when the pools came along with twenty *billions* of dollars. Now, when he wanted to gun the stops by selling the speculative account legal limit of 3,600 contracts, the pools would act in collusion and either each trade several hundred contracts to amass a total of 3,600, or one pool alone could trade the entire 3,600 contracts. (This is especially easy for offshore pools which are not bound by U.S. commodity exchange restrictions and therefore may trade whatever number of contracts they desire.) When this floor trader lost $150 million and found that he could no longer play the game of gunning the stops, he retired.

However, American ingenuity triumphed, and he devised a plan to overcome the 3,600 contract restrictive limit, and he returned to trading. He trained more than a dozen "students," which he called his "hares." They went through an elaborate training class that taught them *one* thing: gun the stops! He gave each of them several millions of dollars with which to trade, telling them that they could keep a percentage of any profit they made using his system. It would be illegal for him to advise them on the trades which they should make, because if each of the dozen hares sold short 3,600 contracts on his instructions, there would be an aggregate sale of 46,800+ contracts (his 3,600 and their 43,200+), which would be a violation of the 3,600 contract limit, but I suspect that it has been *implied*. I doubt that there have ever been many trades made by the hares in defiance of protocol because of Chicago's renown as the home of the Field Museum, the Shedd Aquarium, the Adler Planetarium, and the cement overcoat.

I love it when floor traders and pool operators get into a slugging match. One side drives the price down, then the other side steps in and rallies the market. Or vice versa. As scale traders, we benefit whichever way they move the market.

One subscriber to our newsletter called one time to say that he was formerly employed by one of the giant grain merchants. He said they had always done exactly what I described in the book: They have no limits on positions, so whenever the price dipped on one of the grains, they would buy one to ten million bushels. Their own buying might be enough to signal the chartists that a temporary bottom had been established, and the chartists would rush to buy. The grain merchant would sell to them, taking its 6 cents profit on 2 million bushels — $120,000 — in a matter of minutes. If they did that only twice a week, that was a profit of $12.5 million per year.

Who do you think puts up the $12.5 million for the grain merchant to win or similar amounts for the floor traders and the hares? You do, if you are trading with less than $5,000.

Very few small traders — even if they are lucky enough to show a net profit briefly — manage to survive because of another problem of management of resources. Let us assume that a trader begins with capital of $5,000 and sets as his goal a net profit or loss of $500 on each trade. Let us further assume that he has been right ten times more than he has been wrong. That has given him a net profit of $5,000, and his capital has grown to $10,000. At this point most traders become convinced they have the commodities markets mastered, and they double up. If our hypothetical trader doubles the number of contracts traded and seeks a $1,000 profit or loss per trade, he is back to his original position — that of having the staying power to last through a surplus of only ten losers. His day of reckoning is inevitable. It is only a matter of time before his luck changes, he falls ten losers behind, and his capital is exhausted.

A $5,000 or $10,000 commodity trading account is virtually assured of failure. In my opinion, it would require at least $50,000 of initial capital to afford a commodity trader any chance of success. Even then the only hope he has is to discipline himself to grind out numerous — though nominal — profits and attempt to achieve a reasonable percentage return annually. Obviously, it is of no benefit to the large trader to have $50,000 of capital if he trades ten contracts at the same time a small trader with $5,000 of capital is trading single contracts. They will go broke together.

Many commodity traders with limited resources have found the solution to the problem of staying power in the burgeoning phenomenon of partnerships formed for the purpose of trading commodities futures contracts.

Many such partnerships are formed as general partnerships in which each partner shares the full liability, shares in the profits and losses on a pro-rata basis, and has an equal voice in management. Generally, these are rather small partnerships put together by several people who share a common interest — such as the same employer. Usually, these groups have no more than a few partners, each with but a few thousand dollars in the partnership, so that the account itself may still be smaller than a fair sized account of some individuals. To be specific, such an account might have between $10,000 and $20,000 total assets. The benefits accruing to members of such a small partnership are probably outweighed by the increased risk if one considers the overall liability that each general partner assumes.

The reason the general partnerships rarely are large is because of the unlimited liability aspects of the partnership agreement. Each partner is a general partner and not only shares equally in the losses but bears *full liability* for any deficits the partnership may incur beyond its capital. In other words, if the general partnership has ten general partners and assets of $20,000 but gets locked into a limit move situation so that it loses the $20,000 plus an additional $10,000, each of the partners is liable for his share of the extra $10,000, or $1,000; moreover, each of the ten general partners is fully liable for the entire $10,000. In the event of a default by the general partnership, if nine of the general partners are ribbon clerks and the tenth is a wealthy professional person, it is likely that the brokerage house would not bother to make a claim upon the nine clerks but would take action directly against the one well-heeled individual. It is difficult to imagine that persons of even modest means would accept such liability, so there are few general partnerships being formed to trade commodities.

The more popular type of commodity trading partnership is the limited partnership.

(Before proceeding with my comments about partnerships, I should make it clear that I am only giving you a general description which is intended as merely the simplest guide for you. I believe the things which I say are true, but the law varies from state to state, and the law in your state may vary from my outline. I am not intending to practice law, nor am I offering legal advice. You should consult your attorney before you do anything about getting into a partnership.)

In a limited partnership there will be one or more general partners who act as manager of the partnership, taking full responsibility for all decisions and accepting the liability for possible deficits beyond the capital of the partnership (as described above). All other partners in a limited partnership are "limited" partners. They customarily take no part in the management of the affairs of the partnership (although they usually have the right to replace the general partner). Their financial liability is limited to the amount of their original contributions to the partnership. Because they can never be called upon for additional contributions to the partnership, it is impossible for them to receive a margin call.

Many limited partnerships have hundreds of thousands or even millions of dollars in assets. Thus, they have more staying power than most individuals and should have a better chance of weathering storms while awaiting better times. Size alone cannot guarantee profits, but *lack of size* will guarantee losses.

Those are the three main attractions of limited partnership: (1) size, (2) limited liability, and (3) no margin calls. To compensate the general partner for managing the affairs of the partnership, and especially for assuming the unlimited liability, a fee is usually paid to the general partner from the assets of the partnership. There are innumerable fee arrangements, but most fall into one of two categories or a combination of both. Some partnerships pay their general partners a flat fee per month, while others pay an incentive fee based upon performance. Most partnerships pay a fee which is a combination of the two. The fees I have seen range from a flat $1/2$ of 1% monthly (6% annually) to as much as 9% annually plus 25% of profits. In the case of partnerships with reasonable fees, the interest earned on the U.S. Treasury bills held by the partnership will usually cover the fee.

Before leaving the subject of commodity trading partnerships, I should admonish you to enter into a partnership only if it has rigid withdrawal restrictions. Do *not* get into a partnership which makes it easy for you to withdraw. That may sound odd — as though I had stated it in reverse — but I mean it sincerely. Do not get in if it is easy to get out! You should contribute only spare capital — money you can afford to lose — to any commodity trading account, even partnerships. This speculative capital should never be your reserve or emergency funds. Likewise, everyone else in the partnership should have the same attitude about his capital. If it is too easy to withdraw from a partnership you may find some partners have overextended themselves by committing capital they could not afford to risk; consequently, if things go poorly for the partnership at the same time these individuals have a personal emergency, they will withdraw what remains of their capital. This may place an impossible burden upon the general partner, forcing him to liquidate positions at the worst possible time.

I alluded to this problem in Chapter XI when I mentioned the partnership I managed which was hit by a sudden heavy run of withdrawals. As this book is being written I have witnessed a similar situation. Two friends formed a commodity trading partnership and provided for easy entry and withdrawal from the partnership. Their agreement provided for contributions of new capital any Friday; likewise, withdrawals could be made any Friday upon five-day written notice. Their sole purpose in allowing such easy withdrawal was to provide for emergencies; after all, there were only the two of them in the partnership. As time passed another partner entered, and then another. Eventually there were nine partners. The partnership had a very large position in hogs and pork bellies, and when prices for these two commodities went into a tailspin the asset value per unit of the partnership did likewise. One of the newest partners recognized this as a tremendous opportunity to acquire a substantial position in hogs and pork bellies with limited risk to himself. Had he bought hogs and pork bellies in his personal account he might not have had the necessary staying power if the decline had continued. He also would have been exposing himself to the personal liability associated with personal commodity accounts. He avoided both of these problems by making two very large contributions to the limited partnership. The second of these contributions was made at the precise bottom of the market, and three weeks later — at about the midpoint of a huge rally — he withdrew from the partnership. His withdrawal of 38% (!) of the partnership's assets literally decimated the partnership. It was forced to liquidate positions prematurely, and despite the eventuation of the excellent rally which the partnership had been anticipating, the only partner who benefited was the one who made the "three week raid."

There is an object lesson in this event for all of us: Do not get into a partnership which permits easy withdrawal. In my opinion, the best kind of withdrawal condition is for everyone to be bound to the partnership for a year. Withdrawals should be permitted only on December 31, and then only with ninety days written notice to the general partner. This allows him ample time to dispose of positions and to accumulate cash to meet withdrawal requests without being put into the position of making forced liquidations.

Perhaps a compromise to the once-a-year withdrawal restriction would be permission for quarterly withdrawals as long as the total amount of withdrawals for that quarter does not exceed a certain percentage of the partnership's total assets. It might be fair to allow aggregate withdrawals to a maximum of 25% of the partnership's total assets, with anything over that amount being held over to the following quarter on a pro rata basis. At least this would allow for a partner's withdrawal of some (or all) of his capital in the event of a true emergency.

One relatively new type of partnership which has earned a degree of acceptance is the "zero coupon" limited partnership. It has the advantage of locking investors into the partnership for about five years, but it has the disadvantage of requiring investment of unproductive capital. Here is how it works:

A limited partnership will be formed with numerous investors becoming the limited partners. The capital may be of any amount, but for the sake of this illustration let us assume that the amount is $1 million. The manager of the partnership will use a large portion of the assets of the partnership to purchase five-year zero coupon U.S. Treasury notes. (Zero coupon notes or bonds have been stripped of their coupons; therefore they pay no interest. Because they pay no interest they sell at deep discounts to face value. At the end of the stated period of five, ten, twenty, or whatever number of years, they will be redeemed at full face value. The difference between the discounted cost and the face value is the equivalent of earned interest.) In recent years five-year T-notes could have been purchased for about 65 cents on the dollar, with a guaranteed return of 100 cents in five years. The other 35 cents of each dollar in the pool would be used to speculate in commodities.

The obvious attraction of this type of pool was that the manager could guarantee that in five years the pool would have no less than 100 cents in it for every dollar originally invested because, of the $1 million originally in the pool, $650,000 had been invested in zero coupon notes which matured at the end of the five years at $1 million. If the manager had managed the $350,000 in the commodity portion of the pool so poorly that the entire $350,000 was lost, the investors still got their money back. Investors couldn't lose.

With the terrible drop in interest rates through 1993, it now takes about 75 cents of every dollar to purchase enough five-year T-notes to guarantee a return of 100 cents in five years. That means the manager has only $250,000 with which to work in commodities in a $1 million pool, and if he holds any portion of that in reserve, he is squeezed down to a level where he might be unable to earn an adequate return on the $1 million. But, one of these days we will probably see five-year interest rates over 6% again, and then the zero coupon T-notes will be trading closer to 65 cents on the dollar again, allowing for their use to guarantee against loss in this type of partnership.

My personal objection to the use of zeros is that they are merely a placebo for the person who is unwilling to take a risk and is willing to pay dearly to avoid it. Investing in a zero coupon commodity pool in which the manger buys 65 cents worth of zeros and 35 cents worth of commodities has the effect of saying to the manager, "Here is my $3; please speculate in commodities with $1, but put the other $2 in the bank so that I will be assured of getting back $3 in five years." It seems simpler to me to put $1 in a fully-invested pool and just leave the other $2 in the bank. This would be especially true if the manager were to charge a fee on the entire $3.

It would be unfair to charge a management fee on that portion of the pool which is invested in the zeros, but there would be nothing wrong with this type of pool if the manager charged his fee only on that portion which is used for commodities.

An alternative to the zero coupon pool with the five-year lock-in might be a regular limited partnership with a two-year lock-in and then a 10% charge to withdraw during the third year, 6% during the fourth, and 3% during the fifth. At least this way the investors know that in case of an emergency during the five-year holding period they may withdraw a major portion of their assets. This would be an especially good format for a pool which is designed primarily for IRA and 401(k) plans in which the investor does not expect to withdraw anything within five years.

Below is listed a comparison chart showing the advantages of partnership participation over trading one's own account. I am aware of a few advisors who use the scale trading system in the commodity partnerships they manage. If you desire further information from them please write me at P.O. Box 3882-0882, Westlake Village, California 91359-0882, and I will see that your inquiry is forwarded.

COMPARISON BETWEEN

INDIVIDUAL ACCOUNTS & LIMITED PARTNERSHIPS

I. LIABILITY

Unlimited liability. In lock limit moves, the individual can lose his entire investment and be liable for substantial additional losses.

The Limited Partner's liability is limited to his initial investment. The General Partner is liable for all other losses.

II. MARGIN CALLS

Individual accounts are subject to margin calls at any time. This may even occur in a profitable account if margin requirements are raised. If unable to meet the margin call immediately, positions in the account will be liquidated.

Because each limited partner's liability is limited to his initial investment, margin calls are impossible.

III. U.S. TREASURY BILL INTEREST

Unless the individual account is substantial in size, trading must be limited to a few commodities. This will restrict profit potential. One bad position can ruin an entire account.

Partnerships are usually larger than $20,000, so their entire assets may be invested in U.S. T-bills which may be deposited in lieu of cash for commodity margin. T-bills currently yield about 6%. Thus, the partnership's assets are employed two ways simultaneously, earning 6% interest while seeking commodity trading profits.

IV. DIVERSIFICATION

Unless an account has more than $20 000 in it, only cash may be deposited for margin. Because cash earns no interest, the only potential for profit is through commodity trading.

Because of its size the partnership will trade in numerous commodities simultaneously. The effect of a bad position will be mitigated.

V. PROFESSIONAL MANAGEMENT

Few individuals have the training, skill, or inclination to trade their own commodity accounts successfully.

Commodity partnership managers are usually qualified professionals.

VI. CONSTANT SUPERVISION

Commodity trading is generally the individual trader's avocation. Few people can afford to devote more than a few hours daily to something other than their own profession.

Commodity partnership managers usually devote their full time to commodities.

VII. COMMISSIONS

Individual accounts pay a fixed commission rate. "Take it or leave it."

Large accounts may negotiate for commission discounts. These discounts may be quite substantial, running as high as 70% or more.

VIII. RESERVE ASSETS

Any well-managed account should hold substantial cash reserves to guard against temporary setbacks. This reserve requirement should be 60% to 70% of available capital. Few individuals can afford to hold such large reserves and still have adequate additional funds available for trading.

A partnership would have no problem in setting aside a reserve (which is also in T-bills earning 6%). The partnership would still have substantial additional funds available for trading.

IX. MANAGEMENT FEE

Some commodity brokers charge double commissions in lieu of management fees. Also, some brokers insist upon cash deposits for margin and prohibit clients' use of T-bills regardless of the size of the account. The broker, in turn, invests the clients' cash in T-bills and retains the earned interest for the house.

Partnership managers charge varying fees, ranging as low as 1½% per month. The T-bill interest earnings will usually cover this fee.

XXIV

Trend-Following Systems

In 1946 after the end of World War II, the common sentiment was that the economy would go into a tailspin as it converted from massive wartime production to comparatively limited peacetime production. This ill-considered philosophy lingered from 1946 to 1949. Meantime, the economy surged ahead as people rushed to replace worn-out automobiles, to build homes to house families created by wartime marriages, and generally to provide themselves with the essentials that had either become luxuries during the war or were totally unavailable.

For three years potential investors were reluctant to invest in the stock market while they continued to harbor the notion that the economy would suffer a setback. Despite rapidly expanding corporate earnings, stocks held in a very narrow band. The Dow Jones Industrial Average stayed within a thirty point range — from 160 to 190 — for the entire period of 1946 to 1949. The combination of a booming economy and rapidly expanding earnings concomitant with static stock prices lowered the Price/Earnings ratio on the DJIA to about 7X. Some of the components of the DJIA sold at P/E ratios as low as 3X. It was a rare opportunity to acquire stocks at truly bargain prices.

When investors finally realized that there would be no postwar bust — that, in fact, they were involved in a postwar boom — they rushed to buy stocks, and the stock market rose in a straight-up configuration for more than a decade. By 1963 the DJIA had reached 1,000, an increase of more than 400%. Earnings of the DJIA component stocks during that fourteen years had not quite doubled, so the P/E ratio had expanded to a startling 23X. Stock buyers had grown rich, but their investment castles were built on foundations of sand. The only way the stock market's performance could be duplicated during the next fourteen years would be for the earnings to double again and for the P/E ratios to triple again. That would mean a ratio of more than 70X for the DJIA! Investors failed to heed the obvious danger signals.

Naturally, mutual funds did very well in the period from 1949 to 1963. Regulations restrict funds to the publication of life-of-the-fund records, or five-, ten-, or fifteen-year, etc., records in their sales literature. The fifteen-year records were phenomenal, so they published charts showing the growth of a $10.000 investment from 1948 to 1963. Those charts were called "mountain charts" because in most cases the $10,000 had grown to $60,000 or more while in some cases it grew into a $100,000 mountain. Crafty salespeople implied that this was typical performance and awed potential investors who never took the time to analyze the situation and realize that it would be impossible to duplicate that performance over the next fifteen years. Salespeople had a picnic during the mid-1960's as unsuspecting investors poured billions of dollars into mutual funds. The salespeople got rich, but investors reaped only disappointment when the stock market went into a tail-spin. It took twenty years for the DJIA to match its 1963 level.

Recently another investment fad has come along, and again investors have failed to perceive the fallacy of the method. It is the computerized trend-following method of trading commodities.

The basic principle of trend-following is borrowed from the physics term "inertia." In simplest terms, the principle of trend-following states: "Once a price trend has been established, the trend remains intact until outside influences cause it to reverse, thereby establishing a new trend."

To recognize trend reversals, a typical trend-follower would use a computer to plot the five-day moving average of a commodity's

231

price against its twenty-day moving average. Theory says that the trend has been reversed when the five day average penetrates the twenty-day average.

The theory seems fine, but it has proved unreliable in actual trading. The flaw is that the method requires very large price swings before profits may be reaped. For example, under ideal conditions a commodity such as cattle might end a price decline at 50 cents and make an uninterrupted climb to 60 cents before topping out and starting a new downward trend. The five-day vs. twenty-day crossover makes it impossible to receive a buy signal at the bottom of the trend or a sell signal at the top; by definition, it is only possible for signals to be flashed no less than five days after the new trend has begun. This would mean signals being given perhaps two cents away from both the bottom and the top. Thus, under the ideal conditions of an uninterrupted rise of 10 cents, trend-followers harvest only 6 cents, or just 60% of the move. Unfortunately for trend-followers, uninterrupted 10 cent moves in cattle are rare, for that represents a 20% price change; fluctuations of a few cents are the norm. Thus, the usual actions of a trend-following account in normal markets is to sell and go short near bottoms and to cover the short and go long near the tops of these repeated oscillations. The net result is a series of costly whipsaws.

In 1973 the Nixon administration sold our surplus grains to the Russians who had had severe crop losses due to drought. At about the time our granaries were being emptied it became apparent that we were going to have a production shortfall of our own, due to drought. Grain prices skyrocketed. Soybeans, which had never previously topped $4, exploded to $13. Wheat — normally $2 — ran to $6.50. Corn — normally $1.25 — ran to $4.00. Other commodities, in sympathetic moves, roared to similar levels. Copper, which had never sold above 80 cents, surpassed $1.40. Sugar, which had traded above 10 cents only once before in its history, hit 66 cents. Apocalyptics called it the beginning of the end of the world and started buying gold and silver, which caused those prices to race to previously unseen levels. The prior top on silver was $2.56, but it reached $7. Gold, which had been fixed at $35 for nearly forty years, topped $200. The computerized trend-following systems had a field day.

The commodity price balloon burst in 1974, and by 1975 most prices had returned to something near their former levels — or at 20% to 30% above those former levels to compensate for the effect of inflation. The Computer operators had another field day on that return trip. What has happened since? Consecutive record-breaking crops and a return to sanity have caused commodity prices to stabilize at near-normal levels, influenced only by the factors of inflation which have caused price increases in just about everything. In recent years commodity prices have swung through relatively narrow ranges, and this trendless activity has been anathematic to trend-followers as whipsaws decimate their capital. Unfortunately, they still display records which include the period from 1973 to 1975, which gives the overall record a respectable appearance, but most of them have done very poorly since 1975. Somehow they still find gullible investors who do not recognize that the bulk of the success was garnered in 1973-5.

The operators of the computerized trend-following systems usually produce only the records of hypothetical accounts, rarely willing to produce records of actual accounts. Their hypothetical records are based upon the assumption that the client deposited enough money to trade in all of the 37 most popular commodities available. They claim such an account could have been traded with $50,000 of capital, but I have before me the margin requirements of a major commodity brokerage house (a New York Stock Exchange Member) which sponsored a commodity fund using trend-following methods, and it shows the total required to trade a single contract of these 37 commodities to be $118,800.*

---

* This chapter was written in 1979, and most of it has been left intact. At the time of the original writing, the mentioned firm required only $1,500 margin for gold and silver contracts, $1,650 for platinum, and $1,100 for copper. With the upside explosion and subsequent collapse of the 1979-80 metals markets, margins were raised retroactively to $50,000 , $75,000 , $30,000 , and $20,000 respectively. These increases, plus the increase in margin requirements for the interest rate futures, would have caused the necessary capital to trade a single contract of each of the 37 commodities to exceed $500,000.

Even if you had had that much cash available, it probably would have been impossible for you to trade. There were times when some markets — especially the precious metals — were restricted to liquidation of existing positions only. New positions and reversal of existing positions were prohibited.

This is about normal for the industry, averaging $3,000 per commodity, including $9,000 for the Standard & Poor's stock index and $5,000 each for the currencies. In their hypothetical summaries, the trend-followers ignore the possibility that the account may have been a 40% loser before it caught the runaway move in Afghanistan artichokes which recouped all the losses and gave the account a net profit for the year. The margin calls prompted by the early losses, plus the cash held in reserve against the possibility of further losses before the blockbuster winner comes in, force the fully-invested account to commit about $200,000 instead of the $50,000 claimed. If they do make a profit, it is on the order of $15,000 for a year, which they claim is a return of 30% on the $50,000, but in truth it is more like $7^{1}/_{2}\%$ on the $200,000 actually required. That is less than what could have been earned by leaving the money in the bank.

A worse deception than the creative accounting of the trend-followers and their hypothetical accounts is the results of the actual accounts they manage. Because they are aware that it would require $200,000 to trade all the active commodities instead of the $50,000 their sales literature claims, they tactfully suggest that you omit Afghanistan artichokes, coffee, cocoa, lumber, the currencies, the interest rate futures, and a few others so that your account may be opened for $30,000. At least they will tell you that it takes only $30,000, but you had better be prepared with another $20,000 for the margin calls, since they state in their literature: ". . . odds are that an initial equity will show a loss before showing a profit. . . since it is necessary. . . to continually probe the market (taking losses while awaiting the blockbuster)." This results in your account trading little more than the grains, meats, and metals.

Grains, meats, and metals have given trend traders an exceedingly rough time of it the past few years as record crops have confined prices to a broad but rather clearly defined price range. Relative stability appears in order for the next few years because of projections of additional record crops and the probability that there will be an internationally cooperative effort to build reserve food supplies. Stability is disastrous to trend-followers as demonstrated by their poor 1978 records.

Stable conditions are ideal for scale trading because the minor oscillations which create the whipsaw losses for trend-followers generate repeated profits for scale traders. Trend-followers will reap another generous harvest only if they are able to survive until another runaway market occurs in commodities, but it is possible that that condition may be a long time in coming. They could suffer greatly as they wait. After all, stable commodity markets are the norm, and markets such as we saw in 1973-5 occur rarely.

Trend-following systems have proven to be very popular with commodity brokerage firms because of the steady flow of substantial commissions which they create, but sooner or later any system must generate profits for the customers, or there will be no customers. For this reason, some of the commodity trading firms have abolished trend-following systems from their managed account programs.

Between 1974 and 1979 there were about fifteen major funds formed for the purpose of using trend-following to trade commodities. Because of poor performance, two of them have disbanded already, and several more are barely surviving.

I have been told that one firm became so disenchanted with computerized trend-following that they sent a confidential memo to their branch office managers quietly announcing they had deleted that particular type of program from their managed account offerings. They did this despite the fact they were preparing a public offering of a huge commodity trading partnership which was expected to use this same trend-following method. Obviously, this offering of the commodity fund was a concession to their sales department because the concept of trend-following and the hypothetical performance records are so easy to sell. Some of the firm's longtime employees had used the trend-following recommendations for their clients and had learned through bitter experience (1) trend-following systems lose more frequently than they win, and (2) most accounts cannot survive the repeated losing years while awaiting the occasional winning years.

When the initial copies of the preliminary prospectus first became available in the Beverly Hills office (which has a large Jewish clientele), one salesman commented: "How do they expect us to sell this? We have used this manager's trend-following recommendations in the past, and we buried everybody. This system has exterminated more Jews than Eichmann!" Another salesperson, noting the repeated losses from using trend-following asked: "Do we offer this fund as a commodity speculation or as a tax shelter?"

* * *

The foregoing part of this chapter was written in 1980 and included in the original edition of this book exactly as printed. Trend-following had become the hot item in commodities trading at that time, and it took a lot of nerve to challenge the most popular trading method extant at the time, but I was convinced that inflation was cooling, interest rates would be coming down, and that there could not be another attempt to corner the silver market because Congress had awakened to the threat it posed for our entire financial system and had taken measures to prevent a recurrence; furthermore, huge grain surpluses would put lids on grain prices and indirectly on meat prices. All of these items combined to indicate probable price restraints on the upside, and because prices had already come down so much, it seemed likely that commodity prices would be contained within a relatively narrow range for the next few years. Narrow trading ranges are anathematic to trend-following systems.

As things developed, my prophecy of hard times ahead for trend-followers came true.

Silver started its meteoric rise to $50.00 in late 1979 and then collapsed to $10.00 in 1980. It carried gold, platinum, copper, and palladium with it for a round-trip. Many of the international commodities such as coffee, cotton, and sugar participated in the price increases and subsequent declines. To some extent, even petroleum was affected as buying reached panic proportions and the hysterical buying and ultimate panic selling touched many commodities.

Not all commodities participated, but those mentioned above made virtually straight-line advances, followed by straight-line declines, giving the trend-followers exciting performance records for 1979 and 1980. Commodity prices have moved sideways since 1980, and promoters of trend-following trading methods in most cases have performed very poorly. However, instead of altering their trading methods, they have altered their selling methods and continue to bilk the public.

Here is how one manager of a large trend-following fund has been able to continue to impress potential investors to become managed account clients or to invest in his fund: He works for a giant commodity wire house which has sponsored a series of trend-timing funds. About ten years ago he started using trend-following techniques in assisting his clients in their commodity trading. He was solidly into trend-following when the Texans made their first attempt at cornering a commodity by buying up a major portion of the soybean carryout in 1976, pushing soybean prices from $4.50 to $11.00 in eight months. There was no fundamental reason for the price rise, but numerous commodities participated, and trend-followers did very well, including this man. (Score one for trend-following, for it will make profits when big moves come, regardless of the reason.)

His record was mediocre to poor until 1979 and 1980 when he caught the silver and gold runup and the return trip. Obviously, he had two more very good years.

He began circulating his performance record for the period from 1974 through 1980. The overall performance was excellent because it had included the three exceptional years of 1976, 1979, and 1980. His record again was poor in 1981 and 1982, but he was riding on the performance of the earlier years, and his firm sponsored him as the manager of a huge commodity fund which it underwrote. In the past twelve months his record has been abominable because of the choppy action of commodities markets such as I predicted three years ago, and he is down about 40% with his fund. That makes his record for the last three years a net decline of about 60%, which takes him nearly back to square one with his old customers and to the poorhouse with the new ones. After suffering a 60% decline, it becomes necessary to show a 150% gain merely to return to the starting point.

But don't worry about this chap. He (or, his firm) is very resourceful. They have changed the sales literature. It no longer refers to his "lifetime" record; instead, it breaks the performance record into three-year segments so that they may claim that you would always have made money with him if you had stayed three years. Part of their purpose is to say that it was the client's fault for losing because he had abandoned the program (who wouldn't, after a 60% loss?) before giving it time to work, but the primary purpose was to deceive potential investors. Starting with 1974, there was always at least one good year in every three-year period, for 1976 would be included in each segment through 1978; then the 1979 or 1980 markets would be included in every three-year segment from 1977 through 1982. You may bet your very last dollar that their sales literature next year will be expanded to show that he made a profit in every four year period so that his atrocities of 1982 and 1983 will be covered by the gains of 1979 and 1980. The impression which they try to convey is that all three-year or four-year periods are profitable for their system, but that is true only if you have at least one blockbuster year during the time you are a client, and I consider that circumstance highly improbable over the next few years. Here is why:

Grain surpluses are even greater today than they were in 1980, and there will probably be a reduction in government assistance to farmers through a lowering of crop support prices for next year. The drought of 1983 has pushed grain prices high enough to encourage non-participation in any 1984 farm program, and we should see a return to near-capacity plantings in the United States. It is a cinch that foreign nations will plant every acre in sight to take advantage of the prevailing high prices, and this will guarantee enormous grain surpluses for several years to come. This will clamp a lid on grain prices, limiting them to relatively narrow ranges. Tightly confined price ranges for grains will permit livestock farmers to plan their breeding programs with greater accuracy, thus allowing a continuation of the expansion program which has already begun. This should assure us of an adequate meat supply, obviating any chance of substantial price increases.

An improving economy will keep a little upside pressure on interest rates, but each minor increase in rates tends to have a negative effect on the expansion, so the economic recovery should continue, but not overheat. There will be an improvement in the consumption of interest-sensitive commodities such as lumber, plywood, and copper simply because of the need to produce the autos and homes which were not produced during the recession, but the lessons learned from the ill-famed experiment with high interest rates in the late 1970's should prevent demand from becoming excessive. An ample supply of crude oil will hold petroleum prices in check.

With grains, meats, and industrial commodity prices contained within narrow ranges, there will be little reason for precious metals prices to advance.

Putting it all together, I predict another two or three years of sideways commodity prices, which will be very costly for trend-followers. Sideways price action is perfect for scale trading.

I do not often recommend any form of speculating in commodities other than scale trading, but once in a great while I will call attention to useful phenomena which become additional arrows in the trader's quiver. Among these are the livestock/feed ratios, the cotton/corn/soybean ratios, and one which has become quite obvious during the past few years as trend-following has become more popular. It is the "moving average crossover."

I certainly do not advocate the use of charts to try to foretell commodity price movements, but I keep one or two moving average charts on each of the forty commodities which I follow. Mine are twenty-day moving averages. I have noticed that more and more frequently in the past few years it has happened that a crossover of daily prices above or below the 20-day moving average results in a burst in the price in the direction of the crossover. This spurt may last for a few minutes or a few days. I suspect this is caused by the legion of trend-followers all receiving buy or sell signals simultaneously.

There was a time when these spurts were rare and usually caused only by something really fundamental in nature, but their occurrence has become more common and today occurs almost with predictability. It is this predictability which can afford you an opportunity to enhance your profits, even if you use a trading method as mechanical as scale trading.

An understanding of why this is happening with increasing frequency lies in the development of trend-following as a commodity trading technique and its rapidly expanding popularity in recent years.

Trend-following as a commodity trading technique is generally thought to have been developed about twenty-five years ago by an individual who had great difficulty in acquiring adherents because of the miserable performance record which the system showed as commodity prices drifted sideways. Then came the grain fiasco of the Nixon administration in 1973 and the beginning of the surge in crude oil prices almost immediately thereafter. That gave trend-followers their first good year of performance and anyone who had survived the first fifteen years of crucifixion finally had something to shout about. Quick to respond, they began touting their system everywhere, and they began to acquire some believers. The Director of Research at one of the major commodity wire houses was quoted recently as saying that he believes that no more than one of ten commodity traders in 1973 was a trend-follower, but the good record of trend-following in 1973, 1976, 1979, and 1980 created so many new disciples that today five more of the original ten traders have converted to trend-following. He went on to say that it was logical to assume that at least three of the original ten have subsequently resigned from commodities trading, so that six out of every seven commodity traders with ten years of experience are trend-followers. (I question whether seven out of any group of ten commodity traders have survived for ten years, but the conclusion that six out of seven commodity traders today use trend-following is probably accurate.)

There are many variations to the trend-following system, but basically it requires that two moving averages be plotted on the same chart with one of the averages being of short duration and the other being of longer duration. Some people use a three-day versus fourteen-day combination; some use four versus seventeen; the most popular is the five versus twenty. Some use simple computations in which each day carries the same weight in the calculation as each other day; however, some people use weighted averages in which nearby days carry greater weight than earlier days. Thus, some of the methods are more responsive than others, flashing trend-reversing signals more quickly, but the trade-off is that they receive false signals more frequently and therefore are subject to more numerous whipsaws.

I contend that if it is true that something like six of every seven commodity traders are trend-followers, and if some of them receive signals anywhere from a few minutes to a couple of days ahead of other trend-followers, it should be relatively easy to anticipate when the mob will probably start to respond to a moving average crossover which is beginning. The trend-followers with the most sensitively responsive methods will receive the first signals, requiring that they reverse, and their own trading action may be sufficient to trigger a reversing signal for the next most responsive method. It then becomes like dominoes as the rush to reverse positions causes an increasing number of reversing signals to be flashed until all of the trend-followers have switched from long to short, or vice versa.

One game that has become popular on the trading floors is "gunning the stops." In addition to the traders in the pits who execute orders for their employers are people known as "locals" who trade for their own accounts. They trade virtually without costs, so they can make a fine percentage profit on the smallest of moves. Many locals have traded so successfully for their own accounts that they have developed a clientele which has provided substantial amounts of cash with which the locals trade. The capital of one local may be measured in the tens or even hundreds of millions of dollars, and if enough of them want to perform in collusion, they can actually move markets to their advantage. These people are not stupid; indeed, they usually are very bright. They can read charts, and they watch for a chance to move a market through the weight of their own buying or selling and will move markets just enough to cause a reversal for trend-followers, for they can tell from their own moving average charts just where the trend-followers have placed their stops. When they go gunning for the stops, and when they are actually successful in hitting them, they can force an avalanche of orders to be executed simultaneously. They merely wait for a few ticks change in the price in their direction, and then they harvest their profits on the positions they took to hit the stops in the first place.

If you will remember that the trend-followers usually have entered *reversing* stops, you will realize that they must buy two contracts for each one short, one to cover the short and one to establish a long position, or that they must sell two contracts for each one long, one to liquidate the position and the second to establish a new short position, then you will realize the likelihood that the price movement following a moving average crossover can become sudden and substantial.

If you are a scale trader, there are at least two ways from which you may benefit if you keep moving average charts. You may be prepared to start accumulating a commodity, but if you see the possibility of a price breakdown if the moving average line is penetrated on the downside, you might elect to lower your top one or two buy orders. For example, copper might be trading around 76 cents, and you have been thinking of starting a buying scale at 73 cents; however, you notice that the 20-day moving average line is at 75 cents, and you reason that violation of that price could set off a wave of selling which carries copper's price down to 70 cents. You might lower your first buy-price to 71 cents, thereby saving $500.

The second way to benefit would be on the selling side. If you have accumulated five contracts of soybeans on a 5 cent scale down, and if the price penetration above the 20-day moving average line appears imminent, you might raise your first sell order 2 cents and the second one 1 cent. You should *not* do as some people advocate: cancel all sell orders. That is ridiculous, for you probably need about 20 cents to 25 cents to sell that top contract, and the action of the trend-followers reversing may be worth a spurt of several cents, but it is unlikely that it would be equal to 25 cents.

* * *

This entire chapter has been repeated verbatim from the 1979 edition and the 1984 edition of this book, with minor changes in wording for clarification. As this is written in early 1994, I will include these few current comments on trend-following:

Trend-following depends upon large moves in one direction, moves caused in the grains by a drought, or in lumber by the Northern Spotted Owl fiasco, or in U.S. Treasury bonds by the collapse in interest rates, but it has been five years since we have had a drought, the Northern Spotted Owl incident may prove transitory, and interest rates may now stabilize in a narrow trading range for several years. These are the types of things that kill trend-followers.

Take the 1993 Midwest flood as an example. It was called a 500-year flood. Trend-followers should have made fortunes this past summer, but most of them lost heavily. The reason is that the price breakout at the time of the start of the flood caused trend-followers to buy heavily and to add to their positions as the price rose. It took about $1.20 of the move in soybeans (from about $5.20 to $6.40) to signal the breakout which established the rising trend, and then in a single month the price shot above $7.50. In barely more than the next four weeks the price had dropped $1.40 and the trend-followers had seen their paper profits evaporate.

Trend-followers do not consider fundamental reasons for price moves, but it is crazy to ignore supply and demand factors and to try to guess future price movements by interpreting a lot of lines drawn on a chart. (Some chartists draw so many trend lines on a chart that it looks like a ball of steel wool. *After* the movement is over they will look back at the chart, select the single line that indicated the trend, and say, "See, didn't I tell you so?")

I am a fundamentalist, so in our newsletter, *The Scale Trader*, in that summer of 1993 I called attention to the fact that 1992 had been a record year for the corn crop in the United States, that it had been a record year for the wheat crop throughout the world, and that South America had just completed (remember, their seasons are six months opposite to ours) a record harvest of soybeans. There were no grain shortages anywhere in the world. Indeed, there were record surpluses in storage.

We had been sold out of our scales in all of the grains and the soybeans, and I suggested that subscribers go to the sidelines ("go fishing" was the precise advice) and await the inevitable correction. Once the correction started, it turned into a rout, and trend-followers took a terrible beating in that $1.40 decline in soybeans. This brought soybeans near to the $6.00 range, and we reloaded our scale trading inventories at the expense of the trend-followers who were now reversing and going short. But poor crops of oilseeds throughout the world caused heavy buying of American soybean oil, which again rallied the price of soybeans. This allowed us to unload our soybeans on the trend-followers who were now forced to cover their shorts and go long.

An interesting sidelight to all of this is the commentary of a prominent weatherman who was quoted in a major national daily newspaper during the summer of 1993. *On precisely the top day of the rally* this large article appeared describing how he was claiming to have just purchased numerous contracts of soybeans because his weather work and his trend-following charts had convinced him that we were going to see "beans in the teens." There has been no follow-up article to describe what the $1.40 decline did to him.

The point of all of this is that giant moves in commodities do not occur often enough to make trend-following profitable. We never know which commodity will make the next big move, so to be sure of catching the big move it is necessary to trade them all. That still requires a bankroll of about $400,000, much of which will be eaten away while you sit and wait for the blockbuster.

P. S.: I deliberately left the comments about "gunning the stops" in this chapter after adding the new commentary about that practice in Chapter XXIII. I simply wanted you to see the high level of sophistication to which the practice has been elevated in the decade since that was written.

I couldn't help but chuckle when I recently read an article in a national daily newspaper about "gunning the stops." The coauthors seemed to consider themselves investigative reporters who had uncovered a dastardly practice which had recently been invented. Heck, they have been gunning the stops since soldiers in the Roman Legion traded futures on spears and shields.

My abhorrence for charting is not limited to trend-following. There are several other gimmick trading methods which are just as silly. Here are my comments on just a few:

Stochastics: The first time I heard the word I thought it was a social disease. After hearing it explained I was convinced that it was. It is a system used to measure momentum, expressed as a percentage, with low percentage numbers foretelling a rally and high percentage numbers foretelling a decline. The trouble is, once the low percentage number is registered, the commodity's price can slowly drift lower, and you get stopped out of your long position with a loss. For example, if silver makes a sharp break and gives a low stochastics percentage reading at $4.90, you might buy and then watch the stochastic number remain fixed at a low number as silver's price slowly drifts down to $4.80, $4.70, and so on down to $3.80. If you use stops in quiet markets, stochastics will cause you to be stopped out dozens of times consecutively. If you don't use stops and you are relying on the stochastic low as an indicator of a pending rally, you will have a huge loss in a single contract.

Fibonacci: Get the penicillin. This guy lived from 1180 to 1228 and is recognized as a mathematician who developed a series of numbers which has as its basis a claim that all things react in a natural order. I don't know how people expect a mathematical series developed nearly 1,000 years ago to predict rain today, and it is today's rain — or lack of rain — which will set today's grain prices. Besides,

Fibonacci was one of the two senior engineers who led the work on the Tower of Pisa. I'm not sure that I want to trust my commodity investments to a man who can't design a building to stand up straight.

Gann: William Gann made $50 million trading commodities in the 1920's. He lost it all and died a pauper in 1955.

Jesse Livermore: Probably the greatest stock trader who ever lived. Books have been written about his trading technique. He made fortunes and lost fortunes on Wall Street. One day he lost $5 million and committed suicide.

Elliott Wave: Ralph Elliott was an engineer who developed a charting system which said there are five waves up and three waves down, but apparently he didn't have any faith in his own system because historians say he never made a trade. His chief devotee predicted in 1992 — with the Dow Jones Industrial Average at 3200 — that the stock market was about to drop "90% to 98%." That would take it down to 320 to 64. It is now 3900. Give me a break.

Kondratieff Wave: Nikolai Kondratieff developed his wave theory in the 1920's, theorizing that the world's economy swings in waves which may be measured in 48 to 60 year cycles. The leading U.S. proponent of this theory predicted in 1991 — with the DJIA at 3,000 — that the DJIA would hit 553 by 1993. The Kondratieff Wave and the wave we do at Dodger Stadium serve the same purpose: they are both good for laughs. Besides, do you want to hold a commodity contract for 60 years?

Japanese Candlesticks: This charting method should be called the "Kamikaze Trading System." It is just a warmed over version of the old-fashioned method of buying just above the "support" level and placing a stop order just under the support level. Vice versa for the sells. You still get stopped out as often as before, and it will eventually consume your capital — as often as before. Some broker glamorized the system by giving it an exotic name and tried to promote it at seminars to get new accounts, but he was only replacing the accounts he had lost from previous seminars when he promoted trend-following.

XXV

Why Doesn't Everyone Scale Trade?

Among the questions I hear most frequently is, "If this system is so good, why doesn't everyone scale trade?" I swear I don't know the answer. I don't trade any other way, but there are very, very few people who use scale trading.

Perhaps the answer to the question lies in the performance that people expect when they trade commodities. In Chapter I, I commented briefly on leverage and time compression and their effects upon commodity trading results, but I should repeat those remarks in the context of this chapter.

Unless inflation is brought under control we will never again see normal standards for return on investments, but because I am only trying to illustrate a point I will refer to percentage returns which were extant until the mid- and late-1970's. Investors sought 4-5% annual returns on bonds, 6% on real estate, and 9% in stocks. Aggressive persons attempted to amplify their results by employing margin in their stock accounts. By using 50% margin they could seek 18% annual returns. For the true speculator there was the commodities market. Commodities might fluctuate as little as 20% per year, but under certain circumstances they might move 10% in a single month or less. Commodity margins were as low as 5% to 10%, so a fortunate trader could realize as much as 100% to 200% profits in a month — sometimes faster.

Normally, U.S. Treasury bills and money market funds yield about 6%. In recent years we have seen real estate appreciate 25% per year. Real estate is not currently showing percentage gains of that magnitude, but the current low interest rates and the belt-tightening that corporations have been doing the last few years should bring an end to the recession before long. As the economy begins to improve and corporate employees begin to fear less about the permanence of their employment, we will see a return to home buying, and we could see another surge in real estate, perhaps to 25% annual gains again. Real estate buyers who purchase with 20% down payments in a 25%-rising market are realizing 125% annual returns. Commodity traders have bought 100 ounce gold futures contracts and have seen the price rise $100 in value in a single year, for a $10,000 profit on $1,000 of margin. That is a 1,000% return. Do you think people making 125% annually in real estate and 1,000% in commodities are interested in a 25% to 50% annual return by scale trading? Of course not. They will tell you that real estate is a cinch; you can't lose. So why take ten times the risk for one-third the return?

It is this mania that people seem to have for the triple-digit annual returns that keeps them from scale trading. There is very little chance that a *properly conducted* scale trading account will generate more than 50% profit in a year, and that does not seem to satisfy commodity traders. I have worked with people who knew nothing at all about commodity trading until I suggested scale trading. At first they were satisfied with the 3-4% monthly profits, but usually they wanted to become more involved, so they would clip a coupon from the paper and write for some free commodity research report. This put their name on a mailing list which was then sold to a mailing list broker. Soon the neophyte trader was receiving all kinds of mail offers and telephone solicitations. It did no good for the trader to tell the caller about his 3% monthly gains, for the caller could always top that by telling about the 500% profit that one of his clients made last month in a single trade. The caller fails to mention that this same client (if he actually exists) is a net loser and this single trade is by far the largest profit the account has ever had. The listener succumbs to the temptation of 500% profits in a single month, and the scale trading system goes out the window. I cannot begin to tell you how many times I have seen it happen.

However, consider this: Let us assume that you are so conservative that you seek only 20% profit per year in your scale trading account, and you actually realize that amount year in and year out. Your brother-in-law doesn't use scale trading. He trades commodities, but his aggressive approach shows profits two of each three years. In his winning years he makes 50% each time, and his single losing year shows a drop of only 25%. Who do you think will do better, you making 20% per year, or your brother-in-law making +50%, +50%, and -25%? You will. Your 72.8% profit will top his 68.75%.

I gave your brother-in-law all the benefit of the doubt in the previous paragraph. I assumed that he would win two years out of three. Few commodity trading accounts win two years out of three. Few make money two years out of ten!

I also gave you all the worst of it in the illustration. With your margin money earning a 6% current return, the scale trading activities of the account would only have to show an annual profit of 14% for you to realize a total 20%. If your scale is set to return an average profit of 1% per trade, you would need to realize only one trade each four weeks. Now, that is a conservative account!

I will adhere to my claim that a properly managed scale trading account should realize 25% to 50% profits per year, but I have also seen some aggressive scale traders who do much better. In all honesty, I would have to label these accounts improperly managed, but the distinction simply lies in their approach. I maintain that a properly managed scale trading account will set its scales to retain 50% of the capital at the probable low and 30% at the possible low, but aggressive scale traders consider this far too conservative. I also maintain that it requires $30,000 for the first commodity scaled, $20,000 for the next, and $10,000 for each additional scale. Aggressive traders also consider this too conservative. Some scale traders will estimate the probable low for a commodity and then determine a scale which will retain only about 10% of the capital at that level. They might also trade as many as ten commodities with $100,000 instead of seven. The escape feature of such accounts is that they may abandon certain positions if one commodity has gone completely awry and has imperiled the entire account. As that one commodity is declining and accumulating substantial losses, other positions may be rising and selling out. Buy orders are not reinstated for those positions so that the account retracts from ten commodities, to nine, then eight, seven and so on until the imperiled position corrects itself; then new positions are added until the account is again trading the full ten. It is not uncommon for traders who use this aggressive approach to realize over 100% profit annually, but this type of trading should be undertaken only by persons who are committing funds which they can afford to lose.

If you remember that I said a properly managed scale trading account will produce one roundturn trade annually for each $1,000 in the account, then we get back to the *real* reason why scale trading is not popular: commodities brokers hate it because it does not produce enough commissions for them. That is an unfortunate attitude for them to take, because if they would only take the *long-range* view they could see that they would earn more in total commissions with a scale trader who stays alive for years than they could earn from a trend-follower who goes broke in a few months.

I had brunch one day with a dedicated scale trading commodity broker who was visiting this area from his home state. We had done a great deal of business together, but we had never met. He had a mature young woman also in this area who was a client using scale trading, and she asked if she could join us so that we could all meet. During the brunch she commented that she would be interested in becoming a commodity broker, and she asked the other fellow how to go about it. He told her that it wasn't easy because commodity brokers lose so many clients and must constantly cold prospect by telephone in the evening, advertise regularly at great expense, and should conduct regular seminars in the office to generate new clients. Then he told her, "However, if you take the long-range approach and try to get all of your clients to scale trade, after a couple of years you will have a virtual residual income from the satisfied clients who are still trading and who are sending in new referral accounts." He went on to say, "We have been so successful with our scale trading the past three years that we have had to add two brokers, and we have not run an ad for ten months."

It is fortunate that in this case we are talking about an office manager who had the foresight to take the long-range approach and to let his brokers take the time necessary to build a client "book" slowly with the emphasis on holding satisfied clients. Managers like that are rare. Most managers are under pressure from the home office to hire and retain only people who are capable of producing enormous commissions from the first day. As an example of the kind of commissions which every broker is expected to produce, a long-time broker-friend of mine was contemplating transferring from one firm to another because of his displeasure over office politics. The manager at the office he wanted to join asked what his annual commission production was. He showed his production sheets for the last three years, showing a $300,000 annual average gross. His firm's average payout of 40% netted him average paychecks of $120,000. You won't believe what the manager told him: "Sorry, we can't use you because we would lose money on you." He went on to say, "If I were just a broker and couldn't produce at least $500,000 per year gross, I would get out of the business and look for a new career." To him, you are a failure if you earn less than $200,000 per year. All that means to me is that this manager — as with most managers — puts so much heat on his salespeople to produce that they would not dare to take the long-range view and try to develop a long-term clientele of scale trading accounts.

XXVI

Some Useful Guidelines

It is impossible to promulgate a set of inflexible rules for scale trading, saying that trades may be made only in a particular manner and only when certain conditions exist. There are just too many variables. Breadth of scales and their starting points are functions of the bankroll. Probable and possible bottoms are functions of fundamental analysis, interpretation of which is dependent upon the analyst. Incremental profits are arbitrary and at the discretion of the trader. Risk versus reward considerations are totally within the judgment of the individual trader. The list of variables is virtually endless. However, experience has given me a few useful tools that I like to apply for consideration before initiating scales. They may prove useful to you.

These rule of thumb considerations that I employ are best applied to $50,000 accounts where capital does not affect the trader's thinking, but even in the smallest accounts — once adjustments are made for capital — these guidelines should prove helpful.

1. IS IT FUNDAMENTALLY ATTRACTIVE? Because this system depends upon the Law of Supply and Demand for its success, the price of the commodity at commencement of buying must be reasonable when considered in light of the current supply/demand situation. It is not enough to say that the price has been declining recently and that this has brought it into an attractive buying range. The fundamentals must dictate that a further decline in price would likely prompt a decrease in production and an increase in consumption.

2. IS IT IN THE LOWEST THIRD OF THE RANGE OF THE LAST TEN YEARS? Only when this rule is applied may you calculate your scales with assurance. As long as you stay in the lowest third for your buying, you have a measure of safety which will guarantee your success. Obviously, you must ignore price aberrations created by nonrecurring events. For example, if silver has ranged from a low of $4 to a high of $9 during the last five years excepting a period of a few months during which a syndicate attempted a corner on the silver market and drove the price to $50, the realistic range should truly be considered to be $4 to $9, and the $50 move ignored. Thus, you would commence a scale in silver only in the range below $5.67.

An adjustment may be made for carrying charges. If corn trades between $2 and $4, scales should begin below $2.67, but that applies only to the December contract, the first to be deliverable from the new crop. If annual carrying charges approximate 6%, or ½% per month, that much may be added to succeeding contracts. Thus, a December scale could be started at $2.67, while March would commence at $2.71. May at about $2.74, July $2.77, and September at $2.80. The next delivery option is the succeeding December, and the lowest-third rule would again apply to that contract with carrying charges added to the deferred contracts.

3. IS IT BELOW THE 20-DAY MOVING AVERAGE? It is human nature to be attracted to those commodities which are moving higher in price. You may get the feeling that you should buy that particular commodity before it gets away. Sometimes it will work to buy those things that are rising, but that practice will generally yield but a single winner, so the risk of starting a scale at a top is far greater than the potential reward. Therefore, you should use some type of control mechanism to prevent you from being attracted to commodities which represent great risk to your trading operation.

To avoid that risk, and to temper my enthusiasm for commodities which appear to be running away from me, I keep 20-day moving average charts on each commodity. As defined before, the 20-day moving average is simply the average closing price of each of the last twenty trading days, with the new closing price added each day and the twentieth day back being deleted. I try to initiate scales only in those commodities which are below the 20-day moving average. Upon occasion it will cause me to miss some trading opportunities, but it also forces me to avoid the embarrassment of starting too high and accumulating a large number of contracts and corresponding large paper loss immediately after initiating a scale.

When Rule 3 is combined with Rule 4 you will find that you frequently make but a single trade and cash a winner very quickly. The astute trader who monitors all the commodities may find that he makes very few trades, is compelled to accumulate very few large positions, and can average a winning trade perhaps each ten days. If each of these trades results in a 1% gain, the account will produce 36.5% profit annually.

4. IS IT NEAR THE BOTTOM OF A DECLINING TREND CHANNEL? The reader who is familiar with the use of charts will readily appreciate the significance of this rule, but for the benefit of the reader who is unfamiliar with the basic tenets of technical analysis, a simple explanation is in order

In Chapter VIII, "Worth 10,000 Words," some examples of bar charts were illustrated. The vertical markings on the charts represent the range through which the commodity traded that day, the lowest point on the line being the lowest price of the day, and the highest point on the line being the highest price of the day. To assist a chartist in recognizing the approximate trend of prices, he may draw a line along the extremities of these daily lines. In a *declining* market the line which is drawn upon the chart will connect two or more of these daily *highs*. In a *rising* market the line is drawn to connect two or more of the daily *lows*. (Charting theory says that once the declining or rising trendline is penetrated, a new and opposite trend has begun. I will not debate the issue here.)

To further define the declining or rising trend, a chartist will draw another line parallel to the original line but connected precisely with the deepest low in a declining market or the highest high in a rising market. Thus, all trading which has occurred during the declining trend or the rising trend is contained between the two lines which define those respective trends. These two parallel lines define what is known as a trend channel. Charting theory says that when the price approaches the lower line of a declining channel, the price has reached an oversold position and is possibly due for a technical rally. It should be safe to commence a scale in this area, assuming you have also checked the other rules for corroboration.

5. IS IT LOW ON THE CONTRARY OPINION SCALE? Most of the commodity brokerage firms publish their research reports on Thursday or Friday for mailing in time for the clients to read over the weekend.

Since a vast majority of commodity traders lose, and since a vast majority of traders receive their advice from commodity house research reports, it is safe to assume that these reports are putting out poor advice. It is not that they do it deliberately, it is just that the writers get caught up in their own enthusiasm and recommend buying when things look brightest and selling when things look gloomiest. This results in their recommending buying at tops and selling at bottoms. Thus, to do the opposite of what the masses are doing should prove rewarding. This has come to be known as the Contrary Opinion Theory.

I am aware of at least two commodity research firms which receive and tabulate these weekly brokerage house advices. They report the scores in their own publications the following week. There is a slight lag time, but the reader who follows these tabulations regularly will be able to capitalize on the printed results and in some cases anticipate pending scores because of an accumulating trend. In other words, if cotton has been declining from a 70% favorable status to 60%, then 40%, and then 25%, it may drop to 10% or 15% the next week. According to theory, when a commodity is rated favorably by 25% or fewer of the research houses, it is time for a rally to begin. The reasoning behind this is that most of the clients have either liquidated positions or shorted the commodity, and with few people left holding long positions, the preponderance of new orders would be on the buy side.

The Contrary Opinion Theory has lost some of its validity in recent years because the brokerage house research reports have become less and less dependent upon fundamental information and more and more upon technical analysis and trend-following. A few years ago the research analysts collected as much information as possible on supply and demand factors to draw their conclusions as to the probable direction of the next move. Their reports on each respective commodity would contain five paragraphs of fundamentals and a final paragraph indicating their expectations for the coming move. There were always extenuating circumstances which could be interpreted in several ways, so there could be honest but different conclusions of up, down, or sideways pending movement. It was rare when 75% or more of the analysts would conclude simultaneously that the next move *had* to be in a single direction. On those rare occasions of near-unanimity it was likely that the commodity had reached an overbought or oversold condition and could probably be expected to reverse momentarily. That is what made Contrary Opinion work.

Things have changed. Many of the research analysts have worked in the area of research for less than fifteen years, which is the period during which trend-following has gained its popularity, and they have been tutored by their superiors to believe that trend-following works and that they should always consider the trend when making analyses. Thus, when they consider all of the fundamentals, they tend to ignore their true feelings and make that paragraph which contains their conclusion a restatement of the new adage, "The trend is your friend," and they allow the trend to dictate the conclusion. Therefore, it is likely that at frequent times there will be 98% of the analysts predicting the same directional move — which is simply that the trend will continue. The percentage changes are so rapid that the percentile swings above 75% or under 25% in a matter of days, causing severe whipsaws for the trend-followers and making interpretation through Contrary Opinion very difficult for scale traders.

An example of this evolution is the Commodity Research Bureau's weekly publication "Futures Market Service," familiarly known as the "Blue Sheet." Twenty years ago it was 100% fundamentals, but today it is 85% technical and 15% fundamental. I had a long, pleasant discussion recently with their managing editor in which I suggested that the Blue Sheet could be restored to its position of preeminence as a source of fundamental information, and although he was most cordial, I am sure he recognizes that he has a greater responsibility to the 98% of commodity traders who use technical analysis than he has to the 2% who use fundamental analysis.

The two firms publishing Contrary Opinion figures are:

Consensus, Inc.
1737 McGee, Suite 401
Kansas City, MO 64108

Market Vane Corp.
P. O. Box 90490
Pasadena, CA 91109-3964

These publications are relatively expensive for someone seeking only Contrary Opinion numbers. Most full-service brokerage firms subscribe to one or both of these services and will be pleased to quote the Contrary Opinion number for the week (and several weeks back) on a commodity you are considering scaling.

6. IS ITS RELATIVE STRENGTH LOW? Commodity prices frequently move in a mass, much as stock prices. When the stock market is going down, even the good stocks go down. When the stock market is rising, even the cats and dogs do well. When grain prices fall, soybean prices decline. Soybean product prices also decline. Each of these commodities is linked by the common thread that it may be used for livestock feed. Likewise, the meat commodities will decline, for as feed becomes cheaper, livestock numbers will tend to increase. Cotton competes for the same farmland as corn and soybeans, so cotton prices will be affected to the downside. Staple foods such as coffee and sugar are affected by the lower prices of the other food staples, so they, too, will decline. Lower food prices can mean a reduction in the pace of inflation, so gold, silver, platinum, and, to a lesser degree, copper prices will fall. It is plain to see why commodity prices move somewhat together.

However, if a particular commodity is momentarily moving out of sync with other commodity prices, it is probably an aberration which will be adjusted soon. For that reason I find it helpful to peruse the weekly "Futures Chart Service" published by Commodity Research Bureau (available in most full-service commodity brokerage offices). It no longer contains the very helpful "Moving Averages and Oscillators" section, but it does show a "Current Relative Strength" line on each individual commodity. When I locate a commodity which has a relative strength line indicating that commodity is very weak relative to the performance of all of the other commodities, I apply the tests of the other rules listed in this chapter, and then I make the determination as to whether I should commence a scale in that commodity. As with each of the other rules, a low relative strength rating alone is not sufficient cause to prompt me to buy.

7. IS ITS RATIO TO COMPETING PRODUCTS FAVORABLE?

There is a very close mathematical relationship between certain commodities which, for example, compete as livestock feeds or for farmland. "Mom and Pop" farms are a thing of the past. Today it is the computerized corporation which dominates farming. By knowing some of the relationships between competing commodities, you will enhance your chances of success in commodities trading, for it is these relationships which are fed into the computers to determine whether it is more profitable to feed corn vs. soybean meal; to raise hogs or beef cattle; to plant corn, soybean or cotton on land which may accept all three; etc.

For example, the normal relationship between corn and soybeans is five bushels of corn to two bushels of soybeans. Thus, if corn sells at $2.00 per bushel, soybeans should be $5.00 per bushel. If corn is $3.00, soybeans should be $7.50. If you are about to commence scaling corn at $3.00, you would be well-advised to check the soybeans price. If soybeans are trading at $7.00, it is relatively safer to trade soybeans.

There is also a relationship between soybeans and cotton. The rule of thumb is ten pounds of cotton for one bushel of soybeans. When cotton trades at $0.70 per pound, soybeans should be around $7.00 per bushel. Thus, in the example given in the previous paragraph, if you prefer soybeans at $7.00 to corn at $3.00, you should also check cotton, for if cotton is $0.65 per pound, it is the best buy of all.

You should also compare oats, wheat, and soybean meal, for each of these competes with corn for land use and as a livestock feed. The relative ratios are available in most commodity brokerage offices.

8. *IS THE MARGIN REQUIREMENT FAVORABLE?* Because corn and soybeans have a 5:2 relationship, when the price of corn moves 2 cents the soybean price should move 5 cents. A scale which is devised to buy corn each 4 cents down and to sell each 6 cents up would correspond to a soybean scale buying each 10 cents down and selling each 15 cents up. What percentage is that on the respective margin requirements? At the present time, corn margin is $400, while soybean margin is $1,350. Six cents in the 5,000 bushel CBOT corn contract would yield a gross profit of $300, or a 75% return on margin. A corresponding move of 15 cents in the 5,000 bushel CBOT contract of soybeans yields a gross profit of $750, or a 55% return on margin. Definitely the advantage is to the corn.

You probably should also consider *net* profit. After deducting a $50 commission from each of the above trades, corn nets $250, or 62.5% on the margin, while the soybeans would net $700, or 52%. It still favors the corn, but the advantage has narrowed.

Another way of stating the problem of comparative margins in the previous two paragraphs is to say that the 5:2 price relationship requires a 5:2 margin relationship. The ratio of the $1350 for soybeans to $400 for corn is nearly 7:2. This gives corn a 40% advantage, which we saw in the above calculation when corn netted 75% and soybeans netted 55%. Comparing margins by using your ratios is a quick way to determine the margin advantage.

XXVII

Patience is a Virtue

The most important requisites of the successful scale trader are dedication, discipline, and patience. Most of all, patience!

The temptation to deviate from the original plan may at times become overwhelming, and unless the scale trader is truly dedicated to the system, he may succumb to the temptation to take a flier on gold or silver, to hold for the big move instead of selling at predetermined scale levels, or to do any of the many things that commodity traders customarily do.

It requires real discipline to ignore the taunts of friends who talk about the huge profits they have been making being long sugar or short the interest rate futures. It will only be a matter of time until they give it all back — plus more — when trending markets begin to chop, when lock limits prevent their cashing profits, when stop orders start to consume their accounts, etc., but the scale trader must discipline himself to endure their ridicule in the meantime. If the scale trader hopes for any chance of success, he must have discipline.

It is, of course, at the most tempting times that not only scale traders but all kinds of traders must steel themselves to ignore what is going on around them and to stick to their own systems for trading. Consider, for example, the stock market. When the market is booming and stock prices are reaching all time highs the evening network news telecasts invade the brokerage house boardrooms to televise scenes of pandemonium as brokers and their clients roar with glee at the profits being realized. This is precisely when every clerk in the country withdraws his life savings from the bank to rush to the brokerage office to share in the action. When this occurs (I call it the Cronkite Index), I know it is time to get out of the stock market.

Conversely, when stocks are plunging to new lows, the networks take their television cameras back to the boardrooms to film scenes of gloom for the evening news: little old ladies and retired men telling horror stories of having to sell their stocks because they can afford no further losses. The Cronkite Index says it is time to buy. It rarely fails.

In the 1980 gold runup, the television news coverage was massive. Radio stations were reporting gold price changes each half hour. Gold was the feature article in every magazine with gold-related pictures on every magazine cover. Here in Southern California the local news broadcasts — as well as the network broadcasts — devoted large segments of their reporting time to personal interviews and live telecasts directly from the offices of the gold brokers. Customers, such as the schoolteacher who had invested her "life savings of $18,000 to make a profit of $16,000 in three weeks," were featured interviews. It takes a devil of a lot of discipline for a scale trader to resist the temptation to seize the opportunity to join the masses and make profits equal to a lifetime of savings merely by buying gold and holding it for three weeks. But virtue is its own reward, for gold declined 25% within the next week, and the Johnny-come-latelies (probably including a sadder but wiser schoolteacher) either had surrendered their profits or taken massive losses.

Even under normal circumstances when there is nothing particularly exciting going on and commodity prices are drifting slowly through their usually long cycles, there will be occasions when scale traders are subjected to temptation. These situations will occur when prices of all commodities seem to have advanced simultaneously; nothing seems cheap, and nothing seems attractive for scale trading. This is when PATIENCE will be rewarded. There is no rule which requires you to trade. You may begin to fear commodity prices are going to run away and you will miss opportunities for profit; that is never the case. Simply convert your funds to U.S. Treasury bills, or deposit your funds in the no-load (no commission) money market funds which are available. Bide your time until prices come down to your desired levels again. They always have, and they always will.

During the 1979-80 gold and silver frenzy, I heard people saying, "This time it will be different because gold and silver are unique. They will never again come down in price!" It reminded me of the book "Extraordinary Popular Delusions and the Madness of Crowds," a chronicle of a millennium of incredible crazes which engulfed the masses, including delirious speculations which drove princes and peasants to the poorhouse. It was written in 1841, but it could have been written today. There is a cycle to everything — especially to prices — and all things return to their starting points when the euphoria subsides.

It only takes patience.

XXVIII
Track Records

I entered the securities business as a Registered Representative in 1958. I suppose most young people who enter the business as an outsider — as opposed to those who ride the coattails of relatives into the business and already know the truth — expect to encounter a world in which all dealings are honest, a person's word is his bond, and a handshake is as binding as a written contract. Huh! It didn't take me long to realize that the primary function of a Registered Representative was to unload stocks, bonds, partnerships, flimsy tax shelters, proprietary in-house products, etc., on the public. The primary purpose of Wall street is to transfer assets from the uninformed small investor to the large investors who are equipped with inside knowledge not available to small investors.

By the end of two years I had decided to write a book about the evils of Wall Street, and I conceived the title: "The Dirtiest, Filthiest, Rottenest, Crookedest Business in the World: Wall Street." This was long before the insider trading scandals uncovered by Rudolph Giuliani. Unfortunately, I have never had enough free time to do the necessary research to document even a modicum of the multitude of shenanigans which occur daily on Wall Street. Maybe after I retire.

Did you ever have a stockbroker call you to say the firm was conducting a secondary offering of stock that you could buy *without commission?* (A secondary offering is an existing stock which is being resold by a private entity, as opposed to an IPO in which the stock is being sold by the issuing corporation.) What he is offering you is probably a block being unloaded by some giant mutual fund, pension fund, bank trust department, etc., which has learned through its Wall Street connections that there is disappointing news pending and that the stock is expected to decline. As for the commission, do you really believe that the brokerage firm is playing Santa Claus and is offering you stock without a commission? The truth is that the seller of the stock is paying the commission — usually *triple* the regular rate — and he is glad to do so, because although it might cost him 2%, the pending bad news is likely to drop the stock 20%.

The Securities and Exchange Commission wages a constant war against insider trading, but if they understood the stock market they would recognize that the problem is so pervasive that they would have to shut down all stock trading. Brokerage houses don't exist on the production of a few dozen Account Executives in Turnip Truck, Nebraska and Hayseed Hollow, Arkansas. Those people are there only to sell the secondaries being dumped on the public by insiders. The SEC doesn't even understand the principles of inside knowledge in the stock market. They can't understand how a broker gets inside information.

Inside information is obtained by a broker who is a huge commission producer and can afford to belong to several country clubs which are part of the old boy network. While playing golf with other club members who are also part of the network, they inform each other of the latest *reliable* rumors, and the next morning each broker is on the phone to his biggest clients — such as a mutual fund or a bank trust — telling them the news and recommending they buy (or sell) 500,000 shares. If the news turns out to be accurate, the fund or trust officer to whom he gave the information reciprocates with inside information of his own to the broker. *Quid pro quo.* This kind of information never makes it to the branch offices, but it circulates all around the old boy network in Wall Street.

It never occurred to the SEC that there is a *reason* why some brokers have gigantic clients and earn millions of dollars per year.

(One broker earned over $1 billion in one year!) I suppose the SEC thinks these people stayed late in the office each night and did a lot of cold prospecting and were fortunate enough to open a lot of accounts. Baloney. They got those big clients by producing good information ahead of the other brokers. The more good information they produced, the more big clients they obtained, and the more reciprocal information they obtained. Then it's back to the country club to exchange hot tips with the other members. The cycle only ends when the broker runs out of good inside information.

Speaking of the broker who earned $1,000,000,000 (that's *One Billion,* with a capital B) in a single year, let's compare that to a family living and working in a Midwest city where $25,000 is a good annual income: If there is one wage earner in that family earning the entire $25,000, he/she would have to work 40,000 years to earn one billion. If the spouse gets a job and also earns $25,000 they get a break, because it now takes them only 20,000 years to earn the billion. Do you see why it is inside information that greases the wheels of Wall Street?

Throughout this book I have related stories of doctored track records. Most of those anecdotes dealt with commodity account performance. I expect that most of the readers of this book are also owners of stock mutual fund shares, so I will expand a little on the doctoring of all kinds of track records.

One of the most common abuses in generating phony performance records is for the giant fund in a family of mutual funds to give tons of commissions to dealers in return for a nominal number of shares of a hot new stock making its debut as an initial public offering (IPO) being given to a tiny in-house fund within the same family of funds. This is called *quid pro quo,* or *something for something.* (Among attorneys, the term *quid pro quo* means, "You show me yours, and I'll show you mine.")

Here is how it works: Perhaps this family of funds is comprised of ten funds being managed by the same company. Total assets under management might be $2 billion. The largest of the ten funds — we will call it fund #1 — is $500 million; the smallest — fund #10 — is $500,000. Fund #1 trades tens of thousands of shares at a time and generates thousands of dollars in commissions daily. Everyone in Wall Street is aware that there is a pending IPO for XYZ Xionics Corporation (nobody cares what a xionic is, just so the company name ends in ionics) which is expected to be a "hot deal." A hot deal is one that is originally offered at $18 a share and immediately opens trading at $28 a share so that anyone fortunate enough to get a few shares makes a profit of $10 a share the instant the stock begins to trade. In the weeks prior to the IPO, fund #1 steers much of its trading business to one of the firms underwriting the XYZ Xionics deal, allowing that firm to earn tens of thousands of dollars in commissions. That underwriter then reciprocates by allotting 1,000 shares of XYZ stock on the IPO to fund #10. Fund #10 unloads the 1,000 shares minutes after the offering, taking a $10,000 profit. A $10,000 gain in a $500,000 fund is 2%!

Fund #10 is the beneficiary of numerous 2% *gifts* throughout the year, and by the end of the year it is up 60%, while the average fund is up only 12%. A couple of years like this, and fund #10 is up better than 150%. The $500,000 of seed capital in fund #10 was put there by insider clients of the company which manages this family of funds. With the fund now up about 150%, they open the fund to public investment, but only by the employees of the management company. These employees know the kind of game that is being played, so they eagerly invest a few thousands of dollars each. Soon the fund is four years old, and its size is measured in the millions of dollars, because the hot IPO's continued to give it above-average performance. Before long, fund #10 is $25 million in size, and it is opened for investment by the general public, but there are no more hot IPO's going into #10 because a $10,000 gift is meaningless to the performance of a $25 million fund.

The sales effort is very low key for the first year or two that it is offered to the general public. All that the management company wants at this time is to add to fund #10's longevity so that they may claim that the fund is up 300% in six years, or an average of 26% annually. This makes it the #1 performer for all mutual funds during that period, and with a new aggressive sales program they are able to bring $1 billion into the fund.

If you take the time to analyze it, you will see that during the last four years fund #10 actually appreciated only an average of 12% annually, or the same as the average fund, and the same as the stock market in general. The real record was generated in those first two years that fund #1 was *buying* a performance record for #10.

During those first three or four years all of the hot IPO deals went to #10, but when they become meaningless as the fund grows rapidly as a result of its phony record, the management company launches fund #11 and gives *it* the hot IPO deals.

If you think this isn't being done, please let me assure you that the above anecdote is a *true story* of how one colossal fund got that way! It is done every day with dozens of mutual fund management companies.

The practice of one fund "buying" a hot IPO for its sibling fund is illegal, but it is as common as jaywalking, and the SEC treats it about as seriously. The reason that the practice is illegal is that the commissions generated by a fund are part of the assets of the fund to be used to buy research; or to be given to a brokerage house to apply against the processing charges for securities transactions by the fund, thereby reducing the fund's overall operating expenses; or to buy hot IPO's for the fund itself. When the manager of fund #1 uses those commissions to buy a track record for fund #10, it has the effect of stealing assets from fund #1. I believe the manager of these two funds should be made to forfeit all of the IPO profits earned by fund #10 to fund #1, and all of the management fees earned on fund #10 because of its phenomenal growth as the result of the great track record "bought" for it by fund #10 should be disgorged and awarded to fund #1. But don't look for it to happen because the people who work for the SEC would like to go to work for the management company of these two funds — at five times their present salary — and they would not want to jeopardize their chances by instituting a fraud action.

Another favorite method of "cooking" a performance record is for a mutual fund family to buy large amounts of shares of the stocks of a few select companies in each of their large funds. This heavy concentration of buying pushes the stocks higher, and although it doesn't mean much to the large funds in that family, it is significant to the performance of the smallest fund in the family because it holds large positions in each of the stocks being boosted, and, as a percentage of its entire holdings, it is so significant that a small rise in the value of these stocks results in a huge percentage gain for the fund. This puts the small fund among the leading performers for the year, and hundreds of millions pour into the fund.

This technique was used very successfully in the early 1960's when one management company, as an example, used all of its mutual funds to make constant purchases of three over-the-counter stocks which are today listed on the New York Stock Exchange. To insure diversification, a mutual fund may not invest more than 5% of its assets in any one stock, so their smallest fund ($20 million) held the maximum allowable number of shares of each of these stocks as the larger funds in the family bought the stocks and sent them sky-rocketing. This had a significant influence on the performance of the small fund and caused it to run from $11 a share to $33 per share. Investor money poured in, and in eighteen months the $20 million fund reached $1 billion in size! Unfortunately for the investors, very little money came into the fund when the shares were $11, but most of the money came in above $30. The public took a terrible beating when the stock market topped out and the fund shares collapsed.

The same fund pulled another scam when it bought tons of "letter stock." Letter stock is stock which is issued by a company without the benefit of registration and which is not offered to the public. It is usually purchased by an investor — such as a mutual fund — which agrees not to reoffer the stock for sale for a specified period of time. The price is negotiated, and it may be 30% to 50% below the current market value for the regular (publicly held) stock of the company.

This fund would buy letter stock from promising small companies which needed additional working capital. Because the letter stock could not be sold for eighteen months, the price might be at 70% of the price of the regular stock which trades freely. Amazingly, this fund *immediately valued the letter stock at 100% of the value of the regular stock*. This bought them a 43% gain the moment they wrote the check and signed the letter which made the stock non-transferable for eighteen months!

Despite these heinous crimes of deceit, and despite the millions of dollars lost by the investors, nothing was ever done to the portfolio manager of the fund.

Should it have been any surprise to anyone that after leaving the fund he became president of a tiny insurance company and made it into an industry giant through collusion with junk bond dealers? The insurance company is now in bankruptcy, and there is an excellent chance that innocent purchasers of that company's insurance may get back only a fraction of what they expected.

One method of creating a false track record for a commodity pool which I alluded to earlier in the book — but not in this context — is the practice of changing account numbers on trades and designating the winners for one account and the losers for another. This requires collusion on the parts of two individuals from two different companies. Here is how this one works:

Although there are ways for brokerage firms to earn the trading commissions on the pools they manage, it is usually done only through one giant holding company owning both the management company for the pool and the brokerage company for the pool. Obviously, such subsidiary arrangements can only occur when the holding company is very wealthy and can afford numerous subsidiaries. Fortunately, it is difficult for collusion to occur in such large companies because there are too many people overseeing operations, but it is a simple matter in small companies.

For example, I once saw a pair of one-man companies which acted separately in managing and brokering a commodity pool. Because they could not be owned by the same people, they were separate companies, with the pool manager owning one company and the broker owning the other, but in adjoining offices. To obviate the annoyance of having to telephone orders from one office to the one next door and then to telephone the prices on the fills back to the originating office, *they cut a window in the wall between the offices* and simply handed the orders back and forth. There were rumors that these two men frequently changed account numbers to enhance the performance record of the pool. It was easy for them to get away with it because there was no supervision other than themselves. They could have placed the losing trades in some of their discretionary accounts, but it makes more sense for them to eat the losing trades themselves. That is because if they ever got caught altering account numbers, they could deny the charge. Their defense would be that no winners were ever steered into their own accounts. The losses which they would be forced to eat in their own accounts would be insignificant if they could "buy" an outstanding record for the pool. This could bring millions of dollars into the pool, which would generate substantial management fees and brokerage commissions, easily exceeding the modest losses which they ate.

In the foregoing example, the manager used a deceitful technique to establish a performance record, but there is a simpler method: The method is basically the same as above, except that instead of showing the losers in his personal account, he takes the losers into his personal account and then simply refuses to show the results of his personal trading. A broker-friend of mine recently sent me a copy of the Disclosure Document of a Registered Commodity Trading Advisor which bears the following wording: "In the interest of privacy, clients will not be permitted to inspect the records of Mr. 'X' or other client's (sic) accounts or trades."

Sellers of computerized trading systems are also clever in their deceptive practices. You might purchase the software to a computerized trading method called "Whiz Bang" on April 1. The advertiser claims this system has produced a huge profit over the last four months, so you purchase the system. During the next six months you find the system doesn't work at all, and you lose very heavily. On October 1 you see an ad for "Whiz Bang," again claiming this system has produced a huge profit over the last four months. The advertiser probably doesn't number his editions of "Whiz Bang," but if he did, you would probably find that you purchased "Whiz Bang #8" — which didn't work after it was marketed to the public — and the developer went back to the drawing board last week to update the trading method, basing his new variation of "Whiz Bang" on known results for the last six months, and which could now be called "Whiz Bang #9." He is under no obligation to inform you that he alters the trading method every few months and advertises his *success* at trading over those few latest months — trading *known* results.

There is a master marketer — notice I said marketer, not trader — who keeps the U.S. Postal Service in business with his mass mailings offering a phone number which you may call to hear the recorded voices of some of the people who made money subscribing to his service. I swear to you that the little tale which I am about to tell you is absolutely true and without exaggeration: Over the years I have received many phone calls from people who were new to commodities trading and just wanted to rap a little before they started trading. During the conversation they would ask me, "Have you ever heard of...uh...uh...," and I would interject this man's name. They would exclaim, "Yes! How did you know?" I would tell them I had had the same question asked two or three times each week for several years, so I knew what they were going to ask.

Then I asked them, "Have you made any money using his method?" The answer was always, "No." Finally, I estimated that I had already talked to approximately 200 people who had said they lost money with his method, and I started counting the callers from that point on. I swear to you that I reached 283 before a single person said he had made money using this man's trading method. That person had stumbled into a profitable trade almost by accident. He had opened his account immediately after the top of the lumber market run caused by the Northern Spotted Owl incident in 1993. The marketer was recommending shorting lumber, and this solitary trader made a profit on lumber's retracement of the advance. The entire decline took only eight weeks, so if this subscriber had called two months later he would have become loser #284 instead of winner #1.

These numbers should not surprise you. Do you remember that earlier in the book I mentioned the researchers who canvassed the three commodity brokerage offices and found that *all* 300 accounts of $5,000 or less equity lost money after a year of trading? If those 300 lost money, why shouldn't the 283 who used this man's method?

A very old scam which has returned to popularity is the act of a noted trader who trades gigantic positions quietly accumulating either large long or short positions of futures contracts in a single commodity, and after the position is established to circulate the rumor that "Mr. Midas is buying (or selling)." The attendant publicity hits all of the media, and small investors jump into similar contracts to take advantage of the legendary trading skill of this noted man. Their buying moves the price sufficiently to hit the reversing stops carried by trend-following funds, and the price surges. This permits Mr. Midas to quietly liquidate his position and haul $100 million to the bank. On occasion, he has been brazen enough to oversell (or overbuy) to establish a new position which is directly opposite to that which the public thinks he has. Shortly thereafter, his confederates put out the word that Mr. Midas is now selling his long positions (when, in fact, he is already short), and the public rushes to sell. Again, their selling causes a trend reversal, forcing trend-following funds to sell their long positions and to establish new short positions. As the price is bombing, Mr. Midas is buying to cover his short position. Off to the bank with another $100 million.

I can't use the names of any of the scoundrels I describe in this book because they could sue me and squash me like a bug, but it you are doing any trading you will surely recognize who I am referring to. And if you think the Mr. Midas story is not true, just check it the next time you hear the media report, "Billionaire investor, Mr. Midas, is rumored to be buying gold." Gold runs up about $10 over the next three days, and then it flattens out. Four weeks later the media report that Mr. Midas may have liquidated his position (without mention of his new short position). In three days the price is $10 lower, having returned to the starting point of the scam. He played with 10 million ounces of gold, so his profit is $100 million. He lays off the gold game for six months, but in the meantime he quietly loads up on Deutsche marks, has his cohorts circulate the rumor throughout the media that Mr. Midas is buying Deutsche marks (long after he is finished buying), and then unloads as his adoring public rushes in to follow their leader. Another $100 million.

So why scale trade? Because scale trading takes advantage of all of these scams. When markets are being manipulated downward by scam artists like Mr. Midas, we are buying right along with him. When he manipulates the market upward to capture his ill-gotten gains, we are also cashing our profits — except that ours are legitimate. Besides, scale trading is not really a commodity trading system; it is a money management technique.

An ancillary consideration in the area of track records is the eerie adoration shown by the public for *hot guru du jour*, not recognizing that today's hot guru is tomorrow's leftover turkey. One major daily business newspaper wrote an article a few years ago featuring the hot guru of the day. They described how the attendees at an investment symposium fell silent when their Messiah entered the meeting hall. They then mentioned his prediction that the Dow Jones Industrial Average would soon hit 3,600. Instead of going up, the market went down, and he reversed his upside projection to say the market was going to bomb. Because of his fear of the pending stock market collapse, he retired from the investment business. He quit *precisely* at the bottom! I guess it embarrassed the newspaper to have canonized this man, so they began writing articles about him in which they now called attention to his occasional current predictions, all of which were dead wrong. His personal fall from grace was a resounding crash.

Incidentally, he was right about the 3,600 DJIA. The only problem is that it took six years to reach it.

His story is no different from the hallowed commodity guru who was everyone's hero during the runup in gold and silver prices in 1979-80. Unfortunately for him, he continued to tout the virtues of gold and silver investments all of the way down as gold and silver returned to their levels prior to the silver manipulation. He insisted the precious metals would surpass the highs of 1980 — $900 for gold and $50 for silver. He finally wilted under the embarrassment of his stubborn adherence to a position which was 180 degrees out of sync with reality, and he told his clients to sell. His timing could not have been more perfect. He sold everything on *precisely* the bottom day!

XXIX

Interest Rates and the Federal Reserve

It would be nice to be able to say that all markets are free markets and that all commodity prices move freely, being influenced only by the factors of supply and demand. Unfortunately, there is another factor which must be considered: interest rates. It is not that interest rates are not supply/demand factors; rather, it is that interest rates are used in an attempt to manipulate economies, and they may thereby influence commodity prices suddenly and sharply in a direction which has no relationship to supply and demand. The supply/demand factors will ultimately prevail, and commodity prices will move to their proper levels, but they may be pushed around by interest rate manipulations in the meantime.

Interest rates are used to direct the economy of the nation — and of the world — but the unfortunate part about it is that the people who are doing the directing know absolutely nothing about economics. They are the chairman and the governors of the U.S. Federal Reserve. The current chairman of the Federal Reserve (the Fed, for short) is Alan Greenspan. Alan Greenspan *taught* economics at the University of Chicago, but the poor man knows *absolutely nothing* about economics. In my newsletter, *The Scale Trader*, I call him Bagel Brain because he has a bagel for a brain. He and his predecessor, Paul Volcker, have this screwball theory that inflation can be slowed with high interest rates. Nothing could be farther from the truth.

Four or five years ago I wrote an article for an investment magazine, and I would like to reproduce it here before going on to discuss interest rates and the Fed:

" A few hundred thousand years ago two cavemen were standing on a cliff, trying to obtain the day's meat by dropping boulders on the mastodons which passed below. Somehow, through a series of grunts and arm waves, one of the men indicated to the other that it was better to drop larger rocks because they would fall faster and therefore strike the animals harder. His premise: a large rock would fall twice as fast as one half its weight.

This guy must have been considered quite the sage, for his premise became an axiom, and it was not questioned until Galileo Galilei in the seventeenth century climbed the Leaning Tower of Pisa to drop a brass ball and a wooden ball simultaneously. When they struck the floor together, the world finally awoke to the fallacy of one accepted axiom. The U.S. Federal Reserve system should awaken to the fallacy of its thinking regarding interest rates and their effect on inflation. Its axiom that raising interest rates will slow inflation makes as much sense as expecting a two-pound weight to fall twice as fast as a one-pound weight.

But, don't expect the Fed ever to be able to do anything about inflation. They can't even define it! They look at indicators of unemployment, manufacturing capacity usage, producer and consumer prices, etc., to determine whether there is inflation. That's not the inflation they should be concerned about. Those indicators tell us something about price inflation, but they tell us nothing about monetary inflation.

For the benefit of the Fed, let's define inflation: Inflation is an increase in the money supply without a corresponding increase in goods and services.

It's as simple as that. If you increase the money supply without increasing the number of things which are available to be purchased with that money, prices rise. Rising prices are an effect of inflation, not a cause.

To give an example, let us suppose that there are one million dollars in the money supply, and there are one million "things" available. The price for a thing is $1. But if the money supply is increased to two million dollars and there is no increase in the number of things, the price for a thing is $2. That is the classic example of how inflation of the money supply works. The only way to counteract inflation is to either reduce the money supply or to increase the available number of things. In the foregoing example, if the money supply is reduced to one million dollars, or if the supply of things is increased to two million, the price of a thing is restored to $1.

The money supply can be increased or reduced in two ways: through an increase or reduction in the federal budget, or an increase or contraction in bank lending. The Fed could do something about the budget deficits simply by going to the Congress (or directly to the voters) with a call for a reduction in spending, but Fed members are reluctant to bite the hand that put them in their cushy positions, so they refuse to blame the reigning Administration and instead blame something inanimate: interest rates. It doesn't bother the Fed one whit that the federal deficit continues to soar and that this means the printing presses must run day and night to keep the money supply inflating to keep up with the deficits.

The Fed tries the alternate method of arresting the money supply by raising interest rates in the expectation that businesspeople will be reluctant to pay the higher rates and therefore will refuse to borrow. That is ludicrous. What do the people at the Fed know about borrowing? Most of them are college professors or other theoreticians. They never borrowed a dime in their lives. They pay cash when they buy automobiles, and they put 40% down when they buy a house. They have never worked a day in their lives where their income depended upon performance, such as selling. They stayed at the university until they gained tenure, and then they sat back and wrote books about finance. As far as I am concerned, you can take all the college professor economists and load them on a plane headed for Europe, but fill the fuel tanks only half full.

If they would let me name the Fed chairman, I wouldn't go for a college professor who knows nothing about borrowing.

Give me the guy who borrowed $20,000 from his father-in-law (or, better still, his mother-in-law) to open a dry cleaning establishment. When things got tough for him, he had no tenure to fall back on. He had to increase his daily work load to seventeen hours instead of fifteen; he had to work seven days instead of six. And if he needed to borrow additional capital to survive, he went to as many banks as necessary to arrange a loan, and he never once asked the interest rate on the loan. He only asked if there was money available.

What the Fed doesn't understand about prices is how business people set prices. They compute the cost of the raw materials, the manufacturing costs, transportation, breakage, taxes, operational expenses such as labor, insurance, interest on loans, etc., and a profit. If there were no inflation, all of those items would remain constant except raw material costs, which fluctuate with supply and demand and may be affected by natural causes such as weather. Thus, if the cost of steel increases, all products which contain steel in them will increase in price. The same is true for rubber products if the price of rubber increases. Or the price of bakery goods if the price of wheat increases. But not all products contain steel, nor do all products contain rubber or wheat. Therefore, some products may decrease in price while others are increasing through the Law of Substitution (which says consumers will substitute cheaper products when prices for comparable products get too high), and the forces of a free market will adjust to supply/demand factors, and prices will remain stable.

Although not all raw materials are present in the manufacture of all products, there certainly is one. That is MONEY! And the "price" of money is called interest. When the Fed increases interest rates, they automatically increase the price of all products. The person with the dry cleaning establishment couldn't care less how much the bank charges him for interest. That money he borrows is his operating capital, and without it, his business dies. He knows what he must do to survive: borrow the money, pay whatever interest rate is charged, and increase the cost of cleaning a suit from $5 to $6.

It doesn't make any difference what a person's business is, the solution will always be the same as long as interest rates are increased: borrow, and raise prices, because your cost of doing business has increased.

If the Fed really wanted to reduce inflation (outside of getting Congress to reduce spending), the solution is very simple: increase bank reserve requirements. If present requirements call for banks to maintain 17% reserves, that means they may lend $100 million for each $17 million they have in reserves. If the Fed wants to slow borrowing, let them increase the reserve requirement to 18%, which means they could lend only $94.4 million. Or raise it to 19%, at which level they could lend only $89.5 million.

In my opinion, Paul Volcker was the greatest con man of all time. He told the world that he could stop inflation by increasing interest rates. The highest rates we had seen in our history were around 10%, and that was more than one hundred years ago, at the end of the Civil War. Volcker claimed we were suffering from inflation, so he pushed interest rates above 10% to 12%, then 14%, and 16%. That poor man couldn't figure out why prices kept going up. Commodity prices had surged. Gold went from $200 to $400. Silver ran up to $7. Sugar — normally a 3¢ commodity — went to 15¢. Volcker — like the caveman operating on the bigger rock theory — stuck blindly to the theory that higher interest rates could slow inflation, and he shoved (and I mean shoved in every sense of the word) the prime interest rate to 21.5%. Instead of prices falling, gold shot to $900, silver to $50, sugar to 45¢, etc.

Volcker's misguided thinking about raising interest rates to slow inflation had its effect, but not the way the theory went. Prices simply got so high no one could afford to buy anything, and prices came tumbling down. He had put the world on the verge of bankruptcy and made it impossible for third-world nations to service their bank debt, bringing world banking to the verge of collapse.

Unfortunately, not too many Americans even gave a thought to Mr. Volcker's misdeeds, for their $40,000 homes had risen in value to $140,000, and they weren't even aware that gold was back below $400, silver down to $5, and sugar was under 10¢ again. It was the surge in real estate values which laid the smoke screen of contentment which allowed Volcker to make his heroic retreat from Washington.

Doubly unfortunately, we now have another college professor at the helm of the Federal Reserve. He probably has never in his life done anything more exciting than to carry out the

277

garbage, and I suspect he longs for the recognition which Paul Volcker received. The first evidence of that was when he raised the discount rate ½% within weeks after assuming his post — without any signs of inflation.

Mr. Greenspan, I beg of you, reconsider the theory that increasing interest rates can slow inflation. That is as ill-conceived a theory as the heavier rock theory. If you don't believe me, just look at South America, where interest rates run 20% per month and inflation runs 30%!"

The foregoing was repeated verbatim, but I would like to change one minor part. That would be about my nomination for a chairman of the Federal Reserve. I would like to see a man — or woman, but I will use the generic term "man" — who graduated from college with a wife, a child, and another on the way. His degree isn't much help because the economy is slow, and he finally takes a job as an auto salesman. The economy is slow, so auto sales are poor, and he is laid off after just a few months. In his desperation he accepts a job as a short-order cook, and as the economy improves his status at the restaurant improves to night manager, to assistant manager, and finally to manager. Then another recession hits, business is very poor for restaurants, the owners decide to close his restaurant, and he is pounding the pavement again, looking for work.

He is tired of working for other people, so he borrows the money from his in-laws to lease a gas station and do repair work. He is very adept at managing the business, and eventually he is operating four bays. He expands into tire sales and has eighteen people working for him. The first of the kids hopes to start college next year. Then another recession hits at about the time he had intended to repay the in-laws. He has major decisions to make: does he start laying off people; does he borrow from the bank to increase his tire inventory and try to increase volume in the face of the recession; does he renege on the in-laws right at the time they were hoping to retire? This is a man who has seen adversity and has had to make business decisions based upon *survival*, not theory.

This man would understand that the level of interest rates has no bearing on his business decisions. The people at the Fed can't possibly know what it means to make a business decision. They have done nothing but work in the sheltered environment of the banking system for forty years. They never had to repay a loan to an in-law or to a bank.

The Fed is a tool of big business, so it tries to do the things which they feel will help the large corporations, the banks, the insurance companies, etc. But *big* business is not the heart of America. Small companies which employ fewer than 500 people account for double the percentage of Domestic National Product that big business does.

The recent plunge in interest rates is a perfect example. The Fed wanted to help the federal government and the banks, so it lowered short-term interest rates to levels not seen for thirty years. Ross Perot, in the debates, criticized the federal government for relying so heavily on short-term borrowings, but why not finance the debt at 2.5% instead of 7.5% if you can get away with it? Those short-term rates were great for the federal government in the face of the $3+ trillion debt.

The banks were the ones who really made out. The Fed claimed it wanted to stimulate the economy, so it lowered interest rates. When short-term rates on T-bills plunged to 2.5% the banks were able to cut certificate-of-deposit (CD) rates from 8% to 2.5%. The banks took the money savers were investing in CD's at 2.5% and reinvested it in riskless long-term T-bonds at 7.5%, making 5% risk-free. The banks had no incentive to make loans, so the economy stayed in recession much longer than would have been the case if interest rates had been *raised*.

The real damage was done to the savers. People who did the thing they have been told by the Fed that they should do — *save* — took a devastating hit. People who depended upon interest income for a part of their spending money saw their income literally stolen from them by the Fed. This was the greatest transfer of wealth in history as the banks took $50 billion away from savers (source: Investor's Business Daily).

Mom & Pop, who had a $100,000 CD and depended upon the $8,000 annual interest return for a major portion of their spending money, were crushed when the renewal rate for their jumbo CD dropped to 3.5%. That loss of $4,500 of income prevented them from replacing the car which they usually traded in each three years, or replacing the carpeting which had a worn spot (which is now a hole), or from taking the trip to visit the family and to see the grandchildren at Christmas. The people who work on the assembly line making cars or the people making the carpeting were deprived of work and either were unable to spend because they lost their jobs, or they were unable to spend because they were in fear of losing their jobs. As for that trip, when you consider how many restaurants, gas stations, and motels along the Interstate were deprived of business, you can see why the recession has lingered so long. You can see it, but the Fed can't.

Today everyone is saying that BB has his finger ready to pull the trigger by raising interest rates at the first sign of an improving economy, which he calls inflation. If you go back to my simplistic example of money supply and things, you have to realize that an expanding economy is *deflationary*! When the economy is expanding, we are producing more things, and that keeps inflation down. But when the Fed raises interest rates it raises the price of everything and contributes to price inflation.

Fortunately, BB is too ignorant about economics to understand that the first few interest rate increases will stimulate the economy instead of stifling it as he would like. Higher rates will put additional funds into the hands of savers, and they will be able to buy cars and carpeting, and to take vacations. That will get the economy moving again. *Unfortunately,* BB will react the same as Volcker did, raising interest rates some more every time a new economic indicator says the economy is expanding. Eventually, he will bring inflation back again, and then he will really pour gasoline on his interest rate fire. We could very well see a repeat of the 1979-80 interest rate debacle when T-bills went to 17.5%, the prime rate to 21.5%, and inflation to 20%.

I think it is criminal to give the Federal Reserve so much power, and especially to give so much power to the chairman. Because he has the power to raise or lower interest rates at will, he has the power to control the economies of all nations of the world. Even the President of the United States hasn't that much power. And when you give so much control to a single person like Greenspan, it is like giving him an 18-wheeler and telling him he can drive any way he wants on the freeway. In the case of Greenspan, because he knows as little about economics as he does about driving 18-wheelers, his stupid theory about raising interest rates to reduce prices and vice versa — which is directly opposite to natural law — is the same as him racing down the freeway with his 18-wheeler in reverse.

My real concern is not as much for inflation as it is for what will happen to the stock market when interest rates are raised. I will cover that in Chapter XXXI, "The Stock Market — Look Out Below!" Everything that I say about interest rates considers 4% to be a low rate and 6% to be a high rate. Rates should never move outside of those parameters. If the Fed wants to play with rates, they should remember that when rates are above 6% they are too high and need to be lowered to slow the economy, not raised. When interest rates are under 4% they are too low and need to be raised to stimulate the economy, not lowered. The Fed need not worry about inflation with interest rates between 4% and 6% because prices will maintain a near-equilibrium.

In case you are wondering why I am about the only person who thinks the theory of high interest rates to slow inflation is analogous to the heavier rock theory, you must understand the workings of Wall Street. Brokerage houses *want* high interest rates. They make out like bandits. First of all, when speculators buy stocks on margin, to pay for the purchase they put up 50% of the purchase price, and the brokerage firm borrows the other 50% from a bank. The bank charges an interest rate which is known as the "brokers' call loan rate." The brokerage firm then adds a surcharge to that rate and charges the speculator the higher amount. That surcharge usually runs about 10% higher than the call loan rate. For example, if the call loan rate is 5%, the broker charges the speculator 5.5%; if the call loan rate is 10%, the broker charges the speculator 11%. Thus, the higher the call loan rate, the greater the spread the broker earns.

Secondly, many of the brokers' clients may have free credit balances (cash) in their accounts awaiting reinvestment or withdrawal. The brokerage firm earns interest on those balances. Again, the higher the current interest rate, the higher the interest earnings to the brokerage firm.

Savvy investors may request that the free credit balances in their accounts be transferred to a money market fund account so that the client earns the interest instead of the broker. Even then, the brokerage firm makes out because it charges a management fee on the money market fund.

Don't look for either the Democrats or the Republicans to try to force the Fed to hold interest rates within a narrow band such as I suggest at 4% to 6%. That would be anathematic to the purpose of Wall Street, which is to separate the small investor from his money. Wall Street brokerage houses and banks are bosom buddies (read: large campaign contributors), and if a politician bites the hand that feeds him, he is not a politician.

The heavier rock theory survived for hundreds of thousands of years, so it should not surprise you that this convoluted theory of higher interest rates arresting inflation persists. The reason that it is so easy to perpetuate the theory is because of the media. Take newspapers as an example: When a newspaper reporter has failed at just about everything else on the staff, they assign him to writing obituaries. If he fails at that, they make him a sports writer. If he fails at that, the last straw is to make him a financial writer. He gets his news by calling brokers who tell him about interest rates and their effect on inflation. The writer submits his article, it is printed, and a million readers accept it as truth because they read it in the daily paper. And the brokers chuckle all of the way to the bank.

XXX

So, You Want To Manage Commodity Accounts?

After reading this far you probably have decided that scale trading is simple: Buy every 10 cents down, then sell every 10 cents up. That's so easy a chimpanzee could manage money using this system. And since you feel confident that you have as much intelligence as a chimpanzee, why shouldn't you manage scale trading accounts for fees and supplement your income? Maybe you can develop a good track record and turn pro. Then you could earn a very good living doing something that you really enjoy.

Before you rush into the office tomorrow morning and tell the boss that you are quitting, let me tell you some of the things you will encounter as a money manager.

Finding money to manage is not difficult. If you scale trade for your own account for a year or so and show an annualized rate of return above 20%, people will queue around the block to give you money to manage for them. You might attract a couple of million dollars, and if you charge the 6% fee I recommend, you would earn $120,000 per year, or $10,000 per month. For playing the commodities market!

You should check with an attorney about the regulations concerning managing commodity accounts, and I am not giving legal advice now, but the attorney probably will tell you that you may manage up to fifteen accounts without obtaining any kind of license. There is no limit on the size of the accounts. If your accounts are all million dollar accounts, you may manage $15 million without a license. If you prefer to manage a partnership, the partnership may have up to fifteen partners and a maximum of $200,000 in it. You are not allowed to advertise for accounts; the people must approach you. There are numerous other restrictions, which is why you should consult an attorney before calling yourself a manager.

Your only real problem will be with the regulators. But they may make you rue the day you ever thought of becoming a money manager!

Let me explain: In most cases, the regulators with whom you will be dealing will be attorneys. For perspective, consider the caliber of attorney with whom you will deal by using the following rule of thumb about those who graduate with a degree in securities law. We can rank the graduates in five levels, with the gifted students in the first level and those who barely squeaked through in the fifth level. Here is how their careers diverge:

Level 1:   They go to work for very prestigious Wall Street securities law firms.

Level 2:   They go to work for securities law firms around the rest of the country.

Level 3:   They go into private practice and specialize in writing wills and handling divorces.

Level 4:   They go to work in a car wash.

Level 5:   They go to work for the government.

The brokerage houses get their house attorneys from Level 5. There may be a talented person in that group who majored in party life at college, graduated without cracking a book and then passed the bar. His grade point average is too low for him to get a job, so he goes to work for the government in some kind of enforcement capacity. After a while he tires of working for $38,000, so he finds a target for prosecution — they are easy to find because they are everywhere — at one of the major firms, puts the heat on, and the firm hires him to terminate the prosecution. Time passes through the year, and several of the government attorneys have moved on to cushy jobs, creating openings. It is still a few months from graduation date for the next class of securities lawyers, so government agencies like the NFA go down to Union Station in Chicago and wake people who are sleeping in doorways to recruit replacement employees. They give them clean clothes, a bath, and a shave — including the female recruits — and turn them loose doing audits. Sometimes you hear about "dedicated employees" who put in an entire career with the government. Rarely are these people truly dedicated. It is only that they were so incompetent that they couldn't find work away from the government.

Aside from incompetent government attorneys (there's a redundancy if I ever heard one) being reluctant to prosecute because they are hoping to get better jobs, another reason they do not prosecute is that their targets will be the big firms or their executives. These people or firms will be represented in court by attorneys from Level 1, while the prosecution is represented by attorneys from Level 5. That mismatch is like having a world class heavyweight boxer going a few rounds with Charles Atlas' famous 98-pound weakling.

Probably the best of the government attorneys work in the United States District Attorneys' offices. The best example of a good U.S. District Attorney was Rudolph Giuliani, who was responsible for rooting out some of the inside traders and junk bond collaborators in the 1980's. But the government couldn't keep him, and he became mayor of New York City.

The probable reason that they couldn't hold him is that they don't pay much to the few good people that they have. Instead of paying them a salary, I think they should pay them a bounty for every securities manipulator they convict. You might react by saying that would cause every U.S. attorney to charge everyone with everything in the hope of getting a conviction on 2% of them. But if they made the U.S. Government pay for the defendant's defense counsel, and if the U.S. attorney were forced to state in advance the amount of penalty he is seeking and made it a "pay or take" proposition in which the loser must pay the winner that stated amount, those being charged with crimes would probably be guilty beyond doubt. Allowing the government attorneys to receive a portion of the settlement would insure that the very best people from Level 1 would be working for the government instead of against it. Giving them even a fraction of the action would allow them to earn huge incomes because there are multimillion dollar frauds committed daily on Wall Street and West Jackson Boulevard.

I can say this only because I don't have anyone who can fire me, but one writer who worked for a major daily business newspaper wrote a lengthy expose of futures trading which he called "A High Risk Gamble," and there was such a hue and cry from the futures industry insiders that the newspaper sacked the writer.

In this discussion I will comment only on the U.S. attorneys who are employed by the Securities and Exchange Commission (SEC), the National Association of Securities Dealers (NASD), the Commodity Futures Trading Commission (CFTC), and the National Futures Association (NFA).

The SEC probably has the best attorneys in this group, but even they can do silly or petty things. For example, I was once the president of a stock mutual fund, and the SEC examiners came in for their regular audit. We were as clean as a whistle except for one alleged violation which the SEC auditor refused to reveal to me. You have to picture this scene: This was many years ago when all men wore suits to the office and got a haircut weekly. This SEC auditor was a tall, skinny kid who was totally out of character with blond hair which hung to his shoulders. His name was Ashley Ugh. (Not really, but very close.) He probably was on his first audit because he sat there with the SEC manual in one hand and our books in the other. When he was prepared to leave — still refusing to reveal our transgression — my wife (who many people said was the sharpest woman they had ever met and was our Senior Vice President) and I cornered him in the conference room and told him he could not leave until he told us what was wrong. He finally told us. Only a government employee could come up with one like this:

I can still remember the name of the stock and the brokerage house which was involved. Mr. Ugh told us that we had violated the law (as shown in his manual) in not purchasing our last 2,000 shares of an over-the-counter stock named Church's Fried Chicken from E. F. Hutton, the primary market maker. I explained that the day we bought that 2,000 shares, E. F. Hutton had been quoting the stock 20 at 21, which means you can get $20 per share if you are selling or must pay $21 if you are buying. A broker other than from Hutton had called and said he had seen in our prospectus that we owned some Church's and said if we were interested in buying more that he had a client who was selling 2,000 shares. Rather than sell it to Hutton for $20 and then have us come along an hour or two later and buy the same 2,000 shares from Hutton for $21, would we be interested in "crossing" the stock with the cross being executed at $20.50, thereby benefiting each side by $1,000? Of course we made the deal.

But Mr. Ugh ignored our explanation about how we had saved $1,000 for the stockholders of the fund, and — going by the manual — he claimed that we had violated the rules by not buying the stock from E. F. Hutton, where we would have paid $21 per share. He said he would return to his office and prepare a report which he would send to us. Instead of the lying creep sending the report to us, he sent it to Washington, D. C. The people in Washington weren't any smarter than Ugh, so they wrote a letter to our attorneys in Los Angeles demanding an explanation. It cost us (the management company, not the fund) $4,000 in attorney fees to finally convince Washington that we had done the proper thing for the fund.

An example of an SEC petty action was when a fund (not ours) designed a logo which had an arrow in it. The SEC questioned the significance of the arrow's pointing upward. Did that mean the fund was guaranteeing that their shares would always go up? The fund managers claimed there was no significance intended in the arrow pointing upward. Whereupon the SEC said, "In that case, why don't you point the arrow downward?" It wasn't a question; it was an order. The fund dropped that logo and designed a new one.

The NASD answers to the SEC and is really only a quasi-government agency. I won't bother to comment on them.

The CFTC has some competent employees, but most of them are totally unqualified for the work they do. That is because they are dealing with entrepreneurs who wheel and deal in the most speculative occupation in the world. CFTC attorneys probably have never made a commodity futures trade in their lives, and they really don't understand the markets. They rarely catch any of the conspirators who perpetrate the crimes I have described in this book. That is either because they are not clever enough to understand the frauds being perpetrated, or it could be that the attorney wants to get out of the CFTC and go to work as an in-house counsel for a major commodity house and therefore is reluctant to prosecute when the crimes are obvious.

The best recent example of that was when a major Wall Street brokerage firm was accused of rigging bids in U.S. Government Bond auctions. After two years of CFTC investigation and preparation of a case, the violating firm (which had already pleaded guilty and paid a huge civil fine) saved its officers from being prosecuted on criminal charges by *hiring* the man in charge of the government's investigation. He went to work in a key executive position in this firm, which is famous for paying multimillion dollar bonuses to its key employees each year. Now he is part of the old boy network. Tell me that's ethical!

The CFTC's case fell apart without the chief investigator there to prosecute, and it appears the criminal charges will never be prosecuted.

The firm had been accused of benefiting to the tune of billions of dollars. You, as a taxpayer, paid the bill.

Have you ever had a limit order working and seen your price penetrated by a substantial amount on the opening of a day's trading because of a sharp move following some overnight surprising news, only to wait hours for a confirmation from your Account Executive? The opening range of prices may be very broad, but when you inquire as to your fill price, you are told by your AE that he has wired the floor and they say they are too backed up by the heavy volume to report execution prices. Baloney. The problem is simply that the floor brokers — who are also permitted to trade for their own accounts — are not required to report trades in a timely fashion; thus, they may sit on your execution and go on trading for their own accounts. If the market suddenly reverses, they now confirm the best prices for their own account and the poorer executions for the public's, time stamping all orders with the same time imprint — even though some orders were executed thirty minutes apart. This practice comes up regularly in CFTC investigations, but the floor brokers always win because they can easily convince the CFTC that it is in the public's interest for the brokers not to take time away from executing orders for the public simply to report trades in hectic markets.

In a recent sting operation, government employees posing as floor traders on one of the giant commodity exchanges in Chicago worked their way into the confidence of regular floor traders and were invited to join in scams which defrauded the public out of millions of dollars through phony and rigged trades. The government people wore "wires" to record the illegal proceedings. Nearly one hundred crooked floor brokers were involved, and the recordings made the cases airtight. Incredibly, only a few minor convictions were obtained by the Level 5 government prosecutors, and most of those came from floor brokers who confessed and gave testimony against the other conspirators in hopes of getting lighter sentences. After the smoke settled and the paucity of convictions was revealed, the exchange — in an amazing disregard for justice — barred the floor traders who had confessed and absolved those who had fought and won their cases. The exchange used the specious argument that the floor traders which the government had been unable to convict were obviously innocent because the courts had found them not guilty, while the ones being punished were obviously guilty because they had pleaded so.

The NFA is the worst of the lot, and that is the body with which you will have the most contact if you manage money. One of their former employees called me one day to ask about buying a copy of this book, and we got into a conversation about the NFA. He candidly declared that, "The NFA is the most corrupt of all of the regulatory agencies!" He explained that he didn't mean that NFA employees take bribes — there is no one there smart enough to know how to solicit a bribe, and if one employee ever figured out how to get one, there wouldn't be anyone else there smart enough to catch him — but rather that their abuse of power is a crime unto itself.

What he meant by that is that they never prosecute big firms for violations — because they all want to go to work for the big firms — but they beat up on the small firms who must acquiesce because they can neither afford the money nor the executive time to defend against the charges. The NFA wants to be able to claim at the end of each year that they prosecuted 325 cases and won 320 of them; the five losers were against the industry giants with their Level 1 attorneys who made fools out of the NFA's Level 5 attorneys. Of course, the 320 winners came against small firms who, in most cases, chose not to fight.

I'll give you some examples to show you what you are going to encounter. I will omit names, but the facts are accurate.

One man who had been managing commodity accounts was on a hot streak with recent excellent performance. He joined the NFA so that he could advertise his record and solicit new managed accounts. The NFA periodically sends out three-person audit teams to go over the procedures of all NFA member firms, and when they came to this fellow's office, they questioned why his advertised track record was showing only the recent good times and omitted the prior poor times. He explained that he was publishing only his record since the date he joined the NFA. (I won't argue the merits of his defense, but he could have made it easier on himself by simply stating that he had altered his trading method at the time he joined the NFA, making the prior record immaterial. That's legal.) I couldn't believe it when the person relating this story to me said the NFA simply went back to Chicago and sent him a notice that he was being fined $65,000, but after hearing some of these other stories, I can now believe it. He paid the fine because it would have taken too much of his time to defend the action, and as long as he was on a roll he wanted to devote his full time to bringing new money under management.

Another case involved a man who formed his own company and assisted a number of IB's in opening satellite offices under his direction. The rules require that he supervise all of these offices, including their advertising. As frequently happens in this business, some of the offices got carried away with their advertising claims, and the NFA fined this man $250,000. He admits that they were correct in fining him because he had failed to supervise properly, but he felt the fine was excessive. I agree. That's a quarter of a million dollars! He paid the fine because if he had refused, he would have been barred from the commodities business for life.

I once received a call from a man in a small Southern California town who simply wanted to chat about scale trading. His primary business was insurance sales and estate planning, but he had once joined the NFA so that he could manage scale trading commodity accounts to supplement his income. He said, "The NFA kept hounding me, asking, 'How can you tell people they can make money with this cockamamie scale trading system when they all lose?'" He answered, "Don't blame me. We have winner, winner, winner, for a dozen winners, and then the market sells off a little, they lose their nerve and their stop-loss mentality tells them they should sell, so they order me to liquidate the account, and they quit losers." I told him I was hearing an echo because that was the same argument I had had repeatedly with the NFA. He said the NFA wore him out. He finally quit the NFA to concentrate on his insurance and estate planning business, and now he scale trades only for himself.

One of the most egregious cases of abuse by the NFA that I have ever heard of is what they did to Larry Williams. (This is one of the rare times when I use the person's real name.) Larry is a fabulous trader. He is probably the best commodity trader I have ever known. He is the only person in the world who can trade the way he does because no one else would have the nerve to pyramid the way he does. (Larry says he doesn't pyramid, but if he doubles his margin one day — he rarely holds a position overnight — he will buy two contracts the next day. Then four, eight, sixteen, etc. Pyramiding by any other name is still an exciting rose called Larry Williams.)

Although Larry is a unique trader, he is *as honest as the day is long*! He may curl your hair with his trading, but he would never cheat anyone.

He ran afoul of the NFA. The way he reported his problem in an open letter to all NFA members goes something like this: One of the commodity brokerage firms promotes a trading contest each year. In it, all entrants pony up $10,000 and make live trades to see who can accumulate the highest stake in four months. One year Larry ran his $10,000 to $1.1 million. He won the contest easily.

(Actually, at one time Larry's stake was up to $2.2 million before dropping back to $1.1 million. He likes to call it the year he made $1.1 million trading commodities. His wife calls it the year they lost $1.1 million.)

After the contest was over, someone ran an ad referring to Larry's great gain. I suppose they were trying to imply that million dollar profits are commonplace in commodities trading. The NFA didn't like the ad, so they jumped on Larry. Larry tried to defend himself by saying he had not even seen the ad before it was run. While the fight with the NFA was occurring, the ad appeared again, and the NFA came down hard on Larry Williams, fining him $12,000. Naturally, Larry would not hold still for that, so he got an attorney to defend him. After $90,000 of attorney fees, the NFA still refused to consider Larry's claim of innocence, so Larry finally threw in the towel and resigned from the NFA.

From what I know about the Larry Williams case, the NFA was not punishing Larry for the ads. They were out to get him for a prior event: Each year the NFA holds an election of directors. The slate of nominees is hand-picked by the NFA, and most of the electorate are unfamiliar with the nominees and simply sign and return their proxies, guaranteeing election of the NFA's group. One year Larry sent letters to all NFA members asking them to write in his name for director. In his letter he mentioned how the NFA had started with a handful of employees and a modest budget, but how it now employed 337 people and operated on a budget of $28 million annually. (I have never seen their Chicago office, but I am told it is like the Taj Mahal.) Larry said if he were elected he would do his best to restore the NFA to a semblance of sanity. He was elected easily.

The NFA laid back in the weeds and waited for an opportunity to pounce upon Larry. They got that opportunity with the ad incident. When Larry had his run-in with the NFA, the NFA invoked a new rule which has come to be known as "The Larry Williams Exclusionary Rule." In simplest terms, it says if you have had an action brought against you by the NFA, you may not serve on the board. They kicked him off the board and replaced him with — guess who. That's right, the guy he had beaten from the NFA's handpicked slate.

I had obtained my first securities license in 1958, and I was first licensed by the CBOT as a commodities Registered Representative in 1961. When the CFTC came into being around 1970 and took over the licensing of commodity people from the CBOT, I became licensed with the CFTC. The NFA came into being in 1983, and my registration was transferred to the NFA. I stopped being a commodity broker in 1984 and set up a sole proprietorship to sell books, publish the newsletter, and to manage commodity trading accounts. I had no need for NFA registration, so I allowed it to lapse. However, my success with scale trading caused money to come pouring in, and I could see that I would soon exceed the fifteen client limit, so I applied for reinstatement of my registration. Because I had never had a black mark on my record and because I had been registered longer than most NFA employees had lived, it

292

should have been a rubber stamp approval. You won't believe what I went through.

The first two times that I called to request that the NFA send me registration documents, they failed to mail them. They finally mailed them after my third request, and I submitted completed documents. I heard nothing for several weeks, so I called to inquire as to the progress of the application. I was shuttled back and forth between clerks so many times that I finally demanded to speak to the top banana. He said my application was not being processed because I had failed to submit fingerprints with the application. I knew that was untrue because I had the receipt from the police department which had done my fingerprinting, and I had put the fingerprint cards in the envelope with the application, walked directly across the street from the police department to the post office and mailed them. When I insisted, he got angry and hung up on me. Thirty minutes later he called to say they found the fingerprints.

He informed me that my next step was to mail a check made payable to the National Association of Securities Dealers (they conduct the tests, not the NFA) and request a test date. I did as I was told, and again weeks went by while I heard nothing. When I inquired as to the status of my application, I was informed that it was not being processed because my check had been deposited in the NFA account instead of with the NASD, and they could not forward it. I rushed a new check to the NASD and was scheduled for the test.

It is a computer test, and they give you your test result on the spot. I passed. I went home and waited for written confirmation that I had passed and that I was again a member of the NFA. Instead, after several weeks I received an NFA letter saying that because I had not taken the test they were assuming I was no longer interested in joining the NFA, and they were trashing my application. I got right on the phone and called the NFA.

I told the registration officer that I had not only taken and passed the test but had written confirmation of it in my hand. She was stunned and asked where I had gotten that from. I said, "*YOU MAILED IT TO ME!*" Incredibly, she asked me if I would be kind enough to mail a copy to her for their records. It had taken ten months to accomplish something which should have taken two weeks.

Does it make you feel comfortable to hear that these are the people who are supposed to be protecting you from the commodity charlatans who are cheating people daily?

I received my first NFA audit in 1988. I have my office in my home, and when the three-woman team arrived I greeted them very cordially and stated that I had never fully recovered from the collapse of my former business which cost me $7 million and left me nearly broke. Aside from book sales and subscriptions — which were modest in those days — my principal source of income was from the management fee I earned from one large and growing partnership which had paid me $12,700 in management fees for the preceding year but which netted very little to me after I paid $10,400 out of my own pocket for their audit. The costs of printing and mailing the voluminous monthly statements to thirty-two limited partners probably consumed the $2,300 balance. I said I could not afford an attorney to prescribe all of the proper procedures, so I tried to do it myself by following the NFA manual, and I would be grateful if they would go over my procedures with a fine-tooth comb so that I could alter any improper procedures and would be in compliance with all of the rules.

I might as well have talked to three tree stumps.

The first young lady was the sweetest thing you could care to know. She was the type you would want your son to marry. But she admitted she had just graduated from college and that this was her first job. She was to audit my newsletter. She held my letters in one hand and the NFA procedural manual for newsletters in the other. When it was time for her critique, she asked if I had stored written evidence of all of the comments I had made in the letters about crop production, exports, feed and seed usage, etc., which was required by the manual. I said that it would be ridiculous to store *all* of that information because — as an example — I condensed all of the crop reports into a few paragraphs. Each paragraph might contain six or eight figures, and if I were required to store six or eight photocopies for e*ach paragraph* in each newsletter I would soon have to move out of my home to make room for the paper storage. Furthermore, I said, if I had to verify numbers, they were all a matter of public record, and if I did not have them stored I could get them quickly from the public library.

She gave me an example of the kind of thing I needed to store. She asked, "Where is your written document verifying your claim in the last issue that the discount rate had just been lowered by the Federal Reserve?" I was stunned. I said, "Surely you jest. That was the first discount rate cut in three years and was the biggest financial news event of the year. It made the headlines in newspapers, and it was the lead item on all of the evening TV news shows. That kind of news is on a par with the results of a Super Bowl game. The whole world knows who won the last Super Bowl game, and the whole financial world knows the discount rate was cut last week, but I doubt if anyone kept evidence of either event in his file."

The second lady audited one of the partnerships I managed. I don't know how she could audit the partnership without reading the partnership agreement, but she tried. I find it as easy to report the monthly statements on columnar pads as by computer, so I use pads and send photocopies to the partners. Columnar pads have room for only two numbers in the decimal column, and we carry our unit value to three decimal places, with the third decimal number being shown as a superior number resembling an exponential number. Because she had not read the partnership agreement and did not know about the third decimal place, she had to ask why our unit value was shown as $156.34 "to the ninth power." Again I was stunned, but I calmly said, "Do you have any idea how much $156 to the ninth power would be? It is not all of the money in the world, but it is close to it. And because we have over 4,000 units outstanding, that would *be* all of the money in the world! Do you really believe we have all of the money in the world in our little partnership?"

They were here for two weeks, and during that time my auto license renewal came due. Under the rules, the auditors are obliged to leave if I must leave, and despite my plea that I would be hit with a $150 penalty if I didn't get to the DMV office prior to closing within an hour, they refused to leave, the "exponential" lady saying that she wanted me to produce a balanced statement for this month's partnership statement. I protested that I had worked on it for a couple of days but had put some garbage in somewhere and could not find the error. This $600,000 partnership was out of balance by $840, and she wasn't going to let me get away with that!

I went into my den to try again to find the error. Meantime, the women sat at my dining room table and chatted. They probably talked about the male performers at Chippendale's, but I can guarantee you they were not talking about their kids. NFA people don't have kids because they eat their young at birth. By the grace of God, when I sat down to look at the statement with which I had wrestled for two days, my eye landed on a $40 error item, and when I subtracted that I had only an $800 item to find. I then remembered there had been a $400 item in the report, and sure enough, I had shown it as a credit instead of a debit. After fighting it for two days, I found the solution in two minutes. I hustled them out the door, raced to the DMV, and got in the door eight minutes before closing.

The next day the captain of the team came forward. (As I recall, her name was Kitty. Yes, Kitty Litter.) She was a real witch — or any word you want to use that rhymes. She asked for the daily statements on the partnership for October of last year. I walked her to my garage and showed her that I had just moved into the house and that two bays of my three-car garage were full floor to ceiling with cardboard boxes full of corporate records, commodity trading records, books, linens, and all other kinds of personal items. I asked why she needed them, and she said she wanted to ascertain the amount of commissions we had paid that month. I told her that was easy, and I took her into the den where I produced the *monthly* statement from a file drawer. (If the monthly statement is available, the daily statements are superfluous.) I told her we paid $25.28 roundturn commissions on every trade — never more, never less — and with twenty trades that month we had paid $500 in commissions and $5.60 in NFA fees.

That wasn't good enough. She demanded the daily statements. When I protested that I hadn't a clue as to which box they were in (a couple of months later I found them and sent photocopies to her), she said, "I suggest you take a day off and straighten up your garage. I want those papers!" This kind of person doesn't understand what it means to work for a living, working seventeen hours a day, seven days a week, so she struck a nerve with me. I kept my voice calm, but I said, "Young lady, if I could afford to take a day off, the first thing that I would do would be to race to Las Vegas to visit my mother who was trapped in an apartment house fire three weeks ago. The heat inside her apartment was so intense that it melted *her typewriter*, but she slept through it. When the firemen carried her down the ladder strapped to a gurney, one of them told the spectators she was dead. She survived, but spent a week in the hospital. I have not been able to get over to see her. Secondly, I need some important dental work. (As it later developed, I had to have a very painful and expensive gingivectomy.) Thirdly, my ophthalmologist wants me to complete the eye examination we started. He thinks I may have a serious problem, but I haven't had time to get back to complete the examination."

Incredibly, this witch — or any word you want to use that rhymes — said, "I couldn't care less about your eye. I want those papers!" (Good thing she didn't say she couldn't care less about my mother!)

I had told them when they arrived that it was two weeks to my mother's eightieth birthday, and that I expected to be there for the celebration. They left barely in time for me to reach Las Vegas for her birthday. As they left, they laughingly said, "See, you will be just in time for your mother's birthday." I didn't say anything, but I couldn't help thinking that I had known that I would either be just in time for the birthday or just in time for three funerals.

When the witch — or any word you want to use that rhymes — filed her report in Chicago, it was filled with lies. I had to answer the report, so I went through and simply said, "This is a lie." "This is a lie." "This is an unmitigated lie." When I came to the incident about the garage, her report said I had *refused* to produce the papers. I typed two pages to give my side of the story, and when I came to her crack about my eye I said, "I am not a person of violence, but if she had been a man and made that remark, I would have punched him right in his eye for saying it."

That cooked my goose with the NFA.

The next time the NFA sent in an audit team it was three men. I guess they feared I would make good on my threat because these men were all over six feet tall.

I immediately asked them if they had read this book because I wanted to know if they understood scale trading and our record of consistently having over 90% winning trades. They had not read it. Because the previous team had not read the partnership agreement on the partnership they audited, I asked if they had read the agreement. They had not. Then I asked them if they had read the letter I sent to Chicago. They gave a sly leer to each other and said, "Yeaaaaah." I said to them, "Then this is the Kitty Litter (not her real name) *revenge* team?" They denied that, but that is exactly what it was.

The audit started very poorly because they literally took over my house. I closed all of the doors to each room, but they entered all of them without knocking. I live alone, so it was no great problem, but it was certainly an annoyance. It could have been embarrassing if others had lived in this house. I am convinced that they were hoping to pop in on me and catch me trying to destroy incriminating documents — maybe some bubble gum wrappers.

Among the many harassing things which they did, they asked for the cancelled checks from my *personal* checking account — which has nothing to do with the business. I laughed as I gave them the checks and bank statements for the last three years, and I said, "Despite my great antipathy for the ACLU, I think they would have a picnic with this one." I asked why they wanted these cancelled checks, and they told me they were checking to see if I had been secretly (and illegally, they implied) disbursing funds to any people who might have been previously forced out of the NFA.

When they finished that part of their audit they called me into a room, and the three of them "revealed" that they had found incriminating documents. I expected them to bring out the rubber hoses. When I asked what they had found, the one fellow leaned forward and in his best Perry Mason imitation asked me about the monthly checks I had been disbursing to Discover *Financial* Services. He wanted to know who they were.

We were probably a week into their stay, and I had had a belly full of their harassment by the end of the first day, so I was in no mood to put up with this garbage. I answered, "You moron (it's hard to start a sentence when you talk to NFA people without saying, 'You moron,' in fact, it is hard to start a sentence addressed to them without putting an adjective in front of 'moron'), I have about a dozen credit cards, and one of them is The Discover Card. I make my monthly payments to 'Discover Financial Services.' " (Today the payments are made to Discover Card Services.)

"Okay," he said, "You got us on that one, but what about Infiniti *Financial* Services? There is no Infiniti credit card." I answered, "You moron, I lease an Infiniti automobile, and I make the payments to Infiniti Financial Services."

I'm surprised they didn't ask about the checks written to J. C. Penney, Sears, Domino Pizza, etc.

There were dozens of such stupid incidents, but they finally found something they could sink their teeth into. I had been managing some limited partnerships for which my family members acted as general partner. I explained that it was my plan to have a holding company in Los Angeles which would own ten subsidiary management companies scattered around the country in Houston, Miami, Atlanta, New York, Chicago, San Francisco, etc., and that each of these offices would be headed by someone who might even be one of my relatives. They were all qualified college graduates with brilliant minds. My son's IQ is 155, my daughter's 165, and my ex-wife's 180.

Each partnership was autonomous, and because the general partner stayed under the 15-partner, $200,000 maximum-size rule, the general partners operated under a Declaration of Exemption. The first NFA audit team had found no fault with this arrangement, but that was *before* I wrote that letter about my eye. This second audit team asked if the Declarations of Exemption had been mailed to the CFTC (which not only gives rubber stamp approval in most cases but in some cases has been known to tell general partners not to bother to mail it because it is a nuisance to everyone). I was surprised to hear that question because I was unaware of that requirement, and the first audit team had never mentioned it, but I offered to mail the Declarations to the CFTC immediately. Surely they would be accepted because these partnerships were now two or three years old.

These men refused to allow that, saying the partnerships should be registered with the CFTC. "No problem," I said. "I know you are wrong about that, but I will register them immediately."

Right at that time commodity prices were near the bottom of the second decline caused by the devastating Grain Crop and Pig Crop reports released on consecutive days which were mentioned earlier in this book. This was the opportunity for the NFA to "prove" that scale trading doesn't work and to bury me, so they refused to allow me to send either a Declaration of Exemption or Disclosure Document to the CFTC. Instead, they ordered me to shut down the partnerships immediately. I protested that the then-USSR would be placing fresh orders to buy grains and pork with the new credit we were about to extend to them, and that the prices would rally sharply. That would give us our desired profits. That is the way scale trading works. Because they wanted to crucify me for writing a letter detrimental to "one of their own," and because they didn't want to take the chance that the accounts could move back into the profit zone on a rally, they repeated their order to liquidate the accounts immediately (so that we would take a loss). In fact, they threatened that if I did not liquidate the accounts immediately they would bring me before an NFA panel which would probably give me the same kind of fine with which they hit Larry Williams, and I would then be kicked out of the NFA and barred for life. Remember, these people are charged with the responsibility of protecting the public. How is it protecting the public when you force a money manager to liquidate client accounts simply because you want to punish the manager for writing a letter?

They called my ten-page monthly partnership statements "atypical." They called it a violation for not following the prescribed format of a single page. I protested that my ten-page reports contained enough information for an auditor to audit the partnership from day one if he had only the most recent month's statement and the supporting documents. They didn't care. I was in violation because I mailed more than one page.

That got me riled, so I snapped at them that the NFA's prescribed one-page report was so incomplete that it could be used to deceive partners and to hide embezzlements. (I call those one-page statements the "trust me" statements.) In fact, I said, I was sure that this is what helped one of the large brokerage houses to embezzle 55% of the assets of their public commodity pools and to conceal it from the NFA for nearly a year. Here's that story:

One of the giant brokerage firms acted as a clearing broker for many IB firms. During the late 1970's and early 1980's, when every Account Executive (the new name for Registered Representatives) was leaving some giant firm to open his own IB operation, this firm grew very large by taking on the accounting duties of a huge number of IB's. This kind of firm is known as a brokers' broker. The big firm expanded very rapidly, hiring many new employees and leasing large areas of office space. After the silver debacle in 1980, the public began to turn away from commodities trading, and the small IB firms were dropping like flies. The big firm began to feel the pinch of having less income concomitant with increased overhead. It was operating at a loss, and its reserve assets were being consumed rapidly. It was on the verge of bankruptcy.

Then some schemer at the firm got an idea. The firm managed two public commodity pools, one of $4.5 million and the other of $5.5 million, so why not sell the smaller pool $1 million worth of the brokerage house's own commercial paper? I contend that if you are acting in a fiduciary capacity you do not sell your trust account your own commercial paper. If you want that account to own commercial paper (which is a short-term loan) you buy paper issued by General Motors. Because the firm was hanging by its fingernails, the $1 million did not last long, but because they got away with the first $1 million embezzlement they sold the larger pool $4.5 million worth of their own commercial paper. That couldn't reverse the tide of losses, so the firm folded. Investors in the larger pool got back 15 cents on the dollar.

The NFA stuck to its story that no crime had been committed, but I contend that is pure and simple embezzlement, and the reason the NFA never prosecuted was that one of the members of the NFA's board was from the embezzling firm. No doubt, at one of the meetings of the board, the representative from the embezzling firm looked across the table at the other directors from the other firms and said, "If you don't prosecute us this time, we won't prosecute you when it is your turn."

The man who was the head of that failed brokerage house was also the chairman of the Chicago Board of Trade and was the first chairman in the nearly 200-year history of the CBOT to be forced to resign in shame. He claims that he knew nothing of the poor financial condition of his brokerage house because of his heavy involvement at the CBOT, but rumor has it that he transferred a huge number of the firm's best accounts to another brokerage house in the weeks before his firm's collapse, and he now is comanager of that firm's London office and earns a huge annual income off those accounts. (He probably moved to London to avoid the possibility of extradition.) The principal reason why he was never prosecuted by the NFA is that he was vice chairman of the NFA — boy, talk about the fox guarding the henhouse! But most of the senior officers of the NFA also are senior officers of major commodity brokerage firms, and they just will not prosecute each other. If they did, they might lose one member of their golfing foursomes.

That could never have happened if this firm had been obliged to send out more than a one-page monthly statement showing "Commercial Paper: $1 million." My ten-page statements show on page 1, "T-bills: $50,000" and then name the broker who holds them. The partners may reconcile that by turning to page 3 of the statement, which is a photocopy of that broker's month-end statement. If the T-bills aren't there, they know something is wrong. Page 1 also shows $48,000 in the money market account, verified by a photocopy of the broker's money market account, which is page 5. If a single penny is missing from the account, the limited partners will know immediately.

All of this was part of the heated discussion I had with the NFA people about my "atypical" ten-page statements. They insisted that there was absolutely no way to prosecute anyone from that failed firm because no one had violated any laws. I told them I knew how I would nail them if I were the prosecutor, and I suggested they read this book to find out how.

You have heard the term "full disclosure" as pertains to securities law. It is used to prosecute the president of a public company who embezzles the company bankroll and runs off to Brazil with his secretary. Usually, it is very difficult to prove embezzlement by an executive because he can claim that he used the money to conduct personal research — or whatever. Indeed, if the firm printed a prospectus which stated that the president was going to run off to Brazil with his secretary and a large amount of money but you were still foolish enough to invest in their stock, you would have extreme difficulty in proving fraud. However, if the prospectus does *not* say that the president plans to run off with the money and the secretary, the issuing company (and the president) are guilty of "failure to make full disclosure." That is fraud, and prosecution on the grounds of failure to make full disclosure is a piece of cake because the prospectus — ironically, it is called a disclosure document — failed to disclose their intention to give themselves $5.5 million for worthless commercial paper which they would issue. There is no question of what was or was not said at the time of the sale of the partnership units because it is all in writing!

It is possible that no commodity law was violated when the commodity firm mentioned above embezzled the $5.5 million, but surely there must be a corollary to the securities law involving full disclosure which the NFA could have invoked and locked up the principals of the firm and thrown away the key.

The real reason why no one was prosecuted was that most of the NFA executives are principals of brokerage firms and do not want to stir up trouble for fear that it might come back to haunt them some day when their firm is caught with a hand in the cookie jar, but you might think that one of the NFA middle level employees might step forward and demand prosecution; however, NFA employees want to get cushy jobs at large brokerage firms, so they refuse to prosecute the hand they hope will some day feed them generously. When the firm failed after the embezzlement, all of the principals scurried to different large firms in the business. Can you see what would happen if a tough prosecutor from the NFA is ever considered for a position at one of the firms which employed one of the executives from the embezzling firm? The NFA person would be run out the door by the former principal of the failed firm who simply says, "Wait a minute. This is the guy who caused me to pay a $100,000 fine and to be suspended for a year. Don't you *dare* hire him." Thus, the NFA person misses out on an easy $100,000 salary and is stuck at the NFA at $38,000 per year.

Do you remember the former NFA employee who called them the most corrupt of the regulatory agencies? When I told him about my two audits, he said all they wanted was for me to bow down and lick their boots (although he made it a little stronger than that). He said I should never have defended myself against the witch's (or any word you care to use which rhymes) lies but should have licked her boots.

I understand the NFA has petitioned the Vatican to have all of their employees canonized. If the petition is granted, NFA employees will then want NFA members to kiss their rings, which is an improvement over what they want now.

If you still think you want to manage commodity accounts, I'll tell you about the NFA's charge of fraud against me and how they cost me an eye: After the second audit team returned to Chicago they knew they hadn't any grounds for real charges against me, so they spent all of their time (and mine!) harassing me almost daily with letters or phone calls demanding answers to their letters or photocopies of documents which they already had. For example, on one of their calls the man requested some photocopies. (It's never a request; it's a demand: "You must submit the required documents in five days or you will be in violation and subject to a hearing which could result in a large fine and/or being barred for life.") His first request was for three pages. No problem, except that I ended up unable to locate the specific pages for several days and was then forced to drive twelve miles to the post office — and then twelve miles home again — to meet their 5-day requirement. The second thing was another three pages. Again, no problem, except for the minor inconvenience. The third thing: 400 pages. Now we have a problem.

He wanted photocopies of forty months of statements on my oldest partnership. They averaged ten pages, and they were two-sided copies, stapled together. That meant standing in front of a photocopy machine all day, removing staples, putting a page in the machine to copy one side, taking it and the paper out, reloading the one-sided copy in the paper tray (in those days they didn't have today's sophisticated copiers that do all of that automatically), stapling the copies and re-stapling the originals, etc. I refused to spend a whole day copying something which they already had in their possession but which was "in another department." I told them they could come and pick up the originals and make their own copies. When they came to make the copies they decided they didn't need 400. They copied only the current month, or ten pages. Harassment!

While they were here, one of them showed me a letter I had mailed to the limited partners in one of the partnerships I manage. He asked to whom I had mailed the letter. Because it was addressed to the partners, for sheer stupidity I considered his question to be on a par with the one uttered by every husband who comes home early and finds his wife in bed with another man and asks, "What's going on here?" I said, "What do you do, take stupid pills before you leave for work in the morning? That letter went to the partners to whom it is addressed, you moron." (Sometimes I put the "moron" at the end of the sentence.)

Violation! Fraud! Alcatraz coming up! Lock Wiest up and throw away the key!

I didn't know it at the time, but when he returned to Chicago he turned the letter over to their big hitter, Domas Fluffy, who proceeded to charge me with fraud over that letter. Here is the story:

The letter was a chatty little thing which mentioned my idea of forming a *management company* (it is important that you remember that the letter spoke of a proposed *management company*) using the concept of the satellite companies in Houston, Miami, etc. I said we needed a good track record for the oldest account — in this case their partnership — in each office. I mentioned that we were on a roll in that my newsletter *The Scale Trader* had made 88 trades the previous month with 88 winners; that I had a man in Houston who had run up a string of 57 consecutive winners in his personal account (which we would use as an example to demonstrate the efficacy of scale trading to prospective investors in Houston) and was going to be the head of the Houston office; and that we had had 29 trades, 29 winners last month in their partnership account, which would be the fishbowl account for the Los Angeles office. I suggested that the two real money accounts were only about eight months old and needed additional longevity, perhaps eighteen months total. I was alerting them that in about ten months they might be offered the opportunity to invest in the management company, and I implied that they might want to think about saving a little money preparatory to receipt of an Offering Circular for the management company in about a year. (I didn't mention it, but I had once invested $4,800 in a mature management company, and that $4,800 was worth $550,000 two years later.)

This guy Fluffy came down on me like a ton of bricks. He accused me of using false trading results to attract money *into a partnership*. First of all, he was dead wrong because the solicitation would have been for the *management company*, not the partnership. Secondly, the partnership had its legal limit of $200,000 of subscriptions, and it long ago had reached that limit, so if someone had sent the general partner $1 million, he could not have accepted a penny of it. Thirdly, the claimed performance was absolutely true.

I gave Fluffy the name, address, and phone number of the man in Houston who was waiting for the call. Fluffy never called him. He simply said 57 winners in a row — the Houston broker allowed him to use LIFO accounting — was "impossible," so there was no need to call the man. I finally became so frustrated in dealing with Fluffy that I asked the man in Houston to mail me a spreadsheet showing his 57 consecutive winners. He mailed it to me, but now it was 98 trades, 98 winners. I forwarded it to Fluffy, but he declared that it was fabricated. (He also chose to ignore the CPA's statement I had produced verifying my 130 consecutive winners in my real money account.)

As for the 88 winners in a single month in the newsletter, that was when the terrible Grain Crop Report had been issued on Thursday, June 26, and the terrible Pig Crop Report on Friday, June 27. The newsletter was buying MidAm soybeans each 3 cents down, so it bought 40 contracts. We also bought corn, wheat, oats, etc., plus hogs and pork bellies. This was followed by three weeks of sweltering heat, and prices shot upward, allowing us to cash about sixty winners, including 39 of the MidAm soybeans. Then the temperature dropped 14 degrees on a Saturday plus another 6 degree drop on Sunday, so the grains tumbled again on Monday. Almost simultaneously there was an attempt at a coup in the USSR, bringing prices farther down. We now had 40 contracts of MidAm beans again. But the Russian coup was defeated in four days, and grain prices shot upward again. Some of the 38 soybean winners we cashed on the second rally came in the next month, but most of them came in July, along with numerous others from the other grains and meats. Fluffy refused to read the newsletters, saying 88 consecutive winners was impossible.

As for the 29 winners in the partnership with real money, Fluffy said they had obtained a copy of our monthly statement from our broker. He said, "Yes, you had 29 trades, but it was 13 losers and 16 winners, not 29 winners." I told him that I purposely do *not* allow my brokers to use LIFO accounting because I don't want to deceive anyone (as described earlier in this book about the brokerage firm which put on spreads and lifted only the winning legs), but when I send out the monthly statements for the partnerships I send a photocopy of the broker's statement which shows all trades on a FIFO basis, a cumulative list of all closed trades on a FIFO basis so that they may reconcile my statement to the broker's, plus a cumulative list of all closed trades on a LIFO basis so that the partners — all of whom understand scale trading — could see how we are doing from a scale trader's viewpoint. That partnership had logged 80 trades, all LIFO winners, but Fluffy didn't want to look at any of our documents. He just wanted to hang me for writing that letter about my eye.

He just kept saying over and over again, "Impossible, impossible." I became so enraged in one telephone conversation that I started to shout at him. I shouted nonstop for thirty minutes. I rarely use four-letter words, but I think I invented some for this creep. He didn't need a telephone; all he had to do was lean out the window of that office in Chicago and he could have heard me shouting from California. I am sure he sat back and salivated as he baited me. Indeed, I am just as sure that anyone who has ever dealt with him refers to him as the "master-baiter."

They sent me a 27-page letter accusing me of the things like using that chatty letter to the partners, falsely accusing me of trying to raise capital for a partnership which was already fully subscribed, and they threatened that if I did not respond within ten days I would be prosecuted, probably fined, and barred for life. I was trying to keep this venture going, but the work was overwhelming me because the book had become the #1 best seller, and my newsletter was ranked #1 in the business. In commodities you can be #1 one month and #80 the next, so I was reluctant to hire additional people who might have to be laid off in a few months. This frenetic pace had lasted for three years, and I was working seventeen hours a day, seven days a week, and trying to find extra time to write a forty-page answer to the NFA.

While all of this was going on, my right eye really started bothering me. I had been having light flashes in it every two years, then once a year, then every six months, etc. During this ordeal, I was talking with my lady friend on the phone one day, and in a ten minute conversation I had three of the flashes. She wanted me to call the ophthalmologist the moment we hung up, but I protested that I had to complete my reply to the latest harassing letter from the NFA in five days or risk severe penalties. She has more brains than I, so she declared that my eye was more important than the NFA, and she insisted that I call the ophthalmologist immediately. It was Thursday afternoon, and the receptionist said the doctor was leaving on vacation after the close of business Friday. "What are your symptoms?" she asked. When she returned to the phone she said he wanted me in there tomorrow morning before his first scheduled patient.

Friday morning I took the phone off the hook, thinking I would be back in half an hour with some eye drops. I never got back! The moment he checked my eye he could see I had a serious problem, so he sent me directly to the specialist. The specialist examined the eye, ordered me to go directly to the hospital, followed me over, and performed emergency surgery. He said, "If you had let that go as much as over the weekend, you probably would have lost the eye." (For people who are interested in such things, I had six tears in the retina.)

Upon recovery I got back to typing my answer to the NFA, but by then it was too late. I hadn't answered in the prescribed time, so they informed me that they were going to call me before an NFA board of inquiry. I knew I hadn't a snowball's chance in an NFA hearing because the jury would be comprised of three commodity dealers. There are about 3,000 small dealers, and about 300 large dealers, so the chances are ten-to-one that each member of the panel would be from a small firm. If any of the panel members could ignore what I have stated about so many crooks in the business, he would still be under pressure from the NFA to convict me. It would never be stated, but it would be implied that the NFA wanted my scalp for defending myself and writing that letter about my eye. If a representative from a small firm serving on the panel did *not* convict me, his firm had better be prepared for the audit of their lives next time.

I went ahead and mailed my forty-page answer to the NFA, and in it I said I intended to resign from the NFA. Remember, I was *never required* to belong because the largest number of managed accounts I had ever had was nine, with a total of $2 million.

In that letter I told them they had nearly cost me an eye (it was too soon to know that eventually I would lose it completely) but I was not going to let them cost me my life. I said I felt it was not cholesterol which caused people to have heart attacks and strokes, but stress. They had kept me under constant stress for two years with their badgering and harassment, and I just wanted out. They responded that they were not going to let me out.

In time I received a call from an NFA attorney who offered to let me out if I would "confess." I asked, "Confess to what?" She said, "To all of the charges." I told her I hadn't the foggiest notion what the charges were, but I was so anxious to get out of the NFA that I would confess to anything short of murder.

She accepted that but said there would have to be a penalty and that I must set the penalty. I said, "Six months suspension." She refused to accept that, saying it would have to be more than that. I said, "Okay, seven months." She said it would have be at least a year, and I accepted. Then she changed her mind and said it would have to be two years. Again I accepted because I just wanted out. She changed her mind again and said it would have to be five years. (All of this was happening in a single phone conversation!) She was just pushing me, but she had passed my limit. I dug in my heels and said I would not go beyond two years. She approved of that and sent me the papers to sign.

After I signed and returned their form I didn't hear a word from them, and it was like having an anvil removed from my shoulders. However, after seven weeks she called again and said my offer of a settlement had been refused and the NFA was insisting upon a five year suspension. I had enjoyed working for seven weeks without NFA membership, and she had finally worn me down, so I agreed. She sent the papers with the five-year suspension plus an unannounced extra paragraph which called for two years of some other kind of suspension. At this point I couldn't have cared less, so I signed and returned it.

She called again. This time she said there had been an error with that second paragraph. I figured she meant it should never have been inserted because I had never agreed to it. No! What she meant was that it also should have said five years instead of the stated two.

That was all I could take. "No way," I said. "We are going to court. I am sick and tired of this harassment by the NFA simply because I wrote a letter defending myself against an NFA witch (this time I used a word which rhymes). And it will not be before an NFA panel of robots, it will be in a civil court where human beings will hear the evidence." I had told parts of this story to a great many people who covered the spectrum from complete knowledge of the commodities business to no knowledge at all, and every one of these people said this was pure harassment and that I would win easily in court.

She answered that I could not go to court *because I had waived that right when I joined the NFA*. (Do you still want to manage money and join the NFA?)

Today I am back to selling books, publishing the newsletter, and managing fewer than fifteen accounts. I am at peace with the world and trying to forget the nightmare of dealing with the NFA.

Incidentally, I want to assure you that in all of the years that I have managed money, there has never been a penny missing from my accounts. There has never been a penny missing from any of my partnerships. When I worked as a broker, I never even had anyone write a letter to any of my managers to complain about anything I did. Absolute accuracy in accounting is such an obsession with me that I will never allow any of my partnership account books to go to the auditors while out of balance by a single penny. One year when I was signing the necessary papers to complete the audit of a large partnership done by a huge accounting firm, the Chinese senior partner with whom I was dealing commented that my hand-calculated statements were "pretty accurate." It was a $700,000 partnership which had executed millions of dollars worth of commodity futures trades that year, so I looked him in the eye and said, "No, not pretty accurate. *Precise.*" He blushed — it isn't easy to make a Chinese man blush — and conceded that my statements balanced to the penny. He pointed to a different one on his desk which had been prepared by computer by another commodity manager, and he said it contained twenty-seven errors.

The NFA is without a doubt the most corrupt of the regulatory agencies. Nearly every NFA member with whom I have talked has related one or more horror stories about NFA abuses, but most of them feared allowing me to tell their story — even without the use of names — because they all fear they might be recognized, and there would be retaliation. To a person, they all said the NFA should be abolished and a proper regulatory body impaneled. I hope you consider that if you expect to try to become a professional commodity money manager.

A closing thought about managing commodity accounts: The NFA auditors live an unbelievably plush life style. An audit team will fly to San Francisco for two weeks with all expenses paid, including a car and lodgings at a plush hotel. They dine in the finest restaurants. Then they fly home to Chicago for two weeks before being flown to New Orleans for two weeks at Mardi Gras time. Two weeks in New York City to dine at their fine restaurants. Two weeks in Denver in winter if they want to ski. Two weeks in Miami in the winter when it's ten below in Chicago. They have dozens of audit teams who follow each other on this year-round vacation circuit. Someone has to pay for all of this, and you had better be prepared because the NFA's principal source of income is fines. (Sounds to me like a gross conflict of interest.) The executives of the NFA treat themselves like potentates. The president of the United States earns $200,000 per year, while the president of the NFA earns $300,000 per year.

The NFA recently celebrated its tenth anniversary, and several of the senior officers suggested that a history of the NFA be written and preserved for posterity, but the project fell apart when they couldn't decide whether it should be included in the Old Testament or the New Testament.

In addition to your vulnerability to fines, you must also pay $500 a year to be registered with the NFA, and if you live in a state like California you will pay another $350 for state registration. Your trading record must be presented every six months, and the accounting is so complex that you probably will want to have an accountant prepare the documents for you. Accountants aren't cheap. You probably will want an attorney to prepare all of your filings, but commodity attorneys are rare. You might find a local attorney who will charge you only $200 an hour, but he probably knows so little about commodities and CFTC/NFA filings that his charges for "research" make him more expensive than using a knowledgeable attorney who will charge you $500 an hour.

If you still want to manage commodity accounts, all I can say is, "Good luck."

XXXI

The Stock Market —
Look Out Below!

I feel that the stock market is grossly overpriced and in danger of a rending crash. The culprit behind the problem is the Federal Reserve and its manipulation of interest rates. To give you an idea of what I fear, I must analogize a little:

Tinkering with the economy by manipulating interest rates is like flying an airplane upward through a layer of clouds without instruments other than a compass, a tachometer, an altimeter with a rate-of-climb indicator, and an airspeed indicator, hoping to reach the clear skies above the cloud bank. You keep your eyes rotating around those four instruments, hoping to keep all settings constant. Suddenly you notice that your compass heading has shifted 5 degrees, so you turn the plane to correct the heading. As the plane turns, the outside wing moves a little faster than the inside wing, so that side of the plane rises very slightly — almost imperceptibly. Because the wings are no longer level — which is the maximum lift position — the plane loses a tiny bit of lift, and the nose drops. This causes the plane to pick up speed. To overcome this you can either lift the nose very slightly, or throttle back. Either way, the plane slows, and it loses lift, causing the nose to fall, forcing you to increase the power to maintain lift.

The plane has a natural trim in its design to compensate for the engine torque, so each time you adjust the throttle the torque is increased or decreased and the plane swings ever so slightly on its vertical axis. Again, this causes the outside wing to move faster, and as the plane tilts it loses lift. As you adjust the throttle and ailerons and trim with the rudder the nose of the plane is going up, then down, then up again. The plane gains and loses airspeed, and it gains and loses altitude. Because you can't see anything but white outside the window, you keep trying to correct directional flaws by jockeying the airspeed, the throttle, the ailerons, and the rudder until you reach the point where over-compensation of one control causes under-compensation of another, and you become so disoriented that the plane goes out of control, goes into a spiral, and unless you come out of the clouds in time to orient yourself and halt the spiral, you crash.

This, I fear, is what the Federal Reserve has been doing to our economy by playing games with interest rates. The Fed has itself between a rock and a hard place, and they may have set us up for a terrible stock market crash.

The reason the Fed, commercial bankers, Wall Street investment bankers, and all others of a similar ilk don't understand the problems created by tinkering with interest rates is that they only talk with each other and with industrialists from giant corporations. In their discussions they hold in their ivory towers in Manhattan they are told by executives of giant corporations that their corporation plans to delay building that new $2 billion assembly plant in Tennessee because interest rates have risen too high for them to commit to long-term financing at such high rates; they will wait for lower rates, even if it takes a couple of years.

They shouldn't be talking to industrialists. They should be talking to the man on the street in Middletown, Iowa, if they really want to know what the American public's reaction is to a change in interest rates. They should walk down Main Street and go in and out of doors, talking with the owner of the hardware store, the appliance store, the car dealership, the farm equipment dealership, and the locals who stopped by the diner to enjoy a cup of coffee and to talk about the weather, the high school's chances in the coming state tournament, and the PTA meeting this coming Saturday night. Talk to the local banker to get an idea of the local citizens' probable buying plans. Do it in a hundred towns scattered all over the country to avoid the possibility of aberrations caused by local situations. Never mind what is going on in Manhattan where people pay $1 million for a 1,600 square foot condominium because they earn $300,000 a year on Wall Street. That's not the real world. Get out and talk to real people. They could find them in West Virginia, Idaho, or Missouri. Go to areas where the largest business in the county employs 125 people. Because small businesses employing less than 500 people account for twice the portion of the Domestic National Product that the large corporations account for, it is ludicrous to attempt to manipulate the economy to accommodate only the giants.

A perfect example of that is the age of the autos on the roads of America today. The average age of cars today is eight years. That is the highest average since the Korean War. If Fed members had gone out to talk with the American public two years ago, they would have learned that the public was going to delay buying a car because the drop in interest rates will cause them to earn $300 less interest this coming year than they earned last year, and that caused them to bypass the new car this year and do a little repair work on the old one. Furthermore, their cousin in Detroit got laid off at the auto plant because fewer people were buying cars, and the speaker feared that poor business in America's most basic industry would eventually filter all the way down to his dry cleaning shop as people wore their garments a few extra times before cleaning them in an effort to conserve cash. The sentiment pervaded the entire economy — except in Manhattan and Washington, DC — and kept us in recession much longer than necessary.

If the Fed had talked with the common people they would have decided to *raise* interest rates instead of lowering them. Then the people would have bought cars, and the recession could have ended two years earlier. The cousin in Detroit — and millions of other people — would be back at work, and that corporation probably would have gone ahead and built the new assembly plant in Tennessee to meet the demand for its product. That plant might have employed 8,000 people, and the ancillary employment — suppliers, shippers, salespeople, media people handling the advertising

314

of the product, etc. — might account for 10,000 more jobs. Figuring four to a family, the assembly plant which employs 8,000 has provided income for 32,000 people — and the ancillary employment 40,000 more — all of whom must buy groceries, clothing, homes, furniture, gasoline, etc., and consume electricity, natural gas, water, etc.

The Fed doesn't understand economics. Big time bankers usually are born into the banking family, go to Harvard or Yale, go directly into the bank upon graduation, never work a day in their lives because of their connections, and eventually rise to the top at the family bank. Their entire social life is rubbing elbows with other members of the elite at country clubs and riding to the hounds. They have never known a person who was unemployed or had to worry about missing a mortgage payment or a car payment and feared losing his home or car.

Then the Fed gets a leader who is a college professor theoretician who has a bagel for a brain, and all the Fed does is to accommodate their fraternity brothers from school who are now investment bankers or commercial bankers on Wall Street under the mistaken impression that they represent America.

Enough of that old adage, "What's good for General Motors is good for the nation." I say, "Quit trying to manipulate the economy and both General Motors and the people will be better served."

As I stated earlier, interest rates should be left alone to find their natural level of supply and demand, which would be somewhere between 4% and 6%. But the Fed has brought short-term rates down to 3%, and they have created a monster of a problem for pension funds. Pension funds operate on actuarial schedules which require them to earn at least 6% annually on their interest-bearing securities, net after operating expenses. They can't produce that kind of income with interest rates so low. *You can't get blood out of a turnip.* There is $8 trillion — with a T — in U.S. pension funds, and much of that is underfunded. For example, General Motors is said to be underfunded by $20 billion to its pension fund, so they keep contributing more of their stock to try to meet the actuarial needs. That's fine, but what if the stock market takes General Motors stock down to 40 cents on the dollar? Then what happens to the pension fund?

315

And don't think it couldn't happen. The public went crazy in Japan, thinking the stock market could never go down. Everyone bought stocks with all the money they had. They bid the value of a single utility stock to a greater value than all stocks on the New York Stock Exchange combined. Their Nikkei 225 Stock Index (their equivalent of our Dow Jones Industrial Average) rose to 39,000. The subsequent decline took that average down to 14,000, or nearly a 65% drop. Our DJIA has surpassed 3,900 on the frenzied buying of people leaving bank CD's to get a piece of the Wall Street giveaway. Who's to say that we could not go down to 1,400 when sanity returns?

If the General Motors pension fund is unable to pay its promised payments to its retirees, those approaching retirement age might decide that they had better continue to work instead of retiring. That could mean fewer job openings for the young people coming into the labor force, exacerbating the serious unemployment situation we would likely have if the stock market had dropped enough to take GM down 60%. The nation could already be in depression. If the young people have no jobs, they cannot spend, nor can the older people who have seen their pension payouts reduced sharply. With spending curtailed that critically, there is no doubt that we would be in a depression.

If the Fed anticipates the problem and decides to preempt pension fund catastrophes by raising interest rates, they are like the pilot hitting the plane's throttle to gain airspeed. Something else gets out of adjustment, and in this case it is the stock market.

This screwball idea of lowering interest rates to save the banks caused savers to abandon safe investments such as bank CD's and to go into speculative investments such as the stock and bond markets. Let's look first at the bond market:

When savers talked to bond dealers and asked about total yields — which includes the interest on the bonds *and* the appreciation, the dealer pulled out a chart showing how well bonds had fared over the last ten years. But the results could hardly have been more deceptive. A little over ten years ago the Fed had pushed interest rates to the moon, with T-bills yielding more than 17% and T-bonds yielding 14%. Bonds move inversely to yields, so older bonds plunged to less than 60% of face value during that

316

stupid Fed experiment. Those same bonds are today selling above par (100), at about 120, so the gain in principal alone is a little more than 100% in twelve years, or about 8% per year. Add the 14% actual interest return (8% bonds selling at less than 60% of face yield a current return of 14%), and bonds have netted 22% per year for more than ten years. Savers have gone crazy over that kind of yield when they can only get 3% in a bank CD, and they have pulled their money from the bank to buy bonds. Or to buy bond funds which would show similar results. Many of those bonds which sold at prices under 60% of face have matured or been called to be replaced by lower-coupon bonds selling at par, but even those bonds have appreciated 20% in the last five years, or 4% per year, still giving them an average annual net of about 12%. This dilutes the twelve-year average to about 14% instead of 22%, but it is still impressive to neophyte bond buyers who will weigh that return — even though it is false and cannot be replicated — against the 3% offered by a CD.

While the bond buyers are writing the check the bond dealer doesn't bother to explain that if interest rates rise, the bond market must fall, and it could fall faster than the paltry interest yields the bonds show today. That would mean a *negative* return on the bonds, meaning a *loss* to investors who expected 14% annual returns. If they manifest their disappointment in liquidating their bond and bond fund holdings, a rout could occur.

The Fed can crush the pension funds by keeping interest rates low, or it can crush the bond market by raising rates.

Now let's look at the stock market: The problem is virtually the same as for the bond market. As interest rates have fallen over the last dozen years, savers have talked with stock brokers who have shown them mutual fund performance charts showing average returns of 18% or more annually, and savers have taken the bait. As with bonds, they withdrew their guaranteed-safe bank savings to buy speculative mutual fund shares which today offer little more guarantee than a lottery ticket.

When I started in the stock market thirty-six years ago, the total amount of money in all mutual funds combined was $50 billion, and it had taken more than sixty years to reach that level. Today the amount is $2 trillion, and the money keeps pouring in at the rate of more than thirty billion per month. What happens when the Fed raises interest rates and the stock market begins to decline?

These people who have been taking their money from maturing CD's and investing it in stock mutual funds are not risk takers. They are very conservative bank savers who were forced by the Fed to go into the stock market against their normal nature. When they start to lose money in the stock market, they will cash in their mutual fund shares and rush back to the safety of bank CD's.

Current dividend yields on the stocks in the DJIA average barely 2.5%, the lowest level in years, and looking like Great Depression yields. That has not been a problem so far because the only other game in town — real estate has bombed — is the bond market, where short-term rates are at thirty-year lows and T-bills yield less than 3%. The public feels it is no big deal if their stocks yield less than 3% per year as long as the stocks rise 18% per year. *Where else can you get 21% total return?* But if the Fed pushes interest rates higher and the stock market then moves lower, look out below!

No-load mutual funds (no-load means they charge no commission to get in or out) have become so popular that they dominate the industry. Because of the ease of entering or exiting the funds, if the stock market starts to fall, it is possible that fund investors will opt to liquidate their holdings, telling themselves that they only expect to go to the sidelines to ride out the stock market decline which they hope will be nominal and short-lived. However, the fiendish program traders (please see below) will certainly be selling into the falling market, exacerbating and accelerating the decline. When that happens, other savers who were non-risk types will be panicked into selling their mutual fund shares, and the collapse will be upon us. Obviously, those who said they would merely go to the sidelines for a while will run back to the bank and not return to the stock market for a decade.

Why do I feel so certain that this will happen? Just look at the fundamentals: Stocks are supposed to sell at ten times earnings, although the youngsters who work on Wall Street today and have seen only the rising market of the last twelve years will tell you that seventeen is the normal P/E ratio. I mentioned earlier in the book that stocks at one time had gone from a P/E ratio of 7X to 23X and could not replicate that performance. Two years ago I said in *The Scale*

Trader that the P/E of the Dow Jones Industrial Average was 24X (!), and that I feared a stock market break because the stock market had sold at 23X only twice before in history, and both times that was followed by a bone crushing decline. Ha! A year later the DJIA was at 72X. The only thing that is supporting it is the constant flow of money fleeing from the low interest rates at the bank to the garden spot called Wall Street.

The Wall Street Journal, the developer of the Dow Jones Stock Averages, formerly printed the current P/E's for their three indexes (Industrials, Transports, and Utilities) each Monday. They appear to have stopped printing that number because I can rarely find it. Perhaps it is because they don't want to frighten the public. The last time I saw it in the Journal was in late 1993 at 45X, and the market has been rising ever since, so it must be over 50X now. (Investor's Business Daily shows the P/E ratio of the DJIA to be 22X, but it is the Journal's own index, so I have to accept their 45X number.)

The dividend yields are at the lowest levels in years, but no one seems to care because the stocks rise to new heights daily. Besides, the alternative would be a CD, which yields about the same as stocks, but the CD can't appreciate the crazy way that stocks have been appreciating.

It's no wonder that new investors think the stock market is a gravy train. The stock market usually goes up for two or three years and then has a gentle correction of 10% or so. Sometimes the correction is greater, but we haven't seen one in years. Indeed, not only have we not seen a 10% correction in three years, but we haven't even seen an 8% correction in that time! What will happen if the Fed raises interest rates from 3% to 3.6%? That's a 20% increase, which could send the stock market down 20%, and if it goes down 20% it could panic the new players who thought the stock market was a one-way street going straight up. Once the selling begins, there won't be enough room at the exits for all of the funds to get out at once.

We see a microcosm of what may lie ahead almost daily as companies report earnings a couple of cents lower than The Street had been anticipating. The stock is unable to open trading because of the backup of sell orders which have accumulated overnight. When the stock finally opens, it is 20% lower. The reason for the 20% drop after the company reported quarterly earnings of 24 cents instead of the 26 cents The Street expected, is that many of the funds are being run by young gunslingers who have no thought for long-term investment and only try to maximize performance through rapid in-and-out trading. To them, a long-term investment is something held over the weekend. How are we to expect them to react if the Fed raises interest rates two or three times, the stock market has started its selloff, the program traders are bombing the market, and former-CD holders now want out of their mutual funds to go back to the bank? There won't be room at the exits!

Now! Consider the effect of the program traders! These devils have programmed computers to enter orders to buy or sell millions of shares of a package of stocks in the blink of an eyelash. Most of their recent activity has been on the "buy" side, helping to push the stock market to new records daily. No one complains about that. But what happens when the stock market starts down, and their trading is on the "sell" side? It could be catastrophic.

Program traders were almost single-handedly responsible for the one-day 508 point drop in the Dow in October, 1987, and the outcry against program trading was so great that the New York Stock Exchange placed a collar on program trading, saying that it must be halted whenever the stock market has risen or fallen 50 points during a trading session. That's a smoke screen. The real reason for stopping program trading for even a few minutes is to give the program traders time to race over to the bank to borrow more millions to use as collateral for more short selling as soon as program trading is reopened.

Imagine what it is going to be like when program traders are smashing the market with tens of millions — perhaps hundreds of millions — of shares of stock at the same time that the multi-billion dollar mutual funds are all trying to unload millions upon millions of shares of stock. The frightening part is that there won't be any buyers willing to buy those stocks. Who wants to get in the way of a runaway freight train?

There is no doubt in my mind that program trading should be outlawed because it serves no purpose other than to enrich the already rich Wall Street brokerage houses.

To give you an inkling of the kind of chaos and destruction program traders can wreak on the stock market, consider the following:

Each point move in the Dow is considered to be equal to a $1 billion change in the value of all U.S. stocks combined. Thus, the 508 point decline cost U.S. stockholders $508 billion. Those who defend program trading — after all, some people even liked Hitler — dispute the notion that program traders were responsible for the 508 point drop, but how do they defend the 120 point drop program traders caused in a single day in 1990 *when there was no news to precipitate any decline at all and the stock market was in a generally rising trend?* There is only one answer: The program traders needed lunch money, so they bombed the stock market to the tune of $120 billion, with the last $90 billion of that coming in the final 75 minutes of trading.

The flood in the Midwest during the spring of 1993 was called a 500-year flood because a flood of that magnitude could only be expected once each 500 years. The flood covered parts of a dozen states, lasted for months, and destroyed homes and farmlands everywhere. The corn and soybean crops were reduced approximately 25%. The financial loss was estimated to be around $10 billion.

$10 billion? That's not even walking-around money to program traders. They won't bother if they think they can move the market only ten points. It took six months for the flood to cause $10 billion of damage, but program traders caused $90 billion of damage in 75 minutes!

If you figure that a worker could earn $35,000 a year average over his 44 years of employment, it would take 60,000 such workers to earn $90 billion. The lifetime earnings of 60,000 people burned up in 75 minutes because program traders got bored and tired of yawning, so they bombed the stock market for $90 billion in 75 minutes! That is 5.28 billion hours of labor wiped out in 75 minutes.

Expressed another way, if you figure four persons to a family, that is the lifetime earnings of a town with a population of 240,000 people. The entire earnings for the next forty-four years of every family in Akron, Ohio wiped out in 75 minutes of greed.

XXXII

General Questions

When I do seminars, or when I have a private conference with prospective clients, some questions seem to arise repeatedly. They deserve comment within the context of this book, but they do not warrant full chapter coverage.

Q. *Do you ever use stop orders?*

A. Absolutely not. First of all, the system itself could not possibly employ stop orders. Secondly, I would never use a system which required the use of stop orders, for stops (as they are more commonly known) are a device invented a long time ago by some broker who was hoping to increase his commissions by churning accounts faster. If you are trading commodities in such a manner that your method requires the use of stops, you are using the wrong system. If you have taken a position which goes against you temporarily, and if you bought right in the first place, you should buy more — not sell out.

Q. *If your system becomes popular, what happens if everyone starts using it?*

A. As stated in Chapter XXV, "Why Doesn't Everyone Scale Trade?," it is unlikely that many people will ever adopt this system because of its producing "only" 25% to 50% annual profits, but even if the system acquires some degree of popularity, it is unlikely that it will ever match the popularity of trend-following, for investors (or speculators) are introduced to commodities by salesmen who generally are more interested in the amount of the commissions an account can generate and are, therefore, more inclined to recommend the trend-following method with its high commissions than scale trading with its low commissions. Despite the fact that very few trend-followers made actual trades in gold and silver in 1979 (because of the enormous margin requirements), the salesmen will point to hypothetical results and induce customers to trade the trend-following method.

Unfortunately, as more people are attracted to trend-following, commodities markets become more volatile, for it is their buying on rallies and their selling on declines which exacerbates trends and amplifies volatility. Actually, it would be good for commodities prices in general if more people would scale trade, for that would tend to mitigate volatility.

In any case, it is the cash market prices which ultimately determine futures market prices, and it is the buying support or resistance of the consumer — the housewife, industry, government, etc. — which sets price trends, and that market is so massive that the trading action of neither the trend-followers nor the scale traders can affect the real (cash) markets for any appreciable period of time.

Q. *Do you ever abandon the scale and hold a few positions when it is obvious that a big move is beginning?*

A. Never. There is no such thing as the obvious beginning of a move. I observed one man in 1979 who tried for the "blockbuster" but reaped only what I would have considered a predictable harvest. This man is a self-made millionaire (the worst kind because they are too stubborn to listen to the advice of others), so he could afford to scale trade pork bellies on an exceedingly tight scale. He bought them every half-penny down and sold them each penny up. After acquiring about forty contracts (!) in the crunching belly collapse of 1979 he was able to begin to sell contracts on the ensuing rally and reduced his holdings to about twenty contracts with his properly executed selling scale. However, he declared that he considered it foolish to adhere unswervingly to the scale trading system and to be sacrificing potential profits which were a cinch to come from the obviously developing explosive move." For the next six months he stopped scale trading the bellies as they oscillated through a very broad range, as well as oscillating through the typically wide intraday swings which pork bellies always enjoy. Eventually, they returned almost precisely to where they were when he decided to sit on his twenty contracts and hold for the big move. His money didn't earn a dime in all that time, but with the tight scale he had been using he would have been averaging better than a winner per day, or more than $2,000 per week. His deviation from the system cost him about $60,000 in six months.

1993 is another example of an "obvious big move" that did not occur. Many of the subscribers to *The Scale Trader* called to ask why they should not cancel their sell orders and hold for the obviously giant move which was just starting. I told them they should do whatever their hearts told them to do, and I said I would never insist that they had to trade my way. However, I pointed out to them that we were coming off a record U.S. corn crop in 1992, a record worldwide crop of wheat in 1992-93, and a record South American crop of Soybeans in 1993. It did not appear obvious to me that grain prices were necessarily heading higher. The fundamentals were right, and prices broke sharply.

Q. *Do you use charts?*

A. Yes and no. No, I do not use them to determine my trading strategy except perhaps using a twenty day moving average to isolate a commodity which may be grossly under-priced. But even then I would trade that particular commodity only if I had already determined that it had been nearing time to commence scaling.

But, yes, I do use them to record my personal trades. It is easiest for me to explain the system to prospective clients if I merely show them a chart with all the red and green dots denoting the actual buy and sell points of my personal trades. (This is the same as the "x's" and "o's" on the soybean oil charts in Chapter VIII.) It is readily apparent to them that the green dots are al-

324

ways an increment higher than the red dots. I also keep all Purchase and Sale receipts from the brokers and the brokers' monthly statements to verify my performance claims and to substantiate the accuracy of each red or green dot.

In that sense, I do use charts, but I hope that I have made it abundantly clear in this book that I consider charts, chart patterns, technical analysis — or whatever other name you choose to use — worthless.

Q. *Do you ever consider seasonal trends to initiate a scale?*

A. To a degree, yes. There can be very little question that seasonal trends do occur, it is normal for prices to be depressed during the harvest season for most crops as farmers sell that portion of the harvest which they are unable to store on the farm, so seasonal trends should be considered. However, it is insufficient to say that merely because a price has risen or fallen from October to January in seven of the last ten years that represents a seasonal trend. It is more important to determine the price levels which were extant at the commencement of the rise or decline of the prices annually. Supply and demand conditions in the respective years must also be considered. So, too, must government programs (loan levels) for those years. Seasonal studies may demonstrate that a commodity such as corn customarily declines forty cents in a particular three month period, and has done it eight of the last ten years, but it would seem improbable that it would happen in the pending period under consideration if corn is at that moment selling at the lowest price of the last six or seven years. All of this comes under that very broad heading of "fundamental analysis," which in turn isolates seasonal trends and reduces the necessity for additional concentrated study to a very bare minimum.

Q. *How do you select the delivery month which you intend to trade?*

A. It is usually through a series of compromises. The nearest delivery month generally has the most volatility and the most liquid market, but it also will require the most rollovers. The most distant delivery month will require the fewest rollovers, but it offers the least liquidity, and it may carry a substantial carrying charge premium. The distant month may also be the new crop,

325

which means you might be trading a crop before it is even planted, and subsequent fundamental developments may alter your price projections dramatically. You should note the volume and open interest figures, which are published daily, to determine the necessary compromises between nearby contracts for trading activity and distant contracts to avoid rollovers. Generally, you will find it best to initiate your scales in contracts which have about six months to go before expiration; these will give you adequate activity, liquidity, and volatility.

Q. *Are there any delivery months which are always best to trade?*
A. Yes, in some commodities. Before the scandals ruined potato trading you would almost always trade the May contract. In pork bellies it is the February contract. There is always a good volume of trading in the first and last crop months of agricultural commodities; for example, November and July soybeans. December is good in all commodities because of extensive hedging of year-end deliveries. The few delivery months which are not good ones to trade are those which have an overlap from the old crop to the new crop; an example being September corn or soybean contracts where the price may be attuned to old crop usage and is suddenly disrupted as perfect harvesting conditions make it apparent that some of the new crop may be delivered against the September contracts. Your commodity broker should be able to assist you in the selection of the proper delivery months to trade. With practice you will be able to do it alone.

Q. *Isn't this system basically the same as "dollar-cost-averaging" in stocks?*
A. Absolutely not. In dollar-cost-averaging a stock, the buyer continues to make identical dollar amounts of purchases at fixed decrements so that he is always buying an increasingly greater number of shares for the same dollar amount. That system is sound only if the corporation stays in business long enough for management to effect a turnaround and cause the price of the stock to advance. However, it is possible for a corporation to go bankrupt, and no systematic method of stock purchases may bring about a profit under that circumstance. This is not the case with a commodity, though, for there is no way that corn can go bank-

rupt. Corn may decline in price for an extended period of time, but sooner or later the Law of Supply and Demand will force the price to rise, and the patient scale trader will convert all of his losses to profits. It may seem ridiculous that something as basic and as simple as supply and demand makes this system unique, but it is true.

Q. *If I find a commodity broker who understands the scale trading system, shouldn't I simply turn over my account and let him handle everything through discretionary power?*

A. I would consider that imprudent and unwise. To give a broker total discretion invites problems; it is a simple matter for him to commit all of the frauds mentioned in Chapter XXI, "The Managed Account." Indeed, it may be easier for the broker acting alone because the cooperation of an advisor is unnecessary. Some contact, no matter how minimal, should be maintained.

Probably the best way to work with a broker is to discuss each scale before commencing the scale so there is no misunderstanding about what you expect from the broker. (Until a relationship is established, the broker may send printed copies of the scales for you to initial and return so that there is no question of what the instructions are.) Then, if you have signed the papers giving him limited power of attorney, he may enter orders for you (only to offset new positions) if he is unable to reach you by phone. This can be very important if you have made a purchase and the price is rallying smartly, or if you have made a sale and the price breaks. The *limited* part of the agreement means that he may not withdraw funds from your account or enter orders which were not previously approved by you. You are placing a very limited amount of trust in his hands, but if you do not trust your broker you should not be dealing with him, and if he does not trust you he certainly will not deal with you.

Q. *Do you ever pyramid profits?*

A. Not in the manner in which the term "pyramiding" is generally used. Pyramiding is the practice of using paper profits to accumulate a larger number of positions to generate really substantial profits from a small initial position. That practice is sometimes — though rarely — successful for the true gambler. How-

327

ever, it works only when price trends continue their direction in an uninterrupted move. It is disastrous when prices reverse suddenly.

The form of pyramiding that I employ is to use *realized* profits to tighten scales. For example, if my capital is adequate for scaling pork bellies from 40 cents each penny down to 30 cents, I will begin to enter additional buy orders at 30.5 cents after I have captured three one-cent winners, 31.5 cents after four more one-cent winners, 32.5 after five more one-cent winners, 33.5 cents after six more, etc.

The reasoning behind this is that I have already allowed for a decline to 30 cents with my existing capital, but the first three one-cent winners would give me a net profit of about $1,200, which would be adequate to cover the paper loss in one contract falling from 30.5 cents to 30 cents ($200) plus the $1,000 additional margin required for the additional contract. The next four winners would produce about $1,600 net profit, or enough to cover the paper loss in a position acquired at 31.5 cents if it drops to 30 cents ($600) plus $1,000 additional margin. Etc.

This is not pyramiding in the truest sense, but it is a form of using house money to increase positions without additional risk to one's predetermined capital commitment.

Q. *May commodities be used in IRA, Keogh, and 401(k) programs? (These are forms of tax sheltered retirement programs for the self-employed.)*

A. The suitability and acceptance of the investment vehicle which may be used with tax sheltered retirement programs is generally determined at the discretion of the custodian. Most custodians will never accept an individual's private commodity trading account in a tax sheltered retirement program for the simple reason that the custodian is the legal and technical "owner" of the account. If the custodian allowed you to trade your own $50,000 account in commodities and you lost $75,000, it is the custodian which would owe the $25,000 deficit, not you.

There are some discount brokerage firms which have been advertising that they will allow you to trade commodities as an individual in your retirement account, but that's a gimmick. You may trade only 20% of the capital and must hold 80% in reserve. However, many custodians will approve your investment of all or part of your retirement account funds in a limited partnership which trades commodities. The reason is that the custodian is now a *limited partner* and need not worry about the loss, for if the partnership goes into deficit, it is the general partner who owes that money and not the custodian.

I am aware of several scale trading commodity partnerships which are approved for tax sheltered retirement programs. Please write to me or call me if you are interested.

Q. *Is it better to concentrate on a single commodity or to diversify when scale trading?*

A. That is up to the individual trader. Concentration in a single commodity will usually produce greater percentage returns, but it will also cause more sleepless nights, for there will be times when the accumulated paper losses will be substantial. It takes the constitution of a riverboat gambler to concentrate on one commodity, but the rewards are commensurate with the risk. Few people have the intestinal fortitude (guts, to be more precise) to trade in a single commodity such as pork bellies where the price swings are substantial, the sleepless nights numerous, and the profits incredible.

Near the end of Chapter VI, I commented about fluctuating interest rates forcing all commodity prices to move in a single direction simultaneously. As a rule of thumb, I would suggest that anytime we have interest rates of 10% or higher, beware of those high rates dominating commodities markets, and try to concentrate on a single commodity, regardless of the size of your account. When interest rates are below 10%, supply and demand will dictate prices, and you can diversify again.

Q. *If you were retired and had $200,000 with which to scale trade, how would you trade it?*

A. Pork Bellies. I would construct one scale and put everything on the bellies. I would start at 50 cents, and buy each 2 cents down to 30 cents, at which point I would shift to 1 cent, being prepared to buy each penny down from 29 cents to 15 cents. The lowest price for pork bellies in the last ten years has been 24.5 cents, and the lowest price in the last thirty years has been 20 cents, so I would feel quite comfortable with a scale carrying down to 15 cents. If the price ever fell to 15 cents, the paper loss would be $152,000, and the total dollar commitment would be $178,000, assuming $1,000 margin on each of the twenty-six contracts. That would take me 5 cents below the lowest price of the last thirty years and still give me $22,000 of cash in reserve.

I would seek a 2 cent profit on contracts purchased at 30 cents and above, and I would seek 1 cent for those purchased at 29 cents and lower.

It is highly unlikely that pork bellies will sell as low as 15 cents because they haven't sold at that price since Abe Lincoln was president. Furthermore, any economic condition severe enough to push pork belly prices down to 15 cents would probably also force a general collapse in the economy. This would cause houses which went from $50,000 in 1975 to $400,000 in 1990 to fall all the way back to $50,000, or lower.

The foregoing answer is nearly identical to the one given in the 1980 edition of the book, with adjustments for subsequent events, but I want to expand that answer for this edition:

When the above was written in 1980 we had already had twenty years of pork bellies trading and had a good idea of possible highs and lows for a coming decade or longer. And pork bellies was an extremely active contract. (At one time pork bellies was the *most* active of all commodity futures contracts.) However, a pair of other commodities began to trade in 1979 which were too new to give us an indication as to what we might expect for price parameters, but they have turned into marvelous candidates for scale trading. They are heating oil and unleaded gasoline.

These two traded between 80 cents and $1 per gallon for the first five years until 1984, and then they slipped to about 60 cents. In 1986 Sheik Yemani, Oil Minister of Saudi Arabia (Saudi Arabia is OPEC's largest producer and exporter) grew weary of OPEC members cheating by exceeding their production quotas, so he opened the spigots on Saudi oil and drove the price of crude oil on the New York Merc down to $10 a barrel to punish them. It cost him his job (and nearly cost him his head), but it proved the point that OPEC members must abide by their quotas. This confined crude oil pretty much to a range from $15 to $24 per barrel — except for the Desert Storm period — and heating oil and unleaded gasoline to a range from about 40 cents to 60 cents — except for the Desert Storm period — ever since.

The volatility in these two is superb; 100 point ($420) daily moves are common. And, whereas pork bellies volume has virtually disappeared (4,000 contracts is now a big day), trading in heating oil (40,000 contracts are the norm) and unleaded gasoline (35,000) is extremely liquid.

Neither of them has ever traded below 30 cents in their fifteen-year history, so the same type of scale as recommended above for pork bellies should prove at least as rewarding in heating oil or unleaded gasoline.

Q. *Do you ever scale trade spreads?*
A. Rarely. It is tempting to scale spreads because they seem to offer very low risk when one commodity which bears a very close price relationship to another appears to have moved away from the normal price differential temporarily. It is logical to assume that supply and demand will force the relatively higher priced commodity lower and/or the relatively lower priced commodity higher. Ninety-nine times out of a hundred that it is precisely what will happen, but that one-hundredth time will prove catastrophic.

Take, for example, the gold/silver spread of 1979. The normal relationship between gold and silver is one ounce of gold for thirty-five ounces of silver. This ratio is a carryover from the days from 1933 to 1975 when gold was frozen at $35 per ounce and silver traded listlessly at about $1 per ounce. In many of the nations of the world, it was illegal to trade silver or gold, but there was an active black market. The ratio was always 35:1.

Once it became legal to trade gold in the United States, very active legal trading commenced, but the 35:1 ratio still prevailed. Thus, when temporary price aberrations occurred, it was profitable to short the one which was temporarily higher and be long the one which was lower. The ratio always returned to 35:1, and easy profits were gleaned. The ratio rarely dropped below 28:1, and it rarely exceeded 42:1. Within those parameters, a person might have chosen to initiate scales whenever the ratio rose to 40:1 or fell to 30: 1. In either case, he would never have been obliged to acquire more than three spreads. Generous profits would have been accumulated from what appeared to be low risk trading.

However, if we remember that one side of the spread is a short sale, we have a clue to the possibility of disaster. It happened in 1979.

Before relating the sad tale, it is necessary to first detail the economics of establishing the spread. A gold futures contract is for 100 ounces, and the silver futures contract is for 5,000 ounces. Thus, to carry a *balanced* spread, it is necessary to use three contracts of gold versus two contracts of silver. When gold is $35 an ounce, 300 ounces has a value of $10,500, and if silver is then trading at $1 per ounce, the 10,000 ounces would have a value of $10,000.

When gold trades at $175, three contracts is worth $52,000. Silver should then be selling at $5 per ounce, and the 10,000 ounces would be worth $50,000. The ratio stays the same and the dollar value stays approximately in balance.

Once the ratio begins to spread because of temporary circumstances, the dollar equivalent of a single point change in the ratio is around $2,500. If the ratio changes from 35:1 to 34:1, the dollar value changes approximately $2,500. If it changes to 33:1, that is another $2,500. A scale trader initiating a position at 30:1 could expect to cash a $2,500 gross profit if the ratio closed merely to 31:1. If it oscillated around 30:1, he would pick up a $2,500 profit with each point swing. Sounds easy, and it was — for a while.

But when the Texas oil people and their friends started to corner the silver market, the silver price skyrocketed, and the ratio fell all the way to 20:1. Had a person begun scaling at 30:1 and added another spread (three golds vs. two silvers) each time the ratio fell a point, he would have accumulated eleven spreads with an aggregate loss of 55 "points." (A loss of ten points on the first spread as the ratio fell from 30 to 20; nine points on the second as the ratio fell from 29 to 20; eight on the next; etc.).

332

With each point being equal to $2,500, the aggregate loss is $137,500. In spread trading, the margin requirement is the larger requirement of the two sides, with nothing required for the other side of the spread since there is generally considered to be some semblance of balance in the two positions. The margin on contracts of either silver or gold at the start of 1979 was around $1,000 per contract, so the required margin to initiate this spread would have been but $3,000 on the three gold contracts with nothing required on the silver. However, when the silver exploded in price, the margin was raised *retroactively* to $75,000 per silver contract. To hold the eleven spreads, representing 22 silver contracts, the trader would have been required to deposit $1,650,000! Add to that his $137,500 paper loss, and he has $1,787,500 committed. Few people could afford that.

When the attempt to corner the silver market failed and prices tumbled, silver fell much more rapidly than gold, causing the gold:silver ratio to swing even more dramatically in the other direction. The ratio exceeded 50:1. A person who tried to take advantage of the situation to scale trade that spread would have had nearly the same problems. If he had started scaling spreads at 40:1, he also would have held eleven spreads, with an identical paper loss as the scale trader who had scaled spreads from 30:1 down to 20:1; however, margin requirements had been cut to about one-third of their former levels, so his capital commitment would have been only $687,500.

The preceding part of this answer was reproduced from the 1980 edition of the book. I purposely left the ratio number at 35:1 because I wanted to demonstrate why I don't use spreads. When I wrote the above the ratio had moved out to 40:1, but no one ever expected it to go to 90:1. It did, and it is now 80:1. You would have been butchered trying to buck that spread.

The reason for the extraordinary widening in the spread is the weakness in silver. Rumors keep popping up that the development of a technique which will remove silver from use in photography film — which accounts for 60% of silver consumption — is imminent. This has brought silver down to $5, while gold hovers around $400, the 80:1 ratio.

Similar results would have occurred in 1977 if a person had been scaling old-crop versus new-crop soybeans. The same people who attempted the silver corner in 1979 actually cornered the soybeans market in 1977. The results would have been catastrophic for anyone scale trading that spread.

It is interesting to note how easily they perpetrated that soybean corner. The normal carryover supply of soybeans at the end of a crop year is about 200 million bushels, but in 1977 it was known to all that the carryover would be only 60 million bushels. The cornering people bought 23 million bushels and ran the price from about $6 per bushel to nearly $11. No one knows how much profit they cashed, but if they managed only $3 per bushel, they made $69 million. The margin required was only $1,000 per 5,000 bushel contract, so they were required to deposit only $4,600,000 on their 4,600 contracts. $69 million profit on less than a $5 million investment in six months. Not a bad return.

Q. *Have you ever seen anyone lose with the scale trading system? If so, what was the problem?*

A. Yes, and the problem is always the same — deviation from the system.

People are inclined to make side bets — taking positions which are unrelated to scale trading. If the extra positions turn against them at the same time their scales are forcing them to accumulate large paper losses, the entire account will be jeopardized; the capital which was to be held in reserve for the scaling operation was lost on the side bet.

Trading aggressively with scales which are too tight for the available capital, failing to maintain a cash reserve, trading too many commodities simultaneously with too little capital, trading spreads, and scaling short positions are other forms of deviation.

Q. *Are there any commodities futures contracts which you do not like to scale trade?*

A. I don't like the financial commodities, because their movement is determined more by banking policy than by supply and demand factors; however, there is nothing wrong with shorting U.S. Treasury bills (remember, that is not true shorting, for this is an inverted market) when yields fall. They can only fall to zero, so you have a limit to the possible move, which is necessary for correct scale trading.

I am also a bit apprehensive about the new contracts which settle for cash instead of a commodity. Examples would be the stock indexes and the currencies. Because they do not settle for a physical commodity, the futures price could vary considerably from the cash price. This could happen if there is a manipulation occurring. Scale trading depends upon prices being determined by supply and demand.

Q. *What is the most significant change you have made in your scale trading technique in the last ten years?*

A. Adjusting for high interest rates. The effect which 20% rates had on commodity prices was devastating. Anytime you see interest rates dominating commodity prices such as they did in 1980-82, you must be prepared for very deep declines in commodities prices and the certainty that all prices will move together. Parallel movement is a powerful argument in favor of concentrating on fewer commodities with your capital.

Q. *A scale trader is trying to average a gross profit of only $400 to $500 per trade, and if he pays an average commission of $50 per trade, isn't that an extremely high percentage of his profit?*

A. No. You must remember that the scale trader is cashing a profit 95% of the time when he pays a commission, while the typical in-and-out trader wins only 50% of the time and pays a commission every time. An in-and-out trader makes a $400 gross profit on one trade and then loses $400 on the next, paying a commission each time.

Q. *Do you scale trade options?*

A. Never. In fact, I have been in this business thirty-six years and have never traded an option, period! If I am in the business thirty-six more years I still will not have traded an option. I can't imagine myself trading an instrument which goes to zero 80% of the time. That is tantamount to walking through a heavy mine field. You might take three, four, or five steps without harm (three, four, or five winners in options), but the sixth step

335

will be on a mine (the option which goes to zero), and you are wiped out.

Options serve no economic purpose. I think they should be prohibited.

Brokers like to tell you that there is limited risk in trading options. That is true, but the risk is 100%! And the erosion of value due to extrinsic decay (time loss) is devastating.

Brokers love options because they can get you to pay five commissions by getting you to trade five $200 options on, say, cattle, while the $1,000 margin on a cattle futures contract allows you to trade only one contract and allows him to earn only one commission. Worst of all, if cattle trades in a very narrow range from the time you enter either of the two trades until expiration, you get back your $1,000 margin money from the futures contract, while all you get back from the option is a receipt to verify another loss.

Q. *Do you ever combine option writing with scale trading to maximize your profits?*

A. No. People call me all of the time to tell me that they have developed a system to write options against scale trades. I tell them they should not try to combine the two. Each system must be able to stand alone, and I am sure there is no option trading system which will stand up under close scrutiny.

Several qualified scale traders who are computer *experts* have told me that they have back traded millions of data items and tried to design an option system to work in conjunction with scale trading. No one has ever come up with anything workable yet. (And, PLEASE, don't be the next caller to say that you have found El Dorado. I love you dearly for buying this book, but I just haven't the time to waste.)

Q. *Do you still feel scale trading will provide 25% to 50% profits per year?*

A. Yes. When I wrote the 1980 edition of this book we had soybeans trading over $8, and silver trading near $16, with all other commodities trading at commensurately high levels. With prices at such high levels it was common, for example, for soybeans to range 18 cents every day, with a 50 cent range for the week, only

336

to close the week unchanged. Under those conditions a scale trader could not help making huge profits, and 40% returns for the year were virtually assured.

Today soybeans trade in the high $6 range, and they probably will trade under $6 by late 1995 in the 1996 contracts. Volatility will be reduced to ranges of 8 cents per day, so not as many oscillation profits will be available. However, because of the price's close proximity to the practical low of $5, tighter scales may be utilized, and that will increase the total number of oscillation profits. Profits might be in the lower range of the 25% to 50% target, but the risk will be so much lower that it is a welcome offset.

There was a time in the years from 1989 until the 1993 flood that soybeans hovered in the range from $5.25 to $6.50, and daily trading ranges were 3.5 cents, with the range for the week a mere 8 cents. Under those conditions the risk was virtually nil, and the 20% to 25% profit of that time was certainly commensurate with the exceptionally low risk.

Q. *If I see a commodity which is trading at a twenty-year low, why shouldn't I start a scale with eight or ten contracts and cash some very large profits on the ensuing rally?*

A. If the price is that low, there must be a fundamental reason. Let's use cocoa as an example: Cocoa traded above $4,200 per tonne in the commodity hysteria of 1979, fell to $1,300 in 1982, and then rallied to $2,800 in 1984. At this point the trap was beginning to be baited. Production was beginning to exceed consumption, and by 1988 there had been six consecutive years in which production exceeded consumption, pulling the price down to $1,200 — the lowest price since they invented chocolate bars. The trader who ignores fundamentals might have been tempted to start a scale with ten contracts because of this unbelievably low price. He would have been poorer, sadder, and wiser when cocoa hit $800 in 1991, because the number of surplus production years had grown to eight.

A small discount commodity brokerage house in suburban Los Angeles advocated starting all scales with ten contracts in commodities which had deeply depressed prices. Their scheme was to earn tons of commissions, but they started their sales campaign just before a sharp break in general commodity prices, and they buried everyone. People who opened their accounts with $100,000 were advised to start with ten contracts of each of eight commodities. Thus, they were nearly fully margined when they started. Those people lost $250,000 each when prices broke.

I have had times when I wanted to start a scale in something but had all of my trading capital temporarily committed to other scales, and by the time I closed out a scale and freed some capital, the one I had been watching had fallen so low that I probably would have owned eight contracts. I wouldn't buy all eight, but if the fundamentals had not changed dramatically, I probably would have started with two or three and set the selling scale to take 10 cents, 20 cents, and 30 cents on those contracts while seeking only 10 cents on any additional contracts subsequently purchased on a scale down.

Q. *How much drawdown is a scale trader likely to encounter?*
   (Drawdown is the combined amount of realized and unrealized loss in an account.)
A. The term drawdown was invented by a broker who wanted to scare his clients into using stop orders — thereby increasing his commission revenue. As stated earlier, you must treat commodity trading like a business. You must expect to incur paper losses as you accumulate inventory. No inventory, no winners. Your early paper losses may equal 10% to 20% before you accumulate enough oscillation profits to overcome the omnipresent paper losses.

Q. *Do I need a quote machine to scale trade?*
A. A quote machine is the *worst* thing a scale trader can have. One reason is that he may become so bored with the slow trading that he will deviate from the system and take an occasional flier, which could get him into serious trouble. Also, if he is holding eight contracts of a troubled position, his emotions may suffer as he watches the price rally a few points and then fall away to a small net loss by the end of trading on several consecutive days; meantime, he sees on the computer's news screen the advisors' — who are all trend-followers — reports saying the commodity will

continue its trend lower. It is quite likely that the combination of the deteriorating price and the trend-followers' advice that the price is going lower will cause him to abandon hope and to sell out. He would be better served to rely upon the morning paper for his quotes.

If you have a quote machine, take a baseball bat and smash it to smithereens. Do unto it before it can do unto you.

Q. *Do you ever scale trade the financial futures?*
A. If you insist that you want to trade them, go ahead, but I don't like them because their prices are set by men without regard to supply and demand. For example, if you are scale trading the Japanese yen and hold six contracts, you might awaken one morning hearing on your clock-radio alarm that the Japanese finance minister has devalued the yen 15% during the night. You might want to stay in that bed which you no longer own and force them to evict you from your home — which you no longer own.

Q. *Are the crop reports still as secret as you said earlier in the book?*
A. It is sad to say, but I don't think so. There have been too many incidents of a commodity moving sharply in the last five minutes before the end of trading on a day on which a crop report — or a vital economic report — is due for release half an hour after the close of trading, with that movement being in the direction indicated by the report. Someone peeked.

I can see how a clerk working on compiling the report could easily be bribed. This poor man is trying to support a family, including one daughter in college, on $23,000 a year. Along comes a floor trader who offers him $2,000 to simply wear a transmitting wire under his shirt while the numbers are being compiled in the locked room. The clerk rationalizes that crime is so pervasive that most of the nation's leaders in congress flaunt the hundreds of thousands — in some cases millions — of dollars they steal each year, and he decides to get his tiny piece to recover some of the tax money he pays to subsidize their thefts. It's very sad, but that is the way of life in Washington, D. C.

Q. *Are there any other professionals who have published anything on this trading method?*

A. Yes. There is a fellow in Belgium who has a public relations man in Florida who arranges for him to come to the United States to put on two-day seminars to teach scale trading. He charges $2,000, but he only teaches what you are reading in this book. I have a letter from him in which he thanks me for teaching him the system through this book. By reading the book you saved $1,960.

There is also a fellow in Tulsa who plagiarized this copyrighted book and produced a pamphlet of his own which he sells for $50. I have never seen it, but people tell me it is about 96 pages, including 80 pages of charts and 16 pages of text. This chap promoted scale trading on his national TV show — including blatantly displaying my eight column scale on the screen — as he recommended scale trading cocoa. The system provided five $500 winners in a month, but he demonstrated that he really is not a scale trader when he said on the TV show, "Cocoa is now too high to trade, so we have shorted it." Cocoa ran 250 points ($2,500) in the next couple of weeks, and he lost his entire profit by taking that flier.

Q. *Does your newsletter recommend commodities to trade with suggested scales?*

A. Yes, we call it *The Scale Trader*. It is our policy to publish at least one letter each month, with special letters being sent if a commodity suddenly becomes attractive for scaling. We have averaged twenty-four issues per year since 1981. (We must be doing something right because many commodity newsletters lose their subscribers and close their doors after a year of publication.)

It is impossible to anticipate all contingencies which may arise in commodity trading and to discuss them in this book, so we try to make our newsletter a teaching letter. When an unusual event occurs, we comment on how we handled it in our real-money accounts as a guide to subscribers and to help them the next time that situation arises.

Most editions contain two or three new scales, and all editions contain continuing comments on previous recommendations —

such as telling how and when to do a rollover and then printing the rollover calculation in the next edition. We continue the comments until the price moves up enough to get us out of the scale. We recognize that most of our subscribers will have between $5,000 and $20,000 in their commodity accounts, so we try to include numerous MidAmerica scales in the letters.

We are so certain of the efficacy of scale trading that we run a "Guarantee Account" in *The Scale Trader*. If the "Guarantee Account" fails to provide a profit for the twelve months subscription period, the subscriber receives a full refund of his subscription cost. One man who manages $25 million in trend-following accounts, including a $15 million fund, told us we were "insane" to give a money-back guarantee "because everybody loses trading commodities," but we have had only a couple of times when prices were temporarily low and we were required to make a refund. Prices always snapped back soon.

Inquiries re *The Scale Trader* should be directed to Robert F. Wiest, P. O. Box 3882, Westlake Village, CA 91359-0882.

Q. *Do you have a 900-number for telephone updates on recommendations?*

A. Yes. It is being installed and should be operative before this book is released. It is an excellent supplement to the recommendations contained in "The Scale Trader."

XXXIII

Make Inflation Work For You

Inflation is one of the worst problems facing our nation today, and with both Democrats and Republicans either unable or unwilling to understand the primary cause of inflation, both parties are unable to cope with the problem. As long as this situation persists, the general public will continue to suffer the ravages of inflation. Until we elect officials who will do something to reduce the expansion in the money supply and thereby slow inflation, we are helpless as individuals. We are helpless, that is, unless we invest in commodities which increase in value at a pace commensurate with the inflation rate.

Real estate is an excellent inflation hedge, for real estate values tend to keep pace with the inflation rate. However, real estate is not the perfect investment for several reasons.

One is that property taxes may become excessive to the long-term holder and force him into premature disposal.

Another potential problem is the necessity for a readily available cash flow at all times in order for the investor to maintain payments — regardless of personal reversals which may be totally unrelated to his real estate investments. This can also force premature disposal.

A third — and more critical — problem which real estate investors regularly face is the possibility of price erosion. An area which becomes popular for investment suddenly tops out, and highly-leveraged fortunes come tumbling down. Picture, if you will, Los Angeles in the '80's. The San Fernando Valley becomes the hottest real estate investment spot in the nation. Land values are doubling in a matter of months. Everyone is investing because of the "you can't lose in California real estate" syndrome. Women are forsaking their domestic lives or other careers to get involved in real estate. Fortunes are made almost overnight. Everyone is getting rich as more and more people pour into Los Angeles and buy San Fernando Valley real estate. Everyone owns five pieces of property, and he makes good on his obligations by selling one piece occasionally to keep up the payments on the other four. He uses the excess profit to acquire a new fifth piece of property, and the pyramiding continues. Continues, that is, until there is a diminution in the flow of new people into California. Then real estate holders who need to sell something every so often to keep the pyramid going find there are few buyers around to keep this chain-letter operation going. The condition changes from a seller's market to a buyer's, and prices soften. Some of the players who considered themselves to be investors now realize that they actually were speculators, and they want out. But the exit door is too small to accommodate everyone at once.

The market collapses. Housewives get out of real estate and return to the domestic scene. Men return to their professions. They all have wounds to heal. A scenario for the 1980's? Possibly. I said it is Los Angeles in the '80's — but 1880! It is in your history books. It actually happened in Los Angeles in 1880.

The foregoing part of this chapter was repeated verbatim from earlier editions of the book to demonstrate the veracity of my claim that real estate is not the perfect investment. California real estate suffered a resounding crash after 1989.

One of the requisites of the perfect investment is liquidity, and commodities trading at least qualifies in this area, for it is possible to close out a commodity account with a phone call at 10:00 a.m. and to pick up the check at noon. Clients are obliged to have funds in the account *before* a trade may be executed (unlike stocks where payment is required after five business days), so the brokerage house is

343

also required to pay the day an account is closed. For all practical purposes, brokerage houses usually settle the day after a trade, but technically speaking they may be required to settle the same day. Ordinary commodity trading is not even a good investment, much less *perfect*, because of the extreme risk, but I think that scale trading narrows the risk to a point where a properly managed scale trading account comes very close to filling the requisites for the perfect investment form: risk is low, profits are generous relative to risk, leverage is available to produce substantial profits, liquidity is virtually unmatched, tax treatment is highly advantageous, and the trading method is simple.

Whenever I make a statement about "virtually unmatched liquidity" of a commodity account I run the risk of rebuttal from the person who says a savings account requires nothing more than a visit to the bank or savings and loan for withdrawal. Not so! When interest rates soared a few years ago many people found out about the fine print in their certificate of deposit contracts. People who purchased CD's a few years ago when rates were 7% had seen rates go to 18%; they tried to cash their low-yielding CD's to purchase the higher-yielding new CD's. They were willing to suffer the interest forfeiture penalty which early closure of the account brings, but when they asked for the return of their funds they found the savings institutions had invoked the section of the investment agreement which allowed it to withhold the funds. Why should they let you off the hook at 7% if you are going to reinvest the money with them at 18%?

I drifted from my original point of the chapter. I wanted to talk about inflation and how it can be made to work for you.

The reason why inflation will probably be with us for the foreseeable future is that it comes directly from Washington, D. C., and the people in Washington have no intention — nor even the desire — to control inflation. It keeps them in office. The French statesman and political writer Alexis de Tocqueville (1805 - 1859) said, "America will be a great nation until its politicians discover they can buy the people's votes with their own money." That is what is happening today. Something for everybody. It costs nothing because "the government" pays for it, is the accepted attitude. No one cares as long as he gets his share. We gripe about social programs for the poor, but then we demand subsidies for business. We gripe about an airport or dam being built in a distant state, but then we demand highways in our own states. It is a never-ending cycle: complain about what the other guy gets, but be sure I get mine!

Another reason why inflation will continue is because there are not that many people actually being hurt. The vast majority of people profit from it. Their homes which they valued at $40,000 in the mid-1970's were valued at $340,000 fifteen years later. That means they profited $20,000 per year from inflation during that period, perhaps more than they earned from their jobs. What difference did it make that the price of bread tripled or that gasoline quadrupled? They don't eat that much bread or use that much gasoline — at least not $20,000 worth per year; furthermore, cost-of-living pay raises have helped them to keep pace with the increased cost of the essentials. Meantime, by selling the residence each four years and pyramiding the profit, many families have catapulted in fifteen years from a modest two-bedroom bungalow to an expensive rambler in an exclusive walled subdivision with community tennis courts, swimming pool, and golf course. Without inflation they could never have attained such standard of living. Politicians know that people in these circumstances will not complain about inflation.

As individuals, what can we do about inflation? Nothing. We cannot convince Washington politicians that inflation is truly a very serious problem. Bureaucrats don't know what inflation is; they can't even *define* inflation. They make speeches about its being caused by OPEC nations raising the price of oil. That is not a *cause* of inflation, that is an *effect*. Twenty-five years ago they sold oil for $2 a barrel, and we sold wheat for $1.50 a bushel. Oil was probably underpriced relative to wheat, so they raised prices. Now oil is $15 a barrel, and wheat is $3.50. Today oil is overpriced — or wheat is underpriced — but we cannot do a thing about it. The OPEC nations did not raise oil prices because wheat went up in price; they raised prices because the U.S. dollars went down in value and worldwide oil prices are denominated in U.S. dollars.

The correct definition of inflation is: an increase in the money supply without a corresponding increase in goods or services. In simplest terms, if there are one million "things" available and one million dollars with which to buy them, the cost of one thing is one dollar. But if you increase the money supply so there are now two million dollars available but do not increase the number of things, the cost is $2 per thing. The logic is obvious to any third grader, but not to a politician who does not understand the economics of the marketplace. Most politicians only understand the economics of politics which dictates that you give something to everybody and buy his vote with his own money. Then (as a politician) you blame OPEC for inflation.

We should not blame OPEC for raising oil prices. They watched us operate with huge annual deficits as we tried to fight an expensive war and to promote social programs simultaneously — without raising taxes to pay for either, we simply financed everything by printing more dollars. They suffered a diminished purchasing power in the dollars they received in payment for their oil. Their only defense was to increase the price of oil to compensate for the decreased purchasing power of the dollars they held. At first the price increases were reasonable, for they amounted to nothing more than an adjustment equal to the dollar's inflation rate; however, as time has passed, they have become more and more greedy and are now increasing prices at rates which can only be described as confiscatory. But who will stop them? Not the U.S., for the U.S. oil companies are reaping huge profits from the price increases, and everyone knows the oil companies and the banks dictate policy in Washington.

An alternative way to control inflation would be to increase goods and services at the same pace as the increase in money supply; thus, when money supply increases to two million dollars, if there is a corresponding increase to two million things, the cost of a thing has now returned to one dollar, and the inflation rate is reduced to zero. Unfortunately, the labor unions and the politicians who depend upon the labor unions for their voting support continue to support featherbedding. This keeps productivity low and inflation high. A perfect example of this was the protectionism plan of the Reagan administration under which the number of Japanese cars imported by the United States was limited. Instead of permitting a flood of cars to enter the country, thereby increasing the number of "things" available and reducing prices, limiting the number of cars created a relative shortage and kept prices high. This meant there were fewer things to be purchased with the same number of dollars. That is the corollary definition of inflation.

346

You cannot fight them, so join them. Buy commodities. This will immunize you from inflation's harmful effects.

The banks certainly benefited from inflation when Volcker raised interest rates and set inflation afire. Banks had formerly paid 5.25% interest to savers and charged an 8% prime rate of their most creditworthy borrowers, netting 2.75%. During Volcker's fiasco the banks paid 11% on CD's and charged a 17% prime, netting 6%.

It baffles me how politicians expect to mitigate the rapidly expanding rate of price increases for goods and services by increasing interest rates. They can't seem to comprehend that money is a raw material used in the manufacture of *every* product — the same as steel, rubber, plastics, cotton, or whatever. If the price of steel increases, the price of steel products must increase; the same for rubber and rubber products; for plastics and plastic products; etc. But an increase in the price of steel does not necessarily result in an increase in the price of rubber products. Nor in plastic products. Etc. If the supply of steel is relatively low, the price will rise until it reaches the point where it becomes profitable for someone to produce enough additional steel to bring the supply into balance with demand, and then the price will stop rising. If production continues to expand there will develop an oversupply, and the price will fall again. Only supply and demand should ever be permitted to influence prices in the marketplace.

But "interest" is the price one must pay to acquire the raw material called "money," and as long as the cost of this basic ingredient in the production of *everything* is raised and raised, there can be no alternative but higher prices for everything.

Why can't politicians understand that? I really don't know why, but I shall mount my soapbox for a moment again and expound upon a theory of mine in that area. I feel that too many of the people in Washington who act as advisors to our policy makers are professors who have no concept of life in the real world. They are conservative by nature (philosophically, not politically), and are not risk-takers. They demonstrated this when they chose the relative safety of teaching as a career rather than going into the business world to slug it out for potentially great rewards while chancing bankruptcy. They never took a chance on anything. They never borrowed any money, except to take out a mortgage on a home. Then they paid 40% down instead of the usual 10%, and made multiple payments to liquidate the mortgage in ten years instead of thirty. They paid cash every time they bought a car. They are proud of the fact that they owe nothing. They just never take any risk.

But our nation was built by risk takers, and it continues what little growth it is now showing through the efforts of the few remaining risk takers. So how is a professor capable of understanding that a risk taker doesn't give a tinker's damn when interest rates increase? That will not stop an entrepreneur from borrowing money if it means the very survival of his company or his investments. He will merely proceed with the borrowing and simply tack the extra cost to the price when he sells. Increasing interest rates cannot possibly reduce prices — it can only have the opposite effect.

It is futile to complain, impossible to combat. Inflation seems destined to engulf us interminably. So, get a piece of the action. Start investing in commodities. But only be a buyer. Never go short. Scale trade commodities, and then you not only have the mathematics of the system working for you, and the Law of Supply and Demand protecting you and assuring you of eventual profits, but you also have a high inflation rate pushing your commodity inventory ever higher in price. This one-two-three combination will guarantee your success.

Much of what I have said in this chapter was already stated in the Chapter XXIX, "Interest Rates and the Federal Reserve," but I felt that it was worth repeating in the context of this chapter about the effects of inflation on commodity prices.

XXXIV

The Psychology of Commodities Trading

If you have read this far in the book, you are probably giving thought to trying scale trading. I would like to offer some thoughts on the subject, not just about scale trading, but about commodities trading in general.

It is a well-known fact that more than 90% of the people who trade commodities lose, and I think I have some idea of why that is. Perhaps if I offer my observations about the psychology of commodities trading you may recognize yourself, your commodity broker, or his commodity brokerage firm, and if that recognition alarms you, you may choose not to trade commodities at all. If you sense that you will act in a manner similar to the people in this chapter, you should abandon your thoughts of trading commodities altogether, and the money which you will save will be many times greater than the price which you paid for this book.

It has been my experience that the most successful scale traders are the people who have never traded commodities futures. Typically, the most successful scale trader is the person who has done very little investing even in stocks, preferring to keep his money in a bank savings account. As you will see from the stories which I am about to relate about unsuccessful commodity traders, coldhearted commodity salespeople, and unethical brokerage firms, it is easy for the commodity trader to either corrupt himself through his greed for profits of a magnitude much greater than scale trading can provide, or he may be corrupted by salespeople and firms which promise impossible commodity trading profits to the person who is willing to take high risks and will trade aggressively enough to generate substantial commissions before terminating his losing account.

If you like to gamble, scale trading is not for you. Most people who contemplate trading commodity futures begin with the idea that they can turn $2,000 into $10,000 in six months. I prefer a different approach; I try to use $10,000 to earn a mere $2,000 in six months, which would be right on target for my 25% to 50% annual return.

I have worked around gamblers all my life; first, for ten years in the casinos in Las Vegas, and then for thirty-six years on Wall Street as a stock broker and/or a commodities broker. And don't kid yourself, for if you think Wall Street is anything other than a high-class race track with the local brokerage offices being anything other than off-track betting parlors, you are sadly mistaken. Wall Street ceased to be an area of investment with the advent of discount commissions. Prior to that time, most stock brokers were genuinely interested in the well being of the client and devoted hours to research and financial planning to construct an *investment* portfolio for the client and his wife. If the couple had $20,000 to invest, the stock broker might recommend a solid investment portfolio which would include $10,000 in a good mutual fund, $5,000 in bank and insurance stocks which traded in the over-the-counter market in the days before they became listed on stock exchanges, $3,000 in over-the-counter stocks of what was then called "emerging growth companies" with prospects for rapid growth, and the last $2,000 invested in a popular stock or two on the New York Stock Exchange. The purpose of the NYSE stocks was to give the clients something to watch in the paper each day so that they would not become impatient with the slow movements of the 90% of the portfolio which had been selected for *investment*. It was recognized that everyone wants to have some action, so the 10% consigned to the NYSE stocks was the *trading* money.

The commission on the mutual fund investment was $8\frac{1}{2}\%$, with $700 of that $850 being credited to the salesman's gross commissions. His net commission payout was 50%, or $350. As for the over-the-counter stocks, the salesman was able to add a 5% markup to the price which the brokerage firm had paid for the stock and sell it to the clients at the marked up price; thus, the $8,000 worth of over-the-counter stocks would include a commission of $400, of which the salesman again netted 50%, or another $200. The NYSE stocks carried a commission of only about 1.5%, or a mere $30, of which the salesman retained probably 33%, or another $10. If the salesman devoted an entire week to determining the clients' financial status, their objectives and their needs, the research necessary for tailoring their investment program, and then selling them on his ideas, he was suitably rewarded, for his total payout of $610 would give him an annual income of $31,720 if he matched that sale once a week throughout the year. That would have been about double the income of the average stock salesman twenty years ago. That is why stock salesmen could afford to be professionals in those days. But not anymore . . .

The first thing that went was the 5% markup for OTC stocks. The National Association of Securities Dealers releases a daily list of quotations to the newspapers for the most actively traded OTC stocks, and twenty years ago the quotes were what was called the "outside" market, or the dealers' market with the 5% markup tacked on; thus, if the "inside" market for a stock was $19 bid, $20 asked, the quote printed in the paper would read $19 bid, $21 asked, with that extra dollar being the 5% markup which most brokerage firms charged. However, some firms began to charge OTC commissions which were equal to those charged for NYSE stocks, or 1.5% instead of 5%. This caused considerable confusion, for two different clients making simultaneous purchases of the same stock at two different brokerage firms would pay vastly different total amounts. One client buying 100 shares at $20 plus the 1.5% commission would pay only $2,030, while the client purchasing his 100 shares at the firm charging the 5% commission would pay $2,100. The NASD took a lot of unfair criticism over this, so they changed from quoting "outside" markets to quoting "inside" markets. Then it became the problem of the brokerage firms to do the explaining if they were charging $2,100 while their competitors charged $2,030. It didn't take long for many of the firms to switch, and today most of them charge NYSE rates for OTC stocks (now called NASDAQ).

The 8½% mutual fund commission was next to go, and that exited with the advent of the no-load mutual funds. Investors became more sophisticated and began to understand that the 8½% was merely a sales charge which went entirely to salespeople and not to the people who managed the fund. No-load mutual fund advisory services proliferated, and smart investors stopped paying sales charges to buy that which they could get without a sales charge. Today, only innocents and unsophisticates pay commissions to buy mutual fund shares.

Then came the discount brokers who began to undercut NYSE firms in executing stock transactions. Their commission rates were reduced to 50%, or even 40%, of what the regular brokerage firms were charging. Today we have the "deep discount" brokerage firms which charge only pennies per share to execute trades, or, on supersize trades, charge *no* commission, earning their income from the interest on the cash balances in the accounts.

To top it all off, the brokerage business became engulfed in the computer age, with every salesman having an electronic machine on his desk which not only gave instantaneous quotations on thousands of stocks, but gave every client's equity and securities portfolio as of the previous night's closing of trading; latest earnings, price/earnings ratios, dividends, etc., on thousands of stocks; similar information on countless bonds and commodities; current buy/sell recommendations on hundreds of stocks, bonds and commodities; and in general did everything imaginable to assist the salesman to service his clients. These machines cost a lot of money, and somebody had to pay for them, so the brokerage firms started reducing the salesmen's percentage of payout to 25% from the previous 33%. Although the major wirehouses raised commission rates on minimum sized transactions, competition forced them to grant volume discounts. Whereas it had once been common for a salesman to earn $610 net on a $20,000 transaction, he would now be very fortunate to net $100.

Furthermore, clients began to cheat on the brokers, for the clients learned that they could solicit investment advice from wire house brokers and then execute their trades through any one of the dozens of discount brokers who advertised regularly in the investment media.

At this point, what had once been a relatively honorable profession turned into the greatest crapshoot of all time. In my opinion, it was the advent of the discount commission broker which spawned the enormous popularity of the options markets. Wire house brokers loved it, for they could trade customers (they no longer call them clients) in and out of options profitably on moves as small as a quarter-point, and sometimes less. A quarter of a point is barely more than a tick in many of the volatile stocks, so brokers began recommending buying stock options in the morning and selling them in the afternoon. An account with as little as $2,000 equity could be made to generate $200 or more in commissions on a single transaction, and if the broker could roll the account in and out of options rapidly enough, one such account could earn the broker many thousands of dollars in commissions before being consumed. The slogan in many brokerage offices became: "One good churn deserves another."

But the clients loved it. Most of us have some "gamble" in us, and the options market appealed to a very high percentage of traders, for it was easy to believe the salesman's pitch that all the client could lose was the modest amount of premium he paid for the option while his profit potential was unlimited. Is it any wonder that the Chicago Board Options Exchange became the country's second largest stock exchange only two years after its introduction?

Again I state an opinion, but I believe a monster was unleashed with the introduction of options trading, for the old ideas of buying and holding quality stocks went out the window, only to be replaced by the concept of trading in and out of options for a quarter point. Today brokers would starve to death if they had to make a living from 100 share purchases of General Motors, but they do exceptionally well churning accounts which trade 25 GM options at a time.

The average Account Executive nets about $120,000 per year, which means he is producing gross commissions of about $400,000 per year. That is $1,600 in gross commissions per day, which is a lot of trading with commissions at pennies per share. The only way he can produce that kind of gross is to trade plenty of options, day-trade stocks, and to engage in similar speculative activities which have been forced upon him by an office manager who constantly reminds the sales staff that if they do not produce $33,000 per month in commissions that there are thousands of capable unemployed people who would love to replace them. The office manager must do this because there is a district manager reminding him that his office must produce in excess of $1 million per month in commissions, or the office manager will be replaced. The regional manager is riding the district manager with the same pressure because the national sales manager is riding him.

For many traders, however, even the options market was too slow, and these people went for commodity futures trading where the leverage factor allowed them to win or lose substantial sums of money in a very brief period of time. They had found the ultimate speculation vehicle, for if stock options could condense the normal holding period for stocks down to a few weeks, commodity trading could condense it even further — to a matter of days.

Greedy salesmen introduced speculators to the fast action of the world of stock options, and after the customers were hooked on this marijuana of the investment world, they cocained on commodities.

The point is, there are very few people who trade commodities as an investment. I maintain that scale traders come about as close as possible to being "investors" in commodities rather than speculators, but I also contend that most commodity traders are sick people who are seeking action and really don't expect — or even want — to win. They need to lose.

I will give you some examples, and just see if you don't agree with me:

While working as a commodity broker, I once had a young attorney as a commodity account. He had $10,000 in his account and had made four successful scale trades in MidAmerica corn contracts for a modest profit of $400. He was a player who played all games, and he loved to shoot about $3,000 per month in the oil lease lottery game at $10 a throw. He had had a few small hits, but one month he caught the brass ring — better make that the *gold* ring — for he hit one for $600,000. He walked into the office the next day and handed me a check for $350,000 to be used for all-out scale trading. Four months later we had him $68,000 winners, so that we were averaging $17,000 per month profit. Evidently that was not good enough for him, because he came to the office and announced that he wanted to take over the account himself and do all the trading *without using scale trading*. When I asked if there were a problem, he replied: "I don't like your *dumb* system. My friends tell me that when they have a winner in commodities they make $10,000 or $20,000, but all you make is $400."

I protested that they hadn't told him about the $10,000 and $20,000 losers, but it was to no avail.

He took over the account and traded on the recommendations of a commodity advisory service to which he had subscribed. I had always traded one contract at a time for him, but he wanted action, so he started with five contracts of each of four commodities. He cashed a profit on all four trades within a week, making $8,000 profit. That was all it took to convince him that he had found El Dorado. He doubled up and bought ten contracts of each of their next four recommendations, but this time they were all losers. He had already acquired a small case of gambler's fever, so instead of cutting back, he doubled again and bought twenty contracts of their two latest recommendations. Same results, he lost again. His last trade was twenty-five contracts long in orange juice because his source claimed there was a heavy freeze moving into Florida over the New Year holiday weekend. The freeze didn't come; in fact, I had watched the Orange Bowl football game on television the day before and had seen the spectators dressed in shirt-sleeves. Obviously, that information did not impress him, for he subconsciously wanted — indeed, *needed* — to lose. That was his last trade. He had lost $175,000 in seven weeks of doing his own thing. Tell me he wasn't sick!

Then there was the San Fernando dentist. He opened a $100,000 scale trading account with me, and we probably had had about thirty winning trades before cattle went into a sustained decline, forcing us to acquire seven contracts on our scale. He insisted upon trying to outguess the market by using a chart service to which he subscribed, so he insisted that I buy him an extra ten contracts of cattle "at the market" because his service said cattle had reached a support level. I told him that I would start keeping separate pages in my account book for his account, one for my scale trades, and one for his fliers.

Cattle broke the supposed support level, and he received a substantial margin call. (Actually, he had only deposited $50,000 worth of U.S. Treasury bills as collateral in lieu of cash, so the margin call was against the $50,000 cash he held in reserve in a money market fund.) It was the ten extra contracts he had added to the account which caused the margin call, but he thought he could avert responsibility by telling me to sell everything on *my* page. He pulled this on me three different times, so my page showed what appeared to be a $20,000 loss from scale trading. He used that as his excuse to abandon scale trading and to continue to take his five and ten contract fliers. By the time he gave up, he had lost $110,000. That was $20,000 from his messing up the scale trading and $90,000 from his fliers.

One of the strangest cases was the fifty-five year old aerospace engineer who quit his job and set up an office in his garage for commodities trading. I visited that office one time, and I was overwhelmed. He had at least five computers there, and each was plugged into a television projection screen. He had incoming lines from data banks all around the country, and he had tapes and cassettes which permitted him to project bar charts or point-and-figure charts showing trades by the minute, the hour, the day, the week, the month, and the year, on any of his five television screens. The place looked like a NASA substation. He had had his son resign his position also, and together they were going to beat the commodities markets. I know they were familiar with scale trading, for they had purchased two copies of this book; however, most of that equipment would have been wasted on anything as simple as scale trading.

The father told me that he had started with his life savings of $100,000 and that I would be but one of four brokers he would use because he wanted multiple sources of fundamental information to augment his technical approach. It didn't take me long to learn that he wasn't interested in fundamental information. His real reason for using four brokers was that he expected to earn their adulation as a result of his anticipated successful trading. He never earned any adulation from me, for I considered him some kind of a nut. The results proved that:

After eighteen months of trading and 270 trades with me, and despite his claim that one day he was long twenty-seven contracts which were up the limit simultaneously, he had lost $18,000 with me. I think it is safe to assume that if he had lost $18,000 with me, he had also lost $18,000 with each of the other brokers, so he had to have lost about $72,000 of his original $100,000. I pleaded with him to try scale trading, but he would have no part of it.

If you think he wasn't sick and needed to lose, consider what he said to me one day about federal income tax treatment of commodities trading. The 1981 tax law had made commodity trading profits the most tax-advantaged investment available, but he complained that *the new law was unfair because it would severely reduce the percentage of deductions he could write off on his contemplated losses.* Can you believe that? Instead of being pleased at the prospect of having 60% of his *gains* treated as long-term investments regardless of his holding periods, he felt put upon because his net losses would now be treated as 60% long-term. Here was a man complaining in advance that he was not going to be treated fairly on the *losses* he was *expecting* to incur. He never talked about prospective profits, for he had no expectation of winning. He fully anticipated — indeed, probably desired — that he would lose. What is it that compels a man to trade commodities when he knows he will lose?

I wonder if he ever got his old job back.

Then there was the electronics engineer who had formed his own company and subsequently sold it, making him a young millionaire. He opened a modest trading account with me for the purpose of trading interest rate futures. I told him about scale trading and gave him a copy of this book. He increased his account to $70,000 and suggested that he could add another $30,000 if necessary. We established a rapport very quickly, so I suggested that he segregate that $100,000 into a limited partnership account wherein I would act as the general partner making all the trading decisions, and he would be the limited partner owning all the assets of the partnership. Our purpose in establishing this partnership would be to attempt to develop a "track record" showing the results of an account which had used scale trading exclusively over a period of four or five years. I knew that if we could demonstrate an attractive record we could approach one of the major commodity houses about doing a large underwriting (public offering) of the partnership, which could bring many millions of dollars into the partnership, and he and I could then split the very sizeable management fees. I was certain that numerous firms would be interested in such an underwriting, for they all have limited partnerships which they have underwritten, but nearly every partnership uses trend-following, and underwriters are desperately seeking an alternative form of commodities trading.

He thought the idea was fine, because he recognized that we would eventually have to form a management company to conduct the affairs of the partnership and that this management company would have considerable value because of the large fees it could earn from the partnership. However, he objected to a single point in my proposal, and that was my intention that I should make all trading decisions. I said that I would expect him to make all the decisions if we were jointly forming an electronics firm but it was only reasonable to expect that I would make all the decisions in a scale trading venture. It didn't take long to discover why he was so adamant about participating in the decision making.

We worked only with the original $70,000 in his personal account without forming a partnership, and the account did very well. At the end of four months it showed a profit of $35,000. Unfortunately, however, he revealed that he was a subscriber to a couple of advisory letters published by gold bugs, and that he had been bitten and had gold fever. He took a flier on one contract each of gold, silver, and platinum. He placed appropriate stop orders and was stopped out a week later with a $7,000 loss. He was embarrassed about it, and he knew my feelings about apocalyptics, so he became determined to vindicate his deviation from my system. He bought three contracts of gold. Four days later he was stopped out with a $19,000 loss. He made a couple of other silly trades, losing another $9,000. This meant that the $35,000 profit which we had ground out with eighty consecutive winning scale trades had been completely lost on his four fliers.

I begged him to go back to scale trading, and he actually commenced about three or four minor scales, but he stubbornly held to his thought that he could beat the commodities markets despite all the statistics to the contrary. He traded no more gold, but he tried a form of trend-following with pork bellies. During the next four months of abbreviated scale trading we ground out about $9,000 of profits, but his trend-following system got him into trouble as he found himself locked in with six contracts in a two-day limit down situation. He lost $11,500 by the time he could get out.

He had traded eight months, had never had a losing scale trade, and should have been $50,000 winners, but instead his fliers had cost him all of his profit and left him with a $2,500 net loss.

We talked about the sad plight of his account, and I pleaded with him to return to scale trading, but he refused. He was quite frank about his problem. He said he needed the action more than he needed the profit. He knew he was hooked on the excitement and that scale trading was too dull for him. He confessed that if he returned to scale trading it would only be a matter of time before he would be $10,000 or $15,000 winners, but then he would take another flier and lose it all again. I could see he was sick, but I respected him for at least recognizing that he had a problem — which is more than most people will admit. He closed his account.

The four vignettes I have related were about large accounts, but the problem was the same with small accounts — the typical commodity trader wants action more than he wants profit. The $10,000 account holders were as bad as the $100,000 accounts, for they used the small size of their accounts as an excuse not to scale trade. They always pleaded that they hadn't enough capital to go into scale trading, even though I suggested they could trade low-margin commodities such as corn or oats or they could trade the small contracts on the MidAmerica. I might as well have saved my breath, for all they wanted was action. I would have starved to death if I had had to rely upon scale traders for my commission income. I made my living off traders, and in 95% of the cases I acted only as an order taker, letting them make all their own decisions.

The people who frustrated me the most, however, were the $10,000 accounts who rejected my suggestion that they join a scale trading partnership. It is very difficult to scale trade successfully with only $10,000, and it is next to impossible to win in commodities trading using any other trading method and only $10,000 of capital, so I would come right out and say that they should either forget commodities trading and save their money or find a $100,000 scale trading limited partnership to join. The answer I usually received was that the prospect wanted a little time to think about it and that he would get back to me in a couple of days. Usually, I never heard from him again, and I could guess that he had gone across the street to lose his money by doing his commodity trading with another broker.

I could never get over the feeling that these commodity losers were the same as the losers I had seen in Las Vegas. There I had seen people lose huge sums of money, cars, homes, businesses, property, and marriages. They, too, were sick people, and they could not control themselves or their need to lose. It was not uncommon — although it was very sad — to go home at the end of a shift in Las Vegas, saying goodnight to one of these sick people who was playing and had stacks of $25 chips in front of him, only to return the next morning to find that he had played all night, had lost almost all the money he held the night before, had used all his credit, and was now making dollar bets. I have seen the same thing in commodities trading: the player begins trading five contracts at a time, as his losses grow and his capital diminishes he reduces to two contracts at a time, then he reduces to a single contract at a time, and finally he winds up trading one MidAmerica contract. It is very sad, but that's the way it is in Las Vegas and in the commodities markets.

However, the clients are not totally at fault. In many cases it is the heartless broker who overwhelms the prospective commodity trader with stories of fabulous profits earned by his clients. In most cases the claims of success are absolutely untrue, but there is no way to disprove them, and the broker plants that first seed of greed in the mind of the prospect. After the prospect has heard about the mythical client who turned $10,000 into $100,000 in six months, there is no way in the world that the prospect will ever be satisfied with the thought of making $2,000 in six months through scale trading.

Besides, the broker isn't interested in generating 8% to 10% gross commissions from a scale trading account when he can generate 40% to 50% from a regular trading account.

Perhaps the best example I know of a greedy broker who has only his own interests in mind and not those of the clients is the vice-president of a major brokerage firm — I call them Churnem & Burnham — located here in Los Angeles. He earned his title by producing a million dollars in gross commissions annually. He has been quoted as saying: "The primary objective of a commodity broker is to convert customer equity to broker net worth as rapidly as possible." He does this by churning the accounts as fast as he can to skim massive commissions from even the smallest accounts. This guy earns money the old fashioned way — he steals it!

If you wonder how brokers like that stay in business, you need only to see the mass marketing operation he runs and the support people he has working for him. Big producers like this chap frequently have two or more secretaries who spend the entire day mailing prospecting pieces to long lists of names of wealthy investors, professional people, experienced commodity traders, etc. Those mailings may produce several dozen leads daily. The primary broker may have an assistant or two who are also licensed salespeople, and they will follow up on the leads. The hot prospects are then turned over to the primary broker who moves in as the closer. The whole operation is like a used car lot.

The broker must have something to show the prospects, and this is where the brokerage house comes in. They have produced reams of material claiming exceptional gains in nine of the last ten years with compounded percentage returns approaching triple digits annually. The prospect thinks that because he has seen it in print it must be true, but the usual story is that these performance records are based upon hypothetical trades and that real accounts never do that well.

A perfect example of this is a weekly publication produced by one of the major firms. It shows hypothetical results which they claim you would have earned if you had traded with them, following all of their recommendations since January 1 of the publication year. They use trend-timing, and the hypothetical account trades thirty commodities. Their weekly summary of all open positions will always show net paper profits because of the nature of trend-timing. If you will remember that the trend-timing method requires that winners be held for large gains while losers be closed out quickly with small losses, you will realize that it is probable that a trend-timing account will show about twenty-five winners out of each thirty open positions at any given moment. Any losing positions probably show small losses because positions are generally reversed with small losses before they become large; furthermore, trend reversals are usually signaled by sudden and sizable price movements, and the momentum generated by hordes of trend-followers reversing simultaneously will extend the price movement so that the newly established position immediately shows a paper profit. Never mind that the trend-following account just took another loser, the only thing the prospective investor sees in the account summary is the current open positions, most of which show profits. Some of the winning open positions may show very large profits because the trend has remained intact for several months. Thus, the account may be accumulating numerous realized losses while constantly exhibiting $30,000 to $40,000 of unrealized gains in each weekly publication.

The broker who is soliciting a prospect may simply show him this trading summary with the $30,000 to $40,000 of paper profit, but unless the prospect is terribly gullible he will ask to see a summary of closed out trades for the year to date. Now, this is where the deception arises: the broker will show the prospect that the closed positions have produced a loss of $20,000 for the first six months of the year, but he claims that is more than offset by the approximately $35,000 of paper profits and that the account has actually produced a $15,000 net increase in equity in those six months, which annualizes to $30,000. What he — and the house publication — failed to disclose was that the hypothetical account *always* has approximately a $35,000 paper profit in it, and that it started the year with a $35,000 paper profit (and likely will end the year with a $35,000 paper profit in it), so that the actual performance is a $20,000 net *decrease* in equity in six months, which annualizes to a $40,000 loss instead of a $30,000 profit.

If you think they could never get away with that, let me tell you how they do it. The summary published each week shows (1) the unrealized profits or losses in all open positions, (2) the realized profits or losses from trades completed since the previous week's summary, (3) a cumulative total of all profits or losses from all closed trades since the start of the present year, and (4) a net result combining the year's closed trades and the currently open positions. Their model account does not cancel all open positions at the start of each year and restart at zero. It simply carries the unrealized gains into the new year. The closed positions for each week will probably show a few thousands of dollars of either profit or loss, and this weekly result is cumulated accurately. If the commodities markets have dramatic moves in one direction or the other, the closed positions will show a handsome profit, but in the more likely situation wherein commodities prices have oscillated within normal ranges, the closed positions will show a net loss of a few thousand dollars each week. It would be devastating to the sales efforts of the brokerage house's salespeople if the prospective investor could see a continuous running record showing a steady accumulation of realized losses which ultimately will exceed the $35,000 of paper profits that are always in the account and in which the prospect does not participate. To lay a smoke screen of deception, the brokerage firm omits one part of its weekly summary for the first two months of the year. The omitted number is item #4, the *net result combining the closed trades and the currently open positions*. By doing this, the summary shows only a relatively modest realized gain or loss for each of the first nine weeks of the new year, and when these are cumulated, they are easily offset by the $35,000 of unrealized profit which is always in the account. I assume this brokerage firm has determined that two months is the required amount of time it takes for salespeople and prospects to forget about the $35,000 of paper profit which was in the account at the start of the year, because they do it *every* year, and along about March 1 they resume publishing the combination of realized losses since the start of the year and the current — and ever present — $35,000 unrealized gain. The prospect would have been aware of the deception if the summary had shown the $35,000 of paper profits at the end of the first week of the new year as a debit against the new year's performance, and that is the reason for deleting the combined total for two months. By that time a $35,000 unrealized gain seems plausible, for that is an average gain of only about $1,000 for each of the thirty commodities being traded. If, during this two month period, the closed positions have produced, say, $5,000 in net losses, the open positions will still show approximately $35,000 of paper profit, and the house claims a result showing $30,000 of net profits when the truth is that they have a $5,000 net loss. They conveniently ignore the $35,000 of paper profit which was in the account at the start of the year and hope that the prospect will accept that the $35,000 of paper profit presently shown in the account has been accumulated since the start of the new year.

By utilizing this deception each year the model account needs only to hold its realized losses to less than $35,000 for the year, and the brokerage firm and its salespeople will claim that their trading method provided a profit for all clients who followed the system throughout the year. They ignore the fact that the model account opened the year with $35,000 of unrealized gains, closed the year with $35,000 of unrealized gains, and took $20,000 to $30,000 of realized losses through the year. Then they go through the same charade again for the next year, concealing the paper profits in the account at the start of the year by deleting them from the summary for two months.

This particular firm claims they can show a record dating back more than twenty years with astounding results. Their claim, however, is similar to that of a "salted mine." As long as they continue their practice of inserting approximately $30,000 to $40,000 of fictitious gains in their record each year, an astounding record is guaranteed. Think of it their phony claim of $35,000 of profits each year for twenty years means they have padded their results by $700,000.

These people personify the axiom that figures don't lie, but liars figure.

Perhaps you think the brokers should know better than to be deceived by this fraudulent practice, but most of them are either too gullible to recognize what is going on, or if they do know, they condone it. For example, I alluded to this practice in the first edition of this book, and a Southern California commodity broker who had read the book mailed me a copy of his firm's track record. I suppose he expected me to be impressed, and he probably thought I should eat humble pie. Unfortunately for him, though, he proved his own gullibility, for it was *his firm's* questionable sales practices to which I had referred. I call his firm Dewey, Cheetum, and Howe.

If you fear there is any chance that you might be tempted to over trade, you should not trade at all, for most brokers and brokerage houses will encourage you to trade aggressively. They will try to dissuade you from scale trading because of the low commissions. Instead, they will try to steer you into one of their trend-following accounts, because those accounts generate five times as much in gross commissions as scale trading.

I will give you two examples:

I once worked for a giant brokerage firm which was sponsoring a sales drive which encouraged clients to deposit $5,000 to open personal commodity trading accounts which would use trend-following to trade only those commodities which were available on the MidAmerica Commodity Exchange. I voiced open criticism of the program because of the excessive commission rate which our firm charged for MidAmerica trades. I even wrote to our home office in New York and challenged them to show me an account which had shown successful results from this program. They asked one of the men from one of our southern offices to send me a transcript of his most successful account. I truly could not believe what I received.

The transcript showed this $5,000 account to have been reduced to a remaining equity of $2,400 in exactly a year. Can you believe that? This was the salesman's *best* account. Down $2,600 in a year! The account had had nearly one-hundred trades that year, and the gross profits and losses were exactly equal. So, where did the $2,600 go? You're right, commissions. This account had generated 52% in commissions to total $2,600 for the year. It is hardly any wonder that the broker considered this a very good account.

Incidentally, that broker has since been promoted to the position of Eastern Regional Sales Manager for Commodity Trading Programs, which, I am sure, does not surprise you. If he has the ability to sell that kind of performance, he should be National Sales Manager.

It is possible to scale trade a $5,000 account, but it probably would also be limited to MidAmerica trades. If a $5,000 scale trading account limited itself to MidAmerica trades, and if it sought an average of $100 net profit per trade, it would generate only twenty trades during a year in its quest of the 40% profit objective. That is one-fifth the number of trades in the above account, and it shows you why brokers will try to steer you away from scale trading and into trend-following.

The second example of brokerage house greed happened with the same house as above, but it was with a different person. This person was the National Commodity Sales Manager. He was visiting California offices one time, and while in our office he conducted a sales meeting with all the brokers in attendance. After the meeting, he spent some time at my desk because I was the commodity specialist in the office.

The Resident Manager of the office and I had had repeated arguments about the kind of commodity business he wanted me to do. He wanted me to sell the firm's managed accounts, but I would have no part of it because of the terrible record. I wanted to scale trade. Knowing my feelings about the company's managed account program, he warned me prior to the sales meeting not to say anything contradictory or embarrassing during the National Sales Manager's presentation. The other brokers from our office were primarily stock brokers and did commodity business only rarely, so they were vulnerable to a slick sales pitch, which is exactly what they heard. They came out of that meeting all fired up, ready to go out and hustle the firm's managed account programs. They knew so little about commodities that they had no idea they had been conned.

After the meeting, the National Sales Manager came to my desk, and I kidded him about the liberties he had taken with the truth. For example, he claimed that we had never issued a margin call against any of our managed accounts, but I knew that the firm had some managed accounts which had lost 100% of their capital. He was right; that is not a margin call, it's a wipe-out.

I steered the conversation around to commodity trading systems, and I told him about my scale trading method. He confided to me that the firm was concerned that virtually everyone in research had become a trend-follower, which made us vulnerable to a sideways market, so I told him about this book and showed him the auditor's report verifying the 130 consecutive winning trades. His eyes nearly popped out, and he commented that perhaps the firm should invite me to New York to discuss this trading method with the top-ranked commodity people. He suggested the possibility that they might direct money to me to be managed under the scale trading method.

Then the critical question came. He asked what kind of gross commissions this trading method generated. I exaggerated and claimed 10% instead of the more likely 8%. That killed the subject right there. He said, "No way! If a system can't do 40-50% in annual gross commissions, we are not interested."

I protested that the system was good for the customers because it made profits for them.

He suggested that the customers could go perform a certain anatomically impossible act upon themselves. Then he said, "We are not here to make money for the customers, we are here to make money for (the firm)."

I urge you to take a few minutes to reflect. Did you recognize yourself in any of the examples of the commodity traders? If so, you shouldn't try scale trading. Indeed, you should not trade commodities at all. You are sure to lose.

And did you recognize your broker? If you have a broker who encourages you to trade frequently, and if you have discussed scale trading with him and he has told you not to use the method, get a new broker. If you continue with him, you will join the 90% of traders which even the commodity exchanges say lose.

As for the brokerage firm, that is a tough decision. Many of the firms keep constant pressure on their salespeople to produce commissions. This, in turn, puts pressure on them to encourage clients to overtrade. It is very difficult to recognize that subliminal pressure, but if you know that you might be the type to succumb, stop now. Don't trade commodities.

If you want to try scale trading, but if you feel there is any chance whatsoever that you could be tempted to deviate from the system, please do not attempt it. Give up now, for either you, your broker, or his firm will eventually cause you to lose great amounts of money. Your prospects are bleak enough if you could be tempted by thoughts of larger profits than scale trading can provide, and it is quite probable that the broker will play upon your weakness.

XXXV

Specific Recommendations

In the original edition of this book I commented upon the length of time required to write it. I said it had taken much longer than should have been necessary because of the action of silver. I used silver for many of the illustrations of scales, and I usually showed silver around $6.00 per ounce or less, so I delayed publishing when silver moved to $10.00. Eventually it ran to $50.00. Throughout that entire time I debated with myself over whether I should rewrite the examples, substituting soybeans for silver, or wait for silver to return to reasonable levels. I finally decided to go ahead and publish the book as written since the examples used were intended to be nothing more than that — examples! They were not intended as recommendations.

I have encountered a similar problem with this new edition in that interest rates are so low that they make the carrying charge examples ludicrous. Interest rates will rise soon, and we will return to a range of 4% to 6%, so I used 6% in the examples because short-term rates will spend a lot more time in the future around 6% than they ever will around today's 3%. Most of the original examples have been retained, and you should recognize that they are still just examples and not recommendations.

We have learned from the publication of *The Scale Trader* that it is impossible to anticipate all contingencies which may occur between the time of writing that letter and the time the readers receive it two days later; therefore, it is difficult, if not impossible, to give specific recommendations in a book which requires two months for printing and which may be read four years later. However, I will offer my thoughts on a very broad and general basis concerning the commodities which I feel will offer the greatest opportunities for scale trading profits within the foreseeable future. In all cases, low risk will be a primary consideration:

INTEREST RATES: Any discussion of future commodity prices, unfortunately, must begin with consideration of interest rates because interest rates have come to dominate futures trading, commodity prices, the economy, and every aspect of our lives. I called it "unfortunate" because I believe in free markets, and I consider it a crime to place so much power — the power to control the world — in the hands of a few men at the Federal Reserve, and particularly to make the chairman an icon with almost solitary power to rule and to allow him to operate without controls and without accountability to anyone. He doesn't even answer to the president of the United States, and it is shameful that the only power that the president has is to *hint* that he would like to see interest rates moved one way or the other, but the chairman can ignore him.

It is a favorite pastime of the media to malign economists and to make jokes about their inability to predict the future of the economy, but probably the greatest problem economists face in making projections is coping with the Fed. As an example, an analyst's econometric model may have factored in a 3.8% increase in the Domestic National Product while other economists are projecting only 3.4%. When the latest DNP number is released showing 3.8% — a bull's-eye for our subject economist — it is so shocking to the economists who missed the mark that they fear this is an indication of inflation and that the Federal Reserve will soon raise interest rates to arrest a "perceived" pending bout with inflation, and the bond market goes into a tailspin.

This should not be. If the economy is expanding, let it expand. If natural forces within the economy cause interest rates to rise, that is okay. If rates get too high, The Law of Supply and Demand will bring them down again. There is no need to mess with rates.

Unfortunately, though, the Fed exists, and we must try to think of what the members will do next and what their actions might do to commodity prices.

We are finally beginning to emerge from an incredibly long recession caused primarily by the Fed's lowering of interest rates. (Those low rates took interest earnings away from savers and prevented them from doing the spending that would support the economy. Ergo, recession.) As the signs of an improving economy begin to appear, the Fed has suddenly taken what it calls "preemptive action" to stave off inflation by raising interest rates. How can they be afraid of inflation when all that is happening is that we are picking ourselves off of the floor as the economy regains consciousness?

The Fed says it is raising rates to counter inflation which they claim is evident in rising commodity prices. That shows that these people haven't a clue as to what they are doing. They watch the Commodity Research Bureau commodity price index for indications of rising prices, but evidently they don't know that many prices — the grains, for example — are trading at lofty levels in the cash market today but at substantial discounts to today's cash prices in next year's futures prices. As soon as the 1994 harvest comes in, the CRB will move sharply lower. Unless, that is, the Fed has pushed interest rates higher and forced the prices of basic commodities and consumer goods higher as explained in Chapter XXIX, "Interest Rates and the Federal Reserve," where I demonstrated that increasing interest rates increases the cost of the basic ingredient in the production of all goods and therefore pushes prices higher.

The first two or three rate increases will be good for the economy as that puts additional buying power into the hands of the public and stimulates the economy, but Bagel Brain is sure to interpret that to mean a return of inflation, and he will raise interest rates even more. Then it becomes a problem as the bond market breaks and the stock market goes with it.

There is indisputable evidence available which shows that inflation is lowest when interest rates are low and highest when interest rates are high, but the Fed refuses to look at the record, choosing to rely upon theory, which has proven disastrous.

By his pouring gasoline — in the form of higher interest rates — on the inflation fire, we could see double-digit rates again before the turn of the millennium unless we get a practical person in to replace Greenspan whose second term as chairman expires in 1996. Let us pray that short-term rates stay between 4% and 6%, and that long-term rates stay between 7% and 8%.

There is a powerful cyclical tendency dating back 200 years for interest rates to bottom in years which end in 5, with an occasional bottom occurring in years which end in 4. Couple that with the Fed's stated intention of starting to raise rates soon, and higher rates soon is a virtual cinch. By definition, bonds must fall as interest rates rise, so prepare yourself for that eventuality.

THE STOCK MARKET: This one scares me. If the Fed keeps interest rates down, they bankrupt the pension funds and put life for seniors into chaos. If the pension funds begin to liquidate stocks to make the required income distributions, they could put the stock market into chaos. On the other hand, if the Fed raises interest rates enough to push the bond market lower, it would take the stock market down with it. The combination of rising interest rates concomitant with a declining stock market could put the stock market into a rout as mutual fund shareholders redeem their depressed shares for the purpose of investing the proceeds in guaranteed-safe CD's. A 10% correction in the stock market is long overdue, and it will surely come sooner or later. My worry is that first-time mutual fund investors who have never lost money on investments before because the only thing they ever invested in was a guaranteed CD may liquidate their mutual fund shares to return to the safe haven of bank CD's; their own selling could be enough to push the stock market even lower as fund managers are forced to sell stocks to pay them off, and then the market could fall another few percentage points. That could prompt new liquidations, and as the decline feeds on itself it could turn into a rout.

This scenario of a stock market collapse can be avoided only by keeping short-term interest rates at 6% or less. But, if the Fed pushes rates above 6%, look out below. We could see stocks cut in half.

I am going to assume that the Fed senses that danger and will not allow short-term rates to exceed 6%, in which case the Dow Jones

Industrial Average could reach 5000 by the year 2000. That is a compounded rate of increase of only 4%, but I can't see the market doing any better. Earnings may grow at a faster pace, but the Price/Earnings ratio is already so amazingly high that it would require a surge in earnings just to return P/E's to normal levels.

PRECIOUS METALS: I like to think that the Fed will show some restraint with interest rates, but Greenspan has such an enormous ego and understands so little about economics that I fear that he will tinker with rates just to have something to do. I worry that he will push short-term rates above 6% and inflation will return. But that is good for precious metal prices.

Gold: Gold has traded throughout the past decade in a range from about $280 to $500, with most of the trading in the range from $330 to $430. I think of gold as a $375 commodity, anything under being underpriced, and anything over being overpriced. If gold drifts under $375, I can't see it staying there very long because of the Fed probably pushing us back into inflation. Unless there is a collapse in the stock market which leads to a collapse in the economy, it is safe to start gold scales under $375. Gold could sell again at $500 before the year 2000. If the Fed brings serious inflation back the way they did in 1979 by raising interest rates the way Volcker did at that time, we could see gold as high as $850.

Incidentally, don't pay any attention to the gold bugs who would have you believe that gold will rise if the economy collapses. They cite the Depression years as an example, pointing out that gold rose 75% at the start of the Depression. That is preposterous. All that happened was that the *official* price of gold was raised from $20 to $35 to strengthen our currency. American citizens could not own gold, so there was no free market, and the 75% increase in its price was merely a bookkeeping entry.

If the economy falls, gold will fall. Just remember the old adage: When the tide goes out, all of the ships go down.

Platinum: This one moves up and down with the Japanese economy because the Japanese prefer platinum jewelry to gold. It is also influenced by the world economy because platinum is used in catalytic converter exhaust systems of automobiles, and its consumption is based upon the number of new cars being sold. During the past decade platinum has ranged from a low of $240 to a high of $680. It is good for scaling under $400, but be careful because of the recurring rumors that several auto companies have developed a catalytic converter which uses cheaper palladium instead of platinum.

Barring a collapse in the economy, platinum could trade as low as $300, but it is more likely to sell above $500 with our return to a mild inflation.

Palladium: This is a beauty for scale trading because every six months another auto manufacturing company announces its new palladium catalytic converter to replace platinum, and palladium spurts $25 in the next couple of days. That is usually enough to get you out of any scale.

The problem with trading palladium is that it is a very thin trader, and it is difficult to get executions. However, you can always commence a scale under $110 because it is unlikely to trade under $80, and it is more likely to trade at $175.

Silver: Too many commodity traders consider silver to be a precious metal, when it is actually more of an industrial metal. It can appreciate with inflation simply because of its false reputation as a precious metal, but you should think of the economy's condition before scaling silver. You must also keep in mind that industry is constantly in search of a process to replace silver in film, which accounts for 60% of silver's usage. Each time there is a rumor that someone has perfected a process to replace silver in film there is a sharp break in silver's price of 50 cents or more, so you must be prepared for that kind of action if you want to scale silver.

Silver traded at $3.50 in 1993 as it returned to prices extant before the Texans tried to corner the silver market in 1979. If the economy does not come unglued, that $3.50 low should hold. We will probably see silver hold between $3.50 and $5.00, with an occasional spurt to $7 before 2000. You may scale silver anytime under $4.00.

Copper: This industrial metal is overpriced at 85 cents. It spent the early 1980's around 60 cents, and then it ran to a high of $1.65 in the late 80's as available supplies dwindled to dangerously low levels. The Law of Supply and Demand brought out huge production increases and rapidly expanding warehouse supplies of copper, so the price has fallen to the mid-80's. Consumption of copper should increase as homes are built to replace those damaged or destroyed by

Hurricane Andrew in Florida, the flood in the Midwest, and the earthquake in California. This should give copper a 70 cent base with a potential $1.25 top. All bets are off if the Fed wipes out the stock market and the economy, so start your copper scales under 80 cents.

Keep in mind that there has been a change in the delivery specifications for copper. The purity is greater than before, so it is now called High Grade Copper. Those in the industry say that added two or three cents to the value of a deliverable pound.

THE GRAIN GROUP: The Great Flood of 1993 pushed grain prices to highs since the 1988 drought, but there is plenty of grain around, so don't get carried away. Things have changed since the days when the United States was the breadbasket to the world. There are so many other nations on so many other continents growing grains now that this catastrophic flood could not push corn above $3 or soybeans above $7.50. Now there is a new crop of everything coming into harvest every six months instead of every twelve months, and there is less of a need to make panic purchases to avoid running out of stored supplies.

Corn: Because of the flood, the U.S. corn crop declined 33% — from 9.479 billion bushels in 1992 to 6.344 billion in 1993. But there was plenty of reserve from that record 1992 crop to take up the slack in the 1993 crop and to hold corn's top price under $3.20. 1994 production will probably be lower than USDA projections (which are yet to come) because of so much land either still holding standing water or so many fields that lost their topsoil and are buried under silt. This will give corn scale traders ample opportunity for profit in 1994 and 1995. The carryout at the end of the 1993-94 marketing season (September 30, 1994) has been estimated by the USDA to be a mere 777 million bushels, compared with 2,113 million on September 30, 1993. That is a precariously low reserve, and if there is a weather problem during the 1994 growing season, there could be an upside explosion in corn's price.

Corn should hold above $2.20 for at least a couple of years and could reach at least $3.50 if there is a weather-related problem during 1994's growing season. Start scales under $2.60.

Soybeans: A few years ago if there had been the 500-year flood, soybeans would have traded at $12, but there was a plentiful supply from the 1993 crop still available, and South America was heading for a record harvest of soybeans, so the soybean price stayed under $7.50. We will close the 1993 marketing year (September 30, 1994) with the smallest carryover since the drought of 1988 (155 million bushels versus 292 million last year), so prices could run — in spite of the South American crop — if there are any weather problems during the 1994 growing season.

We saw $4.70 soybeans in 1986, but that won't happen again soon because of the low carryover projected for September 30, 1994. That should keep soybeans above $6 through the trading of 1994-crop soybeans (through the September 1995 contract). Set scales for $5.80 lows and $7.50 highs.

Soybean Oil: There is a worldwide shortage of edible oils, and U.S. soybean oil yields per bushel are off nearly 5% from normal, which has allowed soybean oil to trade as high as 31 cents in 1994. But crops are projected to improve in 1994, so look for soybean oil to decline. Besides, we don't want to start soybean oil scales above 24 cents. Soybean oil should hold above 23 cents in 1994 but could decline to 21 cents in 1995. If normal crops reappear in 1995, 18 cent bottoms are possible. We haven't had a drought since 1988, and we normally get one every three or four years, so we should see one soon. That would push soybean oil above 30 cents again and take you out of any ill-conceived scale.

Soybean Meal: There is a surplus of soybean meal as crushers seek the soybean oil. That has held soybean meal under $200 per ton through most of the year — despite the flood (when the price rose briefly to $238). The December 1994 soybean meal contract trades under $190, and that is money in the bank. Soybean meal should hold above $170 for at least a couple of years, and $250 is a possibility if there is a drought in 1994 or 1995.

Oats: Oat crops keep getting smaller, but nobody seems to like this grain. It traded as low as 95 cents in 1986, but the drought of 1988 took it to $3.93. A practical bottom for oats through 2000 is $1.00, and any weather problems in the 1994 growing season could take oats to $1.60. Unless there is a super crop in 1994, it is safe to start oats scales around $1.35.

Wheat: Winter wheat accounts for 75% of U.S. wheat production, and its harvest begins in May, so it cannot be affected as much as the other grains by summer heat or drought. In fact, the 1993 crop was down only 2% from 1992 (2.402 billion bushels vs. 2.459), and because of a projection in the USDA report of a decline of 129 million bushels, the carryover is expected to rise to 588 million bushels vs 529 in 1992. However, wheat can benefit in that it may be substituted for other grains in feed formulas if those other grains suffer from bad growing weather reducing crop sizes and pushing prices higher. Wheat likes to roam between $2.50 and $4.00. With carryover supplies of all of the grains at precarious levels in 1994, any problems with weather (either early for wheat or later for the other grains) could push wheat to $4 again. The low over the next few years should be just under $3. Set your scales accordingly.

THE MEATS: The high prices of feed grains has caused meat producers to trim their herds, sending animals to slaughter instead of breeding them. This has helped to push prices of nearby contracts lower while raising prices of deferred contracts because of the relative shortage of animals which will prevail late in 1994.

Live Cattle: The normal cycle for cattle prices is seven years as prices rise from bottom to top and then return to bottom. The cycle occurs because of changes in feed prices, but it requires seven years for a full cycle because of the lengthy gestation period of cows (ten months) and the two years required for a calf to mature; thus, the lead time required to alter breeding plans is a minimum of three years. Of course, it takes an equal amount of time to reverse breeding plans, or another three-plus years.

Live cattle prices reached a low of 51 cents in 1985 and rose steadily to 82 cents in 1991 before flattening out and trading in a range of about 70 cents to 80 cents since. We are overdue for a downward swing in cattle prices, but the high grain prices caused by the 1993 flood could start cattle prices on the downward swing toward 60 cents. I would not want to scale trade live cattle until the price gets under 63 cents.

Feeder Cattle: Feeder cattle become live cattle, so everything I said above about live cattle applies to feeders. The range for feeder prices prior to the 1986 bottom was 56 cents to 72 cents, and then the price rose to 84 cents in 1993. I can see prices returning to the 55 cents to 70 cents range, so I would not want to scale feeders until the price dropped below 60 cents.

Hogs: The normal full cycle for hog prices is only three years because the gestation period is only four months, and then shoats feed out to market weight in eighteen months. Hogs have ranged for two decades between 40 cents on the low and 60 cents on the high (with one dip to 35 cents and four runs into the mid-60's), with most tops being closer to 56 cents. Thus, the bottom third would be under about 46 cents. This year's high feed prices have caused the slaughter of hogs instead of breeding, pushing nearby prices lower and distant prices higher. Another factor is the backing up of hogs on farms during the bitter winter of 1993-94. This has kept hogs on the farms because of the inability to truck them to processing plants, and that has caused them to put on extra weight. As soon as the winter weather eases and those hogs are moved to market, prices will decline. That will be your opportunity to jump all over them.

After the run to 67.5 cents in 1990, hog production expanded for about three years, bringing prices down, but 1992 was a transition year as year-over-year comparisons of total inventory and breeding intentions in successive quarterly reports showed some increases and as many decreases; however, 1993 is showing declines in all numbers. Hog prices should hold above 43 cents, with a potential top in the mid-50's. Forays under 40 cents are so rare for hogs that you can count it as money in the bank if you have the opportunity to scale them under 45 cents.

Pork Bellies: Pork bellies (uncured bacon) production increased along with hog production, and storage reached record levels, bringing the price down to 28 cents in 1992, but the recent decrease in production of hogs has allowed the price to return to the mid-50's. Current storage numbers of frozen pork bellies are running 30% under 1992, and if you couple those numbers with the decreasing hog production numbers you can make a good case for pork bellies holding at 45 cents or better for at least two years.

I prefer to start pork bellies scales at 50 cents or under, but the reduction in production this year should allow us to nibble at pork bellies starting around 55 cents. Fitting your scale to your available capital, start with a broad scale at 55 cents, but tighten and become aggressive under 50 cents.

THE PETROLEUM GROUP: There is a real problem with this group because it is virtually a man-made commodity group instead of a supply/demand group. The world is awash in a crude oil surplus, but all of the producers seem to ignore the problem and go on producing at full capacity.

Crude Oil: There was a time when OPEC dominated world oil exports, but today it accounts for only 40% of total exports. The USSR was the world's largest exporting nation, but the dismantling of that Union has so completely disrupted production that it is difficult to calculate their current exports. North Sea producers and IPEC nations have taken up the slack, and the production of Norway (the largest North Sea producer) and Britain — which run at nearly full capacity — have contributed to the glut.

Sheik al-Shanfari, Oil Minister of Oman and leader of the non-OPEC oil producing nations (IPEC), has made repeated appeals to *all* producers to curb production by 10%, but they thumb their noses at him and proceed with their policies of "production restraints are necessary, but let the other guy do it."

Rumor has it that the reason why Norway refuses to curtail production is that this is their way to punish Saudi Arabia for its action in 1986 when it allowed Sheik Yemani, then-Oil Minister of Saudi Arabia, to deliberately drive crude oil prices down. Norway was engaged in a massive development of its newly-discovered oil resources, and it needed a decent crude oil price to pay for it. As a result of Saudi Arabia's action, Norway nearly went bankrupt, and now it is repaying Saudi Arabia in kind. What goes around, comes around.

As for Saudi Arabia, the biggest OPEC producer, they accumulated such massive debts in supporting the Desert Storm action that they must also produce at near-capacity to pay their bills.

It seems strange to me that Saudi Arabia cannot recognize that a 10% reduction in production would boost prices 25%, thus increasing their gross income while reducing their depletion of reserves, but how do you fathom the thinking of a nation which punishes a pickpocket by chopping off his hand? If he does it a second time they chop off the other hand. (If he does it a third time, they call in Lorena Bobbitt.)

Personally, I suspect that the reason why the leaders of these oil-producing nations ignore supply/demand considerations is political instead of economical. Their reigns as the heads of these unstable nations is probably so precarious that they just want to bring in as much money as possible as quickly as possible, convert it to gold, and ship it to banks in Switzerland before they are forced to flee a coup.

Perhaps someone with a degree of sanity will come along and be able to convince all of the oil-producing nations that they are only hurting themselves along with everyone else by producing at full capacity. If that person can cause production restraints to be effectuated, we should see crude oil trade between $14 and $18 through 1994 and up to $20 in 1995. If someone with sanity *does not* come along, you can look for a probable $10 low, and you would have to set your scales for an $8 possible low.

Heating Oil: The blizzard conditions in the Northeast United States during the winter of 1993-94 didn't help prices much because of the basic problem of overproduction of crude oil. However, the price is now so low that it probably is one of the best candidates for scale trading if you can afford it. (The margin requirement is $1,400 per contract, and each penny of price equals $420, so it takes a lot of money to scale trade heating oil or unleaded gasoline.)

One drawback to trading any of the commodities in the petroleum group is that virtually all trading is concentrated in the front months because of these commodities being favorites of trend followers (who always trade the front months). That can cause you to pay numerous rollover commissions, but if you try to trade the deferred months you may find that you are the only person trading that month, and when you need only a 30 point dip to buy your distant contract, and the nearby contract is down 150 points, you might not get an execution because there is no one wanting to take the other side of the trade.

If you will look at the prices of heating oil and unleaded gasoline as shown in the paper you will see that they run like a sine wave in that heating oil prices on futures contracts generally are at their highest in the January contract and decline steadily into the July contract, and then they start up again and rise steadily into the next December contract. That is because heating oil is in greatest demand in the winter and in the least demand in summer. Unleaded gasoline prices have a similar sine wave, but with the highs in the summer and lows in the winter because of summer driving requiring peak gasoline usage. This allows you to commence a scale in the one which is seasonally low (to hold your risk to a minimum) and trade it for a few months until your scale is completed. Then you can switch to the other because it is at a seasonal low, and the risk of commencing a scale is lowest at this time.

Rumors continue to circulate about the United Nations temporarily lifting its sanction against Iraq for its invasion of Kuwait and allowing that nation to sell $1.6 billion worth of crude oil for humanitarian reasons, but it may still be a long time before that is allowed. That is because so much of the world's oil is controlled by American and British oil companies, and they have enough control over politicians to prevent that action.

The record low — during the fifteen years that they have traded — for both heating oil and unleaded gasoline is 30 cents, and that occurred in 1986 when Sheik Yemani opened the spigots on Saudi Arabian oil to deliberately drive the price of crude oil down to punish OPEC members who refused to stay within their quotas. Yemani lost his job over that one (and nearly lost his head), so I doubt that any of his successors would allow that to happen again. I think you can commence broad scales in either of them under 45 cents and get serious under 40 cents.

Crude oil is a $20 commodity, not $14. It will trade again in the 20's, and if you have had the courage to stay with it, you will be rewarded handsomely.

Natural Gas: This is an active and very volatile market which can prove very rewarding for scale traders. My reticence to follow this market is based upon its lack of fundamental information. It seems there are few sources of information to guide a person in making decisions as to what is a low or high price. Natural gas follows the thermometer inversely, so scales which commence in the summertime can prove rewarding.

One problem in trading natural gas is that it moves in very broad swings. This could cause you to become concerned as you accumulate a large inventory, but when it reverses as the first "Arctic Express" of the season moves from Canada into the Northeast the price seems to rally smartly and reward scale traders generously — if you had the courage to ride out the decline.

Natural gas has traded as a futures contract only since 1990, so there is not much price history available; however, the cash market gives us a long history. The price seems to swing from a low of $1.00 to a high of about $3.00. Because of the severe cold across the northern part of the United States in the winter of 1993-94, the price has rallied to $2.80. Wait until the price returns to $1.50 before attempting scales. That may take awhile.

FIBER AND WOOD: There are only two commodities in this group which trade futures contracts, cotton and lumber, and both are too high to scale now.

Cotton: Although U.S. cotton production for 1993 was unchanged from 1992, the rest of the world had severe production problems; e.g., China, the world's largest producer and consumer of cotton, saw its production drop from 26.1 million bales to 19.0. Two years ago foreign stocks were 36.9 million bales, and that dropped to 33.8 million in 1993. The estimate for 1994 is 29.1 million. This is what has pushed U.S. cotton futures prices to nearly 80 cents. Cotton ordinarily trades between about 50 cents and 70 cents, with an occasional run to 80 cents or even 90 cents, so it is grossly overpriced for scale traders. The high price will encourage production, and the price will return to its normal range. Avoid cotton until you can commence scales again at 58 cents.

Incidentally, if you check a long-term chart you will see that cotton traded at 30 cents in 1985. Do not be alarmed by that. The U.S. government unloaded its huge inventory, which accounts for that price. It was announced far in advance, so we had a year in which old contracts were trading at 70 cents while new contracts were selling at 30 cents.

Lumber: The Northern Spotted Owl affair and the low interest rates which spawned a boom in home construction caused lumber to run from its normal $200 to nearly $500 in 1993. The Florida hurricane, the Midwest flood, and the California earthquake will sustain strong use of lumber for at least a couple of years and hold lumber prices above $300, but as interest rates are pushed up by the Fed and disaster areas approach normal again, consumption should ease.

Also, a resolution of differences between environmentalists and logging interest may be achieved, making more timberland available. This would also help to reduce lumber prices.

In the last decade lumber futures prices have ranged from $150 to $480, but the bulk of the trading has occurred in the $160 to $220 range. Do not scale trade lumber until the price falls below $200 again, although that might not happen until 1996.

TROPICAL FOODS: World sugar is the only one in this group which has been immune to price erosion over the last decade, making the other three probably excellent candidates for scale trading as we approach the return of inflation.

Orange Juice: Orange juice has spent the past decade ranging from a low of 65 cents to a high above $2.00 (twice). It is hard to say what the "normal" range is because of the huge swings OJ takes nearly every year, but I think it is safe to say that you should not commence a scale unless the price is under 90 cents, probably under 80 cents.

There was a time when Florida's citrus industry was spread throughout the state, but as groves were destroyed by freezes, the replanting was done to the southernmost area, so the industry is pretty much immune from freeze damage today. Also, Brazil has become the world's largest producer of orange juice, producing about 300 million gallons annually. And 7 million new trees have just recently reached their fruit-bearing stage. Considering all of these factors together would indicate a generous quantity of orange juice available with probably lower prices ahead.

We could see orange juice futures trade as low as 60 cents by 2000, so be cautious about commencing scales. We could also see $1.50 again if there is ever a problem with the Brazilian crop.

The best time to start an orange juice scale is in June. It used to be common that traders took OJ positions October 1 in the hope of catching a freeze rally, but "sooners" began to enter September 1. Then August 1. Now it is June 1. It doesn't hurt to get a little boost from speculators who want to make a freeze play.

Cocoa: This could be the best available commodity for scale trading.

After eight consecutive years in which production exceeded consumption and the carryover supply increased steadily, 1994 is expected to be the third consecutive year in which consumption has exceeded production, reducing the carryover and constructing a base of support under prices. Furthermore, because of the price hovering in the range of $800 to $1,200 per ton for the last four years, plantation owners have been unable to afford proper fungicide and herbicide treatments or proper fertilizer applications. This has left the trees in a state of deterioration from which they could not be expected to recover even if prices rallied sharply and efforts were made to restore the plantations. Cocoa is not like corn where you can take advantage of a high price and plant a large crop in the new year; cocoa comes from trees which take four years to mature and to start to produce beans.

As the economies of the world emerge from the Volker recession, one of the beneficiaries of early spending is the world's sweet tooth. This will help to increase consumption and to accelerate the drawdown of supplies.

The $800 price was seen in four of the last five years, but I expect that we will not see a price under $1,000 for the balance of the 90's. I expect to see cocoa trade at $1,500 in 1994 or 1995, and it should trade at $2,000 before the year 2000.

Cocoa has an impotent cartel comprised of producing and consuming nations. They were supposed to pay dues into a cash pool which the manager would use to buy cocoa if prices declined, and then he would sell if prices moved too high. Their goal was to hold prices in a range from about $1,600 to about $2,000. However, the producing nations reneged on their commitments to pay dues — probably because the leaders in those unstable third-world countries were emptying their nation's coffers directly into Swiss bank accounts — so the cartel collapsed. It is still alive, but it is totally ineffective.

Coffee: This commodity also has a cartel, which is a little more effective than cocoa's. Member nations try to agree upon export quotas to control prices. Unfortunately, the producers are all third world nations which do not enjoy the luxury of being able to withhold product from the market for very long, so every once in awhile some member cheats and unloads a huge quantity on the market. When others hear about it, they also sell, and the market turns into a rout.

Coffee prices fell from a high of $2.75 per pound in 1986 to a twenty-year low of 50 cents in 1992, but bad growing conditions and the restoration of the cartel have pushed prices back to 90 cents. There is still a lot of coffee in storage, and it could hit the market if the cartel weakens, so be prepared for a low of 60 cents before 2000. The high price for that period could be $1.60 if weather damages the crop — which happens as often as weather damage to our Corn Belt.

The practical range for prices, though, would be 60 cents to $1.00, so commence coffee scales only in the low 70's.

Sugar (#11, World): Sugar trading has been an enigma the last decade because of the USSR/Cuba relationship. Cuba — the world's largest producer of cane sugar — formerly traded sugar to the USSR for crude oil and cash, but when it lost that customer with the collapse of the USSR, a surplus of production hung over the market. This caused the price to drop from 16.25 cents in 1990 to 7.25 cents in 1991. The price has held between 8 cents and 13 cents since. I still remember the 2.5 cent price in 1984, so it is hard for me to get excited about scale trading sugar in 1994 at 11.5 cents. Each tick in sugar is $11.20 ($1,120 for each cent), so losses can accumulate very rapidly in ill-conceived sugar scales, so don't be too aggressive in launching scales.

Both Thailand and Cuba, the world's two largest sugar exporters, suffered crop damage in 1992-93, but if production is restored for 1994-95, we should see sugar sell as low as 8 cents in the next year. I would not want to start sugar scales above 9 cents, and I would construct them to carry to a low of 6 cents. On the other hand, we could see another 15 cent price if production problems arise in Cuba, Thailand, India, China, or Russia, we could see 15 cents before 2000.

Sugar (#14, Domestic): Don't trade this one. It is too thin. Besides, at 22 cents per pound, you can see that domestic (U.S.) sugar producers have such a battery of powerful political action committees making political donations (they used to call these bribes, now they call them political donations) to hold the domestic price at double the world price that I get livid every time I see that price. Even if it had liquidity, I suspect I still wouldn't want to trade that market because I wouldn't want to be reminded daily of how we are being ripped off.

FINANCIALS: It is suicide to scale trade the financials because they are not supply/demand commodities. Indeed, they are not even commodities. Worse yet, they are man made because their prices go where certain men want to put them. I have already discussed the Treasury bonds, notes, and bills, and I have recommended against scale trading them. The same applies to the municipal bonds, the Eurodollars, and the U.S. dollar index. Only a crazy person would attempt to scale trade the currencies. (I think you have to be crazy to *trade* the currencies, period.)

If the stock market, as measured by the Dow Jones Industrial Average, drops from its present 3950 to less than 2000, I suppose a case could be made for scale trading the Standard & Poor's 500, but it would require so much capital that it would be out of the reach of 99.9% of the people. Scale trading any stock market index with the DJIA above 2000 is far too dangerous for anyone to attempt.

The only financial index which could be scale traded would be the Commodity Research Bureau Index, but if you consider the enormous amount of capital required, you would see that it is impossible for anyone with less than $500,000. For perspective, compare it with pork bellies: Each penny in pork bellies is $400, and each 100 points in the CRB is $500; but bellies are chancy if traded above 55 cents, while the CRB is currently trading at 230, or more than four times as high. If you seek $400 profit in pork bellies or $500 in the CRB, you could average about four winners per week in pork bellies and perhaps four winners per month in the CRB. Four times the investment, four times the risk, and one-fourth the winners. I see no reason to trade the CRB.

CANADIAN GRAINS: Futures contracts of barley, flaxseed, wheat, and rapeseed trade on the Winnipeg Commodity Exchange, and they certainly are suitable for scale trading, but the contracts are denominated in Canadian Dollars, so a winning trade could conceivably result in a loss to a U.S. citizen who deposits U.S. dollars for margin and expects to be paid in U.S. Dollars if there has been a substantial change in the relative values of the two currencies while the position was held. For the person who cares to take the trouble there is the possibility of hedging his grain positions against futures contracts in the Canadian Dollar, but that gets pretty sticky because of the substantial differential between the value of a grain contract and a Canadian Dollar contract. It really isn't worth the bother. Just ignore the Winnipeg markets and trade the U.S. Markets.

Obviously, if you live in Canada, it is all right for you to scale trade Winnipeg grain contracts.

ADDENDUM

Please accept my apology for several contradictions which appear in this book. An attempt on my part to correct these discrepancies would have delayed publication further, and I decided that the numerous exceptionally attractive scale trading opportunities which exist at this time made it imperative that I publish the book immediately. Encouraging you to take advantage of some of these remarkable situations, and assisting you in understanding how to exploit them, seemed more important to me than altering several of the illustrations used throughout the book to make numbers agree in every case.

For example, I used 6% as the current short term interest rate when it is actually just over 3%. I did that because the 3% rate will probably rise to 6% within in a year or two, and people will be reading this book ten years from now, and they would be confused as to what to do with interest rates double my examples.

I altered many of the examples by rewriting chapters, sometimes rewriting the rewrites, because conditions changed as soon as I finished a chapter. The point is, I finally tired of making repeated alterations which were obsolete as soon as they were typed. The purpose of the book is to explain a commodity trading technique, not to track the gyrations of commodity prices on a daily basis; therefore, some of the examples in one chapter may conflict with those in another chapter. Please excuse it, for that is only my way of admitting that I am tired of making adjustments. The scale trading method will be good forever; the examples were good only the day they were written.

Also, I am so alarmed by the runaway stock market and the way that first-time investors are being enticed into something which I consider to be a stock market trap that I wanted to get my comments on the danger of the stock market into your hands as quickly as possible because I fear a stock market collapse is imminent. In the 1984 edition of this book — with the DJIA at 1200 — I said it would hit 2000 in three years. It hit 2000 in exactly three years. I went on to say that it would hit 3000 in six years. It hit 3000 in exactly six years. Perhaps it was dumb luck, but it might also have had something to do with (then) twenty-six years in the market and observation of the indicators. Signs pointed up then; they point straight down now.

In closing, I wish to express my thanks to the group of friends and relatives who read and criticized rough-draft copies of the manuscript for me before it was submitted to the printer. I am deeply grateful for their assistance.

One of their comments bears repeating: One relative said, "Bob, I know you and understand why you did it, but someone who does not know you might misinterpret your motives in speaking so negatively in the book about so many subjects."

To explain: I felt it was my duty and obligation to tell the public that the investment business is not as pristine as it pretends to be, and that the investor needs to be warned of some of the possible pitfalls. I only scratched the surface in describing some of the most common frauds which occur so frequently they are seemingly condoned throughout the industry. Something needs to be done to clean up the industry and to drive the charlatans out of business. The problem exists at every level. One story, possibly apocryphal, says the notorious "Lucky" Luciano, after visiting the New York Stock Exchange, said flatly, "I spent my life in the wrong racket!"

Glossary

ACCUMULATE: To acquire and collect contracts.

ACTUALS: The physical or cash commodity.

BID: A bid, indicating a willingness to buy at a given price. (Opposite of "OFFER.")

BREAK: A sudden, sharp decline in prices.

BULGE: A rapid advance in prices.

CARRYING CHARGE: The cost of storing a commodity. Interest costs generally account for the bulk of the charge, but other expenses include space rental, insurance, transfer fees, and other incidentals.

CASH COMMODITY: The physical commodity as distinguished from the futures contract.

CFTC: The Commodity Futures Trading Commission.

COMMISSION HOUSE: A brokerage house which employs brokers to execute orders to buy and sell actual commodities or futures contracts for the accounts of customers.

COVER: The cancellation of a short position in a futures contract by the purchase of an equal amount of the same contract.

CROP YEAR: That period from the beginning of the harvest of a new crop to the identical date of the following year.

DELIVERY: The tender and receipt of the physical commodity in settlement of a futures contract.

DELIVERY MONTH: A specified month within which delivery may be made in settlement of a futures contract. Also refers to the months for which futures contracts are trading.

DELIVERY NOTICE: A notice of a clearing member's intention to settle a futures contract by physical delivery.

DELIVERY POINTS: Destinations designated by commodity exchanges at which futures contracts may be settled by physical delivery.

FIRST NOTICE DAY: The first day upon which notices can be issued for settlement of specified futures contracts.

FUTURES: Contracts made on commodity exchanges covering the purchase and sale of physical commodities for future delivery.

GTC: Good till cancelled. Same as "RESTING ORDER." Open orders to buy or sell specified futures contracts at fixed prices.

HEDGE: Purchase or sale of a futures contract to offset cash holdings or contractual obligations. (See Chapter I.)

LIFE OF DELIVERY: The period between the first and last trades in any futures contract.

LIMIT ORDER: An open order which may be executed only within a specified time at a specified price or better.

LIMIT MOVE: The restrictive range beyond which trading may not occur in a single day. Many commodities have variable limits which permit expansion of limits after a specified number of consecutive limit moves.

LIQUIDATION: Offsetting of a long or short position.

LOAN PRICES: The price at which producers may obtain government loans for their crops.

LONG: The buy side of a futures contract. Also, the term used to identify the holder of the long position.

MARGIN: Earnest money deposited to insure fulfillment of the terms of a futures contract. The margin is returned upon closure of the contract, plus or minus any profit or loss.

MARGIN CALL: Demand for additional margin in the event of an adverse price movement. Margin calls may also be invoked when margin requirements are increased (sometimes retroactively) due to an increase in a commodity's volatility or other event.

MARKET ORDER: An order to be executed at the next available price.

NET POSITION: The difference between the open long and short positions held in any one commodity by any individual or group.

OFFER: An offer, indicating a willingness to sell at a given price. (Opposite of "BID.")

OFFSET: Liquidation of an open futures contract by executing an opposing position in the same contract. A long contract will offset a short contract, and vice versa.

OPEN CONTRACTS: Outstanding contracts to buy or sell commodities which are as yet unsettled by offset or delivery.

OPEN INTEREST: The number of open or unliquidated futures contracts. Each open contract represents a buyer on one side and the seller on the other, and the open interest represented thereby is one, not two.

OPEN ORDER: An order which remains good until cancelled.

OPTION: Within the context of this book "option" refers to any delivery month in which a commodity futures contract may be traded. Otherwise, a commodity option is the purchased right to take or make delivery of a specified quantity of a commodity at a specified price within a specified period of time without the obligation to do so if the price has moved adversely.

POINT: The minimum unit in which fluctuations in commodity futures prices may be expressed.

POSITION: A long or short commitment.

PREMIUM: The amount by which one delivery contract sells above another delivery contract of like or unlike commodities.

PRICE LIMIT: See "LIMIT MOVE."

PURCHASE AND SALE STATEMENT: The "P&S." A statement issued by the brokerage firm after the customer has liquidated an open position. It shows all pertinent information such as the exchange upon which the buy and sell orders were executed, the commodity traded, the amount, the transaction dates and prices, the gross profit or loss, the commission, any exchange fees, and the net profit or loss.

RANGE: The difference between the high and low prices at which a particular commodity traded during a specified period.

RESTING ORDER: An open order, good until cancelled, to buy or sell a specific futures contract at a specific limit or better.

ROLLOVER: Liquidation of an expiring futures contract and replacement of that position in a deferred delivery option of the same commodity. (See "SWITCHING.")

ROUND TURN: The combination of the entry into and eventual liquidation from a position in a commodity futures contract.

SEC: The Securities and Exchange Commission.

SHORT: The sell side of a futures contract. Opposite of "LONG." Also, the term used to identify the holder of a short position.

SPOT COMMODITY: The physical commodity as distinguished from the futures contract.

SPOT PRICE: The price at which the cash commodity is trading.

STOP ORDER: An open order either to buy or to sell at the market once a particular price has been reached or penetrated. Sometimes erroneously referred to as a "Stop Loss Order" because of the misconception that it will limit a loss. This is not true, for it only assures execution at the next available price, which may be substantially different from the price specified in the "STOP ORDER" in the event of successive adverse daily limit moves.

SPREAD: (Same as "STRADDLE.") Simultaneous holding of equal long and short positions in different delivery months of the same commodity on different exchanges, or the same or different delivery months of commodities of similar characteristics on the same or different exchanges.

STRADDLE: Same as "SPREAD."

SWITCHING: Simultaneous buying of a contract of one delivery month of a particular commodity while selling a different delivery month of the same commodity on the same exchange for the purpose of retaining the same number of contracts but in a different delivery month. This practice may be used to effect rollovers.

TENDERS: Issuance of transferable notices announcing intention of tendering or delivering the physical commodity.

VOLUME OF TRADING: The number of futures transactions executed within a specified time on a particular exchange. The purchase and matching sale count as a single transaction.

WIRE HOUSE: Brokerage houses which operate branch offices and deal primarily with private speculators as opposed to the actual producers and users of the physical commodities.